Capital Gains Tax

2021-22

Andrew Rainford
Lucy Webb
Stephanie Churchill

WORLD LAND TRUST™

www.carbonbalancedpaper.com
UPM FINE

The carbon emissions of the paper used to produce this book have been offset via the World Land Trust's Carbon Balanced Paper scheme.

This product is made of material from well-managed, FSC®-certified forests and other controlled sources.

Capital Gains Tax

2021-22

Andrew Rainford
Lucy Webb
Stephanie Churchill

Published by:

Claritax Books Ltd
6 Grosvenor Park Road
Chester, CH1 1QQ

www.claritaxbooks.com

ISBN: 978-1-912386-40-6

Main titles from Claritax Books

General tax annuals

- Capital Gains Tax
- Income Tax

- Inheritance Tax *
- Stamp Duty Land Tax

* First published October 2020, this will be part of the general tax annuals series from its second (2022-23) edition.

Specialist tax annuals

- Advising British Expats
- A-Z of Plant & Machinery
- Capital Allowances

- Financial Planning with Trusts
- Pension Tax Guide
- Property Investment

Other specialist titles

- Construction Industry Scheme
- Discovery Assessments
- Disguised Remuneration
- Employee Share Schemes
- Employment Status
- Enterprise Investment Scheme
- Furnished Holiday Lettings
- Living and Working Abroad

- Main Residence Relief
- Personal Representatives
- Research and Development
- Residence: The Definition in Practice
- Schedule 36 Notices
- Tax Appeals
- Tax Losses
- Taxation of Partnerships
- Taxpayer Safeguards and the Rule of Law

See www.claritaxbooks.com for details of all our titles.

About the authors

Andrew Rainford BA (Hons), ATT, CTA is an experienced tax adviser, author and publishing editor based in North Wales. After graduating with first class honours with a degree in accounting and finance from the University of Wales in 2005, Andrew worked in the field of public sector audit until switching to tax in December 2007 – just in time for a busy January.

Andrew trained and qualified with the independent London firm Rees Pollock, before joining Ernst & Young's personal tax centre as a consultant, becoming one of the foremost specialists in EIS-related work. During his time in practice, Andrew regularly contributed to various professional publications, including *Taxation* magazine, the *Practical Tax Newsletter*, Tolleys *Tax Guidance*, Tolleys *Tax Digest* and *Tax for Professionals*.

Making the decision to go into writing and publishing full time, Andrew became editor in chief of Indicator's *Tax for Professionals* publication in June 2015, and a contributing editor to *Whiteman and Sherry on Income Tax and Capital Gains Tax*.

Lucy Webb ACA, CTA is a freelance tax writer. Lucy specialises in writing about recent cases in income tax and CGT, and is a regular contributor to *AccountingWEB*.

Lucy also contributes to other tax publications, writing both short-form articles on the latest trends in tax as well as in-depth guides and CPD courses.

Prior to writing, Lucy worked in the asset management tax team at Deloitte.

Stephanie Churchill CTA (Fellow), AAT, TEP is an experienced tax professional with a wealth of experience in advising wealthy individuals from a personal perspective and in relation to extracting funds tax efficiently from their companies.

She has been in the tax profession for around 25 years. She trained at one of the Big Four accountancy firms and worked in mid-tier accountancy firms for a number of years thereafter.

Abbreviations

AEA	Annual exempt amount
ATED	Annual tax on enveloped dwellings
BADR	Business asset disposal relief
BIM	Business Income Manual
BTC	British Tax Cases
CA	Capital Allowances Manual
CA 2006	Companies Act 2006
CASC	Charities and Community Amateur Sports Clubs
CG	Capital Gains Manual
CGT	Capital gains tax
CGTA 1979	Capital Gains Tax Act 1979
Ch.	Chapter
CIR	Commissioners of Inland Revenue
CPO	Compulsory purchase order
CT	Corporation tax
CTA	Corporation Tax Act
EIM	Employment Income Manual
EIS	Enterprise investment scheme
EMI	Enterprise management incentive
ER	Entrepreneurs' relief
ESC	Extra-statutory concession
EWCA	England and Wales Court of Appeal
EWHC	England and Wales High Court
FA	Finance Act
FB	Finance Bill
FHL	Furnished holiday letting
FTT	First-tier Tribunal
GAAR	General anti-abuse rule
HMIT	HM Inspector of Taxes
HMRC	HM Revenue & Customs
IHT	Inheritance tax
IHTA 1984	Inheritance Tax Act 1984
IPDI	Immediate post-death interest
IR	Investor's relief
ISA	Individual savings account
ITA 2007	Income Tax Act 2007
ITEPA 2003	Income Tax (Earnings and Pensions) Act 2003
ITTOIA 2005	Income Tax (Trading and Other Income) Act 2005
LITRG	Low Incomes Tax Reform Group
LLP	Limited liability partnership
LLPA 2000	Limited Liability Partnerships Act 2000
LP	Limited partnership

LPA 1907	Limited Partnerships Act 1907
NRCGT	Non-resident capital gains tax
PA 1890	Partnership Act 1890
Para.	Paragraph
PIM	Property Income Manual
PM	Partnership Manual
PRR	Private residence relief
Pt.	Part
QCB	Qualifying corporate bond
RDRM	Residence, domicile and remittance basis manual
RNRB	Residence nil-rate band
S.	Section
SAV	HMRC's Shares and Valuation Department
Sch.	Schedule
SDLT	Stamp duty land tax
SDRT	Stamp duty reserve tax
SEIS	Seed enterprise investment scheme
SI	Statutory instrument
SITR	Social investment tax relief
SP	Statement of Practice
SpC	Special Commissioners
SRT	Statutory residence test
TAAR	Targeted anti avoidance rule
TC	Tax Chamber
TCGA 1992	Taxation of Chargeable Gains Act 1992
TIOPA 2010	Taxation (International and Other Provisions) Act 2010
TMA 1970	Taxes Management Act 1970
TOGC	Transfer of going concern
TSEM	Trusts, Settlements and Estates Manual
TSI	Transitional serial interest
UK	United Kingdom
UKFTT	United Kingdom First-tier Tribunal
UKUT	United Kingdom Upper Tribunal
UT	Upper Tribunal
UTR	Unique taxpayer reference
VCM	Venture Capital Schemes Manual
VCT	Venture capital trust
VOA	Valuation Office Agency

Publisher's preface

This keenly awaited CGT volume, published almost exactly on our tenth anniversary, is the fourth book in our new series of general tax annuals, alongside our titles on income tax, IHT and SDLT. NIC and VAT volumes are already underway, with a view to publication of first (2022-23) editions in spring/summer 2022. We hope to complete the series with a major corporation tax volume in 2023.

These general tax annuals are written for three main categories of reader: accountants and others who work as general practitioners and who need an appropriate level of commentary across a wide range of issues; more specialised tax advisers requiring clear and accurate guidance on other tax topics that inevitably interact with their specialist fields; and in-house professionals seeking a practical day-to-day reference work for issues arising.

In addition to the obvious requirement for technical accuracy, this book aims to be the clearest single-volume guide to CGT. The concept of clarity is at the heart of our publishing business, and applies most obviously to the writing style, but also to the layout on the page and to the detailed indexing.

Any feedback from our readers will be welcome, including in particular any views on how we can build on this first edition in future years.

My thanks go to all three authors, and in particular to Andrew Rainford, who has written the bulk of this new work and who has also done an initial edit of the chapters contributed by Lucy and Stephanie, to ensure a consistency of approach.

Thanks go also to our own in-house editorial team, including our new editor Aidan Ellis, and to Jane Moore who has conducted a final review and made innumerable helpful suggestions for this book as she did for the accompanying income tax volume. Many thanks, finally, to Jacqui Allen for her work at the later stages of the process, ensuring that the end result is attractively and consistently laid out.

Ray Chidell MA (Cantab), CTA (Fellow)
Director, Claritax Books
September 2021

Table of contents

PARTICULAR TAXPAYERS

INTRODUCTION

1. Introduction to capital gains tax

1.1 A brief history

1.1.1 The need for a separate tax

The first move towards taxing what we now recognise as capital gains came in 1962, when a short-term gains tax was introduced. This only applied to gains made on shares and securities that had been held for less than three months, or land held for less than three years. However, this was not a true capital tax (as we would now understand it) as the resulting gains were subject to income tax.

This was to change in 1965 with the introduction of capital gains tax (CGT). It was clear from then Chancellor of the Exchequer James Callaghan's Budget speech in 1965 that the move to a distinct tax was an anti-avoidance measure to combat strategies designed to convert income into capital. Of course, at the time a successful strategy would mean paying no tax, rather than just being taxed at a more favourable rate:

> "There is little dispute nowadays that capital gains confer much the same kind of benefit on the recipient as taxed earnings more hardly won. Yet earnings pay tax in full while capital gains go free. This is unfair to the wage and salary earner. It has in the past been one of the barriers to the progress of an effective incomes policy, but now my Right Hon. Friend the First Secretary of State has carried this policy forward to a point which many did not believe was possible six months ago. This new tax will provide a background of equity and fair play for his work.
>
> Moreover, there is no doubt that the present immunity from tax of capital gains has given a powerful incentive to the skilful manipulator of which he has taken full advantage to avoid tax by various devices which turn what is really taxable income into tax-free capital gains. We shall only make headway against avoidance of this sort when capital gains are also taxed."

The 1965 regime included a different treatment for assets held for less than 12 months (short-term gains) and those held for longer (long-term gains). Gains made on disposals falling into the former category were taxed as ordinary income, whereas long-term gains were taxed at a flat rate of 30%. This was subject to a form of rebasing to the 6 April 1965 value.

There was a slight concession whereby an individual could elect to charge two-thirds of his or her gain to income tax (and surtax if applicable), with the remaining third exempted altogether. This was an optional election which the individual could make if it were favourable to do so.

The distinction between the two types of capital gain for individuals was abolished in 1971, since when all gains of a capital nature have been subject to CGT, not income tax. From 1982, it was permitted to make a minimal level of gains each year without incurring any CGT (and prior to this date there were other exemptions and reliefs). Initially, this annual exempt amount (AEA) was set at £5,000, since when it has generally increased each year (with some exceptions in the late 1980s) to its current level of £12,300. This was originally the allowance for 2020-21 but FA 2021 has frozen this for all subsequent years up to and including 2025-26.

From the start, gains realised by companies were subject to corporation tax, irrespective of whether they were short-term or long-term in nature. We do not consider the position for companies in this book.

Law: FA 2021, s. 40

Guidance: James Callaghan – Budget Speech to the House of Commons, 6 April 1965

1.1.2   The inflation problem

Initially, there was no relief for the "time value" increase in capital value through inflation, though retirement relief for business assets was available – many of the modern common law precedents for business asset disposal relief (formerly entrepreneurs' relief) derive from this relief. Due to the lack of indexation allowance, many taxpayers suffered CGT on what was in reality a "paper-only" gain following the high levels of inflation the UK experienced in the 1970s. This was recognised by the new Conservative Chancellor, Sir Geoffrey Howe, following Margaret Thatcher's election victory in 1979. However, the underlying problem was not addressed until 1982.

The first measure to alleviate the effect of inflation was an indexation allowance, introduced in 1982 (and expanded in 1985). This was intended to remove the inflation-related portion of the gain from the charge to CGT. This was a step in the right direction; however, it did not deal with the problem of historic inflation prior to 1982. This problem was not addressed until 1988, from when all disposals could be rebased to their value on 31 March 1982, i.e. coinciding with the commencement of the indexation allowance. This rebasing was initially optional, with an alternative approach available, but use of the March 1982 value became compulsory from 2008-09.

At the same time as the introduction of the rebasing element, it was argued that there was no longer a need for differing rates between the tax applied to income and the tax applied to capital gains, since the inflationary elements had been removed. From 6 April 1987, gains were simply charged at the marginal rate of income tax (up to 40% at the time) instead.

1.1.3 The abolition of indexation, and the return to a separate CGT rate

Indexation for individuals continued to increase until 5 April 1998, when it was frozen (rather than abolished), i.e. became less valuable as time wore on.

Taper relief was introduced at the same time, with enhanced relief for business assets (replacing retirement relief) that could reduce the effective tax rate to 10%. The relief was thought to encourage longer-term investment, particularly in new small businesses (as the taper for unlisted shares was significantly greater than for blue chip stocks).

Taper relief lasted ten years, before being abolished in 2008 and replaced (following considerable objection) by entrepreneurs' relief (ER). In addition, indexation for individuals was abolished for disposals made on or after 6 April 2008. However, this coincided with a return of a flat CGT rate of 18%, irrespective of the level of the individual's income.

ER, which has since been re-named business asset disposal relief (BADR), sought to replicate the 10% effective tax rate given by business asset taper relief, but was far more restrictive. For example, business asset taper relief could apply to a holding of any unlisted shares, but ER could only apply to shares in a company that was the vendor's personal company – meaning that he or she had to be an employee or officer for a minimum holding period, and be entitled to 5% of the ordinary share capital. The relief still exists as of 2021-22 but has been the subject of numerous measures to restrict the gains to which it applies. BADR is discussed in detail in **Chapter 7**.

1.1.4   The two-tiered CGT system

The return of a coalition government in 2010 saw the introduction of what can be thought of as a hybrid system. The relevant rate of CGT then depended on the level of income of the individual, but income tax rates did not apply. Gains were taxed at 18% to the extent that the individual's income tax basic rate band had not been exhausted in the year of disposal, and then 28% for any excess. April 2016 saw these rates fall to 10% and 20% respectively, but the old rates of 18% and 28% continue to apply to disposals of residential property or carried interest gains, as well as to the new "non-resident CGT" regime (see below).

1.1.5   The capture of non-residents' gains

April 2016 also saw a watershed moment in the way non-residents were treated for CGT purposes. Prior to that date, gains accruing to a non-UK resident (as determined by the statutory residence test from April 2013, or by the rules that preceded it) were not subject to UK CGT, unless they were subject to certain anti-avoidance rules for persons whose period of non-residence was short-term in nature (less than five years). From April 2016, non-residents making disposals of UK residential property have been required to declare gains and pay UK CGT. This was extended to all "immovable property" located in the UK with effect from April 2019. This is discussed in detail in **Chapter 18**.

From 6 April 2020, a new reporting and payment regime applies to gains realised on disposals of residential property and, for non-UK residents, immovable property located in the UK. Broadly, the regime requires the declaration of a gain, as well as payment of the estimated CGT due, within 30 days of the completion of the sale. This does not, however, remove the requirement for the vendor to make a self-assessment of the gain for the tax year of disposal. The initial payment is therefore treated as a payment on account of the actual tax due. This regime is considered in detail in **Chapter 2**.

1.1.6   Key legislation

The provisions of FA 1965, and the later *Capital Gains Tax Act* 1979, were subsumed into the *Taxation of Chargeable Gains Act* 1992 (TCGA 1992), and this Act, as subsequently amended, remains the primary source of legislation in respect of taxing capital gains.

Statutory references in this book are to TCGA 1992 unless otherwise stated.

1.2   Trustees and personal representatives

Trustees of settlements, and personal representatives of deceased estates, are liable to CGT, but subject to different rates and allowances. See **Chapters 15** and **16** for further detail on these particular types of taxpayer. A disposal by an individual to a trust may be a chargeable disposal, but a transfer to or from a beneficial owner to a bare trustee (or nominee) is not, as the arrangement of such a trust is fiscally transparent.

Example

Andy opens a non-exempt investment account in the name of his grand-daughter Penelope. Andy retains signatory powers and is able to use funds for the benefit of Penelope. By Penelope's 18th birthday, the funds in the account have accrued to £20,000. Penelope requests that Andy transfers the assets to her absolutely. Doing so does not give rise to a chargeable event.

1.3   Operation

1.3.1   Basic mechanics of CGT

Broadly, a chargeable gain arises on the disposal of a chargeable asset, or part thereof, by a chargeable person, whether by way of a sale or otherwise (i.e. it includes gifts of such assets) where the consideration (or deemed consideration) exceeds the asset's base cost. There are also various provisions that can deem a disposal to have occurred, for example when making a negligible value claim (see **3.5.5**). If the consideration is lower than the base cost, a capital loss arises.

Transfers between spouses or civil partners are deemed to take place for consideration that gives rise to neither a gain nor a loss, an exemption that continues to apply right up to the end of the year of permanent separation if the relationship breaks down.

All chargeable gains made in a tax year are aggregated, including any "same-year" losses, and the net amount is subject to CGT after deducting the annual exempt amount (£12,300 for 2020-21 and subsequent years to 2025-26), and potentially any brought-forward capital losses. In some circumstances, it is also possible for trading losses, i.e. as computed for income tax purposes, to offset chargeable gains. Rates of tax are given at **1.1.4** above, and see **Appendix 1**.

Death is not a chargeable event for CGT purposes, i.e. the deceased is not treated as making a disposal to his or her estate, though of course the assets may be charged to inheritance tax (IHT) instead. The beneficiaries of the deceased's estate are treated as acquiring the asset at its probate value, which means the asset is uplifted to the market value at the date of death.

It is possible to make a partial disposal of an asset, for example where a parcel of land is sold out of a larger holding. In such cases, particular rules apply to determine how much of the base cost has been extinguished. This is discussed at **3.4**.

It is important to know when the disposal takes place for tax purposes – see **3.1.3**.

1.3.2   Base cost

The base cost of an asset will consist of its initial acquisition cost (or deemed cost, e.g. where it was acquired by way of a gift), plus any incidental cost of acquisition, e.g. legal fees or land transaction-type taxes. Any similar incidental costs of disposing of the asset will also be deductible from the disposal proceeds.

The base cost may be affected where there has been a claim for a relief that delays a CGT charge, such as relief under TCGA 1992, s. 165 (gifts of business assets – see **Chapter 12**).

1.3.3   Chargeable persons

The general rule is that CGT is only charged to individuals who are resident in the UK under the statutory residence test (SRT) – irrespective of where the asset is located in the world. As discussed in **1.1.5**, the charge has been extended to include gains realised on disposals of (initially) residential property (from 2016) and then all "immovable" property (from 2019).

There are also rules which capture gains made during a period of short-term non-residence. This is intended as an anti-avoidance measure to prevent a tax advantage from being enjoyed by carefully timing the realisation of a gain to coincide with a tax year in which the individual is able to become non-UK resident under the SRT, e.g. by taking an extended holiday overseas. It is also possible for a non-resident individual to be chargeable to CGT in respect of assets located in the UK connected to a UK branch or agency, or of assets that are not land, but that derive a significant amount of their value from land in which the individual has a substantial interest. These, and other anti-avoidance measures, are discussed in **Chapter 18**.

A non-domiciled UK resident may not need to declare gains accruing on non-UK gains if he or she has made an election to be taxed on the remittance basis – see **Chapter 18**.

Charities and Community Amateur Sports Clubs (CASCs) may be exempt from a charge to CGT in respect of a gain, as long as it is applied for relevant qualifying purposes.

1.3.4   Chargeable assets

A gain is only a chargeable gain if it arises in respect of a chargeable asset. An asset is chargeable unless it is specifically exempt from a charge to CGT. HMRC's guidance in their *Capital Gains Manual* (CG) at CG 11700P states that chargeable assets include:

- shares and securities;
- interests in land;
- options, debts and rights over property;
- any currency other than sterling (sterling being simply the unit of measurement of value); and
- any property that was created by the person disposing of it, such as business or professional goodwill, copyright or a lease (by the granting of it).

As should be clear from the above, an asset does not need to be "tangible" in order to be chargeable. Indeed, CG 11700P specifically states that "incorporeal" property is a chargeable asset (see s. 21(1)), the given example being contractual rights, irrespective of whether those rights are capable of being transferred or assigned (or have a market value). The last bullet also demonstrates that an asset does not have to be "acquired" in the sense of it being purchased, or being given, in order to be a chargeable asset.

It is actually simpler to consider what is *not* a chargeable asset when considering whether a disposal is potentially subject to CGT or not. The table at **Appendix 2** details the main types of asset or gain that enjoy a statutory exemption from a charge to CGT under TCGA 1992, in the order they appear. The following is a summary of the types of asset:

- sterling;
- chattels that are wasting assets;
- gambling winnings and compensation;
- termination of a life interest upon death;

- disposal of a beneficial interest in settled property;
- gilts and qualifying corporate bonds;
- government non-marketable securities;
- shares issued under the enterprise investment scheme (EIS), seed enterprise investment scheme (SEIS) or the business expansion scheme (BES);
- ISAs, etc.;
- shares in venture capital trusts;
- main or only residence;
- shares acquired under employee shareholder schemes prior to 1 December 2016;
- pensions, etc.;
- qualifying woodland;
- debts other than securities;
- foreign currency accounts;
- social investment tax relief (SITR) investments;
- art works and similar;
- moveable tangible property;
- cars;
- renewable energy generation;
- decorations for valour etc.; and
- foreign currency for personal expenditure.

1.4 Capital losses

As noted in **1.3**, CGT is charged on the basic premise of calculation of the excess of the disposal (or deemed disposal) proceeds over the base cost of the asset, allowing for same-year losses. Of course, it is perfectly possible that a chargeable asset will be disposed of for less than it was purchased, in which case an allowable loss arises. "Allowable" here means that it can be offset against other chargeable gains before a CGT charge is imposed. So, if an individual makes two disposals in the tax year, the first realising a gain of £20,000 and the second a loss of £5,000, only the net gain of £15,000 is brought into assessment.

It should be noted that, except in specific circumstances (e.g. EIS or SEIS shares – see **Chapter 10**), a loss arising on the disposal of a non-chargeable asset will not be an "allowable" loss. Additionally, losses realised on disposals made to connected persons are "ring-fenced", or "clogged", such that they may only be offset against gains arising on disposals to the same connected person.

Example

Claire sells listed shares in 2021-22, realising gains of £15,000. She also sells her classic Jaguar Mk. 1, realising a loss of £3,000. She cannot use the loss to offset the gain of £15,000 and so, after the AEA of £12,300, her chargeable gain for 2021-22 will be £2,700.

Once a capital loss arises, it automatically offsets any capital gains realised in the same year, before the application of the AEA. This can lead to "loss wastage" and so should be considered before disposals giving rise to losses are realised, i.e. to determine whether tax efficiency can be improved by delaying a disposal into a later tax year.

1.5   Looking ahead

The government has commissioned the Office of Tax Simplification (OTS) to review CGT and there have been two reports so far.

The second report, in May 2021, made 14 recommendations across a broad range of topics. It is therefore possible that this area of tax law will be subject to significant further change in the years to come.

Guidance: https://tinyurl.com/2tcyabey (OTS second report, May 2021)

2. CGT administration and compliance

2.1 Introduction

The reporting and payment obligations for chargeable gains for those subject to income tax largely fall within the income tax regime (see **2.3** and **2.4**).

However, there are some additional nuances in capital gains reporting that advisers may come across, such as the requirements that can arise where there is a sale of land or property (see **2.3.3**).

This chapter outlines the main issues of which taxpayers should be aware, but does not provide a comprehensive insight into all such administration and compliance obligations.

Persons subject to corporation tax are required to report and pay under the corporation tax regime but this is beyond the scope of this book.

2.2 Registration

Where a taxpayer is required to report and pay CGT through a self-assessment income tax return, they should register for self-assessment with HMRC by 5 October following the tax year end (if not already registered).

There are different ways to register, depending on whether the person is self-employed as a sole trader, self-employed as a partner or not self-employed. They can be found at https://tinyurl.com/2fs4tm7r.

Example

Millie disposes of her shareholdings in January 2022, realising a gain of £50,000. During the 2021-22 tax year, Millie also earns over £100,000 for the first time, and so must register for self-assessment.

As Millie does not currently file tax returns, she should register with HMRC for self-assessment by 5 October 2022.

She must report the disposal in her self-assessment tax return.

If a taxpayer realises a chargeable gain during a tax year, but otherwise would not be required to submit a self-assessment tax return, there are alternative ways to report the disposal that avoid the need to register for and file a self-assessment tax return, namely:

- the real time CGT service (see **2.3.2**); or
- the CGT on UK property account (see **2.3.3**).

Law: TMA 1970, s. 7

2.3 Reporting

2.3.1 Income tax self-assessment

Capital gains and losses are reported in the CGT summary pages (SA108) in self-assessment tax returns.

As HMRC's summary notes for the 2020-21 tax year state, SA108 should generally be completed by persons who, during a tax year:

- sold or disposed of chargeable assets worth more than £49,200;
- have chargeable gains (before losses) greater than the annual exempt amount (frozen for individuals at £12,300 until 5 April 2026);
- have gains in an earlier year that are taxable in the return period;
- want to claim an allowable capital loss or make a capital gains claim or election for the year;
- are not domiciled in the UK and are claiming to pay tax on their foreign gains on the remittance basis;
- are chargeable on the remittance basis and have remitted foreign chargeable gains of an earlier year; or
- made a direct or indirect disposal of the whole or part of an interest in UK property or land when either non-resident, or UK resident and the disposal was in the overseas part of a split year (see **2.3.3**, **Chapter 4** and **Chapter 18**).

There are instances when the SA108 pages do not need to be completed, for example when only the following items are disposed of/sold:

- exempt assets, such as wasting chattels (see **14.2**);
- a main residence, the sale of which is exempt from CGT under private residence relief (see **Chapter 9**);
- stocks and shares held in tax-free investment savings accounts, such as ISAs and PEPs; or

- UK government or gilt-edged securities, such as National Savings and Investments (NS&I) savings certificates, premium bonds, and loan stock issued by the Treasury.

Claims

A number of claims, elections and notices can be made in the CGT summary pages of a self-assessment tax return. This includes where a taxpayer wishes to notify that they have made an allowable capital loss in the tax year.

The codes relevant to claims/elections/notices that can be made are summarised as:

Private residence relief where letting relief does not apply	PRR
Private residence relief where letting relief applies	LET
Gift holdover relief	GHO
Rollover relief	ROR
Provisional rollover relief	PRO
Employee shares	ESH
Business asset disposal relief	BAD
Investors' relief	INV
Negligible value claims	NVC
Social investment tax relief	SIR
Other claims	OTH
If more than one code applies	MUL

The relevant three-letter code should be entered in box 8, 20, 28, or 36 of SA108 as applicable. Full details about the claim, election or notice should also be provided in box 54.

Note that in some cases it is also possible to make a claim outside a tax return (for example, in rollover relief claims – see **Chapter 11**).

Where a claim can be made outside of a tax return, this is indicated in the relevant chapter of this annual.

Filing deadline

The filing deadline for a self-assessment tax return is:

- midnight on 31 October following the tax year end, where a paper return is submitted; or
- midnight on 31 January following the tax year end, where the return is filed online.

Example

Gary needs to file his 2021-22 self-assessment tax return. The return should be filed by midnight 31 October 2022 (if filing a paper return) and by midnight 31 January 2023 (if filing an electronic return).

There are instances where a different filing deadline can apply.

Penalties can apply where a self-assessment tax return is not submitted by its due date. See **2.6** for further information.

Law: TMA 1970, s. 8, 12AA

Guidance: https://tinyurl.com/ytmp6tkr (HMRC self-assessment – CGT summary)

2.3.2   Real time CGT service

Where a UK resident has a capital gain to report, and that gain does not arise from a UK residential property disposal made since 6 April 2020 (see **2.3.3**), the capital gain can be reported through the "real time" CGT service.

Although there appears to have been limited take-up of the service to date, where a taxpayer does use the service, they should report the relevant gain by 31 December in the tax year after the gain arises.

Example

During the 2021-22 tax year, Omar makes a gain that can be reported using the real time CGT service.

If using the real time service, Omar should report the gain by 31 December 2022.

The taxpayer will need a Government Gateway login to access the real time service.

Interaction with self-assessment

Use of the real time CGT service is optional.

If a taxpayer uses the real time service to report and settle the tax due on a gain, there should be no requirement to file a self-assessment tax return (provided the taxpayer does not otherwise need to file a return).

However, taxpayers that are required to submit a self-assessment tax return would still need to report the disposal when they file their return, even if they use the real time service.

Given the above, the real time service is most likely to appeal to taxpayers who have a reportable gain but are not otherwise in self-assessment.

Agents cannot currently use the real time service to report gains on behalf of clients – a taxpayer should report the gain personally.

2.3.3   Reporting property and land disposals

Additional reporting obligations can arise where a disposal of UK property or land takes place. The reporting requirements differ for UK and non-UK residents, and are summarised below.

UK residents

Where a UK tax resident disposes of UK residential property, and the exchange of contracts is on or after 6 April 2020, the resulting gain may need to be reported to HMRC within 30 days of the sale completing. This step is not optional; if a taxpayer meets the criteria to report the disposal of a UK residential property within 30 days of completion, then penalties may apply if this is not done (see **2.6.4**).

The disposal is reported through the "CGT on UK property account". An individual will need a Government Gateway user ID and password to create the account.

For UK tax residents, this additional reporting form is only required where CGT is payable on the disposal of the UK residential property, after reliefs (including losses) and exemptions are considered.

For example, a disposal of a UK resident taxpayer's main private residence that is fully CGT exempt would not need to be reported to HMRC, nor would a disposal where the net gain falls within the annual exempt amount. See **Chapter 4** for further information on the 30-day reporting of gains.

Example 1

Eva sells a UK residential investment property, realising a capital gain on disposal. The exchange of contract takes place on 3 January 2022 and the sale completes a week later on 10 January 2022.

Eva should report the disposal to HMRC by 9 February 2022 (i.e. within 30 days of the sale completing). She should also pay the CGT due by the same deadline (see **2.4.3**).

As Eva would be in self-assessment (to report her UK investment property income) she should also report the disposal in her 2021-22 self-assessment tax return.

Example 2

Shane, a UK tax resident, sells his main residence in February 2022. The gain is fully exempt by virtue of private residence relief (see **Chapter 9**).

There is no need for Shane to submit a 30-day reporting form to inform HMRC of the disposal.

Where a UK tax resident disposes of an overseas residential property (e.g. a Spanish investment property) or of non-residential property (e.g. commercial property) the disposal is not reported through the CGT on UK property account, and the 30-day deadline does not apply.

Instead, the disposal can be reported through a self-assessment tax return, and/or the real time CGT service may be used. See **2.3.1** and **2.3.2** respectively for further information.

Non-UK residents

Generally, non-UK residents are not subject to UK CGT on the gains they realise.

There are exceptions to this. One such exception is where a non-UK resident disposes of an interest in UK land or property, regardless of whether said land is residential or commercial.

Non-residents disposing of UK property or land should report the disposal to HMRC, and pay any CGT due, within 30 days of the sale completing. In the case of non-UK residents, a disposal should still be reported to HMRC even if no gain arises on disposal or if there is a loss. Further information can be found in **Chapter 4** and **Chapter 18.**

Disposals from 6 April 2020 should be reported through the CGT on UK property account. Taxpayers who should report gains in this way include:

- non-resident individuals;
- personal representatives of a non-resident who has died;
- non-residents in a partnership;
- non-resident landlords;
- non-resident trustees; and
- UK residents meeting split year conditions, where the disposal is made in the overseas part of the tax year.

Example 3

India owns a UK residential property which, prior to her moving abroad, was her main residence.

She sells it within nine months of moving out at a time when she is non-UK resident for tax purposes.

Although there is no CGT due on the sale (the gain being exempt by virtue of private residence relief – see **Chapter 9**) India does need to report the disposal to HMRC within 30 days of the sale completing.

If the non-resident is unable to create a CGT on UK property account (e.g. by not having a Government Gateway login) it is possible to submit a paper reporting form to HMRC. A copy can be requested from HMRC's technical team.

Disposals of UK land or property that took place prior to 6 April 2020 were reported using a different non-resident CGT return.

Guidance: https://tinyurl.com/85nsbe (HMRC guidance re CGT); https://tinyurl.com/4vznrrj4 (non-residents' CGT on property)

Agent authorisation

Where an agent reports a disposal on behalf of a taxpayer using the CGT on UK property service, there are several steps to be followed to ensure the relevant authorisation is in place:

- the tax agent will need to create an agent services account;
- the taxpayer should create a CGT on UK property account using his or her Government Gateway details;

- the agent should sign in to their agent services account, and select "ask a client to authorise you" to manage the taxpayer's CGT on UK property account (noting that the agent will need to enter the taxpayer's CGT on UK property account details); and
- a link is then generated, which the agent shares with the taxpayer. This link authorises the agent to manage the taxpayer's CGT on UK property account.

Interaction with self-assessment

As with the real time CGT service discussed at **2.3.2**, if a taxpayer uses the CGT on UK property account to report a gain and otherwise has no need to file a self-assessment tax return, there should be no requirement to file a self-assessment tax return.

However, taxpayers who are required to submit a self-assessment tax return still need to report the disposal when they file their tax return, even if they have had to report the disposal via the CGT on UK property account.

2.4 Payments

2.4.1 Introduction

Taxpayers are subject to CGT at varying rates – 18% or 28% on gains from residential property and 10% or 20% on gains arising from other chargeable assets, depending on whether the taxpayer is a basic rate or higher/additional rate taxpayer respectively.

The following scenarios are considered below:

- the normal payment rules (see **2.4.2**);
- disposals of land and property (see **2.4.3**);
- consideration received in the form of instalments (see **2.4.4**); and
- disposals by way of gift (see **2.4.5**).

2.4.2 Normal rules

CGT arising on a disposal should be paid by the 31 January following the end of the relevant tax year.

Payments on account do not apply to CGT – the full amount is payable by 31 January.

Example

Tessa has CGT to pay for 2021-22 of £5,000.

She should pay the £5,000 by 31 January 2023.

Real time CGT service

The real time CGT service enables a taxpayer to report, and pay, CGT in "real time" (see **2.3.2**).

Once the taxpayer has reported the disposal through the service, HMRC issue a payment reference number and instructions on how to pay.

While the statutory deadline remains 31 January following the tax year end, the taxpayer can pay the CGT due before this date.

2.4.3   *Land and property disposals*

Where a UK resident disposes of UK residential property on or after 6 April 2020, or a non-UK resident disposes of an interest in UK property or land, generally the sale should be reported to HMRC, and the associated CGT paid, within 30 days of the sale completing. See **2.3.3** and **Chapter 4** for further information.

2.4.4   *Consideration payable by instalments*

If either the whole or part of the consideration for an asset is payable by instalments, the person making the disposal may be able to pay the tax arising on the gain by instalments over a period of up to eight years, ending no later than when the last of the instalments of consideration is due.

To qualify, the instalments of consideration should:

- begin not earlier than the date of the asset's disposal;
- last for a period that exceeds 18 months; and
- continue beyond the usual due date for the payment of the tax arising on the gain.

The seller is normally expected to pay instalments of tax equal to 50% of each instalment of *gross* consideration due under the contract until the total tax liability has been discharged.

Where instalments of consideration fall due on or before the usual statutory payment deadline, the respective instalments of tax are payable on that normal due date.

If the instalments of consideration fall due after the statutory due date then the instalments of tax are payable on the dates when the seller is contractually entitled to receive the consideration.

HMRC example (from CG 14910)

Mr X enters into a contract for the sale of an asset which provides for its disposal on 1 June 2021 for a consideration of £120,000 payable by six instalments of £20,000 each, at yearly intervals, commencing on 1 September 2021. The CGT payable by Mr X on the disposal is £35,000 and he asks for TCGA 1992, s. 280 to apply.

The tax instalments are calculated as:

- 50% of consideration due on 1 September 2021 (tax £10,000);

- 50% of consideration due on 1 September 2022 (tax £10,000);

- 50% of consideration due on 1 September 2023 (tax £10,000); and

- 50% of consideration due on 1 September 2024 (balance of tax £5,000).

As the first two instalments of tax fall before the normal due and payable date for disposals in the tax year 2021-22 (31 January 2023) then £20,000 is due from Mr X on 31 January 2023.

As the remaining instalments of tax fall after 31 January 2023, these are due when the instalments of consideration to which they relate are due to Mr X under his contract with the purchaser. Thus, a further £10,000 tax is due from him on 1 September 2023 and the final amount of £5,000 tax is due from him on 1 September 2024.

Law: TCGA 1992, s. 280
Guidance: CG 14910

2.4.5   *Gifts*

Ordinarily, CGT arising on a chargeable gain should be paid by reference to the relevant payment deadlines mentioned above and is payable by the person making the disposal.

However, there are exceptions to this rule where gifts of assets are concerned:

- Certain gifts of assets are eligible to be paid by ten equal yearly instalments (TCGA 1992, s. 281).
- HMRC may also, in certain circumstances, assess the donor's CGT on the donee (TCGA 1992, s. 282).

Further information is provided at **Chapter 12**.

2.5 Record keeping

2.5.1 Introduction

Good quality records should be kept that support any chargeable gain/loss reported.

2.5.2 Retention

The general rule is that records should be kept for at least a year after the self-assessment filing deadline for a given return (assuming the return is filed on time).

Individuals who have a business or rent property should keep their records for five years after the self-assessment filing deadline (again, assuming an on-time filing).

Where the return has not been filed on time records need to be kept until the deadline for opening an enquiry has passed.

Clearly, if an enquiry has been opened, records must be kept until it is completed, whether or not normal deadlines for record retention have passed.

Records relating to the acquisition and/or improvement of a chargeable asset should be kept indefinitely, until the asset is disposed of. Following the disposal, the record keeping timeframes outlined above apply.

Law: TMA 1970, s. 12B
Guidance: CH 10000

2.5.3 Format of records

There is no specific format in which records relating to chargeable disposals should be kept, but all relevant records (e.g. receipts, bills, invoices and contracts) should be retained to show how a gain has been calculated. This could include records that highlight:

- the date the asset was purchased and its cost;
- the date that additional costs or expenditure were incurred (e.g. legal and professional fees) and the amount of these;
- substantiation of any market values used; and
- the date of sale and the consideration received for the asset.

Where inadequate records are kept, penalties can apply of up to £3,000.

Law: TMA 1970, s. 12B and Sch. 1A
Guidance: EM 4650

2.6   Penalties

2.6.1   *Introduction*

With the exception of certain disposals (see **2.3.2** and **2.3.3**) chargeable gains are typically reported via self-assessment tax returns.

This means that the ordinary late filing penalties apply where a self-assessment tax return is filed late.

A broad summary of the penalties that can apply for late filing is provided below.

2.6.2   *Self-assessment income tax return – late filing*

Where a self-assessment income tax return is submitted after the filing deadline (see **2.3.1**) the following penalties can be imposed by HMRC, depending on how late the return is:

- £100 for a return filed up to three months late;
- £10 a day, for up to 90 days, where a return is between three and six months late;
- £300 or 5% of the tax due (whichever is greater) where the return is more than six months late; and
- an additional £300 or 5% of the tax due (whichever is greater) where the return is more than 12 months late.

If the late filing of the return was deliberate, or deliberate and concealed, the penalty for a late submission of over 12 months is either 70% or 100% of the tax due respectively (with a minimum payable of £300). Reductions may be available for these higher penalties – see HMRC compliance check factsheet CC/FS18a for more information.

In respect of the six-month and 12-month late filing penalties, note the provision at FA 2009, Sch. 55, para. 17(3). Under that paragraph, where a taxpayer is liable for a penalty under more than one paragraph of Sch. 55 which is determined by reference to a liability to tax, the aggregate of the amounts of those penalties must not exceed the relevant percentage (usually 100%) of the liability to tax.

As such, where no tax is due, no tax-geared penalty can be raised, thus the £300 penalties cannot be levied. This was confirmed in the FTT case of *Jackson*.

Law: FA 2009, Sch. 55
Case: *Jackson v HMRC* [2018] UKFTT 64 (TC)
Guidance: HMRC factsheet CC/FS18a

2.6.3   *Late payment*

CGT arising on a disposal becomes payable by 31 January following the tax year end. There are late payment penalties where a payment is:

- 31 days late: 5% of the unpaid tax;
- six months late: an additional 5%; and
- 12 months late: a further 5%.

For further information on penalties under the income tax regime, see *Income Tax* (2021-22 edition) from Claritax Books.

Law: FA 2009, Sch. 56

2.6.4   *30-day reporting forms – late filing and/or payment*

As noted at **2.3.3**, both UK residents and non-UK residents may need to report a disposal of UK property or land to HMRC through the CGT on UK property account.

The deadline to report a disposal and pay any CGT due is 30 days from the date the sale has completed, *not* the date of contract exchange.

Where a taxpayer fails to report the disposal within the 30-day deadline, a late filing penalty is charged, in line with the same rates outlined at **2.6.2**. Note that, while HMRC guidance does not mention daily penalties where a return is more than three months late, HMRC do have discretion to levy daily penalties where the conditions are satisfied.

As the 30-day reporting deadline also covers the deadline to pay any CGT due on the disposal, late payment penalties and interest can also apply where the deadline is missed (see **2.6.3**).

Law: FA 2009, Sch. 55, 56
Guidance: https://tinyurl.com/4vznrrj4 (non-residents' CGT on property)

2.6.5   Other penalties

Penalties also apply for failure to notify liability, and for inaccurate returns.

Law: FA 2007, Sch. 24; FA 2008, Sch. 41

2.7   Enquiries

2.7.1   Introduction

This section is a general summary of HMRC's enquiry powers into income tax returns and assumes disposals have been reported on time. Late reporting would extend the deadlines discussed.

Further information is provided in the following Claritax Books volumes:

- Discovery Assessments – How to Challenge Them;
- Schedule 36 Notices – HMRC Information Requests;
- Tax Appeals – Law and Practice at the FTT; and
- Taxpayer Safeguards and the Rule of Law.

2.7.2   Self-assessment tax return

Where an income tax self-assessment tax return is filed on time (see **2.3.1**) HMRC have 12 months from the delivery of the return to open an enquiry.

To make a valid enquiry, HMRC must give the taxpayer written notice of their intention to enquire into the tax return.

During the enquiry, HMRC may amend the tax return under TMA 1970, s. 9C. Once HMRC have concluded their enquiry, a closure notice is issued under s. 28A.

In certain cases, it is also possible for HMRC to raise a "discovery assessment" even where the 12-month enquiry window has passed. A discovery assessment can be made under s. 29 where HMRC discover that:

- there is income or chargeable gains which ought to have been assessed, but have not been;
- an assessment to tax is, or has become, insufficient; or
- any relief that has been given is, or has become, excessive.

A discovery assessment cannot be made where the return followed generally prevailing practice at the time it was delivered.

2.7.3   30-day and real time reporting

If an individual is not in self-assessment and submits a reporting form to HMRC within 30 days to report a disposal of UK land or property (see **2.3.3**) then, for the purposes of HMRC's enquiry window, the reporting form is generally treated as having been delivered on 31 January following the tax year of disposal (FA 2019, Sch. 2, para, 20).

This means that HMRC have an enquiry window of 12 months following the deemed 31 January delivery date.

Taxpayers should ensure they retain appropriate records (see **2.5**) to cover this enquiry period.

Example

Trish, who is not resident in the UK, is not required to submit a self-assessment tax return. She completes the sale of her former UK main residence on 10 October 2021 and reports the disposal to HMRC before the deadline of 9 November 2021.

For the purposes of HMRC's enquiry window, HMRC treats the reporting form as though it was delivered on 31 January 2023. HMRC have until 31 January 2024 to enquire into the reporting form.

Interestingly, the real time service (see **2.3.2**) is not, at the time of writing, formalised as a return within legislation. This means that any potential enquiry window into a transaction reported through the real time service is uncertain. However, it would be a reasonable assumption that the enquiry window would broadly run parallel with that for 30-day returns, as outlined above.

Law: TMA 1970, s. 9A, 9C, 29; FA 2008, Sch. 36; FA 2019, Sch. 2
Guidance: EM 1506

2.8   Rights of appeal

2.8.1   Introduction

The following is a high-level overview of the appeals process as it applies for direct tax matters. In appropriate cases, taxpayers may also wish to consider mediation in the form of the alternative dispute resolution (discussed in depth in *Taxpayer Safeguards and the Rule of Law*, from Claritax Books).

2.8.2   Appeals process

Decisions by HMRC generally carry a right of appeal.

If an appeal is possible, HMRC communicate this fact in their decision letter. The taxpayer then, typically, has 30 days to lodge an appeal.

Where an individual or business has been impacted by Covid-19, HMRC allow an additional three months to appeal any decision dated February 2020 or later. The taxpayer should explain within the appeal that the delay is due to Covid-19. For guidance on this, see the website of the Low Incomes Tax Reform Group (LITRG) – details below.

When an appeal is lodged, HMRC consider the appeal and either uphold their original decision or amend it accordingly.

If the appeal is dismissed, HMRC can offer a review (or one can be requested). The review is carried out by an HMRC officer who was not involved in the original decision, and usually takes 45 days.

If, following HMRC's review, the taxpayer disagrees with the decision, an appeal may be made to the FTT (which again, should typically be made within 30 days of the review decision). Alternative dispute resolution may also be available.

Note that the taxpayer may also appeal directly to the FTT and bypass the review, although if a review has been requested, this must conclude before an appeal may be made to the tribunal.

Most cases that make it to tribunal are dealt with initially by the FTT, although very complex cases may proceed directly to the Upper Tribunal.

The majority of appeals are typically dealt with at the FTT level or below (e.g. upon HMRC review). However, more complex cases may progress to the Upper Tribunal, the Court of Appeal (in England and Wales, or equivalent courts in Scotland or Northern Ireland) or, ultimately, to the Supreme Court.

Law: TMA 1970, s. 31, 31A, 47C*ff.*

Guidance: https://tinyurl.com/pz7m9apy (LITRG guidance re Covid relaxations)

2.8.3   *Extra Statutory Concession A19*

Although a minor point, it is worth remembering that HMRC (in limited circumstances) may cancel the tax owed by a taxpayer where:

- HMRC have failed to act on information they had; and
- there was a delay in informing the taxpayer about the tax due.

This relief is possible under Extra Statutory Concession (ESC) A19, the text of which is reproduced below (with minor reformatting):

"Arrears of income tax and CGT may be given up if they result from the failure of HMRC to make proper and timely use of information supplied by:

- a taxpayer about his or her own income, gains or personal circumstances; or
- an employer, if the information affects a taxpayer's coding; or
- the Department for Work and Pensions (DWP), about a taxpayer's state retirement, disability or widow's pension.

Tax will normally be given up only if the taxpayer:

- could reasonably have believed that his or her tax affairs were in order; and
- was notified of the arrears more than 12 months after the end of the tax year in which HMRC received the information indicating that more tax was due; or
- was notified of an over-repayment after the end of the tax year following the year in which the repayment was made.

In exceptional circumstances arrears of tax notified 12 months or less after the end of the relevant tax year may be given up if HMRC:

- failed more than once to make proper use of the facts they had been given about one source of income; and

- allowed the arrears to build up over two whole tax years in succession by failing to make proper and timely use of information they had been given."

There is no statutory right of appeal should HMRC refuse to cancel tax under ESC A19.

Guidance: PAYE 95000, 95090

COMPUTATIONS

3. The CGT computation

3.1 Introduction

Once a chargeable disposal has been made it must be reported to HMRC under the relevant reporting regime. For disposals generally, this will be via the self-assessment system, although there is an additional system for reporting gains on certain disposals of UK property.

The reporting of the gain, and payment of any CGT due, is considered in **Chapter 2**. Before it can be reported, however, the gain must be quantified, and adjusted for any relief(s) available.

This chapter addresses the basic structure of the computation. The chapters that follow then look at specific considerations for particular asset types, for example land, shares and securities.

3.1.1 Overview of the computation

HMRC set out a general *pro forma* for calculating a chargeable gain at CG 14200:

	Disposal proceeds		A
Less	Base cost	B	
	Other allowable costs	C	
	Unindexed gain		D
Less	Indexation		E
	Chargeable gain		F

This is a useful starting point, but further consideration is needed.

For individuals, partners and trustees, there is no need to consider indexation since it was withdrawn from April 2008.

Indexation is now only relevant to disposals made by companies, and it has been frozen since December 2017. As discussed in **Chapter 1**, this book is not concerned with the position for companies as they are not subject to CGT on their gains. However, the way the gains subject to corporation tax are *calculated* largely follows the CGT legislation set out in TCGA 1992. HMRC's guidance also refers to the position for companies in numerous places.

For our purposes, we are therefore concerned with A, B, C and F from this *pro forma*.

Guidance: CG 14200

3.1.2   *Calculating losses*

Losses are calculated in the same way as chargeable gains, i.e. a loss will arise when the base cost plus other allowable costs exceed the consideration when following the *pro forma*. In some circumstances, the amount of loss actually relievable may be restricted, for example where the disposal is of shares for which EIS relief has been given and not subsequently withdrawn.

3.1.3   *The date of disposal*

It is crucial to establish the date of disposal of the asset in order to report a gain (or loss) in the right tax year.

Generally, for disposals made under a contract, the date of disposal will be the date that contract is exchanged, even if the transfer of the asset occurs later. This is often seen with property sales, for example. If the contract is conditional, the date of disposal will be the date that all of the pending conditions have been satisfied, i.e. the date the contract becomes unconditional.

If the disposal is made by way of gift or settlement, the date of disposal is the date that the beneficial ownership or absolute entitlement passes.

If the disposal is of rights derived from capital assets, e.g. for unascertainable deferred consideration (see **3.2.4**), the disposal of the rights occurs on the date the capital sum in respect of those rights is received.

Where an asset is lost, damaged or destroyed, the deemed disposal occurs at the time the particular event occurred.

3.2   The disposal consideration

3.2.1   *Consideration – the general rule*

In most cases, on a disposal made by way of a bargain at arm's length between two unconnected persons, the disposal proceeds for the computation will be the consideration given in exchange for the asset being disposed of, less any allowable incidental costs of disposal.

In the simplest form, this will be a cash amount. However, consideration can consist of any form of value, and can be money or money's worth. There is no statutory definition of "consideration", but by way of illustration HMRC's guidance states that it can include:

- sterling money;
- the value of any asset, other than sterling money, received in exchange for the asset disposed of;
- the capitalised value of the right to receive income or payments in the nature of income;
- the capitalised value of relief from liability, for example to pay maintenance or rent or to repay a loan;
- the capitalised value of the benefit of free or low-interest loans; and
- the capitalised value of the benefit of rights to obtain goods or services free or at a discount.

Example

Andy sells a chargeable asset to Claire. Claire pays Andy £30,000 in cash, and gives him a painting worth £20,000 to make up the agreed transaction price of £50,000. Andy must use £50,000 when working out his gain or loss for CGT purposes.

If the consideration includes the right to receive income, it is only the capitalised value of that right that forms part of the consideration. The income itself is charged to income tax as it arises. This will be the case whether the payments are income, payments in the nature of income, or a rent charge, ground annual or feu duty (an archaic feudal charge now only applicable in Scotland).

Incidental costs of disposal

The types of expenditure accepted as directly relating to the disposal (and its acquisition) are set out in s. 38, which stipulates:

> "the incidental costs to the person making the disposal of the acquisition of the asset or of its disposal shall consist of expenditure wholly and exclusively incurred by him for the purposes of the acquisition or, as the case may be, the disposal, being fees, commission or remuneration paid for the professional services of any surveyor or valuer, or auctioneer, or accountant, or agent or legal adviser and costs of transfer or conveyance (including stamp duty [or stamp duty land tax]) together—

(a)   in the case of the acquisition of an asset, with costs of advertising to find a seller; and

(b)   in the case of a disposal, with costs of advertising to find a buyer and costs reasonably incurred in making any valuation or apportionment required for the purposes of the computation of the gain, including in particular expenses reasonably incurred in ascertaining market value where required by this Act."

Law: TCGA 1992, s. 38
Guidance: CG 14500

3.2.2   *Non-arm's length disposals and the market value rule*

The general rule in **3.2.1** is superseded in some circumstances by s. 17, which substitutes the market value of the asset in place of any actual consideration. This will apply where the taxpayer makes a disposal:

- otherwise than on arm's length terms, including gifts and transfers that are knowingly made at undervalue, and the making of, or adding to, a settlement;

- in connection with a loss of office or employment or diminution of emoluments, or otherwise in consideration for (or in recognition of) past services;

- for consideration that cannot be valued, whether in whole or in part, e.g. where there is an exchange of assets; and

- by way of a distribution from a company in respect of its shares.

The fact that a bargain is a "bad" bargain does not necessarily mean that the market value rule is invoked. A bad bargain can still be a bargain at arm's length, for example where a vendor accepts a relatively low offer for an asset, e.g. a property, to facilitate a quick sale where there is little or no alternative interest, or where the buyer has better information about an asset than the vendor.

This is often seen with antiques and artwork for instance. The test is whether there is a subjective intention by the vendor to confer a "gratuitous benefit" on the recipient. The most obvious example of this would be where an outright gift is made, but it can also include a sale knowingly made at undervalue.

HMRC's guidance at CG 14545 indicates that the following (non-exhaustive) list should be taken into account when considering whether a subjective intention is present:

- the presence or absence of real negotiations between the parties about the terms of the transaction;
- how the terms of the transaction compare with those in similar commercial transactions;
- whether the parties have separate legal or other professional representation;
- whether the parties have received independent advice;
- the character of any comparable prior dealings between the parties;
- whether the transaction between the parties may be linked with any other transaction between the same parties; and
- the relationship between the parties outside the transaction in question.

Connected persons

A transaction will always be deemed to be "otherwise than on arm's length terms" where the parties to the transaction are "connected persons", and so the subjective intention test does not need to be considered for such transactions.

In addition, any losses arising on such transactions become "clogged" ("ring-fenced") and may only be offset against future gains made on a disposal to the same connected person.

The term "connected persons" is defined in s. 286, and includes the following categories:

Other individuals

- the individual's spouse or civil partner (although there are special rules for disposals between spouses and civil partners);
- certain relatives of:
  - o the individual; or
  - o the individual's spouse or civil partner; or
- the spouse or civil partner of those relatives.

"Relative" has a restricted meaning for tax purposes. It includes siblings and lineal descendants or ancestors, e.g. brothers and sisters, parents, children, grandchildren, etc. but excludes cousins, uncles and aunts and so on. It should be noted that spouses remain connected persons for these purposes until the issue of the decree absolute (per *Aspden v Hildesley*).

Any two or more persons acting together to secure or exercise control over a company can be connected with one another, for example where one shareholder abstains from voting in a particular way in order that another person's vote carries more weight.

Trustees

The trustees of a settlement will be connected with:

- the settlor (as an individual);
- any person connected to the settlor;
- the trustees of any sub-fund settlements to a principal settlement; and
- a limited company or other body corporate connected to the settlement.

Partners and directors

Partners in business together in partnership are connected with one another, and each other's spouses, civil partners and relatives (see above). Directors of a company are not connected with one another unless they are also relatives or partners, unless the transaction is with the company itself.

The market value rule does not apply where there is an acquisition, but no corresponding disposal (or *vice versa*). For example, the issue of new shares by a company is not a disposal, even though someone acquires them.

Law: TCGA 1992, s. 17, 18, 286
Case: *Aspden v Hildesley* [1982] BTC 69
Guidance: CG 14545

3.2.3 Ascertaining market value

Market value means the price that the asset could reasonably be expected to achieve if it were sold on the open market. However, there are special rules that relate to valuations of shares and securities as follows:

Quoted shares and securities	The lower of the two quoted prices from the Stock Exchange Daily Official List, plus 50% of the difference. If the Exchange is closed on the date of disposal, the figures from the most recent date when it was open are used.
Unquoted shares	The open market value assuming the buyer has all the information required for a purchase at arm's length. May need to be agreed with HMRC.
Unit trust units	The buying price of the units on the date of disposal.

Law: TCGA 1992, s. 272, 273

3.2.4 Deferred consideration

In some cases, the consideration for the disposal may not be paid in a single transaction at the date of disposal. The consideration may be made in pre-agreed instalments, for example.

It is also possible that the purchaser will want to link the total consideration to future events. This is common in business takeovers where the purchaser wants to ensure that the acquired trade (or company) remains profitable going forward.

For a discussion of deferred consideration in the context of business asset disposal relief, see **7.6.5**.

Ascertainable consideration

If the full amount of the consideration is specified in the contract, and it is simply a case of spreading this out across a number of instalments, the future consideration is said to be "ascertainable". There is no scope to split the instalments out as separate chargeable events, though it may be possible to pay the CGT in instalments (see below).

Example 1

Morgan agrees to sell the shares in his company. The agreement for the disposal provides for a consideration of £500,000, of which £300,000 is payable on completion and £200,000 will be payable in four annual instalments of £50,000. This deferred consideration is known at the outset, and so is ascertainable.

In these circumstances, the full amount of the consideration is brought into account in the year of disposal. There is no discounting for time value, or for the risk of the purchaser not fulfilling the instalments. If any of the consideration is not received, the vendor may amend the initial calculation to take account of this, and have the difference in tax reduced or refunded (as applicable).

Where the consideration is payable in instalments, it may be possible to request to pay any CGT due in instalments (s. 280). This will be available where the consideration instalments:

- begin no earlier than the date of disposal of the asset;
- extend over a period exceeding 18 months; and
- continue beyond the date on which the tax would otherwise be due and payable.

In most cases, the instalments of tax will be equal to 50% of the instalments of consideration due (or the balance of the amount remaining outstanding, if lower) until the liability has been paid in full, with no adjustment for associated selling costs, etc.

The instalments of tax are due to HMRC on the same day as the instalments of consideration are due to the vendor. However, if the instalments of consideration are contractually due before 31 January in the tax year following the year of disposal, i.e. the normal due date for CGT on disposals in the year, the due date for the instalment of tax will be the normal due date, i.e. 31 January.

Example 2

Jenni enters into a contract on 1 June 2021 to sell an asset for £180,000, payable in six annual instalments of £30,000 starting on 1 October 2021. Her CGT liability is £36,000 and she makes a claim to pay the tax in instalments. Jenni's tax payments will be as follows:

Date of instalment	Date tax payable	Calculation	Amount due £
1 October 2021	31 January 2023	50% x £30,000	15,000
1 October 2022	31 January 2023	50% x £30,000	15,000
1 October 2023	1 October 2023	Balance of tax due, as less than 50% of instalment	6,000
1 October 2024	n/a	n/a	0
1 October 2025	n/a	n/a	0
1 October 2026	n/a	n/a	0

The asset is sold in tax year 2021-22 so the normal due date is 31 January 2023. As the first two instalments fall before this date, the tax on these is due on 31 January 2023 as normal. The tax on the third instalment is then due to HMRC on the day the instalment is due to the vendor.

Contingent but ascertainable

Deferred consideration can also be ascertainable, but contingent on some future event or condition being satisfied. Where this is the case, it is treated in the same way as other consideration, i.e. taxable in the year of disposal with no discount in respect of the deferred portion.

Example 3

Morgan agrees to sell the shares in his company. The agreement for the disposal provides for a consideration of £500,000, of which £300,000 is payable on completion and £200,000 will be payable in four annual instalments of £50,000, as long as the profits of the first year following the disposal exceed £100,000. Morgan's disposal proceeds in the year of disposal will be £500,000.

What makes such consideration ascertainable is that the full amount of the consideration, i.e. the maximum amount receivable, is known at the outset – even though it may not eventually be received. The mere fact that the contingent part may be subject to a cap or maximum does not necessarily mean that it is ascertainable. The consideration will be ascertainable as long as the deferred part can be determined by reference to a contractual amount, or by reference to computations. It can also be ascertainable if all of the events that will establish the amount have already occurred by the disposal date, e.g. if the future consideration is based on profits for an accounting period that has ended before the disposal date.

If any part of the deferred consideration proves to be irrecoverable, the taxpayer may claim to make an adjustment to the original gain under s. 48, and either recover an appropriate amount of the tax already paid, or reduce the amount payable, for example where the liability is being paid in instalments.

Law: TCGA 1992, s. 48, 280
Guidance: CG 14883

Contingent and unascertainable

If the amount of contingent consideration cannot be determined at the date of disposal, there are different rules. HMRC's guidance at CG 14940 states that consideration is unascertainable if events that establish the amount of the consideration do not occur until after the disposal date. They give the following examples:

- The agreement for the sale of shares in a company provides for an initial payment of £100,000, plus three further payments equal to the excess of the company's profits over £300,000 in each of the three years following the date of the contract.

- The agreement for the sale of land provides for a consideration of a capital sum payable in three annual instalments to be calculated by reference to the tonnage of landfill dumped on that site in the three years after the date of the contract.

Following the cases of *Marson v Marriage* and *Marren v Ingles*, it was established that the right to receive the unascertainable consideration is an asset in its own right, i.e. a "chose in action". The payments when received are capital sums derived from assets within the scope of s. 22, and each payment constitutes a separate chargeable event, being a disposal or part disposal of the right to receive the consideration. They are not payments in satisfaction of a debt.

Any ascertainable amount is brought into account in the year of disposal, in the way described in the previous section. The present value of the chose in action is also brought into account, as it represents consideration for the asset being disposed of. Such rights are often referred to as earn-out rights.

Example 4

John bought a trading business in 2013 for £100,000, and sells it to a third party in March 2021. The consideration consists of £500,000 in cash at the disposal date, and the right to two further payments over the next two tax years based on the profits of the business. John agrees with HMRC's Shares and Assets Valuation (SAV) department that the present value of this right is £300,000.

In May 2022, John receives £190,000 based on the profits of the business to 5 April 2022. The remainder of the right is valued at £125,000 by SAV.

In May 2023, he receives a further £130,000 in relation to the profits for the year to 5 April 2023. The way the gains will be calculated is as follows:

2020-21	£
Consideration (£500,000 cash plus value of earn-out right)	800,000
Less acquisition cost	(100,000)
Gain for 2020-21	700,000

First contingent payment

2022-23	£
Consideration paid	190,000
Less acquisition cost: $£300,000 \times \dfrac{£190,000}{£190,000 + £125,000}$	(180,952)
Gain for 2022-23	9,048

Second contingent payment

2023-24	£
Consideration paid	130,000
Less acquisition cost: £300,000 − £180,952	(119,048)
Gain for 2023-24	10,952

In this way, the full proceeds are brought into charge. Initially the right was valued at £300,000 and brought into charge in 2020-21, but £320,000 was eventually received. The additional £20,000 is brought into account as demonstrated here.

Note that the calculation of the cost used up by the first contingent payment is worked out by using the part-disposal rules. These are discussed further in **3.4**, and require a valuation of the remainder of the asset. In this example, the second contingent payment uses the remainder of the base cost as there will be no further payments, i.e. the asset has been completely disposed of. If there were further payments, another calculation would be required, with a further agreement of the value of the remainder.

Losses arising on the disposal of earn-out rights are also subject to special rules. Because the earn-out right is a distinct asset from the original asset disposed of, a loss can arise where the eventual proceeds are less than the original value brought into account in the year of disposal.

In most circumstances, capital losses may only offset gains arising in the same year. Where this is not possible, the loss may be carried forward indefinitely to offset future gains.

However, where the loss arises on the disposal of the right to deferred unascertainable consideration and the conditions in s. 279A-D are met, the loss may be offset against any tax year in which a chargeable gain accrued upon a disposal or part disposal of the asset for which the right to unascertainable consideration was conferred. This is done by making an election, either on the tax return or in writing. This is one of only two occasions where it is permitted to carry back a capital loss (the other being where a loss is incurred in the part of the tax year in which a taxpayer dies).

Example 5

The facts are the same as in **Example 4** above. However, this time John only receives £30,000 in May 2023, so a loss of £89,048 arises. John can elect to offset the loss against the original gain of £700,000 made in 2020-21.

Law: TCGA 1992, s. 22, 279A-279D

Guidance: CG 14940

Cases: *Marson v Marriage* (1979) 54 TC 59; *Marren v Ingles* (1980) 54 TC 76

3.2.5 Series of transactions

Section 19 exists to ensure the market value rule described in **3.2.2** for transactions between connected parties cannot be exploited in regard to a collection of assets that are worth more together than separately. In the absence of a specific provision, it would be possible to make a series of single transactions of the assets and take advantage of the lower value of the individual items.

For example, a collection of valuable items that together make a complete collection or set will almost always be worth more when sold together. Section 19 therefore replaces the market value of the individual item with an "appropriate proportion" of the aggregate market value that would have applied if all the items had been disposed of at the same time.

These rules only apply if all of the following conditions are satisfied:

- A person disposes of assets to a connected person or persons by way of two or more gifts or other transactions.
- Those transactions occur within a period of six years ending on the date of the last of them – they are said to form "a series of linked transactions".
- The "original market value" of the assets disposed of is less than the "appropriate portion of the aggregate market value" of the assets disposed of by all the transactions in the series.

Example

Mary owns four identical antique cabinets that together form a complete set. Taken together, the collection is estimated to be worth £75,000. Individually, each item is estimated to be worth £10,000.

In the absence of s. 19, Mary could gift the items to her daughter in four separate transactions in four different tax years to keep the deemed consideration below the CGT annual exemption. For simplicity's sake, assume that the market values do not change.

Section 19 counteracts this by replacing the market value with the proportional value of the piece when taken as part of a set, i.e. £75,000/4 = £18,750 in this case.

The situation is often described by reference to groups of chattels, but it could equally apply to shareholdings, e.g. where the original shareholding is a controlling holding.

In practice, the numbers will not be as neat as in the example above. The first transaction in a series will initially be brought into account using the proceeds or market value in respect of the individual item as appropriate. The deemed proceeds may then be adjusted by reference to the series of linked transactions as a whole upon the occasion of a subsequent disposal. Where there are more than two transactions, the aggregate market value of the assets disposed of to date would have to be considered, and each earlier transaction within the six-year period ending with the most recent of them would have to be revisited and revised.

Linked transactions made between spouses or civil partners are not subject to s. 19. However, the provisions may still need to be considered where there is more than one recipient, e.g. a shareholding transferred in a series of transactions to both a spouse and a child. A just and reasonable apportionment would then be required.

HMRC provide a comprehensive example of the application of the rules in relation to shareholdings at CG 14740.

Law: TCGA 1992, s. 19, 20

3.2.6   *Spousal etc. transfers made on a no gain/no loss basis*

Where the parties to the transaction have a particular type of relationship to one another, the transaction is deemed to take place on the basis that neither a chargeable gain nor an allowable loss is generated in connection with the disposal. The recipient is deemed to acquire the asset for consideration equal to the allowable expenditure on the asset.

The most common example of a no gain/no loss transaction is one made between two spouses or civil partners under s. 58.

Example

Al and Bert are in a civil partnership. Al owns an asset he acquired for £15,000 in 2003, when he incurred £500 in associated acquisition costs. In May 2021 he gifts the asset to Bert. Al is deemed to receive consideration of £15,500 for the asset, giving him a gain of £nil. Bert is deemed to have paid £15,500 for it, and this amount will be brought into the computation on any future disposal.

The application of s. 58 can cause issues upon the break-up of a marriage or civil partnership. The no gain/no loss treatment applies in any year that the two parties are "living together" for the purposes of ITA 2007,

s. 1011. That is to say, a married couple or members of a civil partnership are treated as living together unless:

- they are separated under an order of a court of competent jurisdiction;
- they are separated by deed of separation; or
- they are in fact separated in circumstances in which the separation is likely to be permanent.

As a result, the inter-spouse exemption can be used following permanent separation, but only until 5 April of the tax year in which the separation occurs. Timing of transferring assets upon a divorce or dissolution of a civil partnership can therefore make a significant difference to the tax position.

Section 58 does not apply:

- if until the disposal the asset formed part of trading stock of a trade carried on by the one making the disposal, or if the asset is acquired as trading stock for the purposes of a trade carried on by the one acquiring the asset; or
- if the disposal is by way of *donatio mortis causa* – that is to say, a gift made independently of a will in contemplation of death.

Other no gain/no loss transactions

A no gain/no loss transaction may arise with the same mechanics as described above in relation to:

- deemed disposals of settled property which revert to the settlor on the death of the beneficiary;
- changes to partnership sharing ratios with no revaluation in the accounts;
- a charity becoming absolutely entitled to settled property;
- gifts to charities, employee trusts (or employee ownership trusts), or housing associations; and
- transfers to a harbour authority.

Law: TCGA 1992, s. 58

3.3 Allowable expenditure

3.3.1 *Amounts deductible from the disposal proceeds*

As HMRC point out in their guidance, it is important to recognise that CGT is concerned with the *gains* made on the disposal of assets. That is to say, only the "profit" element of the disposal should be brought into charge. Therefore, permissible expenditure must be deducted from the disposal proceeds to arrive at the chargeable gain. With some minor exceptions, allowable expenditure will fall into one of the following categories:

- the acquisition cost of the asset, including any associated costs, (e.g. solicitors' fees);
- enhancement expenditure that increases the capital value of the asset, e.g. an extension to a property that is still in existence at the date of disposal;
- amounts incurred in preserving or defending the title to, or rights over, the asset; and
- any permissible incidental costs of disposal.

It is specified that an item of expenditure may only be deducted once, e.g. in the unlikely circumstances where it would fit into more than one of these categories. Where expenditure has only partly been incurred for these purposes, an apportionment on a just and reasonable basis should be made, e.g. a solicitor's bill that partly relates to a boundary dispute on a buy-to-let property, and partly to do with unrelated advice.

Where the transaction is not made on an arm's length basis, including to a connected party, market value is substituted for any actual acquisition cost. Additionally, where the transaction is made on a no gain/no loss basis, the transferor's allowable expenditure is used.

Any VAT incurred should be included, unless the seller was able to reclaim it.

Is it capital?

A distinction must be made between enhancement (often referred to as "capital") expenditure, and expenditure of a "revenue" nature. This is often seen in the context of trading expenses, but s. 39 prohibits the deduction of any sum that *would* have been deducted as part of the computation of the profits of a trade, if the asset had been a fixed asset for the purpose of a trade.

Example

Andy purchases a buy-to-let property for £150,000 in 2010. He incurs £8,000 building an extension, and pays a handyman £1,500 for painting and some minor re-wiring work. Andy sells the property in 2021. His allowable expenditure will be the £150,000 acquisition cost plus the £8,000 spent on the extension, as long as this was still in existence at the date of disposal. However, the £1,500 is not allowable as it would have been classed as repairs and/or maintenance, i.e. revenue, not capital, in nature.

A full discussion of the revenue v capital argument is beyond the scope of this book. However, it is discussed more fully in *Income Tax* from Claritax Books, and see HMRC's *Business Income Manual* from BIM 35001 onwards.

Law: TCGA 1992, s. 39
Guidance: BIM 35001*ff.*

3.3.2   *Excluded expenditure*

In addition to revenue expenses, certain other items of expenditure are specifically excluded from being "allowable" expenditure:

- contingent liabilities;
- discounts given in return for postponement of consideration payment;
- insurance premiums paid to cover the risk of damage, loss, or depreciation;
- expenditure that has been reimbursed from public funds; and
- interest, other than that specifically allowed by s. 40 (interest charged to capital).

Law: TCGA 1992, s. 38(3), 39, 40, 50, 205

3.3.3   *Rebasing*

Generally, the actual acquisition cost will be used, unless the market value rule is in point. However, there are some occasions where the asset's value at a given historic date is substituted instead.

Uplift in value on death

Where an asset is passed via a will, the recipient is treated as acquiring it at the value agreed as part of the probate process. This "tax-free uplift" is a form of rebasing, though death is not a chargeable event for CGT purposes.

Law: TCGA 1992, s. 62

Assets held on 31 March 1982

Another rebasing commonly seen in practice is to an asset's value at 31 March 1982, under s. 35. In order to apply, the asset must have been held at that date.

The rebasing works by deeming a disposal to have occurred on 31 March 1982, with the asset re-acquired immediately at its market value. This date was used to coincide with the introduction of the indexation allowance, though the rebasing was not available until 1988. Where the asset has since been transferred on a no gain/no loss basis, e.g. between spouses or on the reversion of a life interest to the original settlor, the person making the disposal will be treated as having held the asset at 31 March 1982, as long as the only transfers in the interim period were all on a no gain/no loss basis.

Since 6 April 2008 (coinciding with the withdrawal of indexation for individuals), this rebasing treatment has been mandatory (so the alternative treatment is now only applicable for corporation tax purposes).

Example

Jacinda bought a house in 1979, when she was 18, for £15,000. By March 1982, the property was worth £21,000. In 1990 she began letting the property, and in 2006 she transferred it to her husband for income tax planning reasons. The house was sold in 2021 for £180,000. The starting point for calculating the gain is to use £21,000 as the acquisition cost, giving a gain of £159,000 before the calculation of any private residence relief.

The rebasing provisions extend to the situation where the asset being disposed of was not held on 31 March 1982, but is derived from an asset held on that date. An example of where this might apply in practice is where an individual held a leasehold interest in a property on 31 March 1982, and subsequently acquired the freehold reversion. The allowable cost would be the consideration paid for the freehold plus the market value of the lease on 31 March 1982.

In the case of a part disposal (see **3.4**), the March 1982 value will be used to calculate the cost to be brought into account.

Law: TCGA 1992, s. 35

Disposals of UK property by non-UK residents

In general, CGT only applies to UK-resident taxpayers, or those who fall foul of the "temporary non-resident" rules discussed in **Chapter 18.** Broadly, this means that a gain accruing to an individual in a tax year when he or she is not UK-resident (or the non-resident part of a split year) under the statutory residence test is not a chargeable gain. Of course, it may be taxable in the country where the individual is resident for tax purposes, but that country may have lower rates of tax – or even no capital tax charges at all.

As a result of this, UK residential property has been a very attractive investment for offshore individuals. There has been growing suggestion that wealthy offshore landlords are shutting potential buyers out of the property market by holding properties as an investment – in many cases with no intention of letting a tenant occupy them.

To help combat this, the CGT regime was extended to non-residents for disposals of UK residential property from April 2015. By default, the computation would use the 2015 market value where property was held at the date of the change, and so this is another example of rebasing. The regime was expanded to include disposals of all UK-sited "immovable" property in April 2019, bringing commercial buildings into charge. These changes, including the options for rebasing, are discussed in detail in **Chapter 18**.

Law: TCGA 1992, Sch. 4ZZB

3.4   Part disposals

If a disposal consists of only part of a larger asset, such that any part of the asset (or rights derived from it) remain undisposed of, particular rules to determine the portion of expenditure that can be deducted in the CGT computation. A basic example is the sale of a parcel of land out of a larger plot. However, a part disposal can also apply where the disposal creates a separate legal interest or right over an asset, for example where a lease is granted out of a freehold (the special treatment of leases is examined in **Chapter 4**).

Any costs that can be directly ascribed to the part disposed of can be deducted directly, with no need to apportion – for example, any legal costs or valuer's fees solely relating to the part sold. Similarly, any costs that can be wholly ascribed to the part retained should be omitted from the calculation.

Non-specific costs – such as the original acquisition cost, enhancement costs, etc. – will need to be apportioned. This is achieved by using the formula prescribed in s. 42:

$$\text{Allowable cost} = \text{Base cost of asset} \times \frac{A}{A + B}$$

Here, A is the sales proceeds (or deemed proceeds, e.g. where the market value rule applies) and B is the market value of the part retained at the date of the disposal. A valuation will therefore be required.

Example

Gordon bought an asset for £50,000. He sells part of it in 2021-22 for £18,000. It was agreed that the remainder of the asset was worth £70,000 at the time of the disposal. The gain will be calculated as follows:

	£
Proceeds	18,000
Less apportioned cost:	
£50,000 x 18,000/(18,000 + 70,000)	(10,227)
Gain on partial disposal	7,773

The base cost of the remaining asset is £50,000 – £10,227 = £39,773.

Where the part disposal is made in a way that gives rise to no gain/no loss, for example on a transfer to a spouse, it is still necessary to use the formula above to ascertain the deemed acquisition cost and remaining base cost to carry forward for subsequent disposals.

Law: TCGA 1992, s. 42

3.5   Capital losses

3.5.1   *General overview*

Where the allowable expenditure exceeds the consideration for the sale, a capital loss arises. To attract relief, i.e. to be an allowable loss, this must be claimed by giving notice to HMRC via the tax return, or by making a standalone written claim within four years of the end of the tax year in which the loss arises.

As a general rule, these losses must be offset against gains arising in the same tax year in priority to deducting the annual exempt amount. If there is an excess of losses over gains (or if there are no other gains to offset) this will be carried forward indefinitely.

When gains in excess of the annual exemption arise in future years, the losses will be available to reduce these to nil.

As discussed earlier, any losses arising on a disposal to a connected person (see **3.2.2**) will be a "clogged" (ring-fenced) loss, and will not be available to offset against general gains – whether in the same tax year or a later one. Rather, they can only be offset against gains arising on disposals to the same connected person.

A loss may have to be restricted under s. 41 if capital allowances have been claimed in respect of the asset. This is to prevent relief for the same expenditure being claimed against both income tax and CGT. Where applicable, this is achieved by reducing the allowable expenditure in the calculation.

Law: TCGA 1992, s. 41

3.5.2 *Carrying losses back*

As mentioned above, capital losses cannot usually be carried back against historic gains, other than in two very specific circumstances:

- Losses accruing in the year of an individual's death can be carried back to offset gains arising in the three preceding tax years on a last-in first-out basis, i.e. the most recent first (s. 62) after deducting any brought-forward losses.
- Where a loss arises on the disposal of an earn-out right (see **3.2.4**).

The carry-back on death is restricted to the extent to which the gains exceed the annual exemption. For the year of death, the losses must be offset against gains of the same year first, even if those gains would be covered by the annual exemption.

Example

Gilbert died in 2021-22, having made a capital loss of £25,000 and a gain of £2,000. His gains and losses for the previous three years are as follows:

> 2020-21 – gain of £15,000
>
> 2019-20 – loss of £7,000
>
> 2018-19 – gain of £28,000

The mechanism for relieving the loss in the year of death will be as follows:

> **Step 1** – offset against £2,000 gains in year of death. Balance left to relieve = £23,000.
>
> **Step 2** – look at 2020-21 tax year. Position is a £15,000 gain offset by £2,700 brought-forward loss (part of the loss from 2019-20) and the £12,300 exemption. No s. 62 relief available. Balance left to relieve = £23,000.
>
> **Step 3** – look at 2019-20 tax year. No gains to offset. Balance left to relieve = £23,000.
>
> **Step 4** – look at 2018-19 tax year. Position is a £28,000 gain. After deducting the annual exemption (£11,700), some £16,300 of the s. 62 loss can be used to reduce the gain.

No further relief for the losses is possible. The balance of the 2019-20 loss (£4,300) and the remaining £6,700 of the loss from the year of death will essentially die with the individual.

Law: TCGA 1992, s. 62

3.5.3   *Non-allowable losses*

Just as not all gains made on the disposal of assets are "chargeable" gains, so also some losses arising will not be allowable, i.e. no relief is available in a number of circumstances.

Non-residence

If an individual is not a UK resident in the year (or UK part of the year) in which the disposal took place, the loss will not be allowable unless:

- it arises in respect of an asset used in connection with a UK trade;

- the individual becomes subject to the temporary non-residence rules (see **Chapter 18**); or

- the disposal is in respect of UK-sited immovable property after 5 April 2019. Where this is the case, the loss can only offset future gains made on other UK property. But if the individual becomes UK resident again, the carried-forward loss will be available for general offset.

Domicile

An individual who is UK-resident, but not domiciled (or deemed domiciled), can make an election to be taxed on the remittance basis. One of the effects of this is that he or she will not pay tax on unremitted overseas gains.

In the first year that the remittance basis is claimed, it is possible to make an irrevocable election to allow overseas losses to offset UK gains. If the election is not made, overseas losses cannot be used in the UK until the individual becomes domiciled. See **Chapter 18** for further discussion.

Exempt assets

Where a disposal of an asset would not give rise to a chargeable gain (were it sold at a profit), any loss will not be an allowable loss unless the legislation specifically permits it, e.g. for EIS shares (albeit with adjustment for income tax relief given).

The table in **Appendix 2** sets out exempt assets and the corresponding statutory references, and includes cars, qualifying corporate bonds and gilts, wasting chattels, etc. This is summarised at **1.3.4**.

Debts acquired from connected persons

A loss accruing on the disposal of a debt is not an allowable loss by virtue of s. 251(4) if the debt was acquired from the original creditor (or his personal representative or legatee), at a time when the creditor etc. was a person connected (see **3.2.4**) with the person making the current disposal. In other words, the debt is acquired either directly or by one or more purchases through persons all of whom are connected with the person making the disposal.

Artificial losses and anti-avoidance

Where an artificial loss arises as a result of arrangements that fall foul of the value shifting provisions in s. 29, the loss will not be an allowable loss. In practice, this is most often applicable to transactions involving shares or land.

Similarly, loss relief will not be available if the loss accrues to a person directly or indirectly in consequence of (or otherwise in connection with) any arrangements that are intended to secure a tax advantage, i.e. tax avoidance schemes etc.

Law: TCGA 1992, s. 16A, 29, 251(4)

3.5.4   Share loss relief

If a loss arises on a disposal of certain company shares, it may be possible for the individual to offset the loss against his or her general income rather than against capital gains, by virtue of ITA 2007, s. 131. This "share loss relief" is available if the shares are:

- shares which have EIS income tax relief attributable to them (see *EIS and Other Venture Capital Reliefs* – from Claritax Books – for in-depth coverage of the scheme); or
- shares in a qualifying trading company that were subscribed for, i.e. they were newly issued shares.

Share loss relief is only available:

- for an arm's length disposal;
- for a distribution paid in the course of the dissolution or winding-up of the company;
- as a result of a negligible value claim (see **3.5.5**); or
- following the "entire loss, destruction, dissipation or extinction" of the asset (which, intuitively, would only appear to apply where shares are unilaterally cancelled).

There is no requirement for the company to be a UK company or to be carrying on a business in the UK. (The former requirement to carry on the business in the UK was found to be incompatible with the principle of free movement of capital by the European Commission. At the time of writing the requirement has not been reinstated into the legislation following Brexit.)

A company will be a qualifying company if it meets conditions A, B and C.

Condition A is that the company either:

- meets all of:
  - ○ the trading requirement – namely that it must exist wholly for the purpose of carrying on a trade that is not an "excluded" trade (as set out in ITA 2007, s. 192);
  - ○ the control and independence requirement;

      o the qualifying subsidiaries requirement; and

      o the property management subsidiaries requirement; or

- has ceased to meet any of those requirements at a time which is not more than three years before that date, and has not since that time been an excluded company, an investment company or a trading company.

Condition B is that the company either:

- has met each of the requirements mentioned in condition A for a continuous period of six years ending on that date or at that time; or

- has met each of those requirements for a shorter continuous period ending on that date or at that time, and has not before the beginning of that period been an excluded company, an investment company or a trading company.

Condition C is that the company:

- met the gross assets requirement both immediately before and immediately after the issue of the shares in respect of which the share loss relief is claimed; and

- met the unquoted status requirement at the relevant time (the time the shares were issued).

The specific requirements of these conditions may be subject to change, so the contents of the relevant statutory provision should be referred to.

HMRC also discuss potential complications, for instance where there are bonus issues or share reorganisations, and the guidance in HMRC's *Venture Capital Schemes Manual* at VCM 70170 is a useful reference.

Where available, the allowable loss is calculated using the normal capital loss rules, including the share identification rules (see **Chapter 5**) where relevant. The loss may be offset against income in the year in which the loss arises, or in the preceding year. As for other income losses, the individual may choose which year to relieve the losses against first, but the income of the year which is the subject of the initial claim must be exhausted before deduction of the personal allowance (if available) before the balance can be set against the other year. Current-year losses are prioritised before carried-back losses where both are claimed in the same tax year.

The loss will also be subject to the general restriction under ITA 2007, s. 24A, which limits the aggregate of uncapped income tax reliefs to the higher of:

- £50,000; and
- 25% of adjusted total income

in any tax year.

Law: ITA 2007, s. 24A, 131-143, 192
Guidance: VCM 70170

3.5.5 *Assets of negligible value*

A loss may also crystallise where an individual makes a negligible value claim in respect of an asset that has become worthless (or virtually worthless). This is achieved by treating the individual as having sold the asset and immediately reacquiring it at the time of the claim.

This is obviously a deemed disposal, as the individual continues to own the asset in question.

A negligible value claim can be made where it is evident that the asset has lost its value. In the case of quoted shares it is straightforward, and HMRC maintain a list of those shares they accept as being of negligible value. However, with unquoted shares and other assets things can be more complicated,

In particular, an individual subscribing for shares in an already failing company may have difficulty substantiating a loss. In the cases of *Harper* and *Dyer*, the shares in question were adjudged to have been of negligible value at the time of acquisition, i.e. there was no loss in value, irrespective of the fact that they were subscribed for at par value. This can happen when individuals seek to provide financial assistance for sentimental reasons rather than as a commercial investment.

In the case of unquoted shares, HMRC will usually accept that they have become negligible in value if the company is in administration, and if it has been indicated that there will be no payment made to shareholders. The claim must be made before the shares cease to exist.

For other assets, a claim may be made following loss, damage or destruction that renders the asset worthless. Receipts of compensation for these events are covered at **6.4.2**.

In order to be eligible for a claim, the asset must:

- have become of negligible value (i.e. worth nothing or next to nothing) while owned by the claimant; or
- have been of negligible value at the time of acquisition, and:
  - o the asset must have been acquired by way of a no gain/no loss transaction (e.g. between spouses); and
  - o any other disposals between the time the value became negligible and the disposal by the claimant were no gain/no loss transactions.

The loss will be deemed to arise on the date the claim is made. However, it is possible to backdate the claim by up to two years if the asset was already of negligible value.

Where the conditions for share loss relief are met (see **3.5.4**), a negligible value claim can lead to a loss relievable against income tax instead of CGT.

Law: TCGA 1992, s. 24; ITA 2007, s. 131
Guidance: Helpsheet 284

3.5.6   *Trading losses*

In most cases, it is desirable to offset trading losses against income. However, where this is not possible, or it is not possible to use them fully in this way, a claim may be made to offset trading losses against capital gains.

The amount of loss that can be claimed under s. 261B is broadly restricted to the lower of:

- the amount of remaining loss available following other loss relief claims (e.g. a s. 64 claim); and
- the "maximum amount", which is the amount on which the individual would be chargeable to CGT for the year of claim, ignoring the annual exempt amount.

In essence, the maximum amount takes into account the taxpayer's net capital gains in the year of the claim, less any capital losses brought forward (or, exceptionally, carried back).

Law: TCGA 1992, s. 261B, 261C
Guidance: BIM 85025, 85040

4. Land

4.1 Introduction

Land is a chargeable asset for CGT purposes. Generally, the principles discussed in **Chapter 3** apply when calculating the gain on a disposal of land. However, there are specific rules that need to be considered in certain circumstances. This chapter looks at these circumstances and the application of the rules.

Although land is generally a capital asset for tax purposes, there are some transactions where a disposal of land will lead to a charge to income tax or corporation tax (not covered in this book), rather than CGT.

Some of the more important examples of this are:

- an appropriate proportion of a lease premium paid for the grant of a lease of 50 years or less;
- disposals of land held as trading stock, for example by a property dealing or development business; and
- disposals to which the transactions in UK land anti-avoidance rules apply – these rules essentially deem profits that are purportedly capital in nature to be trading profits and hence subject to income tax (or corporation tax, as the case may be) where there is an intention to realise a profit on the sale of the underlying land.

4.2 Key definitions and concepts

4.2.1 Land

Much of the tax treatment of disposals of land derives from land law. The term "land" includes the land itself, as well as (subject to specific provisions or easements):

- all buildings situated on it;
- all fixtures attached to it;
- any minerals below its surface; and
- the air space above it.

TCGA 1992, s. 288(1) specifies that land includes messuages, tenements, and hereditaments, houses, and buildings of any tenure. Additionally, HMRC guidance confirms that chattels that have been brought onto land may become fixtures, and therefore brought within the remit of CGT. For example, a stock of timber is a collection of chattels. However, if the timber is used to build an outbuilding, it becomes a fixture.

Land and the buildings situated on it are therefore treated as a single asset. However, there are provisions that can treat buildings as a distinct and separate asset in circumstances where they are lost or destroyed.

Law: TCGA 1992, s. 288(1)
Guidance: CG 70207

4.2.2 Ownership of land

Theoretically, all land in England, Wales and Northern Ireland is ultimately owned by the Crown, with a different legal framework in Scotland. Other persons may, however, hold a legal interest in land under the land tenure regime. This has its roots in the Norman feudal system.

In the modern day, there are three types of tenure applicable to England and Wales – freehold, leasehold and commonhold. The position in Scotland is different, with tenures being abolished by the *Abolition of Feudal Tenure etc. (Scotland) Act* 2000, replaced by a system of outright ownership termed "heritable title". This is broadly equivalent to a freeholding in English law.

The legal interest (and its extent) in land is referred to as the "estate in land" – essentially the collection of legal and beneficial rights the owner of the interest has. The terms "freehold" and "leasehold" refer to the way the ownership of the estate in land is structured. Generally, a freehold interest will be an absolute title, vested on the registered owner, and will continue indefinitely. A leasehold interest will be for a defined period, granted by the freeholder, and may be subject to additional restrictions or covenants.

There are other types of interest in land which grant lesser rights to their holders, including:

- licences, which generally give implied or express right of usage with no right of exclusive possession, for example a licence to enter a cinema to view a screening is implied in the ticket sale;
- easements, which give some right (either positive or negative) over the land, for example rights of way; and

- *profits-à-prendre*, i.e. the right to take something (e.g. game) from land belonging to another.

Commonhold ownership is a relatively new way of holding interests in land. It is mainly seen in buildings which are subdivided into individual units, such as an apartment complex. The individual units may be held as freehold interests, with each freehold owner being a member of a commonhold association that collectively holds the freehold interest of the common parts of the building, such as the stairwell, entrance hall, and so on.

Law: *Abolition of Feudal Tenure etc. (Scotland) Act 2000*

4.2.3   Co-ownership

In England, Wales and (usually) in Northern Ireland, land held by more than one person will be held either as joint tenants or as tenants in common.

The Scottish equivalent terms are joint owners or owners in common following the abolishment of the system of tenures.

Joint tenancy

Joint tenants (or joint owners) have an equal, undivided share in the land. Broadly, that means that each owner owns 100% of the interest.

Where a joint tenant dies, the interest in the land passes to the surviving joint tenant (or tenants). It cannot be passed by a will, for example to their children.

On a lifetime sale, proceeds would normally be split equally between the owners. It is possible, though, for joint tenants to divide the proceeds in accordance with their actual contributions as long as they all agree and signify this agreement in writing.

For CGT purposes, however, each tenant/owner is entitled to an equal share of the sales proceeds – even if they have not all contributed towards the cost of the land equally.

Tenancy in common

Where the land is held by tenants in common (or owners in common), each of them owns a fractional share of the interest in the land absolutely, rather than jointly owning 100% of it.

As a result, they are able to sell or gift their fractional interests as they see fit. Also, an interest in land held as a tenant in common does not automatically pass to the other co-owners upon death. This means that for tax planning purposes, co-ownership as tenants in common is usually more suitable as it allows for greater flexibility.

If the interest in land is currently held as joint tenants, it is possible to sever this joint tenancy so as to convert the ownership into a tenancy in common. This severance can be done with or without the agreement of all joint owners. There will only be CGT consequences if any of the joint owners reduce their interest. However, there may be other reasons, including non-tax considerations, that do favour a joint tenancy.

Example

Bert and Ernie own Sesame Manor as joint tenants. The house is valued at £1 million, meaning that they have an effective interest of £500,000 each. To facilitate some tax planning, they have decided to sever the joint tenancy and own the property as tenants in common in a ratio of 90 to 10 in favour of Bert. Following the transaction, Ernie's interest is reduced from £500,000 to just £100,000, meaning that he has made a disposal for CGT purposes.

A contract for the disposal of a legal interest in land can only be made in writing, unless (in England and Wales):

- the disposal creates an interest that is a lease at full market rent for a term of less than three years; or
- it is a contract made in the course of a public auction.

In Scotland, the only exception is for the grant of a lease for a term not exceeding 12 months.

It is, however, still possible for a transfer of a beneficial interest to be made by oral contract. Obviously, however, it is advisable for such disposals to be evidenced in writing.

4.2.4 Legal and beneficial ownership

The legal owner of the land is the person or persons holding the legal title, which must be registered with the Land Registry. A maximum of four persons may be registered as legal owners.

Beneficial ownership is the key concept for CGT purposes, as it is usually the beneficial owner who bears the CGT burden. Beneficial ownership refers to the person or persons entitled to benefit financially from the underlying property. This will often, but not invariably, be the same as the legal owner.

Example

Stan is the legal owner of a parcel of land in England. However, he purchased this on behalf of Ollie, who is entitled to 100% of the proceeds of any disposal. If the land is sold at a gain, it is Ollie who will need to pay any CGT, even though his name will not appear on any of the conveyancing documentation.

This is an example of a nominee, or bare trust, arrangement. The beneficial owner may be identified by a written agreement, but where there is uncertainty, it will be necessary to consider certain factors. A person is likely to be a beneficial owner if he or she:

- holds legal title (in the absence of any contrary evidence the legal owner will normally also be the beneficial owner);
- occupies the land;
- receives any rental income from the land;
- provided the funds used to purchase the land; and/or
- received the sale proceeds from a disposal of the land.

However, these factors are not always sufficient to determine the matter. In *Lawson*, the FTT upheld the taxpayer's appeal against HMRC's assertion that Mrs. Lawson, who was the sole legal owner of a property, was also the sole beneficial owner. The taxpayer had prepared her self-assessment return on the basis that her spouse was a joint beneficial owner, i.e. the gain was shared between them with two annual exempt amounts being applied. Following an internal review, HMRC gave their reasons for their decision that she was sole beneficial owner. These included the facts that:

- all rental income and the proceeds from the sale were received by Mrs. Lawson;
- Mr. Lawson had not included any gain on his own return and had never declared any rental income; and
- Mrs. Lawson was also the sole legal owner.

The FTT upheld the appeal, confirming that they were both beneficial owners, stating that:

"It was quite clear to us that the true purpose of purchasing the property at Southampton Road was to provide stable and secure accommodation for Mr. and Mrs. Lawson's daughter as opposed to being held for investment purposes. We found as a fact that a strong indication as to the lack of commerciality could be seen in net income from rents.

... We accepted Mrs. Lawson's evidence that the money used to fund the purchase came from two sources; the inheritance she received and the couple's savings. We found it significant that the savings included the proceeds of an endowment policy which had been held solely in Mr. Lawson's name. In such circumstances, we found that the provision of funds with which the property was purchased came from both Mr. and Mrs. Lawson."

Case: *Lawson v HMRC* [2011] UKFTT 346 (TC)

4.3 Specific rules relating to land disposals

4.3.1 Overview

The general computational rules apply to land in the same way as they do to other assets. However, a number of situations require specific rules:

- residential property (see **4.3.2**);
- part disposals of land (see **4.3.3**);
- leases (see **4.3.4**);
- exchanges of joint interests in land (see **4.3.5**);
- land subject to compulsory purchase orders (see **4.3.6**);
- disposals of qualifying furnished holiday lettings (see **4.3.7**);
- woodlands (see **4.3.8**); and
- disposals by non-UK residents (see **4.3.9**).

4.3.2 Residential property

The basis of calculating a capital gain on the disposal of a residential property follows general principles. However, the rate of CGT applied to gains realised on residential property are 18% to the extent that the basic rate band for the year has not been used, and 28% for any excess. These rates are higher than the 10%/20% rates that apply to gains generally.

Where the residential property has been the only or main residence of the taxpayer making the disposal at some point during the period of ownership, some or all of the gain may be exempted by private residence relief (see **Chapter 9**).

Residential property is defined (in TCGA 1992, Sch. 1B, para. 3) as any land where:

- the land consisted of or included a dwelling at any time falling on or after the date on which the applicable period begins;
- the interest in land subsisted for the benefit of land that consisted of or included a dwelling at any time falling on or after that date; or
- the interest in land subsists under a contract for the acquisition of land consisting of or including a building that is to be constructed or adapted for use as a dwelling.

The "applicable period" means the period beginning with the date the interest in the land being disposed of was acquired and ending with the date of disposal.

It is possible that land that is the subject of a disposal has not always been used for residential purposes. In these circumstances, Sch. 1B, para. 2 requires the gain to be apportioned by the fraction A/B, where:

- A = the number of days in the applicable period on which the land to which the disposal relates consists of or includes a dwelling; and
- B = is the total number of days in the applicable period.

Further, where there is mixed use of the land, i.e. where part is used for residential purposes and part is not, the relevant fraction itself must be adjusted on a "just and reasonable" basis.

Example 1

Morgan owned a parcel of land, subdivided into four distinct but equal fields of five hectares for ten years. After five years, he built a house on one of the fields. The house and its grounds were separated from the remaining field by fencing that Morgan erected. The house and grounds occupied one hectare of the field. The entire parcel, including the house, is sold after ten years. As there is non-residential use, followed by mixed use of the land, an appropriate calculation of the relevant fraction might be as follows (ignoring the minor complication of leap years):

$A = (1{,}825/3{,}650 \times 1/20) \times 3{,}650 = 91.25$ days

$B = 3{,}650$ days

The numerator (A) has been adjusted to reflect both the non-residential use for five out of ten years (calculated on a daily basis), and the fact that the residential use only applied to one hectare out of the total 20 in the parcel.

Temporary unsuitability

Where a dwelling becomes damaged to an extent that it is temporarily unsuitable for use as a dwelling, no adjustment is made to the appropriate fraction, unless the unsuitability:

- arose from accidental damage; and
- the period of unsuitability lasted for at least 90 consecutive days.

This does not apply if the unsuitability arises due to work undertaken to alter the building, including partial demolition.

30-day reporting of gains

For disposals where the date of exchange falls on or after 6 April 2020, if, after taking account of any relief or exemption available, there is a tax liability on a disposal of residential property located in the UK, the gain must be reported to HMRC within 30 days of the completion date. A payment on account of the tax liability must be made by the same deadline. The relevant provisions are contained in FA 2019, Sch. 2.

This will be a provisional payment on account, rather than a final payment, because it only takes account of the taxpayer circumstances at the date of disposal. For example, the taxpayer may later make a capital disposal (before the end of the tax year) which gives rise to an allowable loss which he could offset against the gain realised on the residential property. However, he cannot adjust the original computation of the payment on account to take account of the loss. Instead, this would be reconciled via the self-assessment tax return, with credit given for the payment on account already made.

The requirement to submit a return within 30 days of completion only applies where there is CGT to pay. Therefore, if there is a gain but this falls within the annual exempt amount of £12,300, there will be no need to submit a 30-day return. This will also be the case if there are losses brought forward or arising in the tax year before the date of disposal, or if the disposal of the property itself gives rise to a loss.

There is also no need to submit a 30-day return if a self-assessment tax return containing details of the disposal is submitted before the expiration of the 30-day deadline. This will largely be confined to disposals where the date of exchange and date of completion straddle the end of the tax year, due to the way that the self-assessment deadlines and tax points work. The trigger date for the 30-day return is the date of completion, but the tax point for CGT purposes is the date of exchange, meaning the relevant tax year for CGT purposes can be earlier than the one in which the 30-day return is due.

Example 2

Jenny exchanged contracts to sell one of her rental properties on 30 March 2021. The sale completed on 1 May 2021. If there is a CGT liability, Jenny will need to make a return detailing the disposal and the payment on account by 31 May 2021. However, because the tax year of disposal is 2020-21, Jenny could submit her return for that year including details of the disposal. If she does this before 31 May 2021, she will not have to submit the 30-day return or make a payment on account of the CGT.

Prior to 6 April 2020, there was a broadly similar 30-day reporting regime that was restricted to non-UK residents (see **4.3.9**).

Law: TCGA 1992, Sch. 1B; FA 2019, Sch. 2

4.3.3   Part disposals of land

A part disposal of land may occur where:

- a piece of land is sold out of a larger holding, e.g. a 10-acre plot is sold out of a 100-acre holding; or
- a lease (or sublease) is granted out of a superior interest (see **4.3.4** for the CGT treatment of leases).

The general rules for working out the allowable cost attributable to the part disposal, discussed in **Chapter 3,** apply to part disposals of land. However, HMRC's Statement of Practice D1 allows the taxpayer to use an alternative basis to simplify the calculation, as long as the asset being sold is the entire interest in what is recognisable as a separate asset. An obvious example would be a single field out of a larger estate. However, it could also be an identifiable part of a larger field, regardless of any physical segregation.

In the absence of the alternative basis, an accurate valuation of the part remaining unsold would need to be obtained. Not only may this mean incurring professional fees, but it may also be a complicated process to identify and value the assets disposed of and retained.

Under the alternative basis, the part being disposed of is treated as a distinct and separate asset from the remainder. The taxpayer is permitted to apportion a part of the total cost to it on a fair and reasonable basis. The apportioned cost used in the calculation is then deducted from the allowable cost of the remainder of the estate. Any basis of apportionment will be accepted as long as it is reasonable. For example, cost may be apportioned by area if it is appropriate to do so. Alternatively, a reasonable valuation could be obtained of the part disposed of at its original acquisition date.

Example 1

Melissa purchased a 200-acre farm in 1990 for £200,000. In 1998, approximately one quarter of the land becomes flooded following heavy rain. Melissa incurs £40,000 for remedial work needed to bring the land back into use. In 2021-22, Melissa sells a parcel of ten acres for £100,000. Two of these ten acres were affected by the flooding in 1998.

Melissa's gain will be worked out as follows:

	£
Proceeds	100,000
Less:	
Proportion of acquisition cost 10/200 x £200,000	(10,000)
Proportion of remedial costs 2/50 x £40,000	(1,600)
Gain	88,400
Cost of remaining land (£200,000 – £11,600)	188,400

Care needs to be taken where there have been previous part disposals. The alternative basis can only be used if any previous part disposals made on or after 22 April 1971 have also been calculated on the alternative basis. The taxpayer is entitled to apply the general part disposal rules to any disposal. However, once this is done any subsequent part disposals of the same asset must be calculated on the same basis. This is to ensure that the eventual cost deducted over all disposals does not exceed the total initial acquisition cost.

If HMRC believe that the apportionment of the cost is unreasonable and agreement with the taxpayer cannot be reached, they will replace it with a calculation based on the general rules. The taxpayer would then have to appeal against the calculation by making representations.

The value shifting provisions in s. 29 may apply in circumstances where a transfer of value occurs in a way that does not give rise to a disposal under the CGT legislation – see **6.11.2**.

Law: TCGA 1992, s. 29
Guidance: HMRC *Statement of Practice* D1; CG 72000

Small part disposals of land

If the part of land disposed of is "small" then an election may be made under TCGA 1992, s. 242.

The disposal is "small" where:

- the consideration received for the part disposed of does not exceed more than 20% of the market value of the entire holding at the time of the transfer;
- the consideration does not exceed £20,000; and
- the total consideration for all transfers of land made in the same tax year does not exceed £20,000.

Where the election is made, the transfer is not treated as a disposal for CGT purposes. Instead, the consideration received is deducted from the allowable expenditure of the entire holding, i.e. it reduces the base cost of future disposals or part disposals. The election is not available for a grant of a lease out of a short lease or for a transfer to a spouse or civil partner (or other transfer made on a no gain/no loss basis).

There is also a restriction where the conditions are satisfied but the consideration received for the part disposal exceeds the total allowable cost of the whole holding. Here, s. 244 permits the taxpayer to make an election to deduct all of the allowable expenditure from the proceeds received for the part disposed of. This will extinguish the allowable expenditure incurred up to the point of the part disposal, so there will be no expenditure to deduct from a future disposal unless further expenditure is incurred, e.g. enhancement expenditure.

Example 2

William owns a large field that he acquired 30 years ago for £5,000. In 2021 the field is worth approximately £120,000 based on land values in the area. William sells a part of it for £20,000.

The disposal qualifies as small for the purposes of s. 242. However, because the proceeds exceed the allowable expenditure of £5,000 William cannot make the election to deduct the proceeds from allowable expenditure. Instead, the gain will need reporting, but William can make an election under s. 244 to use the full £5,000 in his computation of the gain; i.e. he will be taxed on the excess of the disposal proceeds of £20,000 over the full cost of £5,000.

The time limit for either of the elections is the first anniversary of 31 January following the end of the tax year in which the disposal takes place.

Law: TCGA 1992, s. 242, 244

4.3.4 Leases

A lease gives the holder a right to occupy land physically for the time specified.

A leasehold interest in land is therefore inferior to a freehold interest as it is temporary in nature. A leasehold interest in an estate only lasts for the term, or duration, of the lease, following which the associated rights revert to the freeholder (the reversionary interest).

The grant of a lease out of a freehold interest is a part disposal of an interest in land. Similarly, the grant of a sublease out of a leasehold interest (the headlease) is a part disposal. The alteration or sale (sometimes called an assignment) of a lease, as well as the merging of a lease with a superior interest, also constitute a disposal for CGT purposes.

In most circumstances, a lease will require the payment of rent. HMRC's guidance at CG 70703 states that if no rent is paid, it is unlikely that an arrangement will amount to a lease. CG 70704 goes on to say that where a right to occupy is granted on a rent-free basis, there is no part disposal for CGT purposes.

Long and short leases

For CGT purposes, a lease may be "long" or "short". The distinction is important, as short leases are categorised as wasting assets, and are subject to particular rules. A short lease is one that has 50 years or less to run. A long lease is one that has more than 50 years to run and is treated in the same way as a freehold interest for CGT purposes.

Grant of a long lease out of a freehold

Where the owner of a freehold interest grants a lease for a term of more than 50 years, it is treated as a part disposal as discussed at **3.4**. Where a premium is payable for the grant of the lease, it will be treated as the proceeds, i.e. A in the formula:

$$\text{Allowable cost} = \text{Base cost of asset} \times \frac{A}{A + B}$$

B will be the value of the reversionary interest retained by the landlord, plus the value of the right to receive rent. The value of B will need to be agreed by the Valuation Office.

Example 1

Joanna holds the freehold title to a property in Basingstoke she purchased last year for £175,000. She grants a 70-year lease on the property to Richard, who pays a premium of £150,000 for it. The value of the reversion is £180,000 as agreed by the Valuation Office. The capital gain is calculated as follows:

Proceeds	£
Premium received	150,000
Less allowable cost: $£175,000 \times \dfrac{£150,000}{£150,000 + £180,000}$	(79,545)
Chargeable gain	70,455

The treatment is the same for the holder of a long lease that grants a long lease out of it, for example a 60-year lease being granted out of a 100-year lease.

Law: TCGA 1992, s. 42

Assignment of a long lease

An assignment of a lease simply means that an existing lease is transferred to someone else, by means of sale or otherwise. The key feature of an assignment is that the owner of the lease relinquishes their rights over the property, and someone else acquires the same rights. This is different from the grant of a new lease, which creates a new asset.

The assignment of a long lease is very straightforward for CGT purposes. As the whole asset is being sold, all of the acquisition expenditure will be deductible in the chargeable gain calculation.

Example 2

After ten years, Richard, from **Example 1** above, decides to sell his leasehold interest to Veronica, who pays £200,000 for it. The lease still has 60 years to run, so it has not become a short lease.

Richard's chargeable gain will be calculated by simply deducting the premium he originally paid, £150,000, from the proceeds paid to him by Veronica, £200,000. His chargeable gain will therefore be £50,000. If Richard had incurred any incidental costs of acquisition or disposal, for example legal fees, these will also be deductible from the proceeds.

Grant of a short lease out of a freehold or long lease

A short lease is a wasting asset. Where a premium is received for the grant of a short lease, part of it is taxed as property income and part is taxed as a capital disposal. Essentially, the shorter the lease the larger will be the proportion that is taxed as income.

The granting of a short lease is still a part disposal, and the method to calculate the proportion of the acquisition cost to be deducted is similar to that for the grant of a long lease. However, the appropriate figure for A in the numerator of the fraction (and in the calculation of the gain) is restricted to the element of the premium that is not taxed as income. Accordingly, this must be calculated first.

To calculate the element treated as a capital receipt, the following formula is used:

$$\text{Capital element} = P \times 2\% \, (N - 1)$$

where:

P is the amount of the whole premium; and

N is the number of years the lease will run for.

Another way of presenting this is to say that the capital element can be calculated as:

$$\text{Capital element} = P \times \frac{(N - 1)}{50}$$

The allowable cost for the calculation of the gain can then be worked out using the revised formula:

$$\text{Allowable cost} = \text{Base cost of asset} \times \frac{a}{A + B}$$

where:

a is the capital element of the premium received (**A**).

The chargeable gain is then worked out by deducting the allowable cost from the capital element of the premium received. As before, **B** will be the value of the reversionary interest retained by the landlord, plus the value of the right to receive rent.

Example 3

John purchased the freehold of a property 20 years ago for £50,000. In the current tax year he grants a 40-year lease for a premium of £100,000. The Valuation Office agrees that the reversionary interest is £200,000.

The first step is to work out the capital element of the premium:

$$a = £100,000 \times 2\% \ (40 - 1) = £78,000$$

John will include the remaining £22,000 as property income on his tax return.

The next step is to work out the allowable cost for use in the calculation of the chargeable gain:

$$\text{Allowable cost} = £50,000 \times \frac{£78,000}{(£100,000 + £200,000)} = £13,000$$

The final step is to work out John's chargeable gain, which will simply be the capital element of the premium, £78,000, less this allowable cost.

John's chargeable gain is therefore £65,000.

Law: TCGA 1992, Sch. 8, para. 1

Assignment of a short lease

A lease with 50 years or less left to run is a wasting asset. Wasting assets that are chattels are generally exempt from CGT. However, leases are not tangible assets and so do not benefit from this exemption. As with all wasting assets, the initial value of the short lease depreciates over time. However, due to the nature of land this depreciation is not uniform as it is for other assets (per s. 46), i.e. the value does not reduce by the same amount each year. Instead, the value of a lease initially depreciates slowly, but the rate of depreciation will be much higher as the expiration date approaches.

Accordingly, TCGA 1992, Sch. 8 provides percentage tables (reproduced at **Appendix 4**) that must be used when calculating the allowable cost appropriate to the assignment of a short lease.

Where a short lease is being assigned, the entire asset is being disposed of. The gain is therefore relatively straightforward to calculate, being the proceeds received for the assignment, less the allowable cost.

The allowable cost is the acquisition cost that has not "wasted" at the date of the disposal. Sch. 8 provides a formula to use to ascertain the disallowed portion of the expenditure, which can then be deducted from the total expenditure to give the allowable cost. However, it is more straightforward to work out the allowable portion directly. To do this, two percentage points are used:

- P_D = the relevant percentage for the years remaining at the date of disposal; and
- P_A = the relevant percentage for the years remaining at the date of acquisition.

The allowable cost is then worked out by multiplying the original acquisition cost of the lease by the fraction P_D/P_A.

Example 4

Charles acquired a 60-year lease from the freeholder 20 years ago for a premium of £200,000. In the current tax year, the lease still has 40 years to run, and so is a short lease. Charles assigns the lease for £450,000.

To calculate the chargeable gain, the percentage tables must be used to determine the amount of the original £200,000 acquisition cost which has not wasted by the date of disposal.

Using the percentage tables, the lease has 40 years to run at the date of disposal. P_D is therefore 95.457%. Charles acquired the lease when it had more than 50 years to run. P_A is therefore 100%.

The allowable cost is therefore £200,000 x 95.457/100 = £190,914.

Charles's capital gain will therefore be £450,000 – £190,914 = £259,086.

If the person granting the lease has incurred incidental costs of acquisition, or enhancement expenditure, these must be similarly restricted, but by using the relevant percentage at the date they were first reflected in the lease, rather than the acquisition date.

For example, if Charles had incurred enhancement expenditure of £10,000 two years before the assignment of the lease in the example above, the relevant percentage point to use for P_A would be the one for 42 years, i.e. 96.593%. P_D would remain as 40 years. The allowable amount would therefore be £10,000 x 95.457/96.593 = £9,882.

If P_A and/or P_D are not whole years then the relevant percentage points must be calculated to the nearest month. Incomplete months are rounded up if they consist of 14 or more days, otherwise they are rounded down. A monthly increment is calculated by finding the difference between the percentage points on either side and then dividing by 12, e.g. if looking for 26 years and four months the percentage points for 27 and 26 years would be used. Once the monthly increment had been calculated it would then be multiplied by four and added to the percentage for 26 years.

Law: TCGA 1992, s. 46, Sch. 8, para 1(6)

Grant of a short lease out of a short lease

The grant of a short sublease out of a short headlease is the most complex scenario for CGT purposes.

The complexity arises because both the sublease and headlease are wasting assets. Sch. 8, para. 4 stipulates that the part disposal rules do not apply. Instead, a proportion of the costs attributable to the headlease is apportioned to the sublease using the percentage tables and multiplying the expenditure by the fraction:

$$\frac{P_1 - P_3}{P_2}$$

where:

- P_1 is the percentage for the remaining years of the headlease at the date of the grant of the sublease;
- P_2 is the percentage for the remaining years of the headlease at the date of acquisition (or at the date the expenditure is reflected in the headlease for enhancement expenditure); and
- P_3 is the percentage for the remaining years of the headlease at the date the sublease ends.

In this way, the rules ensure that only the expenditure that wastes under the duration of the sublease is deductible.

However, there is a further complication as the rent payable under the sublease must be compared to the rent payable under the headlease. If the sublease rent is more than the headlease rent, the allowable expenditure is further reduced. This is because when a higher rent is agreed during negotiations, it is usually in exchange for a lower initial premium, which would reduce the capital gain. A reduction to the allowable amount is therefore made by multiplying the expenditure by the fraction:

Premium paid/Notional full premium

The notional full premium is the premium that would have been payable if the sublease rent were the same as the original rent payable. Again, this will usually need to be agreed with the Valuation Office.

A further complication is that the whole premium must initially be brought into account when calculating the chargeable gain, even though some of it will be charged to income tax. This amount will be deducted from the chargeable gain, but this is done at the end of the calculation and can only reduce the gain to nil – it cannot create or increase a loss.

Example 5

Kirsten acquired a 30-year lease over a property for a premium of £200,000. She pays £8,000 per year in rent. After five years she grants a sublease of ten years to a tenant, in exchange for a premium of £120,000 and annual rent of £10,000. The Valuation Office agrees that the notional full premium is £150,000.

There are several steps to calculate Kirsten's chargeable gain.

The first step is to ascertain the allowable expenditure using the formula and the three relevant percentage points.

Allowable expenditure =

$$£200,000 \times \left(\frac{81.100 - 61.617}{87.330}\right) = £44,620$$

(The headlease is for 30 years, 25 years of this remain when the sublease is granted and 15 years remain when the sublease expires.)

However, this needs to be adjusted because the sublease rent is higher than the headlease rent.

Allowable expenditure =

$$£44,620 \times \frac{£120,000}{£150,000} = £35,696$$

The chargeable gain can now be calculated. Remember, initially the whole premium is brought into account, not just the capital element.

	£
Premium received	200,000
Less adjusted allowable expenditure	(35,696)
Gain	164,304

Less part of premium charged as income
  Capital element
    £200,000 x 2% x (10 – 1) = £36,000
  Income element
    £200,000 – £36,000
	(164,000)

Gain for CGT purposes	304

Sometimes a lease out of a short headlease will only confer rights over part of a property, for example where only a room in the property is subject to the sublease. An extra step is required here: instead of using the total initial expenditure, the part disposal formula from **3.4** must first be used to work out the total expenditure attributable to the part of the property covered by the lease. This attributable expenditure is then used in conjunction with the percentage tables to work out the allowable expenditure. The remaining steps then continue in the way described above. A comprehensive example is provided at CG 71012.

Law: TCGA 1992, Sch. 8, para. 4

Losses restricted for income tax relief given

A capital loss may arise when a short lease is granted out of a short headlease. This loss will need to be restricted if the owner of the headlease is entitled to income tax relief under ITTOIA 2005, s. 292 on the part of the premium they paid that is taxed as income in the hands of their landlord. This relief would be available if they were operating a property business. The amount of restriction will be calculated by multiplying the annual s. 292 deduction by the duration of the sublease and deducting the element of the premium received for the sublease that is taxed as income. The following example is adapted from CG 71016 as an illustration:

Example 6

Petunia acquired a 40-year lease on a property, paying a premium of £300,000. Applying the formula, the amount of the premium taxable on the recipient as income was £66,000 (balance of the premium after deducting £300,000 x 2% x (40 – 1)). She was therefore entitled to claim an annual deduction of £1,650 (£66,000/40 years).

Her intention was to sublet it, but initially she struggled to find a tenant. After five years, she did find a tenant and granted a 21-year sublease over the whole property. The tenant pays a premium of £50,000. For simplicity's sake, assume the rent paid under the sublease is the same as Petunia's rent under the original headlease.

Applying the formula and percentage tables to the original premium of £300,000 gives allowable expenditure attributable to the sublease of £103,744 (see **Example 5** above).

On the face of it, the capital loss will be £53,744 (£50,000 – £103,744). The amount chargeable to income is £30,000 (balance of the premium after deducting £50,000 x 2% x (21 – 1)). This is not deducted as this is only done to reduce a gain to nil; it cannot create or increase a loss. However, an adjustment is needed for the s. 292 relief.

Prior to the grant of the sublease, Petunia was claiming relief of £1,650 against her profits each year. The total deduction over the term of the sublease will therefore be £1,650 x 21 = £34,650. However, Petunia must deduct the amount of the premium that will be taxed as income from this to arrive at the capital loss adjustment.

The appropriate amount to adjust the capital loss by is therefore £4,650 (£34,650 – £30,000).

Petunia's capital loss is therefore restricted to £49,094 (£53,744 – £4,650).

Where a restriction is necessary there will normally be no requirement to calculate the annual deduction, as this should be obvious from the historical claims for relief. As illustrated above, the daily amount of relief is the income element of the landlord's premium spread evenly over the duration of the original lease.

Law: TCGA 1992, Sch. 8, para. 5
Guidance: PIM 2300

Alteration of terms and commutation of rent

It is possible that, during the period covered by the lease, the landlord will agree to a variation of the terms of the lease in exchange for the payment of a capital sum by the tenant.

Alternatively, the tenant may desire a commutation of the rent due for the remainder of the lease and agree to pay a capital sum to the landlord. There may be provision for this in the original lease agreement.

Where the capital sum is received in exchange for a variation of the terms of the lease, or for a commutation of rent provided for in the terms of the lease, the capital sum received is treated as a premium, or additional premium. The tax treatment then follows that for lease premiums and will depend on whether the landlord holds the freehold, a long lease or a short lease.

If the capital sum is received for a commutation of rent, but the terms of the lease did not provide for this, the capital sum is chargeable under TCGA 1992, s. 22.

Law: TCGA 1992, s. 22 and Sch. 8, para. 5
Guidance: CG 71350*ff.*

Mergers of leases

It is possible for a leaseholder to acquire a superior interest in the land, e.g. the longer headlease that their sublease was granted from, or the freehold interest where the lease was granted by the freeholder. The original lease comes to an end on such occasions. The lease and the superior interest acquired are considered merged.

A later disposal of this merged asset requires some work to determine the allowable expenditure. This will be the sum of the amounts paid for:

- the acquisition of the original lease, adjusted to exclude any expenditure that has wasted where the lease had less than 50 years to run at the date of the merger; and
- the acquisition of the superior interest.

If the superior interest is a short lease at the date of disposal, the expenditure on its acquisition must also be adjusted to reflect the wasting nature of the asset by reference to the number of years left to run.

Law: TCGA 1992, s. 43

4.3.5   *Exchanges of joint interests in land*

In some cases, owners may jointly own land but wish to exchange their interests, for example to simplify their holding or to permit succession planning.

As a basic example, consider two individuals who jointly inherit two fields of equal size and value. One may wish to sell the interest, and the other may wish to put it to some other use. They may agree to rearrange their holdings so that each of them owns one field outright. Ordinarily, this will be a disposal by each of them of 50% of the interest to one another. However, if the following conditions are met s. 248A-E permits a form of rollover relief to apply:

- a person (the landowner) and one or more other persons jointly own a holding of land or two or more separate holdings of land;
- the landowner must dispose of an interest in the holding, or one or more of the holdings, to one or more of the co-owners;
- the consideration for the disposal is, or includes an interest in, another jointly held holding in land held by the owner and one or more of the co-owners;
- as a consequence of the disposal, the landowner and each of the co-owners become the sole owner of part of the holding, or the sole owner of one or more of the holdings; and
- the acquired interest is not an interest in excluded land.

Land is excluded land if, and to the extent that, it is a dwelling house or part of a dwelling house that would be covered by private residence relief if there was a chargeable gain at a "material time". A material time means any time during the period of six years beginning on the date of the acquisition of the acquired interest. If the land is not excluded land at the time of acquisition, but becomes excluded within the six-year period, rollover relief is withdrawn, and the gain is recalculated with no regard to the relief previously claimed.

Spouses or civil partners are treated as a single person for the purposes of this rollover relief.

The amount of relief

The amount of relief that can be claimed depends on whether or not the interests exchanged are of equal value, and whether any actual consideration is paid.

If they are of equal value, the landowner is treated as making a disposal on a no gain/no loss basis. The consideration for the acquisition of the acquired interest is reduced by any excess over actual consideration that they are treated as having received.

If the relinquished interest is of a lower value than the acquired interest, the same treatment applies.

However, if the relinquished interest is of higher value than the acquired interest, and the excess consideration is less than the amount of gain accruing on the disposal, the landowner is treated as if the amount of gain on the disposal is reduced to the amount of the excess consideration, and as if the acquisition cost for the new interest is reduced by the same amount the gain is reduced by.

It is not necessary for each joint owner to claim relief where they are eligible to do so, and each may make the decision independently of the others.

The following example is adapted from CG 73000.

Example

A and B, who are not connected persons, jointly own two parcels of farmland, Greenacre and Redacre. The land was acquired by inheritance at market values of £50,000 for each parcel, i.e. A and B both have a cost of £25,000 for each of the two parcels. A and B decide to exchange their joint interests so that A will own Greenacre and B will own Redacre.

At the time of the exchange Greenacre has a market value of £200,000 and Redacre a market value of £250,000. The five conditions in s. 248A are met and A and B claim rollover relief.

The relief on the disposal of the half-share interests is computed as follows:

- In A's case the amount or value of the consideration for the disposal of the relinquished interest (half interest in Redacre) is £100,000 (the value of a half interest in Greenacre). This is less than the market value of that relinquished interest, £125,000. Consequently relief is computed according to the rules in s. 248B(1) – see CG 73000.

- In B's case the amount or value of the consideration for the disposal of the relinquished interest (half interest in Greenacre) is £125,000 (the value of a half interest in Redacre). This exceeds the market value of that relinquished interest. The excess consideration of £25,000 (£125,000 – £100,000) is less than the amount of the gain of £100,000 (£125,000 – £25,000). Consequently relief is computed according to the rules in s. 248B(2), the gain being reduced to £25,000 (the excess consideration) and the rollover relief being restricted accordingly.

Step 1 – Compute B's consideration

Consideration for disposal of Greenacre:

£250,000 x 50% = £125,000

Step 2 – Compute B's allowable expenditure

Cost of Greenacre:

£50,000 x 50% = £25,000

Step 3 – Compute B's gain

Consideration for disposal of Greenacre *minus* allowable expenditure:

£125,000 – £25,000 = £100,000

Step 4 – Compute B's rollover relief amount

The amount that would reduce the gain of £100,000 (Step 3) to the amount of the excess consideration of £25,000 (£125,000 – £100,000), can be rolled over:

£100,000 – £25,000 = £75,000

Step 5 – Compute B's chargeable gain

Gain *minus* rollover relief:

£100,000 – £75,000 = £25,000

Step 6 – Compute B's cost of acquisition for the acquired interest

Actual cost (£100,000) *minus* amount by which B's gain was reduced:

£100,000 – £75,000 = £25,000

Step 7 – Compute B's total acquisition costs of Redacre

Original acquisition cost of half share *plus* cost of acquisition of acquired interest:

£25,000 + £25,000 = £50,000

Law: TCGA 1992, s. 248A-248E

Guidance: CG 73000

4.3.6   Land subject to compulsory purchase orders

Entities such as the government, local authorities, or utility companies may have a statutory right to acquire land. An owner of an interest in land may make a disposal to such an entity.

Usually, the entity will approach the landowner to try to agree a voluntary sale. Where an agreement for sale cannot be reached, the acquiring entity may exercise its compulsory powers by obtaining a purchase order.

Where a disposal is made to such an authority, a number of specific rules apply regardless of whether the disposal is made under contract (i.e. sold voluntarily in circumstances where compulsory powers could have been exercised) or under an order. It is the fact that the authority could have used its compulsory purchasing powers that is crucial under s. 247 (discussed below), subject to the taxpayer not having taken any previous steps to sell the land.

Compensation will usually be due based on either the value of the land for redevelopment, or the current use value of the land, plus amounts due in respect of any fall in value of other land as a result of the acquisition (severance) and also for disturbance.

An apportionment must be made between amounts that represent capital or income.

Income compensation

Where land has been used for the purposes of a business, an element of the compensation may be in respect of disturbance, e.g. a loss of stock or temporary loss of profits. This element is taxable as income.

Capital compensation

The elements of compensation paid in respect of the value of the land taken over, and in respect of any fall in value of other land as a result of the acquisition (severance), are capital in nature.

The amount paid in respect of the value of the land being sold will be treated as proceeds for the disposal or part disposal, and the tax treatment will follow this.

Any compensation attributed to severance will, however, be treated as proceeds for a separate part disposal of the remaining land. Part of the allowable expenditure attributable to the remaining land can be brought into account accordingly.

Small part disposals

There are special rules in s. 243 for small part disposals. For these to apply, the following conditions must be met:

- the interest in the land must not be a wasting asset, i.e. a short lease;
- the market value of the land disposed of must be small in comparison to the value of the entire holding; and
- the owner must have taken no steps to make it known, by advertising or otherwise, that he or she was prepared to sell any part of the holding in the three years prior to the compulsory acquisition.

It should be noted that "small" for the purposes of s. 243 follows the general rule for part disposals, rather than the special meaning used for small part disposals of land. This means that the value of the part disposed must either be less than £3,000, or greater than £3,000 but not exceeding 5% of the total value. Therefore, in theory there is no upper limit to the amount of consideration that can be paid for the special rules to apply, as long as it does not exceed 5% of the total value of the holding.

It may be possible to argue that a higher limit is appropriate, giving consideration to the particular circumstances of the case in question following *O'Rourke v Binks*, which considered the part disposal rules in relation to a company takeover.

Where the special rules apply, and a claim is made, there will be no taxable gain arising on the compulsory purchase, and the compensation received is deducted from the allowable expenditure of the entire holding.

Part disposals which are not small – rollover relief

If the rules in s. 243 cannot apply, for example because the value of the part disposed of exceeds 5% of the total value, then there will be a chargeable gain. This will be charged in the tax year the contract is made, or when the amount of compensation is agreed (or is determined by a tribunal).

Section 247 permits a form of rollover relief to be claimed where there is a disposal of land (the old land) to an authority exercising, or having, compulsory purchasing powers. To qualify, the landowner must apply the whole or part of the consideration received for the disposal of the old land in acquiring new land in the period starting one year before and ending three years after the date of the disposal to the authority with compulsory purchasing powers. There is no requirement for either the old or new land to have been used for the purposes of a trade. The conditions are therefore less restrictive than for rollover relief generally (see **Chapter 11**).

The new land must not comprise a dwelling house, or part of a dwelling house, that will become the landowner's only or main residence for the purposes of private residence relief within six years of its acquisition.

If the new land is a depreciating asset (e.g. a leasehold interest with less than 60 years to run) then there is no adjustment to the acquisition cost in this case. The gain is held over and will become chargeable on the earlier of:

- a disposal of the new land; or
- ten years following its acquisition.

A further claim for rollover relief can be made if a further interest in land is acquired that is not a depreciating asset. This mirrors the position for rollover relief generally (see **Chapter 11**).

Law: TCGA 1992, s. 242, 243, 247
Case: *O'Rourke v Binks* [1992] BTC 460

4.3.7   Disposals of qualifying furnished holiday lettings

Income from the passive exploitation of land through letting activity is not a trade. Instead, it is a special type of business. Accordingly, the business-related tax reliefs – such as business asset disposal relief, rollover relief, and holdover (gift) relief – are not generally applicable to landlords.

However, if a property is let in circumstances where it qualifies as a furnished holiday letting (FHL) it is treated as a deemed trade and a number of CGT reliefs are available, namely:

- business asset disposal relief (see **Chapter 7**);
- rollover relief (see **Chapter 11**);
- holdover relief for gifts of business assets (see **Chapter 12**);
- following the decision in *Ramsay*, incorporation relief in certain circumstances (see **Chapter 13**); and
- relief for irrecoverable loans to traders (see **Chapter 14**).

The qualification criteria for FHLs are contained in the income tax legislation in ITTOIA 2005, s. 323-325. For more detail see *Furnished Holiday Lettings – A Tax Guide* from Claritax Books.

Law: ITTOIA 2005, s. 323-325
Case: *Ramsay v HMRC* [2013] UKUT 226 (TCC)

4.3.8   Woodland

Land that is used by the owner as a woodland operated on a commercial basis with a view to realising a profit enjoys tax benefits, including CGT advantages. Any consideration for the disposal of trees, or "saleable underwood", is excluded in computing any gain on a disposal under s. 250. This applies regardless of whether the trees are still standing or have already been felled. However, this only applies to commercial timber, not timber from trees from agricultural or amenity woodland.

The exemption also applies to any insurance proceeds received in respect of damage to, or destruction of, the trees. Ordinarily, compensation of this type would represent consideration for a part disposal.

The underlying land remains taxable, and so it will be necessary to apportion the proceeds between the exempt trees and the taxable land. It may also be necessary to make a further apportionment if the woodland is used for both commercial and non-commercial purposes.

Christmas tree farms are not covered by the exemption, nor are woodlands used for the intense cultivation of trees, i.e. short rotation coppice; these are both treated as farming activities. Accordingly, business asset disposal relief may be in point.

Interestingly, though the commercial occupation of woodland is exempt for income tax purposes, it can still benefit from rollover relief – the extent to which will depend on exactly what new assets are purchased.

Law: TCGA 1992, s. 250

4.3.9   Disposals by non-UK residents

Generally, gains realised by non-UK residents (as determined by the statutory residence test) are not subject to UK CGT – even if these are UK assets, such as UK-registered shares. As a result, a well-established planning strategy for someone moving abroad, e.g. to retire overseas, is to wait until they have become non-UK resident before disposing of assets that would realise gains. There are, however, some important exceptions to this general rule.

Firstly, there are anti-avoidance rules that apply where an individual becomes non-resident but becomes UK-resident again within five years.

Secondly, non-UK residents are required to report certain disposals of land to HMRC. Since April 2019, this has applied to all disposals of interests in UK land (residential or not) where the disposal is:

- a direct disposal by an individual; or
- an indirect disposal by a company that derives at least 75% of its value from UK land.

There is still, however, a need to distinguish between residential and non-residential property to determine the CGT rates to apply to gains. The rules are discussed in detail in **Chapter 18**.

Where they apply, the gain must be reported to HMRC, with any CGT liability paid, within 30 days of completion in the same way as applies to UK residents making disposals of land. However, where UK residents are only required to make a return if there is a gain and a CGT liability, non-UK residents must report the details of all disposals – whether there is a gain or not. Rebasing of value is permitted (the rebasing point will depend on what type of land is being disposed of), and certain losses may be deducted.

Law: FA 2019, Sch. 2

5.   Shares and securities

5.1   Introduction and definitions

The provisions in TCGA 1992, Pt. 4, Ch. 1, deal with disposals of shares and securities. Any disposals of company securities consisting of shares, securities or other assets of a "fungible" nature are subject to specific identification rules. HMRC's guidance states that:

> "Fungible assets are ones which it is not possible to identify individually in a holding of more than one because they are functionally identical. For example, all ICI ordinary shares and all €100 notes are for practical purposes interchangeable. If a person sells some of their shares, they cannot identify which shares have been sold."

A simple debt, e.g. a loan to a company, is not a chargeable asset in the hands of the person who originally made it, but a debt on a security will be. The CGT treatment of shares therefore extends to assets such as loan notes, depository receipts and units in a unit trust.

The rules for identifying such assets on a disposal are contained in s. 104. Note though that "relevant" securities are excluded and are subject to different rules which are considered in **Chapter 6**. Relevant securities include qualifying corporate bonds (QCBs).

There is no statutory definition of a share. It is taken to mean a definite portion of a company's share capital and represents the shareholder's interest in, or ownership of, a company. The shareholder will enjoy various rights depending on the particular class of shares owned. These rights will be determined by the company and recorded in documentation, e.g. the articles of association.

Different share classes may be issued to achieve different objectives. For example, preference shares usually confer enhanced rights to dividends and to assets in the event of insolvency. They may be issued as part of a finance-raising exercise as they will therefore carry a lower inherent risk than ordinary shares.

It is therefore necessary to group shares of different classes separately from one another. Section 104(3) states that:

> "shares or securities of a company shall not be treated as being of the same class unless they are so treated by the practice of a recognised stock exchange or would be so treated if dealt with on a recognised stock exchange."

For quoted shares, this will be a question of fact. For unquoted shares, it will be necessary to consider whether the shares have sufficiently different features affecting their value. Partly paid shares should be treated as belonging to a separate class from paid up shares unless the balance outstanding is payable within six months of the issue date.

Securities

HMRC's guidance at CG 50220 explains that there are actually two definitions of "security" within TCGA 1992. For the purposes of the share identification rules, s. 104(3) explicitly excludes "relevant" securities, but includes:

- shares or securities of a company; and
- any other assets where they are of a nature to be dealt in without identifying the particular assets disposed of or acquired.

This is somewhat circular, as the definition contains the word it is seeking to define. However, the guidance explains that:

> "The term 'security' is a convenient way of describing all these assets. Fungible assets are ones which it is not possible to identify individually in a holding of more than one because they are functionally identical. For example, all ICI ordinary shares and all €100 notes are for practical purposes interchangeable. If a person sells some of their shares, they cannot identify which shares have been sold.

> The distinction between shares and securities in TCGA92/S104(3) is between share capital and loan capital. This distinction is clearer in the other definition of security, see below. This guidance will explain the share identification rules in terms of shares, but you should bear in mind that the same rules will apply to securities in the wider sense of the term, unless they are relevant securities which have their own identification rules."

Terminology in this book

For the purposes of this chapter, the term "share" is used to encompass both shares and other assets to which the described treatment applies.

Law: TCGA 1992, Pt. 4, Ch. 1; s. 104(3)
Guidance: CG 50200*pp*

5.2 The share identification rules

5.2.1 Introduction

The rules discussed in this section apply to disposals of shares and securities generally. They are modified for EIS, SEIS, SITR and VCT shares – see **Chapter 10**. They do not apply to shares acquired under the now-defunct employee shareholder status.

5.2.2 The share pooling requirement

As discussed in **5.1**, shares are fungible assets (unless they are numbered) meaning one share is indistinct from another. This can present a problem identifying the allowable cost on a disposal unless the entire holding is sold, or all of the shares were acquired on the same date.

Example 1

Jade acquired 600 shares for £60,000 on 1 April 2017, a further 500 shares for £100,000 on 1 April 2020, and finally 900 shares for £200,000 on 1 April 2021. On 1 April 2022, she sells 1,000 shares for £250,000. The problem is to determine which shares should be treated as being sold, and therefore what allowable cost may be brought into the calculation.

A disposal of shares is matched in the following order of priority:

- shares acquired on the same day as the disposal;
- shares acquired in the 30 days following the disposal on a first-in, first-out (FIFO) basis (unless the person acquiring the shares is non-resident); and finally
- shares from the "section 104 holding" (see **5.2.3**).

If these three points do not cover all of the shares disposed of, there is a "sweeping up" provision that matches shares disposed to shares acquired after the 30-day period on a FIFO basis.

The first two bullet points prevent abuse of the annual exempt amount (currently £12,300 until April 2026). In their absence, an individual could make a disposal of sufficient shares to trigger gains just below the annual exempt amount, then immediately (or shortly afterward) use the proceeds to buy back shares of the same class in the same company, with the intention of uplifting the base cost of the shares so that on an eventual disposal, CGT is minimised.

Example 2

Dean acquired 100 shares in Zcom Ltd for £10,000 in 2018. Towards the end of 2021-22 he consults his trading account and finds that the shares are now valued at £18,000. He decides to sell all of the shares, then reacquire them the next day. His hope is that the gain of £8,000 will be covered by his annual exempt amount, and the base cost for the shares will be uplifted to £18,000.

Instead, s. 106A(5) treats the disposal as being matched with the purchase made on the following day. The gain is therefore £nil because the allowable cost is the same as the proceeds. The base cost of the shares is therefore still £10,000.

As can be seen, this "bed and breakfasting" is really a form of deemed short selling, where the shares are treated as being sold before they are acquired. However, there is no provision to prevent the reacquisition of the shares by a spouse or civil partner.

The same day matching rule does not apply where the shares are *deemed* to be disposed of and reacquired, for example upon making a successful negligible value claim.

Law: TCGA 1992, s. 104-106A

5.2.3   *Constructing the s. 104 holding*

Once any shares subject to a disposal have been matched to acquisitions on the same day, or within 30 days as required, the "section 104 holding", or "pool", must be considered. As the name suggests, all acquisitions are pooled together and, upon a disposal, an appropriate proportion of the pooled cost is attributed to the shares disposed of. Effectively, the pool gives each share a cost equal to the total pooled cost divided by the number of shares, based on the pool at the time of disposal.

Example

Andy made the following acquisitions of ordinary shares in Zcom Ltd:

Date	Shares acquired	Price paid £
17 September 2006	3,000	150,000
20 May 2008	500	30,000
31 July 2011	250	25,000
16 January 2015	1,250	80,000
Total	5,000	285,000

After the final acquisition, the s. 104 holding therefore consists of 5,000 shares with a pooled acquisition cost of £285,000.

In 2021-22, Andy sells 3,000 shares for £325,000. We will assume there are no further acquisitions on the same day or within the 30 days following the disposal.

Andy's gain is calculated as the disposal proceeds less the proportion of the pooled cost, i.e. 3,000/5,000 x £285,000 = £171,000. The chargeable gain is therefore £154,000.

The s. 104 holding is treated as a single holding. Where different classes of share are held, a pool must be constructed separately for each class. It may be necessary to adjust a pool where there is any event that affects the pooled expenditure, for example if more shares are purchased, or if shares of a new class are issued as part of a reorganisation. It is also necessary to pool separately where the same person holds shareholdings of the same class, but in different capacities, e.g. as an individual and as a trustee.

As alluded to earlier, relevant securities do not form part of the s. 104 holding.

Shares held at 5 April 2008

A problem can arise where shares were held at 5 April 2008, because the share identification rules changed for disposals on or after 6 April 2008. Such a holding would be the balance remaining of shares bought and sold prior to this date. The pre-existing identification rules would determine the shares entering the pool and the associated costs at this point.

HMRC's guidance shows how to convert an existing holding into the s. 104 pool.

Law: TCGA 1992, s. 104-106A
Guidance: CG 51570

5.2.4 Shares acquired and disposed of on same day under certain schemes

Where a person acquires shares of the same class on the same day they are disposed of, they are treated as being acquired in a single transaction: this is the "same day" matching rule.

However, it is possible to make an election under s. 105A to use an alternative basis if some (but not all) of the shares were acquired through the exercise of qualifying EMI options, or other tax-advantaged employee share option schemes, in a way that leads to no income tax charge.

The alternative basis treats the scheme shares as being acquired in a separate transaction to the other shares, and any disposal on the same day is first matched to the non-scheme shares. This generally gives a higher acquisition cost, and therefore a smaller gain than would otherwise be the case.

Example

Joy acquires the following shares on 22 November 2021:

- 2,400 shares by exercising EMI options; and

- 1,000 shares under a non-tax advantaged option scheme that predated the EMI being set up.

The exercise price for all the shares was £5, but the market value on the exercise date was £10. There is no income tax charge on the EMI shares, but the unapproved option exercise will trigger a charge on the difference between the price paid and the market value, i.e. 1,000 x £5 = £5,000.

Joy is a higher rate taxpayer and so the charge is £2,000. In order to fund this, she sells 200 of her shares on the same day, receiving proceeds of 200 x £10 = £2,000.

If there is no s. 105A election, the 3,400 shares are pooled as £5 x 2,400 = £12,000 and 1,000 x £10 = £10,000. Note that for CGT purposes the cost of the non-tax advantaged option scheme shares is £10, even though only £5 was paid, because the difference has been subject to income tax. This avoids a double tax charge. The pool therefore consists of 2,400 shares with a total cost of £22,000.

Joy's gain would therefore be the £2,000 proceeds, less £1,294 (200/3,400 x £22,000) = £706. As she is a higher rate taxpayer, a CGT charge of £141 would arise on this.

If Joy made a s. 105A election, the 200 shares sold are matched with the 1,000 non-tax advantaged shares, which have a cost of £10. As the proceeds are also £10 per share, no gain arises.

The election must be made on or before the first anniversary of 31 January following the end of the tax year the first relevant disposal takes place in.

For detailed discussion of share schemes, refer to *Employee Share Schemes* from Claritax Books.

Law: TCGA 1992, s. 105A-105B

5.2.5 Clogged shares

Shares acquired in the course of employment may be restricted; for example, there may be a clause providing that they may not be sold for a fixed period of time following acquisition. Such shares must be pooled separately from shares that do not carry such restrictions, even if they are of the same class under s. 104(4). These shares are said to be "clogged".

HMRC's guidance indicates that clogged shares may be moved into the pool with unclogged shares when the restrictions are lifted. The example given is where an individual acquires shares with a three-year block on disposal, acquired at six-monthly intervals. The restriction lifting dates will be at different times. All of these clogged shares will initially form a single holding and will be moved to the main s. 104 holding in separate tranches as the restrictions are lifted.

Where a s. 105A election is made (**5.2.4**), any clogged shares of the same class as the shares to which the election applies are automatically treated as coming within the election from the time the restrictions are lifted.

Law: TCGA 1992, s. 105B(3)
Guidance: CG 51580

5.3 Reorganisations

5.3.1 *Introduction*

Further rules apply where shares are disposed of following certain events falling within TCGA 1992, Pt. 4, Ch. 2 – collectively referred to as reorganisations. These, along with other events, are examined later in this chapter, as follows:

- bonus issues (see **5.3.2**);
- rights issues (see **5.3.3**);
- stock dividends (see **5.3.4**);
- conversions (see **5.3.5**);
- mergers or acquisitions of companies (see **5.3.6**);
- reconstructions (see **5.3.7**); and
- earn-outs (see **5.3.8**).

5.3.2 *Bonus issues*

A bonus issue, sometimes called a scrip issue (not to be confused with a scrip (or stock) dividend – see **5.3.4**), occurs when a company offers free additional shares to existing shareholders as part of a capitalisation of existing reserves. The new shares are treated as having been issued at the same time as the original shares that the entitlement arose on. However, the effect on the s. 104 holding depends on whether the bonus shares issued are of the same class as the original shares.

If they are, the shares are added to the holding but the pooled cost is unaffected. The overall effect is to dilute the cost per share. However, if the shares are of a different class, some of the original cost must be attributed from the original holding. The method of doing so depends on whether the shares are quoted or unquoted.

Quoted shares

For quoted shares, or for shares that become quoted within three months of the issue, the cost is apportioned on the basis of the market values of each class of share on the date that the values are first revised and published to reflect the bonus issue (s. 130).

Example 1

Martin purchased 40,000 shares in Acom plc for £1 each in December 2015. In 2021 there was a 1 for 5 bonus issue of preference shares with a £1 nominal value. On the day after the issue, the ordinary shares were valued at 150p each, and the new preference shares at 105p. The respective values of the holdings are £60,000 for the 40,000 ordinary shares, and £8,400 for the 8,000 preference shares.

The cost attributable to both holdings is £40,000. This is apportioned between the two classes as follows:

Ordinary shares:

$$£40,000 \times (£60,000/£68,400) = £35,088$$

Preference shares:

$$£40,000 - £35,088 = £4,912$$

The newly acquired shares form a new s. 104 holding with the apportioned cost. The original shares form a separate s. 104 holding.

Unquoted shares

As unquoted shares have no published values to make reference to, there needs to be a different treatment, avoiding the requirement for formal valuations of shares each time there is an issue. The original and new shares are treated as being part of the same holding, despite being of different classes.

Upon a subsequent disposal, the cost will be apportioned using the values at the date of disposal and the formula:

$$\text{Pooled cost} \times \frac{\text{number of shares sold}}{\text{number of shares held in class}} \times \frac{\text{MV of class holding}}{\text{MV of all holdings}}$$

Example 2

Louisa bought 1,500 ordinary shares in Zcom Ltd for £10,000. Zcom later made a 1 for 3 bonus issue of preference shares in respect of the ordinary shares. Louisa received 500 shares.

In the current year, Louisa sells 300 ordinary shares for £900, i.e. for £3 each. The preference shares were worth £2 each at this date. To work out the correct base cost for the disposal, the formula is used:

$$£10,000 \times \frac{300}{1,500} \times \frac{(£3 \times 1,500)}{((£3 \times 1,500) + (£2 \times 500))} = £1,636$$

Law: TCGA 1992, s. 127-130

5.3.3   Rights issues

A rights issue occurs when a company offers existing shareholders the right to purchase additional shares, usually at a price that is below the open market value of the shares. These rights will be granted in proportion to the existing shareholdings.

It is possible that a company offers its shareholders the right to buy shares in another company. This is simply treated as a purchase of new shares, i.e. starting a new s. 104 holding for CGT purposes.

Where the rights issue is over shares in the same company as the original shareholding, the correct treatment depends on whether the shares are of the same class as the original holding, and whether the rights are sold before the new shares are allotted, referred to as sold "nil paid".

The most straightforward scenario is where the rights are not sold and the new shares acquired are in the same class as the existing shares. The new shares, and the associated acquisition cost, are simply added to the existing s. 104 holding.

Where the new shares are of a different class, the cost must be apportioned upon a later disposal in the same way as described for bonus issues (see **5.3.2**). The reorganisation is treated as taking place on the day following the date the right to receive the allotment expires. Again, for unquoted shares the cost is apportioned by reference to the values on the disposal date instead.

Rights sold nil paid

A shareholder may not wish to take up the allotted shares, and one option is to sell the rights. Because the rights are over shares, selling them before they have been purchased means that the shares are being sold "nil paid", in contrast to fully paid or partly paid. The proceeds paid for the rights are a capital distribution, and the general CGT treatment is a part disposal of the holding. The appropriate cost to deduct when calculating any gain will therefore be:

$$\text{pooled cost} \times \frac{\text{capital distribution}}{(\text{capital distribution} + \text{MV of remaining shares})}$$

Example

Ian has a s. 104 holding consisting of 1,000 ordinary shares in Zcom with a pooled cost of £100,000. In the current tax year there is a 1 for 2 rights issue of ordinary shares. Ian decides to sell the rights nil paid and receives £20,000. His original shares are worth £180,000 at this time.

Ian's gain will be:

Proceeds: £20,000

less:

$$£100,000 \text{ x } \frac{£20,000}{(£20,000 + £180,000)} = £10,000$$

Thus the gain on the part disposal is £10,000.

Treatment where proceeds are "small"

Section 122(2) provides that where a capital distribution is paid, but is "small" compared to the value of the underlying shares, the distribution does not constitute a disposal. Instead, the amount received is deducted from the original cost of the shares, i.e. there will be a deduction from the pooled cost in the s. 104 holding. This treatment is automatic, so there is no requirement for the shareholder to make an election.

"Small" is not defined in statute, but HMRC's guidance states that an amount will be considered small if it does not exceed:

- 5% of the value of the asset; or
- £3,000 (irrespective of the 5% test).

It may be possible to suggest that an amount in excess of 5% of the value is small, but this will be considered on the merits of the individual circumstances, in accordance with the decision in *O'Rourke v Binks*.

HMRC's guidance at CG 57835 acknowledges that this "no disposal" treatment may not always be to the taxpayer's advantage. For example, where the proceeds are £3,000, this will automatically be deducted from the s. 104 holding cost, increasing any gain on a future disposal. However, if the shareholder had no other gains in the year, a gain on a part disposal (if s. 122 were disapplied) would be covered by the annual exempt amount, preserving more of the base cost for a future disposal. The guidance suggests that HMRC may accept a taxpayer's preference to treat the distribution as a disposal instead. This is not statutory, and presumably needs to be at HMRC's discretion.

If the capital distribution is small under the tests above, but exceeds the allowable expenditure on the entire shareholding, the no disposal treatment does not apply. Instead, the shareholder can elect to deduct all of the allowable expenditure in the s. 104 holding from the capital distribution. This will extinguish the allowable cost in the pool such that there will be nothing to deduct from the proceeds of a future sale unless there are further acquisitions.

Law: TCGA 1992, s. 122, 123
Case: *O'Rourke v Binks* [1992] BTC 460
Guidance: CG 57835

5.3.4 Stock dividends

In some cases a company will make an issue of shares in lieu of a dividend payment, called a stock (or scrip) dividend. Quoted companies may also offer shareholders a "reinvestment" option, whereby dividends are automatically applied to purchase further shares. The amount forgone (the cash equivalent) will generally be taxed as dividend income under ITTOIA 2005, s. 410.

Where a receipt is taxed as income, for CGT purposes the shares received are treated as a new acquisition (i.e. not under a reorganisation), with the acquisition cost being the amount forgone.

Law: TCGA 1992, s. 142; ITTOIA 2005, s. 410

5.3.5 Conversions

Where shares are converted from one class to another, the new holding simply inherits the acquisition history of the previous class. So, if 10,000 preference shares purchased for £1 each are converted to 100,000 ordinary shares, the holding will simply change to 100,000 shares with an allowable cost of £10,000. The conversion itself is not a disposal.

However, where the shareholder receives (or becomes entitled to receive) a premium upon a conversion then a part disposal calculation is required using the same rules as where rights are sold nil paid (see **5.3.3**) using the premium amount in place of the capital distribution. The two treatments for small receipts also apply.

Law: TCGA 1992, s. 132, 133

5.3.6   Mergers or acquisitions

Where a company acquires the shares in another company, the consideration for those shares may consist of shares in the acquiring company, debentures, cash or a combination of some or all of these.

Share issue

Shares will be issued in proportion to the shareholders' existing holdings.

Section 135 provides that the transaction does not give rise to a chargeable disposal, and the new shares stand in the shoes of the original shares, if the following conditions are met:

- the purchasing company acquires (or already holds) more than 25% of the ordinary share capital of the target company;
- there is a general offer made to shareholders which (if accepted) would give the purchasing company control of the target company; or
- the purchasing company acquires (or already holds) the majority of the voting rights of the target company.

The acquisition must be made for genuine commercial purposes and not as part of a tax avoidance scheme.

Where there is a single class of share, the new shares simply inherit the allowable expenditure of the original shares.

Example

Larry owns 1,000 shares in A Ltd which cost him £20,000 several years ago. B Ltd acquires a controlling interest in the ordinary share capital of A Ltd and Larry receives 5,000 shares in B Ltd as consideration for his shares. The B Ltd shares are treated as having been acquired on the date Larry acquired the A Ltd shares and inherit the £20,000 allowable expenditure.

Where this applies, any gain is deferred until the new shares are disposed of. Where business asset disposal relief (BADR) or investors' relief (IR) would be available on a disposal of the old shares but would not be available on a later disposal of the new shares, it is possible to make an election to disapply s. 127 and crystallise the gain in the year of the share exchange. The election is made under s. 169Q for BADR and s. 169VO for IR.

If the new shares consist of shares in more than one class, the allowable expenditure must be allocated between the classes in the same way as for bonus or rights issues.

Law: TCGA 1992, s. 127, 135

Debenture issue

Where the new holding is in the form of debentures, the same rules apply as for shares unless the debentures are qualifying corporate bonds (QCBs).

As QCBs are an exempt asset, s. 116 provides that a deemed disposal takes place at the date of exchange, but any gain is frozen until a later disposal of the QCBs. This rule is necessary as, in its absence, a gain on a chargeable asset could be converted into an exempt gain with relative ease.

Corporate bonds which are not QCBs are treated as any other security, i.e. they are chargeable on disposal. Therefore, no special rules are necessary.

For CGT purposes, a QCB is a security that meets the following conditions:

- the debt on it represents (and at all times has represented) a normal commercial loan;
- it is expressed in sterling; and
- no provision is made for its conversion into, or redemption in, any currency other than sterling (other than a redemption provision at the exchange rate prevailing at redemption).

Law: TCGA 1992, s. 116

Receipt of cash

If any cash is paid in addition to new shares and/or securities, it is treated as a capital distribution in respect of the original shares. The part disposal formula must be used to ascertain the cash gain that becomes chargeable (and how much of the allowable expenditure remains), unless the cash amount is "small", in which case the provisions of s. 122 apply in the same way as for rights issues (see **5.3.3**).

Law: TCGA 1992, s. 122

Advance clearance

It is possible for the taxpayer to request advance clearance under s. 138 that the transaction is accepted as being made for *bona fide* commercial reasons.

Law: TCGA 1992, s. 138

5.3.7   Reconstructions

A scheme of reconstruction will also qualify as a reorganisation to which s. 127-131 will apply. Schedule 5AA defines a scheme of reconstruction as a merger, division or other restructuring that meets the first two, and either the third or the fourth, conditions set out in that schedule. An example of a reorganisation to which this may apply is a division of trading activities, where part of the business is hived off to a new company.

Where the conditions are met, there is no disposal or acquisition, and the new securities simply stand in the shoes of the original holding. However, a deemed disposal will take place if any of the new securities are QCBs (see **5.3.6**).

Condition one

The first condition is that the scheme involves the issue of ordinary share capital of a company or of more than one company:

- to holders of ordinary share capital of another company or, where there are different classes of ordinary share capital of that company, to holders of one or more classes of ordinary share capital of that company; or

- to holders of ordinary share capital of more than one other company or, where there are different classes of ordinary share capital of one or more of the original company or companies, to holders of ordinary share capital of any of those companies or of one or more classes of ordinary share capital of any of those companies.

Furthermore, it does not involve the issue of ordinary share capital of the successor company, or (as the case may be) any of the successor companies, to anyone else.

Condition two

The second condition is that under the scheme the entitlement of any person to acquire ordinary share capital of the successor company or companies by virtue of holding relevant shares, or relevant shares of any class, is the same as that of any other person holding such shares or shares of that class.

Condition three

The third condition is that the effect of the restructuring is:

- where there is one original company, that the business or substantially the whole of the business carried on by the company is carried on:
  - by a successor company which is not the original company; or
  - by two or more successor companies (which may include the original company);
- where there is more than one original company, that all or part of the business or businesses carried on by one or more of the original companies is carried on by a different company, and the whole or substantially the whole of the businesses carried on by the original companies are carried on:
  - where there is one successor company, by that company (which may be one of the original companies); or
  - where there are two or more successor companies, by those companies (which may be the same as the original companies or include any of those companies).

Condition four

Condition four is that the arrangement was carried out as part of a compromise or arrangement with members under *Companies Act* 2006, s. 899.

Law: TCGA 1992, s. 136, Sch. 5AA

5.3.8   Earn-outs

Where an earn-out arrangement is used (see **3.2.4**) the value of the earn-out right is a separate asset. Its value must be included as proceeds. If the earn-out is to be satisfied by the later issue of securities, s. 138A may be used to treat the unascertainable consideration as a security (unless the recipient elects for it not to be so treated). This brings the receipt of the right as being within s. 135, i.e. not chargeable in the year of the reorganisation.

If the earn-out is payable partly in shares and partly in cash, the two elements must be treated separately.

Law: TCGA 1992, s. 135, 138A

6. Other assets

6.1 Introduction

In addition to land (see **Chapter 4**) and shares and securities (see **Chapter 5**) there are other assets that require particular consideration for CGT. This chapter considers those often seen in practice:

- wasting assets – see **6.2**;
- relevant securities – see **6.3**;
- capital sums derived from assets – see **6.4**;
- options – see **6.5**;
- debts – see **6.6**;
- appropriations to or from trading stock – see **6.7**;
- plant subject to a long funding lease – see **6.8**;
- foreign currency – see **6.9**;
- assets of closely held non-resident companies – see **6.10**; and
- assets subject to value shifting – see **6.11**.

6.2 Wasting assets

6.2.1 Introduction

The concept of the wasting asset has already been considered in the context of short leases (see **4.3.4**); however, the rules for leases are different from the general rules considered here.

6.2.2 Key concepts

A wasting asset is one with a predicted useful life of no more than 50 years. It is likely to become less valuable over its life.

The predicted useful life is measured at the time the asset is acquired, with reference to what the acquirer will use it for, not at the time of disposal.

Some asset types, such as copyrights and licences, have their predicted lives set out in HMRC's guidance at CG 76706. By way of example, copyright normally runs for 70 years after the end of the calendar year in which the work is published or the author dies. So if copyright is acquired 20 years or more after that calendar year end, it will be a wasting asset.

It will often be necessary to estimate the residual, or "scrap", value that the asset will have when it reaches the end of its useful life. This is also determined by an estimate at the date of acquisition. Any enhancement expenditure does not affect the predicted useful life but, per CG 76700, it can affect the residual value.

If the wasting asset is also a chattel, i.e. it is tangible moveable property, there is a general exemption from CGT under TCGA 1992, s. 45. However, where the wasting chattel has been used solely for the purposes of a trade, profession or vocation, and capital allowances have (or could have) been claimed in respect of the initial acquisition or subsequent expenditure, the exemption does not apply. See **Chapter 14** for the treatment of non-exempt chattels.

Plant and machinery is always deemed to have an expected useful life of less than 50 years, and so is always a wasting asset. It makes no difference if the asset ends up having an actual useful life in excess of 50 years. However, there are special rules that apply where capital allowances have (or could have) been claimed (see **6.2.4**), or where the assets have been used in a business carried on by someone else as explored in CG 76722.

The term "plant and machinery" has no statutory meaning for CGT purposes, and so takes its normal meaning. Machinery is straightforward, but there is a plethora of case law surrounding what does or does not constitute "plant". For further information, see *A-Z of Plant & Machinery* and *Capital Allowances,* both from Claritax Books.

Livestock and bloodstock are wasting assets (and are obviously tangible and moveable), so are not subject to CGT.

Law: TCGA 1992, s. 44
Guidance: CG 76700, 76706, 76722

6.2.3   Allowable expenditure

If a disposal of a wasting asset is subject to CGT, i.e. it is not an inter-spouse transfer or other exempt disposal, then the allowable expenditure is restricted under TCGA 1992, s. 46.

The acquisition cost is deemed to be used up (i.e. to waste away) on a straight-line basis over the predicted life of the asset. The residual value also needs to be considered, as this amount does not waste (as implied by the name).

The following example demonstrates how to calculate the gain.

Example

Winston purchases an asset with a predicted useful life of 43 years. He pays £50,000 and it has an estimated scrap value of £2,000. He sells the asset after 20 years for £100,000.

The following steps are used to calculate the amount of allowable expenditure:

Work out the length of time that has expired between acquisition and disposal:

T(1) = 20 years.

Determine the predicted life of the asset:

L = 43 years.

Divide T(1) by L:

20/43

Deduct the residual value from the acquisition cost to determine the "wasting" expenditure:

£50,000 – £2,000 = £48,000

Apply the fraction to this amount to determine how much of the expenditure has been used up:

20/43 x £48,000 = £22,326

Calculate the gain, omitting the wasted expenditure from the computation:

£100,000 – (£50,000 – £22,326) = £72,326

Where any enhancement expenditure has been incurred, this will also depreciate from the date it was first reflected in the nature of the asset.

Law: TCGA 1992, s. 46

6.2.4   Assets qualifying for capital allowances

The restriction of allowable expenditure under s. 46 does not apply to an asset:

- that has always been used solely for the purposes of the trade, profession or vocation and the person making the disposal has claimed, or could have claimed, capital allowances in respect of any expenditure attributable to the asset; or

- on which the person making the disposal has incurred any expenditure that has otherwise qualified in full for any capital allowance.

The effect of this provision, which is contained in s. 47, is that any gain or loss on the disposal is calculated in the normal way. However, where a loss arises, s. 41 requires that the expenditure in the calculation is excluded to the extent that any capital allowance has been, or may be, made in respect of it. The effect of this is to reduce the allowable loss or to restrict it to nil – it is not possible for s. 41 to turn a loss into a gain.

It is possible that a wasting asset only qualifies for capital allowances in part, for example where it was only used for business purposes for part of the period of ownership, or where there was mixed use of the asset.

In such cases, it is necessary to apportion both the consideration and allowable expenditure into two parts. The apportionment of the consideration should follow any apportionment that has been made for capital allowances purposes.

Example

Neil purchases an asset for £10,000 in March 2018. The asset has a predicted life of 20 years, and an estimated residual value of £1,000. Neil uses the asset for the purposes of his trade, but only for six months each year. He leases the asset to a third party for the remaining time. Neil claimed capital allowances on half of the cost, i.e. £5,000.

Neil sells the asset in March 2022 for £9,000 and, based on the allowances claimed, a balancing charge of £2,000 arises. To calculate the CGT position, the £9,000 proceeds must be apportioned between the business and non-business parts. Fortunately, in this case it is relatively straightforward as we know the capital allowance apportionment was 50%.

Business part

	£	£
Proceeds (50% x £9,000)		4,500
Less		
Allowable cost (50% x £10,000)	5,000	
Less		
Adjusted capital allowances (£5,000 – £4,500)	(500)	(4,500)
Allowable loss		0

Non-business part

	£	£
Proceeds (50% x £9,000)		4,500
Less		
Allowable cost (50% x £10,000)	5,000	
Less		
Amount "wasted" during ownership 4/20 (£5,000 – £500) Residual value = £500 (50% x £1,000)	(900)	(4,100)
Gain		400

Had the figures in the business part of the calculation been such that the proceeds less the allowable cost had resulted in a gain, there would be no need to make the adjustment to the capital allowances. For instance, if the sales proceeds had been £11,000, the gain would simply be £500, i.e. £5,500 less £5,000. The non-business part of the calculation would still need to account for the wasting of expenditure though so the gain here would be £1,400 i.e. £5,500 – £4,100.

Law: TCGA 1992, s. 41, 46, 47

6.3 Relevant securities

6.3.1 Introduction

As discussed at **5.1**, "relevant securities" are outside the scope of the s. 104 pool. Instead, s. 106A applies to match disposals of such securities with other relevant securities of the same company, type and class on a last-in, first-out basis. However, the requirement to match with securities acquired within the 30 days following the disposal still applies.

Relevant securities are defined as:

- qualifying corporate bonds (QCBs) (see **6.3.2**);
- securities within the accrued income scheme (see **6.3.3**); and
- securities that are interests in a non-reporting fund, within the meaning of the *Offshore Funds (Tax) Regulations* 2009 (see **6.3.4**).

6.3.2 Qualifying corporate bonds

There is a general exemption from CGT for QCBs (and any loss realised is not an allowable loss). However, their disposal may trigger a gain that has previously been "frozen" following a reorganisation, e.g. after a share for share exchange where some of the new securities were QCBs (see **5.3.6**).

6.3.3 Accrued income scheme

Where the accrued income scheme applies to a security (e.g. gilts), part of the consideration is for the amount of any accrued (but unpaid) interest and must be taxed as income. The CGT consideration is therefore reduced accordingly.

HMRC's *Helpsheet* 343 contains guidance on how to work out the income profit, which is deducted from the consideration in the computation.

Likewise, a corresponding deduction must be made from the allowable expenditure, as some of the amount paid will be in respect of any accrued interest.

6.3.4 Offshore funds

Offshore funds are investment schemes where the trustees or operators are non-UK resident. Unless HMRC have designated the fund as a "reporting" fund, any gains are subject to income tax (as an offshore income gain) and not CGT.

The type of funds that this applies to are broadly those that accumulate or "roll up" income in a way that means the investor is not subject to income tax during the accumulation period.

If the disposal results in a loss, this remains a CGT loss, not an income loss.

Non-domiciled individuals may be able to mitigate a charge if they are using the remittance basis, and the proceeds from the disposal are not brought into the UK in a way that constitutes a remittance (see **Chapter 18**).

6.4 Capital sums derived from assets

6.4.1 Deemed disposals under s. 22

A deemed disposal arises where there is a receipt of the capital sum derived from an asset that is made in money or money's worth by the beneficial owner of the asset. This may be in respect of:

- compensation for damage, loss or destruction, e.g. insurance proceeds (see **6.4.2**);
- a right to receive unascertainable contingent consideration (see **3.2.4**);
- compensation for surrendering rights over an asset, or for refraining from exercising such rights; or
- consideration for the use of, or exploitation of, assets.

Certain capital sums are excluded, and therefore do not give rise to a deemed disposal. Any winnings from betting, lotteries or other games with monetary prizes are one such exclusion. Additionally, any compensation or damages for wrong or injury suffered by an individual in either a personal or professional capacity are excluded capital sums by virtue of s. 51.

Law: TCGA 1992, s. 22, 51

6.4.2 Compensation payments

Where a payment of compensation is made in respect of an asset that has been lost, damaged or destroyed, the correct CGT treatment will depend on what has happened to the asset. Relief may be available if the capital sum received is subsequently used to restore or replace the asset in question. We will look at each scenario in turn.

Asset lost or destroyed – introduction

Where a capital sum is paid in respect of an asset that has been entirely lost or destroyed, any amounts received, including insurance proceeds, are treated for CGT purposes as consideration for the disposal of the asset.

Of course, it is possible that no compensation will be paid in respect of a lost or destroyed asset, for example where there is no insurance and a claim cannot be brought for financial redress. The loss or destruction is still a deemed disposal by virtue of s. 24. In this case, the loss (allowing for any salvage or scrap payments) is an allowable loss for CGT purposes.

Where the asset subject to the deemed disposal rules is an interest in a building or structure then further rules are needed. Strictly, under general UK law the asset is the interest in the underlying land which can never be destroyed and is unlikely to become of negligible value.

To overcome this, s. 23(6) and s. 24(3) permit a building that has been destroyed to be treated as a separate asset from the land and subject to the deemed disposal rules. However, there will also be a deemed disposal and immediate reacquisition of the related land at the market value on the date of the deemed disposal of the building. This permits the deemed disposal of the destroyed building to reflect a fall in value accordingly. If the value of the land has increased there may be a gain if the increase exceeds the loss on the deemed disposal of the building.

A form of relief may be due where the capital sum is used, or partly used, to acquire a replacement asset.

Asset lost or destroyed – capital sum reinvested in replacement asset

If the whole of the sum is used within 12 months of its receipt to acquire assets to replace the one that was lost or destroyed, an election under s. 23(4) would deem the disposal proceeds of the original asset to be such that neither a gain nor a loss applies.

The base cost of the replacement asset will then take into account the difference between the capital sum received, plus any residual value, and the deemed disposal proceeds of the original asset.

Asset lost or destroyed – capital sum partially reinvested in replacement asset

If the capital sum is only partly used to purchase a replacement asset, some relief is still available if the amount not used is less than the gain on the disposal of the original asset under s. 23(5).

Any gain chargeable on the deemed disposal of the original asset will be restricted to the amount not used in acquiring the replacement asset.

The reduction in the base cost of the replacement asset will be equal to the reduction in the gain on the deemed disposal.

Example 1

Jhooti purchased an asset in April 2007 for £10,000. The asset was stolen from her home in 2021 and she received an insurance pay-out of £17,000.

Within 12 months she purchases a similar asset to replace the stolen one for £14,000.

The gain on the original asset is £7,000 (£17,000 – £10,000). However, on election Jhooti may restrict this to £3,000, i.e. the amount not used in replacing the original asset (£17,000 – £14,000).

The base cost for the replacement asset is reduced by the difference in the gain on the deemed disposal and the actual amount charged following the election, i.e. £4,000 (£7,000 – £3,000) giving a base cost of £10,000 (£14,000 – £4,000).

Asset damaged – introduction

The situation where an asset is not lost or destroyed but is sufficiently damaged to affect its value is slightly different. In most circumstances, a capital sum received in respect of damage to an asset is treated as proceeds for a part disposal as long as ownership has been retained.

The allowable expenditure is calculated using the normal part disposal formula discussed at **3.4**, i.e.:

$$\text{Allowable expenditure} = \text{Base cost of asset} \times \frac{A}{A+B}$$

For these purposes, A is the capital sum received and B is the market value of the asset at the date of receipt of the sum.

However, there are some further considerations. If any expenditure is incurred on restoring the asset, e.g. so it may continue to be used, *before* the receipt of the capital sum, this is treated as enhancement expenditure and included in the base cost to be apportioned.

Asset damaged – capital sum used for restoration – no disposal

The general rule, above, is revised if the capital sum is wholly or partly used to restore the damaged asset. Under s. 23(1), an election may be made such that there will be no deemed disposal if one of the following applies:

- the whole of the capital sum is used in restoring the asset;
- the capital sum is applied in restoring the asset except for a part which is not reasonably required for the purpose of restoration and which is "small" as compared with the whole capital sum (but see below for capital sums that exceed the allowable expenditure); or
- the capital sum itself is "small" compared with the value of the asset.

The full capital sum is then deducted from the allowable cost of the asset.

"Small" for these purposes is not defined in the legislation, but CG 15703 gives the HMRC view that this should be taken to mean not exceeding 5% of the total capital sum or value of asset as appropriate. HMRC also accept that a capital sum is small if the amount or value of the receipt is £3,000 or less, regardless of whether it meets the 5% test.

Asset damaged – capital sum used for restoration – part disposal

If the whole of the capital sum is not applied in acquiring a replacement asset, and the unused part is not small, then it is not possible to claim that there has been no deemed disposal.

Instead, a claim may be made under s. 23(5) that the unused part is consideration for a part disposal. The element of the capital sum not used in the restoration is deducted from the base cost.

The same part disposal formula as above will be used, but A will be the unused part of the capital sum rather than the total receipt and B will be the value of the asset after restoration.

113

Example 2

Jade buys an asset for £30,000 and insures it against fire and theft.

In 2021 the asset was partly damaged in a fire and Jade receives £10,000 from the insurance company.

She manages to find a specialist who restores the asset for £6,000. The restored value is £50,000.

The unused amount is not small, so it represents proceeds for a part disposal.

If Jade makes the claim under s. 23(5) then the allowable expenditure is £30,000 x (£4,000/(£4,000 + £50,000)) = £2,222. Part of the restoration cost is also deductible using the same fraction, i.e. £6,000 x (£4,000/(£4,000 + £50,000)) = £444.

The gain on the part disposal is therefore £1,334 (i.e. £4,000 – £2,222 – £444).

On a future disposal of the asset, the allowable expenditure will be reduced accordingly. The capital sum used for the restoration is deducted from the allowable expenditure.

Jade sells the asset in 2022 for £55,000. The CGT computation is as follows:

	£	£
Proceeds		55,000
Less allowable expenditure		
Balance of acquisition cost (£30,000 – £2,222)	27,778	
Balance of restoration cost (£6,000 – £444)	5,556	
Adjusted capital allowances (£5,000 – £4,500)	(500)	
Less		
Capital sum used in restoration	(6,000)	
Allowable expenditure		(27,334)
Gain		27,666

Asset damaged – capital sum used to restore asset exceeds allowable cost – no disposal

If there is no allowable expenditure, or the capital sum received exceeds it, full relief (i.e. that there is no part disposal) will only be available if the whole of the capital sum is used to restore the asset – the disregard for small capital sums under s. 23(1)(b)-(c) does not apply.

Asset damaged – capital sum used to restore asset exceeds allowable cost – part disposal

Where only part of the capital sum is used to restore the asset, a claim under s. 23(1) cannot be made. But the taxpayer may make a claim under s. 23(2) that the entire allowable expenditure (immediately prior to the receipt of the capital sum) may be deducted from the capital sum, i.e. there is no need to restrict the expenditure using the A/(A + B) formula. The allowable expenditure carried forward is therefore nil. On a later disposal, only any amounts of subsequent enhancement expenditure would be deductible.

Wasting assets – introduction

Where capital sums are received in respect of wasting assets (see **6.2**), the rules regarding replacement or restoration are modified.

Wasting asset lost or destroyed – capital sum reinvested in replacement asset

Relief will be available in respect of the replacement of a wasting asset following its loss or destruction if either s. 23(4) (capital sum fully applied in acquiring a replacement asset) or s. 23(6) (buildings and structures treated separately from land) apply.

Wasting asset damaged – capital sum used for restoration

Relief is available under s. 23(1) if the capital sum is wholly used to restore the asset. No relief is available if part of the capital sum is not used for the restoration, even if either of the "small" provisions are met.

Relief under s. 23(3) is available if part of the capital sum is used for restoration. The amount deducted from the allowable expenditure must be made from the wasted cost of the asset at the time the capital sum is received, not the original cost.

Law: TCGA 1992, s. 22, 23, 24
Guidance: CG 15700

6.5   Options

6.5.1   Introduction

Options are an asset in their own right and their disposal is the disposal of a chargeable asset and not a part disposal of an underlying asset. As a result, an option is unlikely to have any allowable expenditure other than any associated costs incurred by the option holder relating to the grant.

An option may be a "call" option, which (if exercised) gives the option holder the right to purchase an asset from the grantor at a price fixed by the option agreement (the exercise price). Alternately, a "put" option gives the holder the right to sell an asset to the grantor at a price fixed by the exercise agreement.

Options are frequently granted over company shares or securities, but in theory can be granted over any asset. The agreement will contain a date specifying how long the option is available for. If it is not exercised before that date, the option simply expires.

Options which have an expiry date within 50 years of grant will be wasting assets, except for:

- quoted options to subscribe for shares in a company;
- traded options;
- financial options; and
- options where the underlying asset is intended to be used for the purposes of a trade by the option holder.

6.5.2   Disposal before exercise

if an option holder disposes of the option without exercising it, any gain or loss is calculated according to general CGT principles. If the option is a wasting asset the allowable expenditure (if there is any) will need to be restricted in accordance with the rules discussed in **6.2.3**.

It is possible that an option holder may receive a capital sum in exchange for abandoning an option as opposed to disposing of it. In general, abandonment of an option will not be a disposal. However, where a capital sum is received this will be treated as consideration for a disposal.

Law: TCGA 1992, s. 144

6.5.3 Exercise of an option

Where an option is exercised, the CGT of the grantee and the grantor differ, and the consequences depend on whether the option is a call option or a put option.

When an option is exercised, the granting of the option and the transaction undertaken by the grantor (i.e. the sale or purchase of the asset subject to the option) are treated as a single transaction.

Call options – grantor implications

Here the transaction is a sale of the asset by the grantor. The consideration brought into the CGT calculation is any amount received in respect of the grant of the option plus the consideration received in respect of the underlying asset (usually the exercise price, but this may be substituted for market value if the bargain is not on arm's length terms).

Call options – grantee implications

There are no immediate CGT consequences for the grantee (i.e. the option holder). The allowable expenditure for a future disposal will be the sum of the exercise price and any amount paid for the grant of the option, as well as any associated costs and subsequent enhancement expenditure in respect of the asset.

Put options – grantor implications

Here the transaction is a sale of an asset to the grantor. The acquisition cost for the grantor is the consideration for the acquisition (usually the exercise price, unless market value applies) less the consideration received for the grant of the put option.

Put options – grantee implications

With a put option, it is the grantee who is making the disposal of the asset and for whom a CGT computation is therefore required. The consideration will be the full amount for the asset (i.e. the exercise price or market value as applicable). If there was a cost incurred when the option was granted, this will be treated as an incidental disposal cost, i.e. it will increase the allowable cost of the underlying asset.

Law: TCGA 1992, s. 144

6.5.4   Cash-settled options

Where the grantor is required to make a payment to the grantee in full or partial satisfaction of their obligations under the option agreement, the option is said to be "cash-settled" and the general rules described above are modified. There are useful examples in CG 12321 and 12322 respectively.

Law: TCGA 1992, s. 144A

6.5.5   Employee share options

Options over shares acquired and exercised by reason of an employment are subject to different rules, under the employment-related securities regime. A detailed discussion of employee share schemes is beyond the scope of this book, but broadly the rules work to prevent the conversion of income to capital subject to lower tax rates.

Generally, where the exercise price of the option is less than the market value of the underlying share, the shortfall is subject to income tax. For example, if an option is granted with an exercise price of £2 per share and is exercised when the shares are worth £5, an income tax charge will arise on an amount equal to £3 per share. For CGT purposes the base cost of the shares is the amount paid (£2) plus any amounts charged to income tax (£3). This usually means that the base cost of the shares is equivalent to the market value at the exercise date (£2 + £3 = £5) and this is a useful shortcut.

If the option is successfully exercised under an approved share option scheme (such as the enterprise management incentive), no income tax charge arises on the £3 difference. This is charged to CGT on a subsequent disposal instead. The base cost here would therefore be the price paid, i.e. £2.

This brief summary is an extremely simplified overview of the employment-related securities regime. For further information and detailed commentary, reference should be made to *Employee Share Schemes* from Claritax Books.

Law: TCGA 1992, s. 119A-120, 144, 144A

6.6   Debts

6.6.1   Ordinary debts

In general, the disposal of an "ordinary" debt (a debt which is not a debt on a security (see **6.6.2**)) will not give rise to a chargeable gain or an allowable loss. However, where the debt is acquired from the original creditor and subsequently disposed of, this subsequent disposal is a chargeable disposal for CGT purposes.

Example 1

In March 2019, Bert lent £100,000 to Barry. In 2021-22, Bert sold the debt to Hopper for £80,000. Barry pays Hopper in full in 2022. For CGT purposes, the sale of the debt by Bert is not a chargeable event. However, Barry's satisfaction of the debt gives rise to a £20,000 gain in the hands of Hopper.

Any loss arising is an allowable loss.

If the original creditor disposes of a debt to a connected person, any gain realised by the connected person on subsequent disposal of the debt will be a chargeable gain. However, if there is a loss it will not be an allowable loss.

If property, rather than cash, is received in satisfaction of a debt the transfer is treated as being made for a consideration that cannot exceed the market value of the asset at the time of the disposal. If the person receiving the property is the original creditor, any subsequent gain on a disposal of the property is restricted to the gain that would have arisen if the person had acquired the property for an amount equal to the outstanding debt.

Example 2

John owes a creditor £100,000. After negotiation, the creditor agrees to accept a parcel of land worth £80,000 in full satisfaction of the debt. John is treated as making a disposal of the land for consideration of £80,000, not £100,000.

The creditor's position depends on whether the debt was a chargeable asset. See HMRC's guidance for detail.

Law: TCGA 1992, s. 251
Guidance: CG 53513, 53514

6.6.2   *Debts on securities*

A "debt on a security" is not defined in the legislation, despite the wording in s. 251(1) implying that it is. HMRC's guidance acknowledges that the legislation is of limited use in this respect but does state that a debt does not have to be secured to be a debt on a security, and therefore the term "debt on a security" must be distinguished from the term "secured debt".

However, there are certain characteristics that distinguish a debt on a security from an ordinary debt. The case of *Ramsay* highlighted that a debt on a security should be capable of being:

- held as an investment; and
- realised at a profit.

HMRC's guidance at CG 53426 states that for a debt to be held as an investment, it should either:

- carry a commercial rate of interest;
- carry a premium on repayment, equivalent to the interest which would have been paid; or
- be issued at a discount, so that repayment at face value reflects the interest which would have been paid on the debt.

Failure to meet any of these benchmarks is likely to see a debt being classified as an ordinary debt instead of a debt on a security.

The level of premium, or rate of interest which the debt carries, will be an important factor when considering if a debt can be realised at a profit. However, a debt carrying an attractive rate of interest may still not be regarded as a worthwhile investment, for example due to terms which favour the borrower rather than the debtholder. HMRC's guidance gives the example of a loan which carries the right to repay early. Each case will need to be judged on its own merits.

Where the status of a debt is established as a debt on a security, a disposal by the original creditor will give rise to a chargeable gain or allowable loss.

For these purposes, "securities" excludes mortgages, charges or other debts in respect of securities given. However, it can include loan stock (including government loan stock) as well as debentures issued by a company after 15 March 1993 if they are issued in respect of reorganisation or a qualifying scheme of reconstruction (see **5.3**).

Law: TCGA 1992, s. 132, 251
Case: *W T Ramsay Ltd v IRC* (1981) UKHL 1
Guidance: CG 53426

6.7   Appropriations to or from trading stock

If a chargeable asset is acquired otherwise than as trading stock, but it is subsequently appropriated as trading stock, the general rule is that the asset holder is treated as having sold the asset at market value at the time of the appropriation, giving rise to a chargeable gain or allowable loss. However, an election may be made to treat the asset as being transferred at cost instead.

Law: TCGA 1992, s. 161

6.8   Plant subject to a long funding lease

Where plant or machinery is used for the purpose of leasing under a long funding lease, the lessor is treated as making a deemed disposal at the "relevant disposal value" at the date of commencement of the lease, and immediately reacquiring it at the same value.

The relevant disposal value depends on whether the lease is an operating lease or a finance lease. If it is the former, the market value at the date of commencement of the lease is the relevant value. If it is the latter, the figure to use is the greater of the qualifying lease payments or the market value of the plant or machinery at the start of the lease term.

When the lease is terminated, the underlying assets are deemed to be disposed of and immediately reacquired at current value at the time the lease terminates.

If a loss arises on the deemed disposal, it must be restricted. If the plant or machinery has only been leased once, the restriction will be an amount equal to the fall in value of the asset during the period of the lease. If it has been leased more than once, the restriction will be an amount equal to the aggregate value over every period it has been leased, i.e. not just the most recent one. The fall in value is measured by the difference in market value between the two relevant dates.

Law: TCGA 1992, s. 25A, 41A; CAA 2001, s. 61(2)

6.9   Foreign currency

6.9.1   Introduction

Sterling is not a chargeable asset for CGT purposes. However, currency in any other denomination is, and its disposal can give rise to a chargeable gain or allowable loss.

6.9.2   Disposal of a foreign asset

In practice, foreign currency gains or losses will most likely be seen where overseas shares or other assets are acquired and disposed of for foreign currency.

Such transactions require the foreign currency to be treated as a separate asset from the underlying investment. As an example, if some shares are purchased in a foreign currency, the acquisition cost must be converted into sterling for UK CGT purposes at the date of acquisition. Upon a later disposal, the consideration received must be converted into sterling at the date of disposal. Any change in the exchange rate between sterling and the relevant other currency or currencies in the interim period will therefore be accounted for.

The gain or loss on the underlying shares themselves will also be accounted for by following these steps as long as the bargain is made at arm's length as the value of the shares in sterling is highly likely to be the same as their value in the relevant other currency once the exchange rate is taken into account.

The gain or loss in the foreign currency is not calculated and then converted into sterling. This was confirmed in *Capcount Trading*.

Case: *Capcount Trading v Evans* [1993] BTC 3

6.9.3   Foreign currency for personal expenditure

Any gain on the disposal of foreign currency for personal expenditure outside the UK by the taxpayer or his or her family is not a chargeable gain, including provision or maintenance of a residence outside the UK. Since April 2012, the treatment of foreign currency bank accounts for individuals, trustees and personal representatives was aligned with the treatment of ordinary debts discussed in **6.6.1**, i.e. they do not give rise to chargeable gains or allowable losses in the hands of the original creditor.

6.9.4   Cryptocurrency

Cryptocurrency is a chargeable asset and gains must be calculated in the same way as other foreign currency. However, care should be taken that the activity does not constitute a trade, in which case profits would be taxable as income. This is a specialist area and reference should be made to HMRC's *Cryptoassets Manual*.

6.10   Closely held non-resident companies

Without specific provisions, it would be possible for UK-resident individuals to use a non-UK resident company with no UK permanent establishment to accumulate gains on UK assets.

To counteract this, anti-avoidance provisions exist to attribute such gains to UK-resident shareholders if the company would be a close company if it were resident in the UK. Where these provisions apply, gains are apportioned between the UK-resident participators (and possibly non-UK resident trustees). However, this only applies to participators who would be attributed more than 25% of any relevant gain using a straight allocation corresponding to their interest.

These apportionment rules do not apply to annual tax on enveloped dwellings (ATED) related gains, or to carried interest gains.

Where an individual is subject to split-year treatment – i.e. the individual arrives in, or leaves, the UK partway through the tax year – any gains arising in a non-resident part of the split year are ignored.

Law: TCGA 1992, s. 3

6.11   Value shifting

6.11.1   Introduction

The value shifting provisions in s. 29 and 30 seek to counteract situations where value passes from one holding or interest into another without there being a disposal for CGT purposes, or where the value of an asset is deliberately reduced prior to a disposal. Without these provisions, it would be possible to create an artificial loss by manipulating certain assets.

6.11.2   Section 29

The rules in s. 29 work by deeming the shift in value to be a disposal, or part disposal, by the person transferring the value. The person who receives the value makes a corresponding acquisition. The transfer is deemed to take place at the amount that the transferor could have obtained in respect of the transfer if it were made at arm's length. Where some actual consideration is paid, the rules add the difference so that the CGT computation is made using the full hypothetical amount.

HMRC's guidance at CG 13230 states that s. 29 is applicable in three situations:

- Where a person, or persons, who control a company use that control so that value or valuable rights pass out of shares which they own (or are owned by persons connected with them) into other shares in, or rights over, the company.

- Where the owner of land (or any other property) sells it and becomes lessee, and there are subsequent arrangements generally favourable to the lessor.

- Where rights or restrictions over any asset are reduced or removed by the person entitled to enforce them.

Example

Aaron owns 75% of the share capital of the company. Aria owns 25% of the shares. There are 10,000 shares in issue. Aria subscribes for 20,000 additional shares at the nominal value.

Following the subscription, Aaron's shareholding has fallen to 25% (i.e. 7,500 shares out of the total 30,000 in issue). Because this is now a non-controlling shareholding, value will have passed from Aaron's holding to Aria's holding – even though Aaron still owns all his shares.

Section 29 operates to deem Aaron to have made a disposal of an interest in his shares for consideration equal to the market value of 50% holding prior to Aria's subscription.

Law: TCGA 1992, s. 29

6.11.3   Section 30

Section 30 applies where there is a scheme or arrangement resulting in a material reduction in the value of an asset that has been disposed of and any person has received a tax-free benefit.

A person will have received a tax-free benefit if they become entitled to any money, money's worth, increase in the value of an asset, or release from any liability, and this entitlement is not otherwise charged to corporation tax, income tax or CGT.

Where s. 30 applies, the CGT computation is amended by increasing the consideration for the disposal by a just and reasonable amount having regard to the benefit obtained.

For CGT (as opposed to corporation tax) purposes, the s. 30 provisions do not apply to:

- transfers between spouses or civil partners;
- transfers from personal representatives to a beneficiary; or
- transfers which result in a shift in value for *bona fide* commercial reasons and not as a result of a scheme or arrangement to avoid tax.

Law: TCGA 1992, s. 30
Guidance: CG 13260-13280

CGT RELIEFS

7. Business asset disposal relief

7.1 Introduction

7.1.1 Background

The former entrepreneurs' relief (ER) was renamed as business asset disposal relief (BADR) in 2020. The fundamentals are unchanged, with the important exception of a big reduction in the maximum relief that can be claimed.

The rationale behind the relief is that if you encourage wealth creators to invest in trade and industry, they will in turn create jobs and help to redistribute that wealth.

7.1.2 BADR at a glance

BADR applies a flat rate of 10% on eligible gains made by taxpayers, irrespective of whether they are basic, higher or additional rate taxpayers. The eligibility criteria are primarily designed to encourage investment into trading businesses.

There is a maximum lifetime limit on which BADR can be claimed. This is currently £1 million (compared with £10 million under the former ER regime) but gains made before 6 April 2008 do not count towards this limit.

The relief can be claimed on multiple qualifying disposals during the taxpayer's lifetime until this limit is reached. Thereafter, any further gains are taxed as normal according to the CGT rates in force at that time.

Spouses and civil partners are treated as separate individuals, each of whom is entitled to relief up to the maximum amount, provided that the relevant conditions are met.

When determining the rate of CGT to be applied to other gains that are not eligible for BADR, gains that are eligible for BADR are treated as being taxed first, thus taking up any unused basic rate band.

Law: TCGA 1992, s. 4(6), 169N
Guidance: CG 63970

7.1.3   Who can claim?

BADR is available to reduce the CGT charge arising from "qualifying business disposals", which are defined to include any of the following:

- a material disposal of business assets (which may include an unincorporated business or shares in certain trading companies, see **7.2**);
- a disposal of trust business assets (see **7.10**); or
- a disposal that is associated with a "relevant material disposal" (see **7.5**).

In some cases, relief is only given on part of the qualifying business disposal, i.e. on the part constituting a disposal of "relevant business assets" (see **7.8.2**).

Typically, BADR will be claimed by the following:

- sole traders and partners disposing of all or part of their business (see **7.7** and **7.9**);
- company directors and employees disposing of qualifying shares in a qualifying company (see **7.3**); and
- trustees disposing of qualifying business assets where there is a qualifying beneficiary (see **7.10**).

BADR is not available to companies, to personal representatives of a deceased person's estate or to trustees of a discretionary trust.

A taxpayer does not have to be UK resident in order to claim the relief, although in most instances the non-UK resident will not be within the UK CGT net. Similarly, the asset does not have to be situated in the UK in order to claim the relief.

Law: TCGA 1992, s. 169H

7.1.4   Legislation and guidance

The legislation covering BADR is found at TCGA 1992, s. 169H to 169V.

HMRC guidance can be found in the *Capital Gains Manual* at CG 63950 onwards.

It is possible to approach HMRC for a non-statutory clearance prior to undertaking a transaction. This could be useful, for example, to give certainty as to whether a company is a qualifying trading company, or to determine if the "whole or part of a business" condition is met.

Guidance: CG 64100 (clearance)

7.1.5   Claims

BADR is not automatic. It requires a claim to be made, the time limit for this being on or before the first anniversary of 31 January following the tax year in which the qualifying business disposal takes place.

The claim is not irrevocable and can therefore be amended or revoked within the time limit. Furthermore, the time limit for amendment may be extended in the case of an enquiry.

Where a notice to file a return has been issued, the claim can be made in the taxpayer's (or trustees') self-assessment return for the year of disposal. Where no notice has been received, the claim is made in accordance with the provisions of TMA 1970, Sch. 1A.

A claim can only be made if, after taking account of all relevant gains and losses on disposals of material business assets, a gain arises. The interaction with losses is illustrated by the following HMRC example:

HMRC example

K ran a confectioner/tobacconist business for several years. He then sold it and made a gain of £38,000 ("relevant gains") on the goodwill, but a loss of £8,000 ("relevant losses") on the premises. Assuming he qualified, BADR is applied to the net gains of £30,000.

The £30,000 would be the "chargeable gain" and, subject to reduction by other allowable losses and the AEA, would be charged to CGT at 10%.

The loss of £8,000 on the premises is not otherwise allowable.

Law: TCGA 1992, s. 169M
Guidance: CG 63970, 64130

7.1.6   Pitfalls and planning points

In order to minimise the CGT due, the annual exempt amount (AEA) should be allocated in priority to gains not eligible for BADR, i.e. those that suffer tax at the highest rate, as can be seen in the following example.

Example

In January 2021, a higher rate taxpayer realised a gain on the disposal of asset 1, which was eligible for BADR, of £100,000 and a gain on asset 2, which was a residential property not eligible for BADR, of £25,000.

The optimum position will be to allocate the annual exempt amount to gains not qualifying for BADR, which achieves an overall tax saving of £2,214 (being £12,300 @ 18%).

Option 1 – allocate AEA to non-qualifying gains

	BADR gains £	Non-BADR gains £
Asset 1	100,000	
Asset 2		25,000
Less AEA		(12,300)
Chargeable gains	100,000	12,700
CGT @ 10%/28%	10,000	3,556

The total CGT charge is therefore £13,556.

Option 2 – allocate AEA to qualifying gains

	BADR gains £	Non-BADR gains £
Asset 1	100,000	
Asset 2		25,000
Less AEA	(12,300)	
Chargeable gains	87,700	25,000
CGT @ 10%/28%	8,770	7,000

The total CGT charge is therefore £15,770.

Guidance: CG 64125

7.2 Material disposal of business assets

7.2.1 Key principles

As previously mentioned, BADR is available where a taxpayer makes a "material disposal" of "business assets". These concepts – and the notion of associated disposals – are defined below.

7.2.2 Disposal of a business asset

This can be broken down into the following main categories:

- a disposal of the whole, or part, of a business – this can be a sole trade or partnership;
- a disposal of assets used in the business at the time that the business ceases, whether sold at the date of cessation or later; and
- a disposal of shares or securities in a company.

There are various conditions that must be met for each of the above categories, discussed later in this chapter.

Law: TCGA 1992, s. 169I(2)

7.2.3 Material disposal

Whole or part of a business

In the case of the disposal of the whole, or part, of a business, a material disposal means that the taxpayer must have owned the business for at least two years before the disposal.

Assets used at cessation of business

Where there is a cessation of a business, in order to qualify as a material disposal, the assets being disposed of must:

- have been used in the business at the time the business ceased;
- relate to a business owned by the taxpayer for at least two years before the business ceased; and
- be sold within three years of cessation.

HMRC make the point that they have no discretion to extend the statutory three-year limit. They also state that the guidance in the

Business Income Manual will be applied if there is doubt about the date of business cessation.

Law: TCGA 1992, s. 169I(2)
Guidance: CG 63975

Shares or securities

In the case of a disposal of shares or securities in a company, a material disposal means that for at least two years before the disposal:

- the company is the taxpayer's "personal company" – i.e. broadly the taxpayer holds 5% of the shares (see **7.3.2**);
- it is either a trading company (see **7.4.2**) or the holding company of a trading group; and
- the individual is an employee or officer of the company (see **7.3.1**).

In the case where a company has ceased trading, the material disposal conditions will continue to be met provided the shares are disposed of within three years of cessation. This could include a liquidation.

Law: TCGA 1992, s. 169I, 169S(3)
Guidance: CG 63975

7.2.4   Associated disposals

A disposal associated with a material disposal will also qualify for BADR provided all of the following conditions are satisfied:

- The taxpayer makes a material disposal of:
  - the whole or part of a business in which he or she was a partner; or
  - shares or securities in a company.
- As part of the withdrawal from that business, the taxpayer makes a disposal of an asset that has been used in that business.
- The asset has been used in that business for at least two years.
- If the asset was acquired on or after 13 June 2016, it has been owned for at least three years.

If the disposal relates to a business in which the taxpayer was a partner, the disposal must be of at least 5% of the partnership assets or partnership share (or, subject to further conditions, of the whole partnership interest if it is less than 5%). A similar condition applies for disposals associated with share disposals.

Associated disposals are covered in depth at **7.5**.

Law: TCGA 1992, s. 169K

7.3 Qualifying shareholders

7.3.1 Introduction

An individual wishing to claim BADR in respect of a holding of shares must meet the shareholder tests:

- the shares (or loan stock, securities, etc.) must be in the individual's personal company (see **7.3.2**);
- the company must be a trading company or holding company of a trading group; and
- the individual must be an officer or employee of the company, or of a company within the group.

Law: TCGA 1992, s. 169I(2)(c)

Two-year rule

Generally, the individual must satisfy the conditions for the period of at least two years prior to disposal – this increased from one year from 6 April 2019. There are exceptions to this, for example in the case of a takeover or reorganisation, or in spouse transfers, but these are discussed specifically in later sections.

Where the company has ceased trading:

- the conditions must be met for the period of two years prior to disposal, but for one year if:
  - o the disposal took place before 6 April 2019; or
  - o the cessation took place before 29 October 2018; and
- the shares must be sold within three years of trade ceasing.

In the case of shares held in an EMI scheme, the requirement is two years from the date of grant.

Law: TCGA 1992, s. 169I(6)

Office or employment

To determine whether the individual making the disposal is an officer or an employee of the company, the CGT legislation requires us to look at the meanings given in ITEPA 2003, s. 4 and s. 5(3).

"Employment" for these purposes includes:

- a contract *of* service;
- a contract *of* apprenticeship; and
- any employment in the service of the Crown.

To satisfy the employment condition, the individual must have held the position, or office, for at least two years up to the date of the disposal of shares.

There is no minimum working hour requirement to satisfy this condition, so part-time employees and officers are eligible

Case law in relation to ER has considered this matter. In *Hirst*, an individual was held not to be a director or shadow director but was nevertheless held to have an employment relationship with the company. The case is of interest for anyone giving up their formal post prior to the sale of shares, providing the individual demonstrably continues to work for the business.

The FTT case of *Corbett* concerned a wife who provided clerical services to her husband, who was a director of the company. The taxpayer's appeal was allowed in the circumstances of the case.

Law: TCGA 1992, s. 169I(6), 169S(5); ITEPA 2003, s. 4, 5

Cases: *Hirst v HMRC* [2014] UKFTT 924 (TC); *Corbett v HMRC* [2014] UKFTT 298 (TC)

7.3.2   Personal company

For a disposal of shares to qualify for BADR, the disposal must be in the individual taxpayer's personal trading company.

A personal company means that the individual owns at least 5% of the ordinary shares in the company, together with at least 5% of the voting rights.

There is no minimum level of disposal that qualifies, so if (for example) a person owns 10% of the shares and the shareholding reduces to 9.9%, that will qualify, provided the other conditions are met. This is no longer the case for associated disposals, however, as explained at **7.5.2**. See

7.6.6 for the modification of these rules in relation to shares acquired under EMI schemes.

In addition, since 6 April 2019 the taxpayer must also either (or both):

- be beneficially entitled to at least 5% of the company's distributable profits and 5% of the assets available to equity holders on a winding-up; or
- be entitled to at least 5% of the proceeds on the sale of the company's entire ordinary share capital (in determining whether this test is met at any time during the requisite two-year period, the whole of the ordinary share capital is deemed to be sold at its market value on the last day of that two-year period).

HMRC guidance confirms that the personal company condition can be met:

"if throughout part of the period of two years the company was a trading company and throughout the remainder of the period was the holding company of a trading group".

HMRC have also confirmed that the condition:

"is not failed if another share transaction takes place earlier on the same day as the disposal which results in the 5% shareholding requirement not being met at the time of the disposal".

FA 2019 also introduced new protections for shareholders who have previously met the personal company test but whose shareholding is subsequently diluted as a result of a new share issue. An election can be made to treat the shares as being disposed of and immediately reacquired at their market value immediately prior to the dilution. BADR can then be claimed on the resulting gain.

Of course, this is a "dry" tax charge as the shares have not actually been sold. A further election can therefore be made to defer the payment until the shares are actually sold. The two elections are separate. Care must be taken, as where the shares subsequently fall in value, tax will still be payable on the notional gain based on the share value at the election date. There is no scope to offset the fall in value against the original gain (and if a capital loss crystallises on the actual disposal it cannot be carried back) although, of course, it would be possible to offset a loss against gains arising in the same, or a subsequent, tax year. The two elections are detailed in s. 169SB-SH.

Ordinary shares are given the same meaning as in ITA 2007, s. 989, which states that ordinary share capital is:

> "... all the company's issued share capital (however described), other than capital the holders of which have a right to a dividend at a fixed rate but have no other right to share in the company's profits."

An arrangement involving preference shares was considered in *McQuillan*, while a contrasting decision was reached in the *Castledine* case in 2016.

The *McQuillan* case was later appealed to the Upper Tribunal. The outcome restored order and agreed with the outcome of the *Castledine* case. On the basis of these two cases worthless zero-dividend shares should be included when considering the total share capital issued by a company.

The trade requirement is considered in detail at **7.4.2**.

Law: TCGA 1992, s. 169S(3), 169SB-169SH; FA 2019

Cases: *Castledine v HMRC* [2016] UKFTT 145 (TC); *McQuillan & Anor v HMRC* [2016] UKFTT 305 (TC); *McQuillan & Anor v HMRC* [2017] UKUT 344 (TCC)

Guidance: CG 63975

Voting rights

Two or more individuals (e.g. a husband and wife) may jointly own shares, and in this case they will each be attributed the respective proportion of the total. So if they jointly own a 100% shareholding, they will each (assuming no complicating factors) be treated as owning 50% of the shares and of the voting power.

If an individual is also a trustee of a settlement, any shares he controls in that capacity cannot be counted towards his personal 5% total. Similarly, a qualifying beneficiary of a settlement cannot include shares held in the settlement in determining whether or not he or she personally holds 5% of the shares.

Voting rights that are conditional upon some external factor are not counted if that external factor remains merely a theoretical possibility. HMRC illustrate this as follows:

> "Preference shares in a company may entitle the shareholder to a vote only if the dividend on these shares was six months in arrear at the date of the company's annual general meeting. Such votes

would not be exercisable if the preference dividend never fell into six months' arrear."

Guidance: CG 64050

7.3.3 Pitfalls and planning points

Timing of multiple disposals

Where individuals dispose of shares over a period of time, it is important that they monitor their status as qualifying individuals throughout. At each disposal it is necessary for them to qualify for the relief.

Example

Nicole is a director who owns 10% of a trading company's share capital and voting rights, which she intends to sell to another director over a five-year period. Without planning, the following situation would occur in relation to BADR:

Year	Shareholding prior to sale	Qualifying individual
1	10%	Yes
2	8%	Yes
3	6%	Yes
4	4%	No
5	2%	No

It is therefore important, in order to avoid loss of the relief, to consider the overall position in relation to BADR before undertaking multiple disposals.

Formalising family arrangements

To prevent issues with HMRC when an eventual claim for BADR is made, it is important to ensure that the correct documentation is in place.

For family-run businesses it is important to formalise the position for adult children and spouses to ensure that the relief is available on sale.

Spousal transfers

If one spouse (or civil partner) already qualifies for BADR as a qualifying individual, but the other does not, it may be helpful to transfer shares to the qualifying spouse prior to a sale of the shares.

The transferee does not need to own the additional shares for 24 months. However, in the current environment (with HMRC very sensitive to potential avoidance) it is not advisable to carry out this type of planning immediately before a sale, particularly if large amounts are involved.

Where both spouses own 4% of the share capital, this means that neither of them will qualify for BADR. It is therefore sensible to ensure that at least one of them owns 5% of the share capital. This transfer will need to be carried out at least 24 months prior to any potential sale.

Examples of problem areas

Example 1 – share reorganisation

There is a share reorganisation whereby a new company acquires the shares of the trading company by way of share-for-share exchange. After the transaction, the individual needs to have 5% or more of the ordinary share capital and voting rights. If his or her shareholding falls below 5% after the transaction, BADR will no longer be available on a subsequent disposal of the shares.

Example 2 – share reorganisation – preference shares

There may be a reorganisation within the company which results in preference shares being created. It is important that the preference shares are created in such a way as not to dilute the existing shareholdings for the purposes of BADR.

Example 3 – amending share rights

If a decision is made to amend the rights of shares, for example if voting rights are stripped from a spouse's shares, it is important to realise that they will no longer qualify for BADR.

Example 4 – implementation of share schemes

Where a company decides to put a share scheme (e.g. an EMI scheme) in place, it is important to assess the impact on the existing shareholders and to ensure that their shareholdings are not inadvertently diluted to such an extent that they will be denied BADR.

This is particularly important where the options are automatically exercised on sale of a business. HMRC have confirmed that they will not take dilution on the day of the sale into account but if the options are exercised too early (say the day before), then this could cause an issue for existing shareholders.

However, FA 2019 provisions now allow shareholders to make an election where their shareholding will be diluted as a result of a new share issue (see **7.3.2**).

7.4   Qualifying companies

7.4.1   Introduction

One of the key concepts in relation to BADR for shares is the trading company. There is a very specific definition of trading, different from other areas of tax.

As BADR is an "all or nothing" relief – i.e. as a general principle you either qualify for the relief on the whole value or you get no relief at all – it is vitally important to monitor the trading status of the company to ensure that the relief is not inadvertently lost.

7.4.2   Trading company

BADR is only available when the disposal of shares is in a trading company or the holding company of a trading sub-group.

A trading company means:

> "a company that is carrying on trading activities whose activities do not include to a substantial extent activities other than trading activities".

Trading activities are activities carried on by the company in the course of, or for the purposes of, a trade carried on by it, or for the purposes of a trade it is preparing to carry on.

In most situations, it will be clear whether activities are carried on in the course of, or for the purposes of, a trade. However, similar transactions can be carried on by different companies for different reasons, and it is therefore important to look at the facts in each case. HMRC guidance gives examples of what may constitute trading activities, what normally would not, and where there may be exceptions.

Law: TCGA 1992, s. 165A, 169S(4A)
Guidance: CG 64060

Substantial

There is no definition of "substantial" in the legislation for these purposes. HMRC acknowledge that most companies/groups will have non-trading activities and, in this context, substantial is taken to mean 20% or more. HMRC may typically look at the following in determining a company's trading status:

- income from non-trading activities;
- asset base; and
- time/expenses relating to non-trading activities.

These should not be regarded as 20% tests in their own right. However, they are factors and indicators that are helpful in establishing a company's trading status.

Guidance: CG 64090

Income from non-trading activities

A company that generates 20% or more of its income from non-trading activities (e.g. investment income or rental income) would normally be regarded as non-trading.

HMRC have confirmed, however, that if a company has particularly poor trading results for a given year, with the result that the income from investments makes up an unusually large percentage of the overall turnover, this would not in itself cause the company to lose its trading status.

HMRC would instead look back over the history of the company to take a more balanced view. By building up a bigger picture and looking at the historic position and results of the company, it may be possible to demonstrate that this is not the norm and therefore to defend the trading status, though care should obviously be taken if the circumstances persist.

Asset base

If the value of non-trading assets held on the company's statement of financial position (balance sheet) is substantial, this can be an indicator that a company is non-trading. Examples of such assets can include investment properties and shares.

Long-term investment of cash balances is discussed below.

Intangible assets (e.g. goodwill) are not always recognised on a company's statement of financial position, but HMRC argue that these may need to be taken into account when determining if the 20% test applies.

Current market value or amounts given in consideration for those assets are both appropriate ways of measuring this.

There is a further question as to what constitutes an investment property; for example, a company could let surplus business premises. CG 64085 offers guidance here and states that the following should not necessarily be regarded as non-business activities:

- letting part of the business premises;
- letting properties that are no longer required for the purposes of the trade in question, where the company's (or group's) intention is to sell them;
- sub-letting property where it would be impractical or uneconomic to assign or surrender the lease; or
- the acquisition of property (whether vacant or already let) where it can be shown that the intention is to bring it into use for trading purposes.

As with most guidance from HMRC, it is obviously necessary to look at each case based on the facts and circumstances when deciding whether the company may be likely to breach the substantial test.

Time/expenses relating to non-trading activities

If a substantial amount of staff time/resources/expenses is spent on non-trading activities, this can jeopardise the company's trading status. In practice, however, this is the least likely indicator to be breached when applying the "substantial" indicators.

Excess cash and investments

Large cash balances and investments can be a strong indicator that a company is non-trading.

Sometimes, however, the investment is so closely linked to the trading activity that it becomes an integral part of the trade. CG 64060 gives the specific example of a travel agent, who is required to retain a fixed level of cash on deposit for bonding requirements. Therefore, it is necessary to consider the underlying reason for the cash balances or investments.

Example – sale of property

A company sells its trading premises and is holding the cash balance on deposit until suitable replacement premises are found. This cash may constitute more than 20% of the asset base. However, whilst the cash is currently in excess of the 20% indicator, it derives from the underlying trading activities and, as such, would not normally count towards the company's non-trading activities.

Care needs to be taken to retain evidence that the intention remains to use the funds in the business. If the cash remained in the bank for a number of years and there was no suggestion that the company had searched for new premises or even had any intention to purchase new replacement premises, this could become an issue over time.

Guidance: CG 64080

7.4.3   Clearance

The responsibility for ascertaining the trading status of a company for the purposes of making a claim for BADR lies with the individual making the claim. This can be difficult for an individual, particularly where any excess cash balances or rental properties held within the company may compromise the trading status of the company.

There is no statutory procedure for confirming the trading status of a company. However, if there is genuine uncertainty, it is possible for the company to approach HMRC for an opinion under the non-statutory clearance route, for the purposes of the shareholders making a BADR claim.

A non-statutory clearance is a written confirmation of the view of HMRC's application of tax law where there is genuine uncertainty as to the application of the rules to a specific transaction or event.

The trading status of a company is a question of fact which may change based on the balance of its activities. For this reason, it is not possible for HMRC to give certainty on the future trading status of a company, and therefore it is preferable to wait until all of the relevant facts are known.

When making a request for a non-statutory clearance from HMRC, the company must provide all the information contained in the HMRC checklist. This can be found on the "non-statutory clearance" section of the HMRC website.

Guidance: CG 64100; https://tinyurl.com/hf4wjskf (clearance application)

7.4.4   Holding companies and groups

BADR is only available when the disposal of shares is in a trading company or the holding company of a trading sub-group.

A group for these purposes means a company and its 51% subsidiaries. A company is a 51% subsidiary if more than half of its ordinary share capital is owned directly or indirectly by another company.

A trading group is taken to mean a group of companies, one or more of which is carrying on trading activities and whose activities, when taken together, do not include, to a substantial extent, other activities.

It is therefore necessary to consider the indicators as set out above to decide the trading status of a group of companies.

Law: TCGA 1992, s. 165A(7), (12); CTA 2010, s. 1154-1157

7.4.5   Joint ventures

A "joint venture company" is a trading company where at least 75% of the ordinary shares are held by five or fewer persons, and the shareholder company (or group as a whole) owns at least 10% of ordinary shares.

In the past, it was possible to look through a joint venture or partnership and attribute the underlying trade to the corporate vehicle in which the individual holds his or her shares. An individual could claim BADR on a disposal of shares in a trading company where that company held shares in a joint venture company, even where the underlying holding in the joint venture company was less than the required 5% for the shares to be considered qualifying for BADR under normal circumstances. This is no longer possible.

Instead, the company is treated as carrying on the proportion of trading activities of the joint venture company that corresponds to the percentage of ordinary share capital held.

HMRC, in a policy paper published on 16 March 2016, give the example of a person who holds 20% of a company which does nothing but hold 40% of a trading company's shares. The individual will be treated as holding 8% (20% x 40%) of the trading company and 40% of that company's activities will be taken into account in deciding whether the person's shares are shares in a trading company for BADR purposes.

Guidance: https://tinyurl.com/ykbac8e5 (HMRC policy paper)

7.4.6   Liquidations

For BADR purposes, a disposal of shares includes a distribution made during a winding-up. This covers both solvent members' voluntary liquidations (MVLs) and insolvent creditors' voluntary liquidations (CVLs).

This means that relief is available in respect of the distribution if the other conditions for BADR are satisfied.

There has, however, been a perceived abuse of the rules where people have used a series of companies to obtain capital treatment on their profits rather than extract the value at income tax rates. HMRC therefore introduced a targeted anti-avoidance rule (TAAR) to combat what they describe as "phoenixing". This TAAR is intended to prevent a company being wound up, with the shareholders receiving a capital distribution rather than a dividend, before going on to start up a business in a similar field. Various conditions apply, one of which is that the TAAR will only apply (in HMRC's words) to "circumstances where, when considered as a whole, the arrangements appear to have a tax advantage as one of the main purposes".

Law: TCGA 1992, s. 122; ITTOIA 2005, s. 396B(1)-(10), 404A; CTA 2010, s. 1030A, 1030B

7.4.7   Pitfalls and planning points

It is important that the trading status of a company is constantly monitored. As the company needs to have been a trading company for at least 24 months prior to any potential sale or company purchase of own shares, it is not possible to carry out last-minute changes.

Excess cash

Particular attention should be paid to large cash balances. If the cash balances cannot be justified and are clearly excessive (and therefore risk breaching the 20% indicator), consideration should be given to extracting the cash.

Tax-efficient cash extraction will depend upon the circumstances of the shareholders. The company can pay dividends or bonuses in the usual way. Or it might consider making a top-up pension payment for the directors or key employees (providing the individuals have sufficient annual allowance remaining to make such payments).

The company could consider a non-statutory demerger to extract the cash into a separate company if the balance is sufficiently large.

Property

Care should be taken whenever there is property not used in the trade held within the company. Given the tendency for property prices to increase over time, the company could easily find that it breaches some of the trading indicators without realising it has done so.

Changes over time

Over time the company might find that it becomes less trading in nature and more investment-biased. When it becomes apparent that the company is "winding down", it might be more tax-efficient to cease to trade and close the company down (claiming BADR providing it is within the three-year window) and to restructure as two businesses going forward.

7.5 Associated disposals

7.5.1 Introduction

An individual may own an asset personally that is used by the business. Under the main conditions for BADR, this would not be a qualifying disposal. However, BADR may also be due on an "associated disposal" of an asset that is owned by an individual but used for the purposes of a business carried on by either:

- a partnership in which the individual is a partner; or
- a company which is the individual's personal company.

Law: TCGA 1992, s. 169K(1)

147

7.5.2   Conditions

There are four conditions, all of which must be met.

Condition A

The individual must dispose of all or part of:

- his or her interests in the assets of the partnership; or
- shares or securities in a company.

This disposal must also be a material disposal of business assets, as discussed at **7.2**.

If the disposal relates to a business in which the taxpayer was a partner, the disposal must be of at least 5% of the partnership assets or partnership share (or, subject to further conditions, of the whole partnership interest if it is less than 5%). A similar condition applies for disposals associated with share disposals.

Reference should be made to the detailed legislation, but one requirement is that there must be no "partnership purchase" or "share purchase" arrangements. See also CG 63996.

Law: TCGA 1992, s. 169K

Condition B

The associated disposal must be made as part of the individual's withdrawal from participation in the business of the partnership or trading company: see **7.5.3**.

Law: TCGA 1992, s. 169K(3)

Condition C

The asset being disposed of must have been used in the business carried on by the partnership or company, for at least two years ending with:

- the date of the material disposal of business assets; or
- if earlier, the cessation of the business.

Law: TCGA 1992, s. 169K(4)

Condition D

If the asset being disposed of was acquired on or after 13 June 2016, it must have been owned for three years ending on the date of disposal.

If the asset is co-owned and the ownership interest has changed during that three-year period, the relief is restricted to the element of the ownership interest that was constant throughout that time.

For example, relief would be restricted if the ownership interest rose from one quarter to one half during the three-year period.

Example

Alan, Bill, Charlotte and Donna are equal shareholders in AB Ltd. They personally (and jointly) acquired a building which has been used by the company for its trade for several years. Charlotte and Donna both retired in 2020, selling their joint interest in the building to Alan and Bill.

In 2021, Alan retires and sells his half interest in the building to Bill, realising a gain of £40,000. The proportion qualifying for relief will be restricted to the proportion of the minimum holding throughout the ownership period to the holding at the disposal date, i.e. one quarter divided by one half = 1/2 x £40,000 = £20,000.

Law: TCGA 1992, s. 169K(4A)

7.5.3   *Withdrawal from the business*

Condition B requires a withdrawal from the business. This means that the disposal of the asset must relate to a reduction in the individual's interest in the assets of the partnership or shares in the company. In HMRC's words (in relation to partnerships):

> "relief will not be due unless the disposal of an asset (held outside the partnership) is related to the individual's reduction of his or her interest in the assets of the partnership."

It does not mean that the individual has to reduce the amount of work done in the business.

In the absence of any statutory guidelines regarding the meaning of "withdrawal from a business" it is helpful to see how HMRC approach the matter.

HMRC give the following examples of situations in which they accept that relief would in principle be due.

HMRC example 1

G owns a shop from which he trades in partnership with his son. The asset sharing ratio is: G 60%, son 40%. He wishes to reduce his involvement and the ratio is then altered to: G 20%, son 80%. G also gifts the premises to his son but continues to work full-time in the shop.

HMRC confirm that:

> "the material disposal (G's reduction of his interest in the assets of the partnership) together with the associated disposal (G's gift of the premises to his son) would represent a withdrawal from participation in the business".

HMRC example 2

R owns a small factory unit which is used by her personal company, S Ltd, of which she is the full-time managing director. She sells both her shares and the unit to another company in a takeover but remains managing director.

Here too, HMRC accept that this would represent a withdrawal from the business.

According to the HMRC guidance, the material disposal and the associated disposal must be "part and parcel of one single withdrawal from participation in the business" and therefore "there should normally be no significant interval between the two disposals".

This may not always be practical. For example, in the event of a partnership or company ceasing to trade, it is possible that there may be an interval between the two disposals. Therefore, HMRC accept that a disposal will still be an "associated disposal" if it takes place:

- within one year of the cessation of business;
- within three years of the cessation of business, provided the asset has not been leased or used for any other purpose after the cessation of business; or
- where the business has not ceased, within three years of the material disposal, provided the asset has not been used for any purpose other than that of the business.

HMRC give the following example.

HMRC example 3

W, M and S are in partnership running a chain of retail chemists. W owns one of the shops used by the business. He decides to leave the partnership and move abroad.

M and S continue in partnership. W intends at the time of leaving the partnership to sell the shop, which continues to be used by the partnership, to M. However, M needs time to arrange his finances to allow the sale to proceed.

W disposes of the shop to M 18 months after leaving the partnership. So, the sale of the shop qualifies as an "associated disposal" under the third bullet point above, as the business does not cease, the shop continued to be used in the business and the disposal of the shop takes place within three years of W leaving the partnership.

The three tests above are not statutory so there may be cases where they are not met but where it is still possible to show that the disposal is made as part of the individual's withdrawal from participation in the business.

HMRC will consider such cases "carefully on their particular facts to see whether they meet the requirement" but take the view that the conditions are not likely to be met "if the asset has been used for any other purpose for a significant period following the material disposal". The following HMRC example illustrates the point.

HMRC example 4

Mr and Mrs J own 100% of the shares in a company. It carries on a manufacturing and retail trade. But the premises from which the company trades are owned personally by them, not by the company.

They decide to retire and in 2008 they close the business but sell their shares in the company to a competitor who wants to acquire the intellectual property. The premises stand empty until 2010, when they sell them to a local developer to convert into apartments. Gains arise upon both transactions.

If all the necessary conditions for BADR are met by both Mr and Mrs J in respect of the disposal of their shares, their gains on the disposal of the premises will also attract relief, as that disposal is an "associated disposal".

If Mr J qualified for BADR in respect of his disposal of shares but Mrs J did not, only Mr J's gain on disposal of the premises would qualify as an "associated disposal".

It should be noted, however, that if the premises were used for some other purpose following disposal of the shares, for instance converted into apartments by Mr and Mrs J (as opposed to being sold to a developer), the eventual sale is unlikely to be an "associated disposal".

This is because the later disposal of the property did not arise as part of their withdrawal from the business.

Law: TCGA 1992, s. 169K(3)
Guidance: CG 63998, 64000

7.5.4   Restrictions

Various situations may result in the amount of BADR available on an "associated disposal" being restricted. Any such restricted gain is chargeable to CGT as normal, i.e. without the benefit of BADR.

The conditions which can lead to a restriction of BADR are where:

- the asset owned by the individual subject to the associated disposal rules was only used by the business for part of the period of ownership;
- only a part of the asset owned by the individual subject to the associated disposal rules is used by the business;
- the individual making the associated disposal was involved in the business for only part of the period for which the asset subject to the associated disposal rules is used by the business; or
- the use of the asset subject to the associated disposal rules is dependent on the payment of rent.

See below for further detail on these points and for other anti-avoidance restrictions.

Law: TCGA 1992, s. 169P(4)
Guidance: CG 64145

Asset not used throughout ownership period

Where an asset owned by the individual making the claim for BADR under the associated disposal rules is not used by the business for the entire period of ownership, it is necessary to apportion the availability of BADR on a "just and reasonable" basis.

For this restriction, the availability of BADR is based on the period of time that the asset was used in the business.

Example 1

CJD had owned a commercial property for some years. He purchased it in April 2011 and rented it out to various tenants until April 2015. At that date he moved his own business to the premises and used it exclusively for the purposes of his limited company.

In April 2021 CJD sells his shares in the limited company, which qualifies for BADR. The purchaser also wants to buy his property, on which the capital gain stands at £100,000.

The gain could be apportioned as follows:

Total ownership	10 years
Rented out (April 2011-April 2015)	4 years
Used in business (April 2015-April 2021)	6 years
Total gain	£100,000
Gain not qualifying for BADR	£40,000
Gain qualifying for BADR	£60,000

HMRC guidance states, however, that "no adjustment is required for periods when an asset is not in active use for the business if this is simply a reflection of the seasonal nature of a particular activity".

Law: TCGA 1992, s. 169P(2), (5)(a)
Guidance: CG 64145

Asset only partly used in the business

BADR under the associated disposal rules is restricted where only part of an asset is used for business purposes.

Again, a just and reasonable apportionment is necessary, in this case based on the extent to which the asset was used in the business. This part of the gain will be subject to BADR, and the remainder will be taxed at the appropriate rate based on the individual's income levels.

Law: TCGA 1992, s. 169P(5)(b)

Individual not involved in the business for the whole of the ownership period

An asset may have been used in the business before the individual making the claim for BADR became involved in the carrying on of that business. BADR is in that case restricted on the associated disposal. The involvement can be as a partner, or as an officer or employee of the individual's personal company.

In these circumstances, the restriction is based on the amount of time that the individual is involved in the business.

Example 2

A building used in a family partnership was gifted to a family member, KLD, in April 2008 whilst she was an employee. She was made a partner in April 2010.

KLD sells the property in April 2020 and makes a capital gain of £500,000.

The gain might be apportioned as follows:

Total ownership	12 years
Non-qualifying period for BADR	2 years
Qualifying period for BADR	10 years
Total gain	£500,000
Gain not qualifying for BADR	£83,000
Gain qualifying for BADR	416,667

Law: TCGA 1992, s. 169P(5)(c)

Payment of rent

Where rent is paid for the use of an asset that is subject to a claim for BADR under the associated disposal rules, the relief will be restricted. Rent in relation to an asset includes any form of consideration given for the use of the asset.

The "just and reasonable" basis for this restriction depends on the level of rent charged by the individual.

If a full commercial rent is charged, there is no BADR available on the associated disposal. If rent is charged at below market rent, some BADR is available based on the rent received as a proportion of the market rent.

Rent for these purposes is defined at s. 169S(5) to include "any form of consideration given for the use of the asset".

The restriction only applies where rent has been received after 5 April 2008.

Example 3

JJD purchased a property on 6 April 2005 which was used in his limited company from the date of purchase. The company paid rent for the use of the property until 5 April 2012, at which date, on the advice of his accountant, the rent ceased.

JJD sold his shares in the limited company, together with the property, in April 2021, making a gain of £1 million on the property.

His gain might be apportioned as follows:

Total ownership	16 years
Period arising prior to April 2008	3 years
Period between April 2008 and April 12	4 years
Period from April 2012 to sale	9 years
Total period qualifying for BADR (3 + 9 years)	12 years
Total period not qualifying for BADR	4 years
Gain qualifying for BADR (12/16)	£750,000
Gain not qualifying for BADR (4/16)	£250,000

Law: TCGA 1992, s. 169P(5)(d), 169S(5)

Anti-avoidance

A claimant must normally dispose of at least 5% of the partnership assets or 5% of the ordinary share capital of a company. Relief is denied where arrangements exist for the acquisition of shares or increased partnership share by anyone connected with the claimant.

However, the disposal does not have to be a minimum of 5% of the partnership or company shares provided the claimant is disposing of all of his or her residual interest and the asset subject to the associated disposal has been owned for a continuous period of at least three years in the eight years ending with the date of the disposal.

Further examples

Example 4

EB Ltd is a trading company that has been very successful. OB and her brother JB each own 50% of the shares in EB Ltd. OB also owns personally the property from which the business trades.

OB decides to exit from the business and to allow JB to continue as the sole shareholder. JB therefore arranges for financing to take the business forward. The financing package allows him to buy out his sister, purchasing both her shares and the property.

OB qualifies for BADR on her shares. Also, as she is selling the property alongside making a material disposal of shares, she can claim BADR on the sale of the property.

Example 5

NA, FJ, HJ and SHB are partners of a trading partnership sharing profits and capital in the ratio of 10:30:30:30.

NA owns the building from which they trade. She has never received rent from the partnership for use of the asset.

NA decides to raise funds for a round-the-world trip and agrees to reduce her share to 7%, increasing the other three partners' shares by 1% each. Furthermore, she agrees to sell the property to the other three partners.

As NA has reduced her partnership share by less than 5%, she will not be treated as making a material disposal and therefore BADR will not be available on the sale of the property.

Example 6

On 5 April 2021, SD sells the shares in his personal trading company in which he has been a director for ten years. SD also owns the premises from which the business trades.

The business paid a half market rent to SD from 6 April 2011 to 5 April 2014 but has not paid rent since that date. SD makes a gain of £1 million from the sale of the property.

Because rent has been paid to SD it is necessary to make a reasonable apportionment. This would be calculated as follows.

	£	Eligible £	Non-eligible £
Total gain on sale of premises	1 million		
Gain accruing between 6 April 2011 and 5 April 2014	1 million x 3/10	150,000	150,000
Gain accruing since 6 April 2014	1 million x 7/10	700,000	

7.5.5   Pitfalls and planning points

Where there is a withdrawal from the business, or a material disposal of shares, ensure that the property has been owned for three years.

Where the material disposal is a sale of part of a business, it is important to review the situation properly and to ensure that HMRC are likely to accept that part of the business has been sold (discussed further at **7.7.3**).

A disposal for associated disposal purposes must consist of 5% of the partnership or of the company shares, *not* 5% of the individual's interest in the partnership or company.

7.6   Share exchanges

7.6.1   Introduction

When a person sells shares, the proceeds may consist of a combination of cash, shares and deferred consideration. The BADR rules dictate when relief will be available in such cases.

It is not uncommon, in the context of a sale or reorganisation, for a mixture of shares and loan notes to be issued as consideration. There are two types of loan notes that can be issued – either qualifying corporate bonds (QCBs) or non-qualifying corporate bonds (non-QCBs).

A bond cannot be a QCB unless it is "expressed in sterling and in respect of which no provision is made for the conversion into, or redemption in, a currency other than sterling". This is normally the main distinguishing factor.

QCBs are exempt from CGT (and therefore any losses are not allowable). Non-QCBs are subject to CGT.

For a general review of the CGT issues relating to reorganisations, see **5.3**.

Law: TCGA 1992, s. 117(1)

7.6.2   Qualifying corporate bonds

Where consideration is received partly in the form of QCBs, the capital gain is calculated as though cash had been received. However, as no cash is actually received, the resultant gain is "frozen" and deferred until such time as the QCB is redeemed. When redeemed, this frozen gain will be charged to CGT at the rate appropriate to the individual, depending on whether he or she is a basic or higher rate taxpayer.

BADR is potentially available on the gain relating to the QCB element, as long as the BADR conditions are met in relation to the "old asset", namely the original shares.

An individual wishing to claim BADR on a transaction involving QCBs will have to make an election under TCGA 1992, s. 169R. The downside to this is that CGT becomes payable on the whole transaction prior to the redemption of the loan notes; the tax will be due on 31 January following the end of the tax year in which the exchange takes place.

The election must be made by 31 January, 22 months following the end of the tax year in which the exchange takes place.

Law: TCGA 1992, s. 116(10), 169R

7.6.3   Non-qualifying corporate bonds

Non-QCBs work differently from QCBs.

The issue of non-QCBs will fall into the "share-for-share" rules (see **7.6.4**). This means the non-QCBs are deemed to have been acquired at the same time and for the same base cost as the original shares.

The effect of this is that when the non-QCBs are encashed a capital gain will arise in the usual way based on the proceeds received less the original cost of the shares.

This gain can qualify for BADR providing the individual qualifies for the relief at the date of encashment. Whilst this is possible, it is not very likely and therefore the individual may wish to bank the BADR in the same way as a QCB holder.

This is achieved by making a TCGA 1992, s. 169Q election (see **7.6.4**). This will ensure that the full value of the transaction is taxed at the date of exchange and BADR will be available providing the individual qualifies at that point.

This election should be made by 31 January, 22 months after the end of the tax year in which the gain arises.

Law: TCGA 1992, s. 127

7.6.4   Share-for-share exchanges

Where a share exchange takes place, and the relevant conditions are satisfied, no disposal or acquisition is deemed to take place for CGT purposes. The new shares issued in exchange for the old shares are treated as the same asset; they "stand in the shoes" of the old shares, taking on the history and base cost of the original holding.

When this exchange takes place, it may be that the disposal of the old shares would be eligible for BADR but that the new shares do not satisfy the relevant conditions; for example, it may be that the company is no longer the individual's personal trading company.

Where this occurs, the legislation provides relief for qualifying disposals, and allows the individual to elect for the reorganisation provisions not to apply. What this means is that at the time of the exchange, a disposal is deemed to take place based on the market value of the new shares. This then allows the individual to claim BADR on the old shares.

This is an all-or-nothing election, so it is not possible to crystallise only a part of the gain by making a partial election.

The time limit for making a claim is the same as the claim for BADR itself, i.e. 31 January, 22 months after the end of the tax year in which the reorganisation takes place.

Law: TCGA 1992, s. 169Q(2), (4)

7.6.5   Earn-outs

Where a disposal occurs, the consideration can be structured many ways, for example, wholly cash, wholly shares or a mixture of both. Furthermore, it can be paid up front, or it may be deferred to a later date, perhaps on satisfaction of certain events.

For details of how to calculate the chargeable gain when there is deferred consideration, see **3.2.4**.

159

Deferred consideration can be specified at a later date, typically by using an agreed formula, such as a percentage of post-acquisition profits. This arrangement is known as an earn-out.

The basic CGT rule is that the date of disposal is when there is an unconditional contract for sale. Where a disposal includes an earn-out element, the value brought in at the date the contract becomes unconditional depends on whether the earn-out is ascertainable at that date.

Ascertainable deferred consideration

Where the deferred consideration is ascertainable – i.e. it is fixed at the date the contract becomes unconditional – there is one disposal for CGT purposes and all proceeds are taxed up front, i.e. the amount paid now and the future amount. This means, for BADR purposes, that there is only one disposal to consider, and the relief will apply as normal.

Unascertainable deferred consideration

Where the deferred consideration is unascertainable – i.e. the additional amount is unknown at the date the contract becomes unconditional – it is still necessary to value the earn-out at this point.

This is known as the *Marren v Ingles* principle.

The earn-out right is treated as a separate asset. It is valued and included as part of the initial consideration for sale, and then when the condition is eventually satisfied and the earn-out received, this is treated as a further disposal for CGT purposes.

From a BADR perspective, the initial disposal is the same as discussed above. However, when the earn-out is received, no BADR will be available as the gain relates to the disposal of the earn-out, which is not a qualifying business asset.

Deferred consideration in the form of shares

Where the earn-out will be satisfied in the form of shares or debentures and this deferred consideration is ascertainable at the disposal date then, as discussed above, a single chargeable event occurs at the time of disposal. The normal shares and securities exchange rules would therefore apply per **7.6.3** and **7.6.4**, i.e. no disposal occurs at this point and a chargeable gain would only arise when the new securities are subsequently sold.

Where the earn-out will be satisfied in the form of shares or debentures and this deferred consideration is not ascertainable at the disposal date then, the position is more complex. Refer to CG 58070 and 58090 for HMRC examples illustrating how the rules will then operate.

When the shares are eventually sold, BADR will only be available if the conditions are met in relation to the new shares, i.e. the individual qualifies for BADR in relation to the acquiring company.

However, as discussed above, the share exchange rules can be disapplied at the disposal date, in which case the ascertainable earn-out or the unascertainable earn-out right is treated as cash and, as such, BADR can be applied. See CG 58020.

Law: TCGA 1992, s. 138A

Case: *Marren v Ingles* (1980) 54 TC 76

7.6.6   *Enterprise management incentive options*

Where shares are acquired from a share scheme, the general rule is that they will be eligible for BADR if the conditions are met in relation to a disposal of shares in a company, as discussed at **7.3**.

An EMI is a share option scheme, with tax benefits, that is aimed at smaller companies. The company grants share options to selected employees who are then able to exercise the options when certain trigger points are met.

The qualifying ownership period for BADR in relation to pre 6 April 2013 EMI schemes begins on the date that the shares are acquired. In practice, it was difficult for employees to meet the necessary conditions, so changes were brought in from 6 April 2013.

As a result (for share options exercised on or after 6 April 2013), it may be possible for shares acquired under an EMI scheme to be eligible for BADR even where the personal company conditions are not met.

To qualify for BADR:

- the shares must have been acquired on the exercise of a qualifying option granted under the EMI scheme;
- they must have been acquired after 5 April 2013;
- they must be disposed of at least two years after the option was granted; and
- the individual must be an employee of the company, or group company, and the company must be a trading company or the

holding company of a trading group throughout the period of two years ending with the disposal.

There are two fundamental differences here. First, there is no longer the 5% holding requirement. Second, the qualifying period for BADR begins when the option is granted, not exercised.

These shares are known as "relevant EMI" shares. Where relevant EMI shares are disposed of, the matching rules in relation to shares must be considered.

Relevant EMI shares are never pooled. Instead, the disposals are matched on a first-in, first-out (FIFO) basis. This means that BADR is always given at the earliest opportunity.

Law: TCGA 1992, s. 106A(6A), (6B), 169I(7A)-(7R)

7.6.7   *Pitfalls and planning points*

If a person elects under either s. 169R (see **7.6.2**) or s. 169Q (see **7.6.3** and **7.6.4**) to bring forward the tax point on receipt of QCBs or non-QCBs, it is important to ensure that sufficient proceeds are received up front to pay the tax liability when it becomes due. This might mean negotiating the cash element of the deal.

There will be a trade-off between deferring the gain into the future, with the uncertainty of the future rate of tax that will be paid and the availability of BADR, and the cash flow disadvantage of paying the tax liability earlier. It is important to give both scenarios proper consideration.

Depending upon the nature of the transaction, it might be possible to structure the deal so that the individual retains qualifying status for BADR after the sale. This would require him or her to retain at least 5% of the share capital and voting rights in the acquiring company and to remain as a director or employee. This may not be feasible in many situations, but the possibility should be considered.

If the individual elects to pay the tax under s. 169R, and the QCBs subsequently become worthless, there is no statutory right to recovery of the tax paid. The individual could consider requesting a bank guarantee as part of the deal, whereby the bank agrees to underwrite the liability of the purchaser and will pay if the purchaser defaults on the loan notes. This can be a very expensive option if available, but often banks will not agree to underwrite the debt.

Alternatively, if there is a risk of a bad debt arising, non-QCBs might be a better option as they create a capital loss that can be used against future capital gains.

A further option might be to request that there is no loan note but a simple debt that would be taxable under s. 48 as deferred consideration. This means the individual will be taxed up front on the whole proceeds but the gain can be reduced if subsequently the debt becomes irrecoverable.

Where employees would not be entitled to BADR under normal circumstances, consider whether the company qualifies for an EMI scheme.

7.7 Sole traders – disposal of whole or part of the business

7.7.1 Introduction

Individuals who act as sole traders may be able to claim BADR on a disposal of business assets, which may be either:

- a disposal of the whole or part of a business (see **7.7.3**); or
- a disposal of one or more assets that were used for the purposes of the business at the time it ceased (see **7.8**).

A general condition for relief is that the business (rather than the individual assets) must have been owned for two years before a claim for BADR can be made.

Mixed-use assets

BADR restrictions normally apply where there is private or mixed use of the assets. However, there are no such provisions relating to sole traders. This means that even if part of the property is used for private purposes, there is no restriction on disposal of that asset providing it is sold as part of the sale of the business or within three years of cessation of the business.

Law: TCGA 1992, s. 169I(2)

7.7.2 Qualifying business disposals

BADR is given in respect of a "qualifying business disposal".

This term is defined to include a "material disposal" of "business assets". The legislation goes on to define these key concepts, including what is meant by a business, a business asset and a material disposal.

For BADR purposes, a "business" means anything that is:

- a trade, profession or vocation; and
- conducted on a commercial basis and with a view to the realisation of profits.

There is extensive case law from other tax contexts (e.g. in relation to the offset of losses) to define what is meant by being conducted on a commercial basis.

HMRC guidance confirms that relief may be available where the business consists of the commercial letting of furnished holiday accommodation in the UK (see **7.11.2**).

Law: TCGA 1992, s. 169H, 169I, 169S(1)
Guidance: CG 63965

7.7.3   Whole or part of the business

The disposal of the whole or part of a business will constitute a material disposal of business assets if the business is owned by the individual throughout the period of two years ending with the date of the disposal.

An important distinction is drawn between the sale of an *asset* of the business on the one hand and a sale of a *part* of the business on the other; the disposal of business assets does not necessarily constitute a disposal of part of the business.

If business activities continue after a disposal, the whole of the activities relating to the assets sold must cease. If the assets are sold and there is no corresponding reduction in the activity, HMRC will argue that the disposal was a sale of assets.

Various cases have considered this distinction, mostly from the days of retirement relief. HMRC's guidance at CG 64035 is also helpful in determining whether a disposal constitutes the sale of part of the business or merely of surplus business assets.

McGregor v Adcock

In this retirement relief case, it was held that the sale of 4.8 acres from a 35-acre farm was the sale of an asset and not the sale of part of the business.

In the High Court the judge drew a distinction between the business and the individual assets used in the business. On the facts of the case, he found that substantially the same business continued after the sale of the 4.8 acres as had been carried on before.

Case: *McGregor v Adcock* (1977) 51 TC 692

Pepper v Daffurn

In this, another retirement relief case, Mr Daffurn sold 83 acres of his 116-acre farm in 1986. He later sold a cattle yard in 1988 and claimed retirement relief on the basis that he had sold part of his remaining business.

In this case, the judge found that Mr Daffurn had sold a surplus business asset rather than a part of the business as, after the original sale, Mr Daffurn had changed the nature of his business (he changed from rearing to grazing cattle on a much reduced scale). The cattle yard was not needed for his new business and hence it was a surplus asset.

Case: *Pepper v Daffurn* (1993) 66 TC 68

Jarmin v Rawlings

This was another retirement relief case, which may again have application for BADR.

A farmer owned 64 acres of land with a milking parlour and yard. He had a dairy herd of 34 animals. He sold the milk parlour and yard then within three months he sold 14 of the animals. He then transferred most of the remaining animals to his wife's farm. He ceased dairy farming and used the remaining land to rear cattle.

The courts found that the sale of the milking parlour and yard was a separate trade to that of rearing cattle and that the "sale of the milking parlour and yard, coupled with a cessation at completion of all milking operations for the taxpayer's benefit, amounted to a disposal by him of his dairy farming business".

Case: *Jarmin v Rawlings* (1994) 67 TC 130

Gilbert (t/a United Foods) v HMRC

Mr Gilbert was a sole trader selling for commission to wholesalers. He sold part of his business to one of his suppliers – including brands, trademarks, customer database and all relevant goodwill that related to that part of the business.

The taxpayer claimed ER (the forerunner to BADR – see **7.1.1**) but this was rejected by HMRC on the basis that he had not disposed of "an identifiable part of the business which on its own was separately identifiable". HMRC argued that it was a sale of assets and the taxpayer appealed.

The FTT decided that that the inclusion of the goodwill in the sale made it the sale of a going concern rather than the sale of individual assets.

The tribunal held that the correct test in this type of situation is whether the taxpayer can show that the part of the trade being sold is a "viable section of a composite trade" which would be capable of being recognised as a trade if separated from the whole.

Case: *Gilbert t/a United Foods v HMRC* [2011] UKFTT 705 (TC)

Russell v HMRC

In *Russell*, three individuals owned equal interests in land which they farmed as a partnership. They sold one third of the land and continued farming the remaining land. The farming activity was subcontracted before and after the sale and there was no change in the activities of the partners.

It was found that the sale of the land was a disposal of an asset, and not the disposal of part of the partnership business.

Case: *Russell v HMRC* [2012] UKFTT 623 (TC)

Amin v HMRC

In *Amin*, the taxpayer was denied ER on a partial disposal of his accountancy business premises.

The taxpayer had a sole trade accountancy business. He transferred 50% of his beneficial interest in his business premises to a pension fund over a two-year period. He also disposed of some audit clients as he was unable to carry out the audit work. He then claimed relief on the sale of the business premises on the basis that the transfer of the audit clients was a disposal of part of his business.

HMRC denied relief and this interpretation was upheld by the tribunal. Interestingly, the FTT found that if the taxpayer had sold distinct office space as he no longer needed it to carry out the discontinued audit work, then he might have been entitled to relief.

Case: *Amin v HMRC* [2016] UKFTT 515 (TC)

7.7.4   Pitfalls and planning points

This is a difficult area and caution should be taken when planning for part disposals of a business. HMRC will look at all the relevant facts when deciding whether there has been a disposal of part of a business rather than a mere disposal of a business asset or assets.

The taxpayer should consider the following:

- According to guidance at CG 64035, HMRC do not consider it is possible to dispose of a business, or part of it, in stages.
- A disposal of even a substantial asset is not sufficient to constitute the disposal of part of a business. Simply scaling down activities is not sufficient to evidence a disposal.

HMRC have argued (at CG 64030) that:

> "for relief to be due, the activities included in the disposal need to be capable of being carried on as a business without the addition of anything further".

Arguably, that is an incorrect test as it seems to consider the matter from the point of view of the purchaser rather than that of the vendor. Indeed, this therefore appears to contradict HMRC's other observation (at CG 64035) that:

> "It must be looked at from the vendor's point of view. The question is whether the business (or part of it) has been disposed of, not whether any business has been acquired by a purchaser; there need be no acquisition of a business as a going concern."

It is difficult, however, to argue against HMRC's further comment that:

> "if an asset or assets have been sold but no particular activity or set of activities disappeared with the asset disposal, it cannot be said that any part of the business has been disposed of".

HMRC guidance starting at CG 64010 includes extensive commentary on the "whole or part of a business" issue, with numerous further examples.

Guidance: CG 64010*ff.*, 64030, 64035

7.8 Sole traders – post-cessation disposals

7.8.1 *Material disposal*

It is not unusual for a business to cease trading (rather than to be sold on as a going concern). The business owner may then sell off the assets of the business after cessation.

As the business has ceased, the sale of these assets will not qualify as the sale of the whole or part of the business under the rules considered above, but it may qualify as the disposal of assets sold after the cessation of the business.

In relation to assets in use at the time the business ceases, there will be a material disposal of business assets if:

- the business is owned by the individual throughout the period of two years ending with the date on which the business ceases; and
- the disposal takes place not more than three years following the date of cessation.

It is important to note that the three-year period is a statutory time limit and HMRC have no discretion to extend it.

There is, however, a further requirement that the assets in question must be "relevant" business assets (see below).

Law: TCGA 1992, s. 169I(2)

Date of cessation

The date of cessation is a question of fact.

The taxpayer will need to take care when the facts are not straightforward and there could be a range of dates which could be considered as constituting the date of cessation.

There is also the potential for an argument with HMRC as to whether a cessation has taken place at all.

These issues were considered by the FTT in *Rice*, which held that a significant change in a business was the cessation of the first trade and the commencement of a second trade. This allowed the taxpayer to claim ER against the gains that arose on the disposal of the property used in the first business.

Mr Rice was a used sports car salesman. Due to vandalism and for other reasons he stopped trading at his original premises in 2005 and sold the property in 2008. He then started selling cars closer to his home, which necessitated changes to the way he ran the business. This included no longer displaying the cars, advertising on the internet and selling four-wheel drive and family cars instead of sports cars.

HMRC refused the claim for ER. However, the tribunal found that Mr Rice had had the changes forced on him by external factors (in particular the vandalism). Furthermore, the type of vehicle sold after the cessation was different and the way the businesses were operated was also different.

Taking these factors into account, the tribunal decided there were two separate businesses and therefore a cessation (of the first) had taken place.

Case: *Rice v HMRC* [2014] UKFTT 133 (TC)
Guidance: CG 64105

7.8.2   *Relevant business assets*

To qualify for BADR, the disposal by the sole trader has to be a disposal of "relevant business assets". These are assets used for the purposes of the business apart from "excluded assets".

Excluded assets are:

- shares and securities;
- assets, other than shares or securities, that are held as investments; and
- goodwill (in some circumstances, see below).

Goodwill is an excluded asset where:

- a person (P) disposes of goodwill to a close company; and
- immediately after the disposal P, and any "relevant connected person", together own 5% or more of the ordinary share capital or voting rights of the company or of any company in the same group.

Note that for these purposes a close company is defined to include a non-UK resident company which would be a close company if it were UK resident.

The exclusion of goodwill also applies to the disposal if the person making the disposal is a party to arrangements and one of the main purposes of these is to secure that the exclusion does not apply to the goodwill.

The goodwill exclusion is, however, disapplied in certain circumstances.

The rule is relaxed if all the shares are then sold within 28 days, provided that the purchaser is a company. If the purchaser is a close company, the original vendor (together with any connected persons) must not own 5% or more of it.

This enables relief to be obtained in the circumstances where a company wishes to buy an existing business from a sole trader or partnership but wants to buy it as a company rather than as a separate trade.

Law: TCGA 1992, s. 169L, 169LA
Guidance: CG 64006, 64007

7.8.3 Pitfalls and planning points

Two years of ownership

The two years test applies to the business rather than the asset itself. Therefore, in a husband/wife situation where the husband runs the business but his wife owns half of the assets used in the business, it is possible to transfer the wife's half of the assets to the husband to claim BADR on the full gain.

Conversely, when the sole trade itself is transferred from one spouse to another, the two-year clock restarts. Although there is no gain on transfer, there is no deemed transfer of the ownership period and therefore the receiving spouse will need to run the business for two years before the relief is available.

5% test

A disposal for associated disposal purposes must consist of 5% of the partnership or of the company shares, *not* 5% of the individual's interest in the partnership or company.

7.9 Partnerships

7.9.1 Introduction

It is possible for individuals who are partners in a trading business to claim BADR on the sale of the whole or part of their partnership share or to claim the relief when they sell assets within three years of cessation of their business.

A "partnership" in this case refers to both a traditional partnership and a limited liability partnership (LLP). A traditional partnership is not considered a separate legal entity distinct from its partners. Whilst an LLP is a separate legal entity, it is still treated as transparent for tax purposes providing it is carrying on a trade or business.

HMRC guidance summarises the effect of the BADR rules in relation to partners (at s. 169I(8)) as follows:

"[The legislation] enables partners to qualify for BADR upon:

- a disposal of the whole of their interest in the partnership – by treating it as a disposal of the whole of a business;

- a disposal of part of their interest in the partnership – by treating it as the disposal of part of a business;

- a disposal *by the partnership* of the whole or part of the partnership business – by treating the business as owned by the individual;

- a disposal of partnership assets following the cessation of the partnership business – by treating the business as owned by the individual partner.

An individual may also qualify when their business becomes a partnership.

Relief may be available in respect of an asset owned by a partner personally and used in the partnership business under the associated disposal rules [see **7.6**].

But relief will *not* be available for disposals of partnership assets, unless the disposal constitutes the disposal of part of the partnership business."

Law: TCGA 1992, s. 59, 59A, 169I(8)
Guidance: CG 64040

7.9.2   *Period of ownership*

The partner must have been a partner for two years at the date of disposal before a claim for BADR can be made.

Law: TCGA 1992, s. 169

7.9.3 Disposal of a partnership asset

Relief is not generally available for disposals of partnership assets, unless the disposal constitutes the disposal of part of the partnership business (but see **7.9.5** for disposals of assets owned personally by partners but used for partnership business).

Example 1

A business is run from a building owned by the partnership, which also owns six acres of land. The partnership sells two acres of this land. It is unlikely that this will constitute a sale of part of the business. Assuming that to be the case, BADR is not available.

This may be contrasted with the following:

Example 2

A farming partnership sells two acres of its six acres of land. The two acres were used for pig farming and, after the sale, the partnership no longer carries on any pig farming. This would appear to be a sale of part of the business and therefore relief would be available.

The question of whether there is a sale of part of the business is considered in greater depth at **7.7.3** above.

Law: TCGA 1992, s. 169I(8)(c)
Guidance: CG 64040

7.9.4 Disposal of a partnership share

Where an individual disposes of the whole or part of his interest in the partnership, it is treated as a disposal by that individual of the whole or part of his business.

This is by virtue of the deeming provisions which treat the partner as having owned the business for the purposes of BADR providing that the disposal comprises at least one relevant business asset as defined by s. 169L (assets used for the purposes of a business carried on by the individual or a partnership of which the individual is a member).

Law: TCGA 1992, s. 169I(8)(b), 169L(3)(a)
Guidance: CG 64040

7.9.5 Associated disposals – assets used in partnership

A partner may personally own some of the assets that are used by the partnership business. Gains on the disposal of such assets may qualify for relief, but only if the disposal is associated with another disposal (a "relevant material disposal") for which BADR is available (see **7.5.3**).

7.9.6   Associated disposals – restricted relief

The amount of BADR that may be given for associated disposals may be restricted, for example in relation to non-business use of the assets in question (see **7.5.4**).

7.9.7   Pitfalls and planning points

Spouses and civil partners

A business partner needs to have been in the business for at least two years. Therefore if (for example) a husband and wife jointly own an asset, but only one is a partner in the business, there are two options. Either the non-participating spouse must be brought into the partnership at least two years prior to sale, or ownership of the asset must be transferred to the spouse who is already a partner in the business.

Charging rent

Consider whether rent should continue to be paid for assets used in the business, as this will dilute the BADR rate over time. If it is not necessary, and if the income can be tax-efficiently replaced elsewhere, then an alternative route should be considered.

7.10   Trustees

7.10.1   Introduction

BADR is a relief for individuals and is therefore not available to trustees in their capacity as such.

However, it is possible for trustees to make a claim in very restricted circumstances. They are not then using their own lifetime allowance but instead agree with a beneficiary to use all or part of his or hers.

If the trustees carry on a business in their own right, they will not be entitled to claim BADR when they sell that business.

A full discussion of the different types of trusts is outside the scope of this book, but in essence there are two types – those that provide beneficiaries with an entitlement to income ("interest in possession" trusts) and those that provide the trustees with discretion over the distribution of income and capital ("discretionary" trusts).

For further information see *Financial Planning with Trusts* from Claritax Books.

In short, trustees of a discretionary trust can never make a claim for BADR. In certain circumstances, as noted above, the trustees of an interest-in-possession trust may be able to make a claim.

Law: TCGA 1992, s. 169J*ff.*
Guidance: CG 63995

7.10.2   Overview

To claim BADR the trustees must be disposing of either:

- shares or securities of a company that is the personal company of a qualifying beneficiary; or
- one or more assets used for the purposes of a business carried on by a qualifying beneficiary.

The legislation uses the term "settlement business assets" to denote the shares, securities or business assets in question, forming part of the settled property.

Law: TCGA 1992, s. 169J(2)

7.10.3   Commentary

See **Chapter 15** for more detailed coverage of BADR in relation to trusts.

7.10.4   *Pitfalls and planning points*

Beneficiary also making personal gain

On the sale of assets used in a business or partnership carried on by the qualifying beneficiary, it is likely that the beneficiary will be making a personal gain and will use part of his or her BADR lifetime allowance. In this case, only the balance can pass to the trustees. Where large amounts are involved, this should be factored into any calculations.

If there is a same-day disposal of trust business assets and of business assets owned by the qualifying beneficiary, the personal disposal is treated as taking place first. The trustees can then use only any balance remaining of the individual's lifetime limit.

Law: TCGA 1992, s. 169N(8)
Guidance: CG 64125

No qualifying beneficiary

Many trading companies are wholly owned by trusts (often due to old retirement relief planning). Where this structure exists, it is impossible for the trustees to obtain any BADR as there can be no qualifying beneficiary.

Where all of the company shares are held by a trust, it may be worth appointing at least 5% of the share capital out to a beneficiary who is also an employee or director and ensuring that the individual has a life interest in the relevant assets. After a 24-month period has passed it should be possible to share the beneficiary's lifetime allowance.

It is, however, important to consider the tax consequences of distributing the assets out, and other reliefs might need to be claimed, such as CGT holdover relief and IHT business property relief.

7.11   Other issues

7.11.1   Introduction

As with all tax reliefs, there are particular topics that require further consideration.

This section will look at various specific areas of the legislation, namely:

- furnished holiday lets (see **7.11.2**);
- spouses and civil partners (see **7.11.3**);
- interaction with holdover relief (see **7.11.4**);
- interaction with rollover relief (see **7.11.5**);
- interaction with enterprise investment scheme (see **7.11.6**);
- interaction with incorporation relief (see **7.11.7**); and
- overseas issues (**7.11.8**).

7.11.2   Furnished holiday lets

To qualify for BADR, the business activity must constitute either:

- the commercial letting of furnished holiday (FHL) accommodation in the UK where this activity is treated as a trade by virtue of TCGA 1992, s. 241; or
- the commercial letting of FHL accommodation outside the UK but within the EEA where this activity is treated as a trade by virtue of s. 241A – note that this provision currently remains unchanged following the UK's withdrawal from the EU.

Where the property falls within either of these provisions, BADR may be available on sale or transfer of the property.

As elsewhere, however, it is necessary to have a disposal of a business or part of a business in order to qualify for BADR. A simple sale of a property from a portfolio of FHL properties may therefore be unlikely to qualify for BADR as it will not form part of a business but is rather an asset within the business. However, this is not clear cut and there may be exceptions, depending on the facts.

Law: TCGA 1992, s. 169(2)(a)

Conditions to qualify as FHL

A full examination of the FHL rules is outside the scope of this book (but see *Furnished Holiday Lettings* from Claritax Books). However, in order to qualify the property letting must meet the following criteria.

The pattern of occupation condition

The total of all lettings that exceed 31 continuous days cannot be more than 155 days during the year.

The availability condition

The property must be available to the general public for letting as furnished holiday accommodation for at least 210 days in the year.

The letting condition

The property must be let commercially as furnished holiday accommodation to the public for at least 105 days in the year. It is not possible to include days when the property is let to friends or relatives at an uncommercial rental.

These tests are normally applied to the tax year under consideration. However, where the business commences or ceases during the tax year, the relevant period, i.e. the period in which the tests above must be met, is defined as follows:

- If the accommodation was not let as furnished accommodation in the previous tax year, the relevant period is two years beginning with the first day in the tax year under review on which it is let by the person as furnished holiday accommodation.

- If the accommodation was let by the person as furnished accommodation in the previous tax year, but is not let by the person in the tax year following the tax year under review, the relevant period is two years ending with the last day in the tax year on which the property was let by the person as furnished accommodation.

In all other situations, the relevant period is the tax year under review and the previous one.

Law: ITTOIA 2005, s. 324, 325; CTA 2009, s. 267

Averaging

Averaging is allowed, in relation to the period of letting test, where some properties are in excess of the minimum period but others might not reach the minimum.

HMRC consider that any property which benefits from the averaging provisions is part of the business for BADR purposes.

Law: ITTOIA 2005, s. 326

Qualifying conditions for BADR

To meet the conditions within s. 169H to 169S, it will be necessary to show that:

- the business was owned throughout the period of two years ending on the date on which the business ceases;

- an asset disposed of on or after the cessation date was in use in the trade at the cessation date; and

- the disposal of the asset takes place within three years of the cessation date.

7.11.3   Spouses and civil partners

Spouses and civil partners are each entitled to make their own separate claim for BADR. Provided the relevant conditions are satisfied, this offers the opportunity to double the lifetime limit with some simple planning.

Disposals of shares

There is no aggregation of holdings between spouses for BADR purposes. What this means is that if the husband owns 3% of a company and his wife owns a further 3% of the shares, neither will be eligible for relief.

In this scenario, a spouse transfer of shares could be made, on a no gain/no loss basis, so that the 5% requirement is met. Here, to be eligible for BADR, the recipient spouse would need to wait two years before disposing of the shares as the company was not previously his or her personal company.

Suppose, instead, that the husband owns 7% of the shares and his wife owns 2%. In this scenario, the husband already meets the 5% minimum holding for BADR purposes, whereas his wife does not, so she would not be eligible for relief. Here, if the shares are transferred to the husband prior to disposal, the entire gain would be eligible for relief; as it is already his personal company, there is no requirement for him to hold the additional 2% for a further two years.

A final option is to transfer 5% of the shares to the other spouse who could then work part-time in the business. This would then enable both spouses to benefit from the lifetime limit provided they waited the requisite two years. This would need to be a genuine commercial arrangement, to avoid the risk that HMRC might challenge the transaction.

Disposals of other assets

Now consider the position where assets other than shares are disposed of, a common example being jointly held property used for trading purposes.

The most straightforward scenario is a husband and wife jointly owning a property, which is used in the trade of their partnership, where the building is sold and the partnership is dissolved. Assuming that all of the relevant conditions are satisfied for BADR, both spouses will therefore benefit from the relief on their fractional share of the gains.

If a jointly held asset is used in the sole trade by only one spouse, then only that spouse's share would be eligible for relief. The couple could consider transferring ownership of the property into the sole name of the spouse who satisfies the conditions.

However, there are practical considerations here; for example, legal title has to be transferred, which will incur legal costs. There are also stamp duty land tax (SDLT) issues to consider, and if there is any debt attached to the property, this will trigger a liability to SDLT.

An alternative, more straightforward, option here would be for the spouse to be involved in the running of the business as a partner. Again, the settlements legislation should be considered before implementing any changes.

7.11.4   Interaction with holdover relief

It may be necessary to consider the interaction of BADR with various other CGT reliefs. In particular, it may sometimes be better to claim BADR and pay tax at 10%, but in other cases the preferred route will be to claim holdover relief to avoid any immediate tax charge, but potentially incurring a higher charge later.

It is possible that a material disposal of business assets which might qualify for BADR could also qualify for holdover relief under TCGA 1992, s. 165. This provision enables a gain to be "held over" by reducing the amount of gain that accrues to the transferor on disposal with a corresponding reduction in the base cost of the asset for the transferee. For full details, see **Chapter 12**.

Business assets for holdover purposes broadly align to the type of asset that qualifies for BADR.

Holdover relief normally applies to gifts of business assets, very often (but not exclusively) between family members.

According to HMRC (at CG 64137):

> "If the whole of the assets comprised in the 'material disposal' for the purposes of BADR are gifted and the subject of a claim under TCGA 1992, s. 165 then no chargeable gain will arise at that time. In consequence there will be no 'relevant gain' for the purposes of TCGA 1992, s. 169N (1) – see CG64125 – and a claim to BADR would not be appropriate."

It is therefore clear that the provisions of s. 165 (holdover relief) take priority over a claim for BADR.

However, if only a part of the assets is gifted and a claim is made which results in a chargeable gain remaining on some of the assets, then it is possible to make a claim for BADR on the gain that comes within the charge to tax.

To qualify on a subsequent disposal, the transferee must meet the qualifying criteria in his or her own right at the date of disposal of the assets. The status of the transferor will not be relevant for a future disposal of those assets.

The same analysis would apply to a holdover election made under the provisions of TCGA 1992, s. 260 (gifts subject to an inheritance tax charge).

Example 1

JMB owns 1,000 shares in Taxation Limited, a trading company with a total base cost of £1,000. He qualifies for BADR in relation to the shares. He gifts 500 shares to his daughter and sells the remaining shares to his business partner for £750,000.

In this scenario, the gain on the 500 shares gifted to his daughter (£750,000 – £500 = £749,500) could be held over, with the result that no tax would be due. His daughter would receive the shares with a base cost for tax purposes of £500.

The gain on the shares sold to his business partner is chargeable and would therefore qualify for BADR. His business partner will receive the shares with a full tax base cost of £750,000.

In both cases, the transferees would need to qualify for BADR in their own right to claim relief on any subsequent sale.

Example 2

JMC runs a sole trade. He retires and passes the business to his son. The gains are:

Goodwill £100,000

Property £250,000

As JMC is gifting the business to his son, he could claim holdover relief on the gains and pay no tax. However, he cannot choose to hold over the gains on (say) the property whilst claiming BADR on the goodwill – it is effectively all or nothing for claiming BADR in this situation.

7.11.5   *Interaction with rollover relief*

Where a person replaces a business asset, it is possible to claim rollover relief under TCGA 1992, s. 152 (see **Chapter 11**).

If all sales proceeds are reinvested in a new asset and a rollover claim is made, the gain on the disposal of the first asset is deferred until, usually, the replacement asset is sold. If only some of the proceeds are reinvested, then it may still be possible to defer some of the gain.

This means that rollover relief takes priority over BADR. The HMRC manual (at CG 64136) states:

> "If the whole of the gain accruing upon the disposal of the old asset is rolled-over against the acquisition cost of the new asset then no chargeable gain will arise at that time. In consequence there will be no 'relevant gain' for the purposes of TCGA 1992, s. 169N (1)... and a claim to BADR would not be appropriate.
>
> If however only part of the gain accruing upon the disposal of the old asset is rolled over against the acquisition cost of the replacement asset then a chargeable gain will remain at that time and a claim to BADR may be made in respect of the amount of gain that remains chargeable.
>
> On a subsequent disposal of the replacement (new) asset any gain is calculated in the normal way. This gain may be subject to BADR if a claim is made and the relevant conditions are met in respect of this subsequent disposal."

Example

In 2010 Sammi Diddles bought a factory building for £100,000 which was used in his business, Diddles Widgets. In April 2015, he sold the factory for £150,000 as he needed more space. He replaced it with a factory which cost £200,000. In 2019 Sammi decided he wanted to downsize the business and spend more time abroad. He therefore sold his factory for £230,000 and bought a smaller factory for £200,000. Finally in 2021, he decided to retire and sold the factory for £220,000.

Sale of factory 1

Without claiming relief, the chargeable capital gain would be £50,000 (£150,000 – £100,000).

As the proceeds of the factory were fully reinvested into the second factory, the gain may be rolled over and so there is no chargeable gain in

April 2015. The acquisition price of the new factory is reduced to £150,000 (£200,000 – £50,000).

There is therefore no reason to consider BADR as there is no chargeable gain.

Sale of factory 2

Without claiming relief, the chargeable capital gain would be £80,000 (£230,000 – £150,000).

In 2019 not all of the proceeds are reinvested into the new factory (£230,000 – £200,000 = £30,000).

Therefore the amount of gain that can be rolled over is restricted (£80,000 – £30,000 = £50,000).

This means the acquisition price going forward is £150,000 (£200,000 – £50,000).

The taxable gain that comes into charge (the amount not rolled over) is therefore £30,000.

In this scenario, as Sammi Diddles is not ceasing to trade, he will not be able to claim BADR and will pay the normal rate of CGT.

Sale of factory 3

In 2021, the full gain will come back into charge.

The proceeds received from the factory sale are £220,000. The acquisition price of the factory following the previous rollover was £150,000. The chargeable gain is therefore £70,000 (£220,000 – £150,000).

As the business has ceased to trade, BADR will be available providing the business qualifies.

7.11.6   Interaction with enterprise investment scheme

Where a gain is deferred, such as under the enterprise investment scheme (see **Chapter 10**), the interaction with BADR has changed over the years.

Prior to 3 December 2014 it was not possible to claim BADR on a deferred gain being brought back into charge, even if the original gain would have qualified for relief but for the deferral. For gains arising between 23 June 2010 and 3 December 2014, the individual had to choose between claiming BADR and paying tax or deferring the gain with a loss of BADR.

Prior to 23 June 2010, BADR operated in a different way, namely by reducing the chargeable gain instead of applying a special rate. For details of how to deal with gains that were deferred before that time, refer to CG 64135

Deferred BADR

FA 2015 introduced new legislation, now at TCGA 1992, s. 169T-169V, which was designed to allow a person to defer a gain using EIS relief and also claim BADR for gains arising on or after 3 December 2014 (i.e. the gain that is being deferred). The rules are not retrospective, so gains arising before 3 December 2014 that were deferred cannot benefit from BADR when brought back into charge.

This relief may be claimed when the deferred gain is assessed providing the relief could have been claimed had the gain not been deferred.

The relief applies if the following conditions are met:

- a chargeable gain (the "first eventual gain") accrues as a result of a chargeable event under EIS or social investment tax relief;
- the disposal which originally gave rise to the first eventual gain was a relevant business disposal (or if there is a series of deferrals, the first disposal was a relevant business disposal); and
- the first eventual gain is the first gain accruing in relation to a particular gain.

The last condition means that if a deferred gain has already been partially realised and no BADR claimed, the remaining gain cannot benefit from BADR. Where a BADR claim is made on the first eventual gain, any subsequent crystallisation events linked to the original gain will also qualify for relief.

There can be a timing issue on the disposal of an asset qualifying for BADR. There is a window of three years after the date the gain was made to claim deferral relief. However, BADR needs to be claimed by 31 January after the tax year in which the gain is realised.

Therefore, if the taxpayer claims BADR on his or her tax return in relation to the disposal and then later chooses to defer the gain, the relief in s. 169V would not be available. It is therefore important that the BADR claim is made when the deferred gain comes into charge, not when the original gain arises. This could be problematic in reality as, at the time of the BADR deadline, the taxpayer may not have made a qualifying EIS investment or be contemplating one in the immediate future.

Law: TCGA 1992, s. 169T-169V
Guidance: CG 64135

7.11.7   Interaction with incorporation relief

Like holdover relief, incorporation relief (see **Chapter 13**) prevents any chargeable gain arising.

Incorporation relief applies where a person transfers a business as a going concern to a company and receives shares in the company in return.

If the incorporation relief conditions are met, the relief is mandatory and applies automatically. The conditions are broadly:

- the business is transferred to a company;
- the transfer is as a going concern;
- all assets are transferred excluding cash; and
- the transfer is for a consideration partly or wholly in shares.

As no chargeable gain is triggered when incorporation relief applies, no claim for BADR is required.

If the taxpayer wishes to trigger BADR, it will be necessary to ensure that incorporation relief conditions are not fully met, perhaps by excluding one asset (other than cash) from the transfer.

Law: TCGA 1992, s. 162

7.11.8   Overseas issues

BADR has no jurisdictional boundaries and therefore it is possible for an individual to claim relief in respect of a qualifying investment in another country.

Where a UK-resident individual owns an interest in an offshore company, it may therefore be necessary to consider whether the relief will be available on an ultimate sale of the asset.

It is therefore important to establish whether the entity has share capital and voting rights (to meet the personal company test). Some entities do not have share capital, such as companies limited by guarantee. This type of company will never qualify for BADR.

Furthermore, the individual must be an employee or director of the company.

A common example of a problematic offshore entity for BADR purposes is that of a US limited liability company (LLC).

The US authorities treat the LLC as a partnership (this is a statutory fiction which creates a deemed partnership). However, as a matter of fact, the individual is not in partnership with others and therefore will not be a partner for the purposes of the BADR rules.

Therefore, to claim the relief, the relevant tests must be met – the company must be the individual's personal company and he or she must be an employee or officer, both for a 24-month period leading up to the sale.

Double taxation relief

Whenever considering the sale of an asset that is situated abroad, consideration must be given to the tax that will be paid in the other jurisdiction. Under many double tax treaties, the country in which the asset is situated will also have taxing rights.

Where double tax relief is claimed, the taxpayer will always pay the higher of the two tax rates. It is therefore ineffective to plan to achieve BADR in the UK, if the tax rate in the jurisdiction in which the asset is situated would tax the gain at, say, 40%.

Temporary non-residents and remittance basis users

Where an individual leaves the UK to become resident elsewhere, but later returns to the UK, he can become taxable on gains realised whilst living abroad.

When an individual owns shares that qualify for BADR and he sells them whilst non-resident, at that point they are outside of the CGT net. However, if he returns to the UK within the relevant period (dependent upon the date he left the UK), the gain could come back into charge.

HMRC have confirmed that the gain is treated as accruing to the individual in the year of return to the UK. However, they still consider that the original disposal date for the purposes of claiming BADR is 31 January after the tax year in question. It is therefore likely that he will be out of time to make the election on return. HMRC therefore recommend putting a protective election in place.

The same principle applies to remittance basis users. A disposal might arise in a year in which the taxpayer has paid the remittance basis charge. It may be many years later that the proceeds of the sale are remitted to the UK. Based on HMRC's contention that the disposal for BADR purposes occurs when the original disposal is made, and not when the funds are remitted and the gains come into charge, then the taxpayer would be out of time for a claim.

It is therefore important that remittance basis users also make a protective claim for BADR within the statutory timeframe if they are to benefit from the relief at a future date.

There is no prescribed way to make the claim. However, *BADR Helpsheet 275* states that if a taxpayer is unable to make a claim in a tax return then a claim may be made to HMRC either in writing or by filling in section A of the form at the end of the helpsheet.

Law: TCGA 1992, s. 10A

8.   Investors' relief

8.1   Overview

Investors' relief (IR) was introduced in Budget 2016 for external investors in unlisted trading companies, as an alternative to the enterprise investment scheme (EIS) and the seed enterprise investment scheme (SEIS). These are generous reliefs but contain many restrictions (see **Chapter 10**).

While IR is a different relief from business asset disposal relief (BADR – see **Chapter 7**), the rules are very similar, with some of the definitions and conditions being the same.

This chapter provides an overview of the IR rules and explains how they may be of benefit to an individual who cannot not make a claim for BADR because he or she fails to meet the necessary criteria.

In some exceptional cases, it may be possible that BADR and IR both apply to a gain. Where this arises, the taxpayer can apportion the gain into amounts to be covered by either relief.

The relief is also available to certain trustees, subject to conditions being met (see **8.8**).

Law: TCGA 1992, s. 169VA-169VY

8.2   Amount of relief

Where the relief is claimed, a rate of 10% will be applied to the "relevant gains", subject to a lifetime limit of £10 million. This is similar to BADR, albeit the lifetime limit for BADR was reduced to £1 million for disposals made on or after 11 March 2020.

Where a gain consists of both qualifying and other shares, relief is given for an appropriate proportion (see **8.7** and **8.10**) of the overall gain. If there are losses to be offset, those losses are deducted before the calculation of IR.

Special rules apply for joint holdings of shares. HMRC's guidance at CG 63610 has a useful example of their application.

Law: TCGA 1992, s. 169VC, 169VD, 169VJ, 169VK
Guidance: CG 63610

8.3   Commencement

IR can only be claimed in respect of shares issued by the qualifying company on or after 17 March 2016 (and held for at least three years thereafter, see **8.4**).

Shares cannot qualify for relief if they were acquired before 17 March 2016, even if the other conditions are met.

Law: TCGA 1992, s. 169VB

8.4   Three-year rule

Relief is only available if the shares have been held by the individual for a continuous period of three years (in contrast to the BADR rules where the general rule is for two years).

Where shares were issued between 17 March 2016 and 5 April 2016, the three-year period is counted from 6 April 2016.

In practical terms, therefore, the first claims for IR were not possible until 2019-20.

Law: TCGA 1992, s. 169VB

8.5   Conditions relating to the shares

The shares must be new, ordinary shares subscribed for by the individual in cash on or after 17 March 2016. The shares must be subscribed for and issued for genuine commercial reasons, as a bargain made at arm's length.

The "ordinary share" condition must be met both at the time:

- it is subscribed for; and
- immediately before its disposal.

Ordinary shares are given the same meaning as in ITA 2007, s. 989, which is the same as for BADR.

At the time the shares are issued, the company must not be listed on a recognised stock exchange. As with EIS relief, the shares will not cease to be qualifying shares if they become listed during the three-year holding period, as long as there were no arrangements in place for the listing at the time of the investment.

Unlike BADR, there is no minimum shareholding requirement for an IR claim to be made. The investor does not need 5% of the voting rights for this relief.

The issuing company must be a trading company or the holding company of a trading group:

- at the time of the issue; and
- throughout the subsequent three-year holding period.

The definition of trading company is the same for IR as it is for BADR (see **Chapter 7**).

Provided that it has been done for genuine commercial reasons and not for tax avoidance purposes, a company will not be regarded as ceasing to meet the trading company condition if:

- it is in administration; or
- a resolution has been passed or an order made for the winding-up of the company (or any subsidiaries).

Law: TCGA 1992, s. 169VB, 169VU

8.6 Conditions relating to the individual

IR is only available to an individual who is not a "relevant employee" of the company.

The concept of the "relevant employee" contrasts with the approach taken for BADR, where the individual must be an officer or employee.

For the purposes of IR, the individual (or any connected person) must (broadly) not be a director or employee of the company during the three-year holding period.

An unpaid director will not be treated as a relevant employee, provided that he or she has never been involved in carrying on the whole or any part of the relevant trade, business or profession carried on by the issuing company or a connected company.

An individual will not be treated as a relevant employee if he or she becomes an employee more than 180 days after the share issue, provided there was no reasonable prospect that the individual would become an employee at the time the shares were issued.

Law: TCGA 1992, s. 169VB(2)(g), 169VW

8.7 Identification of shares

Shares may be qualifying, potentially qualifying, or excluded.

On a disposal it is therefore necessary to establish which shares have been disposed of.

If there have been previous disposals it will be necessary to identify the remaining shares currently held.

Qualifying shares are treated as being disposed of first, then excluded shares, and finally potentially qualifying shares. In this way, relief is prioritised and any potentially qualifying shares have the maximum chance of becoming qualifying shares later.

The examples in **8.10** show how this works in practice.

Law: TCGA 1992, s. 169VE-169VG

8.8 Trustee disposals

Disposals by trustees only qualify for relief if there is at least one individual who is an "eligible beneficiary" in respect of the disposal.

To be an eligible beneficiary in relation to a disposal, the individual must meet all the following conditions:

- Immediately before the disposal, the individual must have, under the settlement, an interest in possession (which must not be restricted to a fixed term) in settled property that includes or consists of the holding of shares.
- He or she must have had such an interest in possession under the settlement throughout the period of three years ending with the date of the disposal.
- At no time in that period must the individual have been a relevant employee (see **8.6**) in respect of the company that issued the shares.
- The individual must (by the time the claim is made in respect of the disposal) have elected to be treated as an eligible beneficiary in respect of the disposal. The individual elects by telling the trustees ("by whatever means") of the wish to be so treated. The election may be withdrawn by the individual, but only if this is done before the claim is made.

Where necessary, the legislation specifies how the gain qualifying for relief is calculated where there are two or more people with an interest in possession in the settled property.

The £10 million cap applies, but subject to modification, for trustees as for individuals. Restrictions apply, for example, where there are two or more people with an interest in possession in the settled property.

Law: TCGA 1992, s. 169VH, 169VI, 169VL

8.9   How to claim the relief

There is no upfront relief (as with EIS, for example) and so there is no requirement for HMRC to approve an investment at the time it is made. Instead, a claim must be made following a disposal of qualifying shares.

Like BADR, IR is not an automatic relief but must be claimed in the tax return for the year of disposal. The time limit is 12 months after 31 January following the end of the tax year in which the disposal is made.

Where the disposal is made by trustees, the claim must be made jointly by the trustees and by *the* eligible beneficiary (or by the trustees and *all* the eligible beneficiaries).

In some circumstances, it may not be clear if a gain will arise, for example where the shares are gifted for no consideration and so market value needs to be established. To avoid missing the time limit it is possible to make a claim on a provisional basis.

Law: TCGA 1992, s. 169VM

8.10   Calculating relief

Where all the shares are qualifying, the 10% rate is simply applied to the taxable gains. Current and/or prior year losses and the annual exempt amount are applied as normal.

However, where only some shares are qualifying, only part of the gain can attract IR. To calculate the correct portion of the gain subject to relief, the following fraction must be applied:

$$\text{Gain} \times Q/T$$

where:

> **Q** is the number of qualifying shares in the holding; and
>
> **T** is the total number of shares disposed of.

If Q is greater than T, then Q in the calculation is restricted to the number of shares disposed of, i.e. the amount of relief can never be more than 100% of the gain. In this way, qualifying shares are treated as being disposed of in priority to potentially qualifying shares, giving the remaining shares the maximum chance of qualifying for relief later.

Example 1

Arrianna sells 3,000 shares from a total holding of 5,000.

Of the 5,000 shares, 1,000 are qualifying and the other 4,000 are potentially qualifying.

The gain is £30,000.

The gain eligible for relief is: £30,000 x 1,000/3,000 = £10,000.

1/3 of the gain qualifies for relief, even though only 1/5 of the holding are qualifying shares.

If Arrianna's holding had consisted of 4,000 qualifying shares, the fraction in the calculation would be restricted to 3,000/3,000, i.e. the whole gain would have qualified for relief.

Where there is a mixed holding of qualifying, potentially qualifying and excluded shares, it is necessary to treat the excluded shares as being disposed of in priority to the potentially qualifying shares. This is a crucial exercise for part disposals as it will be the starting point for subsequent disposals.

Example 2

As of 30 September 2021, Megan has 10,000 shares in A Ltd, a qualifying company. The shares were acquired as follows:

- 2,000 shares in January 2016 (excluded as prior to commencement of relief);

- 4,000 shares in January 2018 (qualifying as have been held for at least three years); and

- 4,000 shares in January 2020 (potentially qualifying as not excluded, but minimum holding condition not met yet).

On 1 October 2021, Megan sells 7,000 shares at a gain of £50,000.

IR can be claimed on £50,000 x 4,000/7,000 = £28,571.

- All the qualifying shares are treated as sold.

- Because the total number of shares sold exceeds the number of qualifying shares, the 2,000 excluded shares are treated as being sold next.

- Finally, 1,000 of the potentially qualifying shares are treated as being sold, to make up the 7,000.

The remaining 3,000 shares will become qualifying shares after January 2023. If they are sold before that, no relief can be claimed.

8.11 Reorganisations

The IR rules are modified where there is a reorganisation or reduction of a company's share capital.

The tax treatment will depend in part on whether or not any consideration is given in relation to the reorganisation.

An election may be made to disapply s. 127 (which treats the new shareholding as being the same as the original shares). Where this is done, the IR rules will apply as if the reorganisation or exchange of shares involved a disposal of the original shares, so that relief is available and the new holding has an uplifted base cost.

Such an election must be made by the first anniversary of 31 January following the tax year in which the reorganisation or share exchange takes place.

Law: TCGA 1992, s. 169VN-169VT

9. Private residence relief

9.1 First principles

9.1.1 Introduction

Section 222 of TCGA 1992, titled "relief on disposal of private residence", is one of the most important CGT reliefs available. The relief is known variously as private residence relief, or principal private residence relief, although the word "principal" does not appear in the legislation. The term that appears most frequently in the legislation is "only or main residence relief". In this book, we have opted for "private residence relief" (PRR) to reflect the section title.

The aim of the relief, according to HMRC, is:

> "...to enable a person to replace their existing home with another home of similar value by ensuring that the proceeds of sale of the old home are not diminished by a charge to CGT. So in most cases the gain arising on the disposal of a person's home is relieved from CGT."

This makes things sound reasonably simple, as generally people who buy property to live in do not have a capital investment motive – even though they may hope for some capital appreciation over time. But in practice the relief is fraught with complications. What is a "home"? How long does someone have to live in a property before it becomes a home? What if a person has more than one home? What if the property comprises several buildings and substantial land? And so on. In this chapter, we start by examining the operation of the relief in the most straightforward circumstances, and then look at different complications that can require closer consideration to determine how much relief is available, if any.

Law: TCGA 1992, s. 222
Guidance: CG 64200

9.1.2 Defining "residence" and "dwelling-house"

Relief under s. 222 can only apply to a residence, or interest in a residence, that is a dwelling-house.

There is no statutory definition of the term "residence". HMRC's view is that a person's residence is the dwelling in which the individual habitually lives, i.e. his or her home. The problem with this is that the term home can feasibly encompass holiday homes, second homes, etc.

"Dwelling-house" is similarly undefined. However, there is a statutory definition of "dwelling" in TCGA 1992, Sch. 1B, which provides that:

> "In relation to UK residential property gains, a building is a 'dwelling' at any time when:
>
> (a)   it is used or suitable for use as a dwelling, or
>
> (b)   it is in the process of being constructed or adapted for such use."

In addition, land that at any time is, or is intended to be, occupied or enjoyed with a dwelling as a garden or grounds (including any building or structure) is taken to be part of the dwelling at that time (see **9.5**).

Of more practical use is the definition of what does *not* count as dwelling for these purposes. A building is treated by the legislation as not used (or suitable for use) as a dwelling if it is an institutional building or used as:

- residential accommodation for school pupils;
- residential accommodation for members of the armed forces;
- a home or other institution providing residential accommodation for children;
- a home or other institution providing residential accommodation with personal care for persons in need of personal care by reason of old age, disability, past or present dependence on alcohol or drugs or past or present mental disorder;
- a hospital or hospice;
- a prison or similar establishment;
- a hotel or inn or similar establishment; or
- student accommodation.

The definition of "dwelling" for the purpose of residential property interest disposals is limited to "buildings", so other places which could potentially be used as a dwelling (like boats or caravans) are excluded. This can be contrasted with the much wider definition of "dwelling-house" given in case law for PRR.

There have been numerous key cases on the definition of residence, occupation, dwelling-house etc.

For a more detailed discussion refer to *Main Residence Relief* from Claritax Books.

Law: TCGA 1992, Sch. 1B, para. 5(3)

9.1.3   Scope of relief

Relief is available to individuals, trustees of settled property, and personal representatives. It is also possible for an individual to claim relief on a property that was occupied by a dependent relative before 6 April 1988, as long as the residence was provided rent-free.

9.1.4   Period of ownership

The legislation and HMRC's guidance both make reference to the "period of ownership". It is important to understand that, following the Court of Appeal case of *Higgins*, the period of ownership does not commence until the completion date of the conveyance, i.e. the date that the individual takes full ownership of the property and is *able* to occupy it.

This is different from the trigger date for a disposal under the CGT legislation, which is based on the date that contracts are exchanged. Usually, this will make very little difference, but in *Higgins* the property had been bought "off-plan", and there was a significant delay between the exchange of contracts (when the building did not even exist) and the date of completion. At the time, an extra-statutory concession permitted a period of one year (increased to two at HMRC's discretion) of delay in taking up occupation to count as deemed occupation. The two-year period has since been put on a statutory footing (see **9.2.2**).

The period of ownership may not include any period before 31 March 1982. However, any occupation prior to that date will secure the final nine-month exemption (see **9.2.1**).

Where a transfer of a relevant property (or part of one) is made between spouses or civil partners who are living together on or after 6 April 2020, the recipient inherits the ownership history of the property, i.e. the period of ownership and periods of occupation. This can have positive effects, e.g. inheriting a fully qualifying entitlement to PRR, or negative effects, e.g. where the property has been unoccupied and is standing at a substantial gain.

Law: TCGA 1992, s. 223(7)
Case: *Higgins v HMRC* [2019] EWCA Civ 1860

9.1.5 Interaction with gift holdover relief

An important anti-avoidance measure is in place to prevent PRR being claimed if the property has previously been subject to a claim for gift holdover relief under s. 260 (see **Chapter 12**). In practice, this is commonly seen where property has been transferred into a trust. The trustees cannot subsequently claim PRR on a disposal of the property, unless the claim under s. 260 is revoked.

This prevents gains from being washed out by making an indirect gift of the property via the trust to a beneficiary, with holdover relief claimed on both occasions (i.e. into and out of the trust). In the absence of the rules, neither the original owner nor the trustees would pay CGT; the beneficiary would acquire the held-over gains but would otherwise be able to claim PRR if occupying the property. This is no longer possible.

Law: TCGA 1992, s. 226A, 226B, 260

9.1.6 Losses

If the disposal of a residence crystallises a loss, that loss will not be allowable to the extent that any gain would have been exempt or otherwise not a chargeable gain. This is subject to three exceptions, as below.

Lettings relief due

Section 223(4) restricts the gain made during a period the dwelling-house was in shared occupancy with a tenant by three limits (the lowest of: the amount of chargeable gain arising as a result of the letting, the amount of PRR due, or £40,000) but these limits cannot be applied if no gain arises. There is no further restriction of the allowable loss in such cases (see also CG 65080). Lettings relief is considered at **9.4**.

Occupation under terms of a settlement

Where the dwelling-house is occupied under the terms of a settlement, the trustees may make a claim for PRR under s. 225. If a loss is made, there will be no scope for a claim pursuant to s. 225 and therefore any losses will be allowable (see also CG 65080).

Dependent relative

Where a dwelling-house is provided for a dependent relative, a claim by an individual may be made under s. 226, but if no claim is made then s. 226 will not apply. Any losses made may be restricted by any periods of occupation of the dwelling-house as the individual's private residence but will not be affected by the occupation of a dependent relative (see also CG 65080).

Law: TCGA 1992, s. 223(4), 225, 226
Guidance: CG 65080

9.1.7   *Claims and reporting*

Where relief applies, it is automatic and does not have to be claimed. So, if an individual is not within self-assessment, no tax return has to be filed. Additionally, where all of the gain is covered by PRR, there is no requirement to report the gain within 30 days via the UK Property Reporting Service.

Where two or more residences could qualify for relief, it is possible to elect for one of them to be the main residence, see **9.3**.

9.2   Operation of the relief

9.2.1   *Key principles*

The most straightforward scenario is where an individual makes a disposal of a property (or an interest in a property) that is a dwelling-house that has been his or her only residence ever since it was acquired. Provided that the property has actually been occupied as a home, PRR will exempt any gain in full.

Where the property has been occupied as a residence, but not throughout the whole period of ownership, it is necessary to look at the reason for the periods of absence and their respective lengths. Some unoccupied periods can be deemed to be occupation, helping to preserve maximum entitlement to relief (see **9.2.2**).

However, where the property has been occupied only part of the time as the only or main residence and the absent periods do not count as occupation, partial relief will be available on a proportionate basis.

Final nine months

The final nine months of the period of ownership always count as deemed occupation as long as the property has been occupied as the only or main residence for at least some of the period of ownership. The period of nine months has applied since 6 April 2020, reduced from more generous periods that applied in the past.

This final period exemption is extended to 36 months if either the individual or the individual's spouse or civil partner is a disabled person or long-term resident in a care home, and does not have any other relevant right in relation to a private residence.

Example

James purchases a property in April 2010 for £100,000. He lives in it for nine years before moving in with his girlfriend in April 2019. The property remains empty from that date and is sold in April 2022 for £180,000. As the property has not been James's only or main residence throughout the period of ownership, PRR is restricted.

There are 108 months of actual occupation. In addition, the final nine months of ownership can be added as deemed occupation. The total period of ownership is 144 months. James's gain qualifying for PRR is therefore:

£80,000 x 117/144 = £65,000.

The remaining £15,000 will be taxable but may be reduced by any available losses and/or annual exempt amount.

Law: TCGA 1992, s. 223(1), 225E

9.2.2   Permitted periods of absence continuing to qualify

In addition to the final nine-month ownership period, certain periods of absence can be deemed to be periods of occupation depending on the reason for and length of the absence. Some of these require the property to become the only or main residence again at some point after the period of absence, though not necessarily immediately.

Absence for any reason not exceeding three years

Any cumulative periods of absence, subject to a maximum of three years, may be deemed as occupation as long as the dwelling-house in question was occupied at some point during the ownership period both before and after the absence. The occupation after the period of absence must be *actual* occupation, i.e. the final nine-month exempt period cannot be used to secure the additional relief if the property was not actually occupied following the period of absence.

The legislation ("a period of absence not exceeding three years") could be interpreted as suggesting that if the period of absence exceeds three years, no relief is available. However, HMRC's guidance (see the example at CG 64970P) makes clear that they interpret this more generously, so (for example) if the period of absence was four years, three years would qualify as deemed occupation and one year would be non-occupation.

Absence of any length due to employment or office outside UK

If there is a period of absence (i.e. where the residence is not the only or main residence) that arises because the individual (or his or her spouse or civil partner with whom the individual lived) is employed, or in an office, outside the UK, the period will count as occupation. The following conditions must both be met:

- All of the duties of the employment or office are performed overseas during the entire period of absence.
- No other residence is eligible for PRR.

Again, this requires actual occupation before and after the period of absence.

Absence of up to four years due to place of work

Absences not exceeding a cumulative total of four years count as occupation where the individual (or a spouse or civil partner with whom the individual was living) was prevented from residing in the dwelling-house because of his or her place of work. This includes absence due to any condition imposed by the employer requiring the employee to reside elsewhere, being a condition reasonably imposed to secure the effective performance of his or her duties.

For the deemed occupation to apply, there must be actual occupation before and after the period of absence.

Prevented from reoccupying residence

In respect of the last two deemed occupation periods (i.e. the unlimited absence due to employment abroad and the absence of up to four years because of employment), the requirement to reoccupy the residence after the period of absence is subject to an exception. This exception (s. 223(3B)(b)) applies where the individual was prevented from reoccupying the property because the terms of employment require him or her to work elsewhere. This exception does not apply to the permitted period of absence of up to three years.

Delay in occupation

Section 223ZA gives statutory force to a previous extra-statutory concession which ignored a short period of non-occupation where there was a delay in taking up residence following acquisition, due to particular circumstances.

The provision broadly means that PRR may be due to an individual who has disposed of a dwelling-house that he or she was prevented from occupying for up to 24 months due to the construction or extensive repair and refurbishment of a dwelling which is then used as the same individual's residence.

The provisions apply where an individual:

- purchases an existing dwelling and, before occupying it, undertakes alterations or redecorations; or
- completes the necessary steps for disposing of his or her previous residence which, immediately before the disposal, was the individual's only or main residence.

The new dwelling-house is treated as being the individual's only or main residence "from the beginning of the individual's period of ownership until the moving-in time". This effectively means that the individual would obtain relief for two dwelling-houses for the same period of ownership, provided that neither of the two dwellings was another person's residence during the overlapping ownership periods.

Example

Alison and Mark purchase a three-bedroom detached house in Croydon on 26 July 2020. The house was previously owned by an elderly couple who had to be taken into care. As a result of the couple's deteriorating health, the house had not been updated for decades so Alison and Mark have to undertake extensive works of updating and renovation.

They start work the day after completion and essentially remove all of the interior decorations. They plan to introduce a new kitchen and bathroom, renew the electrical and plumbing systems, carry out some minor structural work to the living room and add a new shower room downstairs. They move in with Alison's parents in the interim and obtain exemption from council tax because their dwelling-house is uninhabitable.

They expect to complete the work within nine to twelve months but in May 2021 the builders discover subsidence. The subsidence had not been caught by their surveyor's report, the cost of repairing the damage is outside their budget and therefore they have to make a claim against the surveyor, which takes a further eight months. The house is finally made safe and completed on 25 April 2022 and Alison and Mark move in straight afterwards.

The total delay of 21 months falls within the terms of s. 223ZA(1), and the property will be treated as their only or main residence for that period for the purposes of claiming relief on a future disposal.

Law: TCGA 1992, s. 223, 223ZA

9.2.3   *More than one property*

Where more than one property is used as a residence and the periods of ownership overlap, the focus shifts to the *main* residence, rather than the *only* residence. It is necessary to determine which of them was the main residence for the purposes of the relief. The relief then applies to the relevant property.

There are two possibilities here. Either the individual will have made a valid election under s. 222(5) (see **9.3**), or the question of which was the main residence, and for which periods of time, will be determined as a question of fact.

Assuming no valid election has been made, the main residence must be determined by reference to the available evidence. The burden of proof is on the individual, so if HMRC disagree with the designated main residence and challenge a claim for relief, the taxpayer will be required to convince an officer, or the tribunals, that the asserted designation is correct.

Two key factors in determining the main residence will be the time spent in the property (in comparison with other properties) and the quality of that occupation.

In some cases, it will be reasonably easy to determine which property the individual spends the most time in. For example, if someone owns a flat in a city centre and lives in it during the week for work purposes but has a cottage in the country for weekends, it should be obvious that, in the absence of an election, the city flat will be the main residence.

In some cases, the time spent between the different residences may be relatively even. The High Court case of *Frost v Feltham* determined that:

> "If someone lives in two houses the question, which does he use as the principal or more important one [main residence], cannot be determined solely by reference to the way in which he divides his time between the two."

That case was concerned with a publican who occupied the living accommodation that accompanied the public house he had leased. Although he spent most of his time there due to work, he had bought a house that was fully furnished, and on which he was entitled (under the tax rules then applying) to claim mortgage interest relief. The decision of the General Commissioners in the taxpayer's favour was upheld by the High Court. In short, periods of time spent in a particular property may be highly persuasive, but do not provide a conclusive answer in all cases.

HMRC may try to argue that no relief is due because the residence has never been occupied with sufficient "quality of occupation". A question that clients frequently ask their advisers is how long they need to live in a property before they can secure at least some PRR on it. HMRC's guidance, and indeed the tax tribunals, make clear that it is the *quality* of occupation that counts, not the quantity.

As a basic example, consider an individual whose family home is well established. He spots a property with exceptional potential that he feels is significantly undervalued and purchases it. He refurbishes the property, staying it at weekends for several months on a camp bed before selling it after 18 months at a substantial gain. The overnight stays may be intended to facilitate a main residence election to secure at least partial exemption, e.g. the final nine months of ownership. However, it is unlikely that HMRC would accept that the quality of occupation is sufficient to have made the property a genuine settled living place. In fact, in the circumstances it might be necessary to argue that any gain is even within the remit of CGT, rather than a trading transaction subject to income tax.

A recent case regarding quality of occupation in circumstances where there were multiple properties was *Simpson*. In that case, the individual sold a one-bedroom flat which she had owned for approximately six months, claiming that it was her main residence throughout the period of ownership. She had another flat a short walk away which she tried to claim was her main residence immediately before and immediately after her occupation of the flat sold. She had moved in some spare furniture but could not produce any evidence to persuade the FTT that she had occupied the flat sold with the necessary degree of permanence, continuity or expectation of continuity for it to be considered as a residence.

However, a short period of occupation is not necessarily fatal to a PRR claim. In *Core*, the FTT concluded that an occupation period of around eight weeks was sufficient to secure relief. In that case, the taxpayers

203

were found to have genuinely occupied the property with the intention of making it their permanent family home but had received an unsolicited offer at a price modestly above what they had paid for it. This underlines the importance of proving *quality* not quantity of occupation.

HMRC's approach

Where HMRC are considering the matter, a non-exhaustive list of questions they may consider is provided at CG 64545:

- If the individual is married or in a civil partnership, where does the family spend its time?
- If the individual has children, where do they go to school?
- At which residence is the individual registered to vote?
- Where is the individual's place of work?
- How is each residence furnished?
- Which address is used for correspondence?
- Which address is used by banks, building societies and credit card providers?
- Which address is used for HMRC correspondence?
- Where is the individual registered with a doctor/dentist?
- At which address is the individual's car registered and insured?
- Which address is the main residence for council tax?

Generally, the property that appears as the answer to most of these questions is likely to be the main residence unless there are significant factors that suggest otherwise. In *Oliver*, the taxpayer presented good evidence as to the quality of his occupation of a particular residence, but ultimately failed to convince the tribunal that it was his main residence.

Things may be more straightforward where a valid main residence election is made, as discussed at **9.3**.

Cases: *Frost v Feltham* (1980) 55 TC 10; *Oliver v HMRC* [2016] UKFTT 796 (TC); *Simpson v HMRC* [2019] UKFTT 704 (TC); *Core v HMRC* [2020] UKFTT 440 (TC)

9.3 Main residence elections

9.3.1 Overview

Where an individual acquires a second property that is available to him or her, and both properties are actually used as a residence for at least some of the time, the individual may nominate one of them as the main residence for the purposes of the relief within a given time limit (see **9.3.3**).

In fact, the opportunity to make an election arises at any time there is a change in the "combination of residences". So, an election window will begin if there is an increase or decrease in the number of residences available for use as a residence. This does not necessarily require a new acquisition or disposal as (for example) letting a property to a third party will generally make it unavailable for the owner to use as a residence, changing the combination of residences.

The election cannot be challenged as long as it is valid and (in particular) as long as the property is actually occupied as a residence at least some of the time – even if a different property is occupied more frequently. However, HMRC may challenge a claim to relief if there are doubts over whether the nominated property has actually been occupied with sufficient quality to have made it a residence in the first place. In other words, it must as a question of fact be a residence before it can be elected as a main residence.

Law: TCGA 1992, s. 222(5)

9.3.2   Making an election

HMRC specify that the following conditions must be met for an election notice to be valid:

- A nomination by an individual must be made to an officer of the Board and must be signed by the individual.
- Spouses or civil partners who are living together can only have one main residence between them for the purpose of the relief. If a nomination affects both of them it must be made by notice in writing to an officer of the Board and must be signed by both of them.
- Where one of more of the residences is occupied by a person entitled to occupy it under the terms of a settlement, the notice must be in writing to an officer of the Board and must be signed both by the trustees of the settlement and by the person entitled to occupy the residence.
- The signature of an agent is not sufficient.

This appears to be more extensive than the legislation requires. However, it is advisable to follow HMRC's guidance so as to avoid arguments and investigations later on. It will also make matters easier when completing the CGT calculation, particularly where there have been multiple elections involving several properties.

Law: TCGA 1992, s. 222(6)
Guidance: CG 64520

9.3.3   Time limits

Notice of an election must be given within two years of a change in combination of residences.

Each time there is a change in the individual's combination of residences a new period begins and there is a new opportunity to make a nomination. This interpretation of the legislation was confirmed in *Griffin v Craig-Harvey*. The relevant date for the two-year window is the date that the relevant property is first used as a residence, or ceases to be used as a residence. These may not be the same as the dates of acquisition or disposal. HMRC give the following example at CG 64495.

HMRC example

An individual has a single residence until 1 April 2017. On that date she acquired a dwelling-house and immediately began to use it as a second residence. She has until 31 March 2019 to nominate which of these residences is to be treated as her main residence.

On 23 November 2017 she acquired another dwelling-house and began to use it as a third residence on 1 June 2018. A new period for nominating begins on 1 June 2018 giving her until 31 May 2020 to nominate which of her three residences is to be treated as her main residence.

On 30 September 2018 she ceased to use one of her dwelling-houses as a residence and subsequently disposed of it on 30 November 2018. A new period for nominating therefore begins on 30 September 2018; she has until 29 September 2020 to nominate which of her two remaining residences is to be treated as the main residence.

HMRC may extend the time limit in circumstances where the individual has not:

- at any time previously given a notice under subsection (5)(a) (whether in respect of the period concerned or any other period); or

- at any time during the period concerned held an interest of more than a negligible market value in more than one of the residences.

Once made, a nomination lasts until the combination of residences changes again (whereupon a new election may be made), the nominated property is disposed of, or a variation is made.

A valid election may be varied at any time, and a variation may be backdated for up to two years in the ownership. It used to be relatively common for individuals to nominate a second property for a short period of time to secure the final period exemption, before "flipping" the election to a property with better growth prospects. This came to widespread public attention in 2009 as one aspect of the MPs' expenses scandal. Flipping was more popular when the final period exemption covered three years rather than just nine months but is still an important strategy for CGT mitigation.

Example 2

Kevin owns two residences – Trundle Place and Hayworth Cottage – and has occupied them as residences since 2003. In 2009, he nominated Hayworth Cottage as his main residence. On 3 April 2022, he accepts an offer too good to pass up for the sale of Trundle Place and disposes of it, realising a significant capital gain. As matters stand, the gain accrued on Trundle Place will not benefit from PRR unless the election made in favour of Hayworth Cottage is varied.

On 3 May 2022, after advice received from his accountants, Kevin submits a notice of variation under s. 222(5)(a) of the original election, changing it to benefit Trundle Place. This variation is backdated to 3 May 2020. The effect of this election would be to treat Trundle Place as Kevin's main residence for a period of time in 2020. Kevin may then flip his election back to Hayworth Cottage in a relatively short space of time (a week or two afterwards).

The end result of this election "flip" is that Kevin will be able to claim PRR on the disposal of Trundle Place for the last nine months of ownership, from 3 July 2021 to 3 April 2022. If the circumstances permit, lettings relief may also be available though, from 6 April 2020, lettings relief is given only if the dwelling-house has been in shared occupancy with a lodger.

The downside of this planning is the loss of PRR on the actual main residence, Hayworth Cottage, for one or two weeks of the ownership period. The modest relief gained on the disposal of Trundle Place is likely to compensate for this loss of relief even in cases where the annual exemption could not cover it.

It is advisable to make the elections separately, i.e. not to make two elections in a single notice.

Law: TCGA 1992, s. 222(5)(a), 223

Case: *Griffin (Inspector of Taxes) v Craig-Harvey* (1994) 66 TC 396

9.3.4   Spouses and civil partners

Spouses and civil partners can only have one main residence, and a single nomination, if they live together. The nomination must be made by both parties to the relationship where it affects both of them. Where the individuals each own a residence and continue to use both after the marriage, the two-year window for making the nomination begins on the date of the marriage or civil partnership.

Law: TCGA 1992, s. 222(6)

9.3.5   Non-residents

Non-UK residents have been liable to CGT on disposals of UK residential property since April 2015 (and all non-moveable property since April 2019). The entitlement to relief, and the provisions regarding making a main residence election, are discussed at **18.3**.

9.4   Lettings relief

9.4.1   General application

Relief for residential lettings is essentially an extension of PRR, as lettings relief cannot apply unless there is some PRR.

Lettings relief was severely curtailed from 6 April 2020. Prior to that date, up to £40,000 of a chargeable gain (per individual) could be claimed on a property that had been the individual's only or main residence at some point during the period of ownership if it was also let as residential accommodation. It was irrelevant whether the let period occurred before or after the period of occupation as a main residence and was therefore extremely valuable to "accidental" landlords, i.e. those who had struggled to sell a property and so let it out to avoid losing money.

For disposals on or after 6 April 2020, relief is available only for periods where the owner occupied the property as shared accommodation with a third-party tenant, i.e. relief is restricted to periods of co-occupation. Further consideration is needed to determine the extent to which the property was available to the owner during such a period. The maximum relief is still £40,000.

Example

Jasminder purchased a property on 1 April 2006. She lived in it alone for six years, before letting three rooms, which represented one third of the property, to a tenant on an exclusive use basis. The tenant used the partitioned property for residential purposes.

Jasminder sold the property at the end of March 2022, realising a gain of £230,400.

The property was solely occupied by Jasminder for the first six years of its ownership as her only or main residence, so the last nine months qualify for full PRR, along with the 72 months of actual occupation, giving 81 months of full relief. Note that the final nine-month exemption is given on 100% of the property, even though only two thirds of it was occupied by Jasminder during that time. The final nine months can therefore effectively be ignored in the next part of the calculation

The 111-month period from April 2012 to June 2021 (nine months before the sale date) will partly qualify for PRR, i.e. on two thirds of the gain attributable to that time. The PRR entitlement will be as follows:

	£
£230,400 x 81/192	97,200
£230,400 x 111/192 x 2/3	88,800
Total	186,000

The lettings relief is the lowest of:

- the gain attributable to the qualifying let period not covered by private residence relief, i.e. 1/3 x 111/192 x £230,400 = £44,400;

- the private residence relief of £186,000; and

- £40,000.

The lettings relief is therefore £40,000.

The chargeable gain is therefore £230,400 – £186,000 – £40,000 = £4,400.

Lettings relief cannot reduce the residual gain below nil, i.e. it cannot create a loss.

Where the owner takes in a lodger on a basis that qualifies for rent-a-room relief, there is no requirement to apportion the PRR. The owner is treated as occupying the whole property, so lettings relief will not be in point. However, there may be a need to exercise caution where there are multiple lodgers as HMRC may take the view that there is a lodging house being run as a business.

The changes to spouse and civil partner transfers made on or after 6 April 2020 (see **9.4.1**) also extend to lettings relief, i.e. the recipient inherits any entitlement to lettings relief from the original owning partner, as well as the occupation for PRR. The real question is whether the owner of the dwelling-house has given away exclusive occupation of part of his or her home to the lodgers taken in. This is ultimately a question of fact to be determined looking at all the circumstances of the case, and a broad-brush approach may result in a hardline view being taken by HMRC (and the tax tribunals).

Law: TCGA 1992, s. 224A

9.4.2   *Lettings relief and furnished holiday lets*

Care is needed where a property:

- is let as a qualifying FHL let; and
- is, or has been, occupied as an individual's only or main residence for any given period of time during the period of ownership.

On a strict interpretation of the legislation, a fraction of the gain arising from an eventual disposal of the property could be exempt from CGT according to the principles in s. 223(2).

If the property is sufficiently large to accommodate its owner(s) and holiday-makers at the same time, lettings relief could also be available for any shared occupancy of holiday accommodation. The availability of lettings relief may, of course, be subject to the terms of the letting being truly commercial. It may also be necessary to consider a potential argument of "acquisition for the purposes of making a gain" under s. 224(3).

A further complication in respect of furnished holiday accommodation arises from the interaction of rollover relief if:

- a chargeable gain has been deducted under TCGA 1992, s. 152 or 153 from the cost of furnished holiday accommodation; and
- PRR applies on the disposal of that accommodation.

On a disposal of an FHL property that has a gain rolled over and that has been occupied as an only or main residence, PRR is applied and calculated by reference to the chargeable gain that exceeds the gain rolled over.

Law: TCGA 1992, s. 152, 153, 223(2), 224(3)

9.5 Grounds, gardens and ancillary buildings

9.5.1 Overview

Full relief from CGT is given for gains on adjoining land that an individual has for his or her own occupation and enjoyment with the residence as its garden or grounds, up to a "permitted area".

The permitted area is defined in the legislation as:

- 0.5 hectares; or
- such larger area as may be required for the reasonable enjoyment of the dwelling-house (or the relevant part in question) as a residence, having regard to the size and character of the dwelling-house.

To qualify for PRR, there is therefore a two-limbed test.

First, the land must be occupied as garden or grounds for the enjoyment of the residence. Following the decision in *Varty v Lynes*, this test is made at the date of disposal. In that case, the dwelling-house was sold prior to a part of the garden which had been retained. Upon a subsequent sale of that part, relief could not apply because the land was not being used as the garden of the dwelling-house (as the taxpayer had already sold it). There is a slight relaxation of this (confirmed at CG 64385) if the land is sold separately after the date of exchange of contracts for the dwelling-house, but before completion of the conveyance.

Second, the land must not exceed the permitted area, considered more fully at **9.5.3**.

Land used as garden or grounds is still subject to s. 223, i.e. the requirements to apportion relief where the dwelling-house was not the only or main residence throughout the period of ownership, taking into account the permitted periods of absence discussed at **9.2.2**.

Law: TCGA 1992, s. 222(1)(b), 223

Case: *Varty (HMIT) v Lynes* (1976) 51 TC 419

Guidance: CG 64385

9.5.2   Defining "garden or grounds"

There is no statutory definition of either "garden" or "grounds", and these terms must therefore take their ordinary meaning. A garden is taken to mean an area of land (often enclosed) where fruits, flowers, herbs or vegetables are cultivated, especially one adjoining a house or other residential building.

HMRC's guidance at CG 64360 mentions a useful dictionary definition of grounds as close land surrounding or attached to a dwelling-house or other building serving chiefly for ornament or recreation.

From these definitions, it follows that gardens may include vegetable patches, flowerbeds and pots, ponds and lawns. Grounds may include fruit trees, orchards and areas that are less maintained than gardens, e.g. fields, meadows or paddocks, as long as these are not used commercially. Land that has been developed into amenity areas, such as swimming pools or tennis courts, may also qualify.

HMRC take the view that where land is physically separated from the main dwelling-house, it is unlikely to be part of the garden or grounds of the residence. However, there may be some limited exceptions to this, for example small rural villages where gardens are located on the opposite side of the street or bridleway.

Land that has traditionally been the garden and grounds of the residents, but that is unused or overgrown at the date of sale, should not necessarily be excluded.

Land that has been fenced off, e.g. for development purposes, will not qualify for relief as it will not be accepted as part of the grounds.

It is clear that the term "grounds" is far more extensive than "garden". In *Hyman & Hyman*, the FTT found that land of just over 3.5 acres – including a secondary garden, a large barn, a pond and the meadow crossed by a bridleway – were all parts of the grounds of the house. While this was an SDLT case, the CGT legislation was examined and cited.

Case: *Hyman & Hyman v HMRC* [2019] UKFTT 469 (TC)
Guidance: CG 64360

9.5.3   The permitted area

The statutory permitted area is 0.5 hectares, including the area taken up by the site of the dwelling-house. If the garden/grounds (including the house itself) do not exceed 0.5 hectares, there will be no need to justify that they are required for the reasonable enjoyment of the dwelling-house as a residence, i.e. relief will be automatic.

Where the garden or grounds (together with the house) exceed 0.5 hectares, it will be necessary to consider whether the additional area is required for the reasonable enjoyment of the dwelling-house as a residence, and so whether relief may apply. This test will take into account the size and character of the dwelling-house, so a commonsense approach is that a more substantial property will justify a larger area. However, there is no rule of thumb here.

In *Longson v Baker*, the High Court dismissed the argument by the taxpayer that his personal interest in horses, and the equestrian character of the property as a whole, meant that an area of 7.5 hectares was required for his reasonable enjoyment of the property. The court took the view that while an individual taxpayer may subjectively wish to keep horses close to the dwelling-house for personal enjoyment, it was not objectively required in order to enjoy the dwelling-house as a residence.

It can therefore be inferred that the area exceeding 0.5 hectares must not merely be desirable, but *necessary* for the enjoyment of the dwelling-house as a residence, i.e. the occupier would be adversely affected in terms of amenities or convenience without it. Providing evidence of this, as well as evidence that the land was used as garden or grounds at the date of disposal, will normally form a crucial part of any argument if a larger permitted area cannot be agreed with HMRC

HMRC acknowledge that the extent of the permitted area is one of the most common areas of disagreement with taxpayers. HMRC rely heavily on the District Valuer for determinations. HMRC's guidance on the matter starts at CG 64800.

An important point is that the permitted area will be a single piece of land; it cannot consist of a series of "islands" of land.

Law: TCGA 1992, s. 222(2)-(4)
Case: *Longson v Baker* (HMIT) [2001] BTC 356
Guidance: CG 64800*ff.*

9.5.4   Part disposals of land

Relief may be available where part of the garden or grounds is sold but the dwelling-house and remainder of the potentially qualifying land is retained. For example, if a developer offers to purchase one quarter of the grounds within the permitted area, relief can potentially apply to the sale as long as the land is used as grounds at the date of disposal.

However, HMRC may point to the sale as proof that the land was not required for the reasonable enjoyment of the dwelling-house as a residence (i.e. if it were so required it would not be sold) in cases where the permitted area exceeds 0.5 hectares. In particular, it may challenge such transactions where there is a series of disposals.

In any event, it is essential that the land retained its character as garden or grounds prior to the part disposal. It should not, for example, be fenced off before the disposal date or relief will not apply.

9.5.5   Ancillary buildings and the concept of curtilage

HMRC accept that a dwelling-house may be made up of several buildings if they are appurtenant to, and within the curtilage of, the main house. "Curtilage" (according to the *Shorter Oxford Dictionary*, quoted at CG 64230P) means a small court, yard or piece of ground attached to a house and forming one enclosure with it.

HMRC's view is that the curtilage must be small, though CG 64245 acknowledges that there may be occasions where buildings that are more dispersed can form a single curtilage, depending on the past history in terms of ownership and function. Relief is more likely to be accepted for a group of buildings if there is a clear relationship between them, and they constitute an integral whole. It is unlikely that buildings separated by walls, fences, or roads will be accepted as constituting such an integrated whole.

In legal terms, buildings are part of the land that they stand upon. Therefore, if a building is outside the curtilage of the dwelling-house but located inside the boundary of the permitted area, relief can apply as long as it is used for residential purposes.

In *Markey* v *Sanders*, it was held that a bungalow built for occupation by a gardener was not part of the main building. The bungalow was located 130 metres from the main house and was screened from its view by a number of trees. The court concluded that it did not form part of the main residence, partly because the screening was clearly intended to provide privacy for the occupants.

By contrast, in *Williams v Merrylees*, a lodge located 200 metres from the main house was held to be part of the main building for the purposes of PRR. As in the *Sanders* case, the lodge was occupied by domestic staff. However, there was a clear relationship between the buildings. The lodge was supplied by the same water main and was initially powered by wiring from the main building. It is interesting that the court found that the distance between the buildings was not a conclusive factor, which appears at odds with HMRC's focus on "smallness" of curtilage.

In *Lady Rook*, a gardener's cottage situated 175 metres from the dwelling-house was found to fail the "appurtenant to, and within the curtilage of" test and so relief was not available.

Cases: *Markey v Sanders* (1987) 60 TC 245; *Williams v Merrylees* (1987) 60 TC 297; *Lewis v Lady Rook* (1992) 64 TC 567
Guidance: CG 64245

9.6 Divorce and dissolution of marriages and civil partnerships

9.6.1 CGT consequences of separation

Married couples and civil partners may only have one main residence between them and may only make a single main residence election (see **9.3.3**).

Where a transfer of a relevant property (or part of one) is made between spouses or civil partners who are living together on or after 6 April 2020, the recipient also inherits the ownership history of the property, i.e. the period of ownership and periods of occupation.

Transfers between spouses or civil partners are also treated as being made on a no gain/no loss basis.

The tax treatment of the main residence, as described here, will apply as long as the couple are "living together". This term is not defined but appears to be more than simple physical occupation of the same building, and to imply a more interpersonal relationship. For the purposes of PRR, where a marriage or civil partnership breaks down and the couple separates the following consequences arise:

- Any main residence election made jointly will cease to have effect for the spouse or partner who moves out of the marital home.

- Each partner will be considered separately again for the purposes of PRR and will be entitled to make separate main residence elections.

- If the departing partner owns another dwelling-house, he or she will be able to make an election in respect of the other dwelling-house.

Care must be taken where a spouse or partner moves out of the main residence on a temporary, or trial, basis. If there is a view to eventual reconciliation, i.e. the separation is to assist survival of the marriage or civil partnership, then HMRC will normally treat any capital gain arising on a property that the departing partner occupies in the interim period as not being eligible for PRR. The argument is that occupation must be intended to be permanent for the relief to apply.

The tax-free treatment of transfers between spouses or civil partners applies until the end of the tax year of permanent separation. This can, with some forethought, allow for tax-efficient division of assets.

9.6.2   *Divorce and dissolution*

In practical terms, final divorce or dissolution of a civil partnership has no direct implication for PRR. In most cases, at least one partner will cease to live in the property, and so will no longer accumulate entitlement to PRR, though the last nine months of ownership exemption will apply.

Where the departing partner transfers his or her interest in the dwelling-house to the other spouse or partner as part of a financial agreement, s. 225B may allow the one who is leaving to treat the dwelling-house as the only main residence from the date of moving out until the date of the transfer of the interest. Five conditions must be met for s. 225B to apply:

- The departing partner ceases to live in a dwelling-house which was his or her only or main residence.

- The departing partner subsequently disposes of, or of an interest in, the dwelling-house or part of the dwelling-house to his or her former partner – not a third party.
- The said disposal is a result of:
  o an agreement between the parties made in contemplation of divorce or dissolution of a civil partnership; or
  o a court order confirming a divorce, dissolution or annulment.
- In the interim period between the departing partner ceasing to live in the dwelling-house and disposing of the interest to his or her former partner, the remaining partner has occupied the same dwelling-house as his or her main residence.
- The departing partner has not given an election notice in respect of any other residence for any part of the interim period.

This offers some protection in cases where the transfer takes place many years after the departing spouse or partner leaves the property. However, it is crucial that the remaining partner occupies the property as his or her main residence, failing which relief may be lost permanently.

Law: TCGA 1992, s. 225B

9.6.3   Mesher orders

Following the case of *Mesher v Mesher and Hall* – and taking account of the statutory duty of care in respect of the interests of any minor children upon divorce – the court may make a "Mesher order". This directs that the marital home should be retained by both spouses or civil partners in their joint names on trust and that (usually) the mother should remain in occupation until the children reach a specified age (normally 18 years).

For the purposes of PRR, HMRC treat a Mesher order as the creation of a settlement. So, the party holding the interest in the dwelling-house is transferring his or her interest into a trust for the benefit of the children or former partner. The trust property, i.e. the dwelling-house, can be eligible for PRR as long as it is occupied as a main residence by the remaining spouse or partner under the entitlement of the order. When the period in the order comes to an end, the settlement will end and the former spouses or partners will become absolutely entitled to the dwelling-house. This will be a deemed disposal by the trustees at the market value of the property.

HMRC illustrate the tax treatment of Mesher orders as follows.

HMRC example

Mr C bought a house in 2000 and occupied it with his wife as their only residence until 2004, when they separated. Mr C moved into rented accommodation while Mrs C continued to reside in the house. They divorced in March 2008. By a court order in May 2008, Mr C was ordered to hold the property on trust for Mrs C and the children until the youngest child, who was then 14, was 18. The youngest child reached 18 in January 2012 and the property was sold in February 2012.

The court order in May 2008 results in a transfer into trust and so is an occasion of charge on Mr C under TCGA 1992, s. 70. Mr C makes a claim for TCGA 1992, s. 225B to apply and so PRR will be due in full.

There is a second occasion of charge on Mr C in January 2012 when the youngest child reaches 18. [HMRC] will allow full relief under TCGA 1992, s. 225, see CG 65400+. No relief is due when the dwelling-house is sold in February 2012 but any increase in value between January and February is likely to be negligible and so a chargeable gain is unlikely to accrue.

Law: TCGA 1992, s. 70, 225, 225B
Case: *Mesher v Mesher and Hall* [1980] 1 All ER 126
Guidance: CG 65400*ff.*

9.7   Restrictions on relief

9.7.1   Introduction

As discussed at **9.2**, relief is restricted where there are periods of non-occupation. However, there are further provisions to restrict the amount of relief available where there is:

- exclusive business use;
- a change of what is occupied as a dwelling-house (reconstructions, conversions or any other such reason); or
- an acquisition made wholly or partly for the purpose of realising a capital gain.

This final section considers each of these in turn.

Law: TCGA 1992, s. 224

9.7.2   *Business use*

Where a dwelling-house, or part of one, is used exclusively for the purpose of the trade, business, profession or vocation, any gain arising on its disposal must be apportioned between the gain eligible for PRR and the non-eligible gain.

A key test here is whether a distinct part has been used exclusively for business purposes. Where a room is used for both business and domestic purposes, no apportionment would be needed. As an example, consider a room that is used as an office by one member of the family, but is also available to use as a reading room or study by the family as a whole. PRR would be available on the whole gain, even if business expenses have been deducted for income tax purposes in respect of household bills on a proportionate basis.

Where part of the dwelling-house is used exclusively for business purposes, it will be necessary to consider how to apportion the gain.

HMRC's guidance at CG 64663 states that simply apportioning the gain on the basis of any fraction used to split overhead costs for income tax purposes is unlikely to give a satisfactory result, and should only be used where there is no other option. Instead, an approach giving consideration to the particular facts relating to the property is required. It may well be that an apportionment based on floor area, or the number of rooms, is appropriate or at least acceptable. However, HMRC state that in a mixed property like a public house with residential accommodation above it, such an approach would not be appropriate because it is likely that the business part of the property is more valuable than the residential part.

HMRC also seem to object to an apportionment based on two separate assets: a dwelling-house and a business property. The distinction between a mixed property and two separate assets lies in the apportionment of consideration. If the business part of a dwelling-house is treated as a separate asset, an apportionment of expenditure and consideration must be made in relation to it; whereas if the business part is treated as part of the dwelling-house, any apportionment is made as the last stage of a tax computation. This may make a significant difference for the individual who has expended significant sums on the business part and who could claim an allowable loss if this part were treated as a second asset.

Farms

In general, as long as a farmhouse has been occupied as a residence by the farmer there will be no apportionment of the gain. If there is exclusive use, for example of an office or dairy, then an apportionment is necessary, and the relief should be regarded as extending only to the part of the farmhouse occupied partly or wholly as a residence.

Rollover relief

If PRR is not available in respect of part of the dwelling-house used exclusively for business purposes, it may be possible to use rollover relief if replacement business property is purchased. This can present a planning opportunity where the business is likely to continue following a move.

Example

Suki has run a successful acupuncture practice (one room and the hallway used as a waiting area) from her home in Staines since 2012. Her tax adviser has informed her that this business use would mean a restriction of PRR of 20% on any accrued gain. She was offered a place at a brand new private holistic clinic in Birmingham and has decided to sell her house, relocate to Birmingham and move her practice to the clinic. This being the case, she will not have a replacement business property in which to roll over her restricted gain.

A planning opportunity would be to relocate to Birmingham before the clinic is completed and continue to practise from her new home as she has done thus far. This would enable her to defer 20% of the gain accrued on her former dwelling-house into the new residence. Once the clinic is ready she may move, and the cessation of business occupation of her new home will not trigger any tax liability. If the Birmingham dwelling-house is not disposed of, the deferred gain may never be clawed back or become chargeable. In the event of a disposal, and depending on the period of ownership, a few months of exclusive business use would mean a very modest apportionment pursuant to s. 224(2).

Business asset disposal relief

If an apportionment of the gain has to be made, it is worth considering whether the business is ceasing at the time of the disposal of the dwelling-house. If so, a claim for BADR may be available if the strict conditions are met. For more information, see **Chapter 7**.

Law: TCGA 1992, s. 224(2)
Guidance: CG 64663

9.7.3   Changes of use

Relief will also need to be restricted via an apportionment of the gain where there is a change in what is occupied as the residence. This will occur where there is a change of use (from residential to business), or where the dwelling has been substantially reconstructed or converted into smaller units or for any other reason.

The apportionment must take into account the floorspace, rooms or extent to which the dwelling-house was occupied as a residence, as well as the period of time for which it was occupied as a main or only residence.

The question of correct apportionment in s. 224 is ultimately a matter of valuation evidence. In cases where apportionment is at issue, it is not uncommon for HMRC to instruct the Valuation Office Agency (VOA) to provide an opinion as to the correct method of valuation. Indeed, the VOA has extensive guidance on these matters – see the VOA technical CGT manual.

Law: TCGA 1992, s. 224
Guidance: VOA *Capital gains and other taxes manual*

9.7.4   Acquisition made for the purposes of a gain

No relief will be available if a dwelling-house is acquired wholly or partly with the aim of realising a capital gain. This is intended to exclude speculative or development gains from being relieved. The restriction also applies where expenditure is incurred after the acquisition date wholly or partly for the purpose of realising a gain from a subsequent disposal. In this case, an apportionment may need to be made if the initial purchase was not made wholly or partly with the aim of realising a gain.

HMRC's guidance at CG 65210 stresses that anyone who buys a dwelling-house is likely to hope that, in the fullness of time, a gain will be realised on its disposal and that this may be a factor in choosing one property over another. Such a motivation could, on a strict reading of the legislation, mean that the restriction applies. However, the guidance makes clear that it would be unreasonable to apply the legislation in this way, and that it should only be applied where the primary purpose is essentially a quick profit.

There are a number of helpful examples in the guidance, which starts at CG 65200. In practice, the restriction is most commonly applied where a leaseholder acquires a freehold shortly before disposal in order to increase the value of the asset, or where a large single property is divided into self-contained units which are then sold separately.

Law: TCGA 1992, s. 224(3)
Guidance: CG 65200P

10. Relief from CGT under the venture capital schemes

10.1 Introduction

To encourage private investment by individuals into entrepreneurial companies, the UK government periodically introduces statutory tax-geared incentives to reward investors. These include what are commonly referred to as the venture capital schemes.

There are four schemes currently available:

- the enterprise investment scheme (EIS) – see **10.2 to 10.6**;
- the seed enterprise investment scheme (SEIS) – see **10.7**;
- social investment tax relief (SITR) – see **10.8**; and
- venture capital trusts (VCTs) – see **10.9**.

The broad hallmarks of these schemes are similar – namely an individual makes an investment satisfying the relevant conditions in exchange for a collection of tax reliefs. Usually, it is the income tax relief that receives the most attention due to income tax rates being higher and the fact that the relief is received in the year of investment. However, there are also CGT benefits for making such investments that are often overlooked.

In this chapter, we consider the CGT relief available under each scheme in turn. For a fuller discussion of the schemes, refer to *Enterprise Investment Scheme* from Claritax Books.

10.2 Enterprise investment scheme

10.2.1 Threefold relief

The EIS is the best known of the venture capital schemes for a reason – it is by far the most generous, particularly from an income tax perspective. However, there are also three CGT reliefs to consider:

- CGT reinvestment relief – see **10.3 to 10.4**;
- CGT exemption upon disposal – see **10.5**; and
- loss relief – see **10.6**.

The term "Period A" is relevant for income tax relief purposes, but is mentioned several times in this chapter. This is the period that begins two years prior to the investment date (or the incorporation date of the company, if later), and ends with the "termination date" (see **10.2.3**) relevant to the shares in question.

10.2.2   Application process

For any of the reliefs to be available for a particular investment, the company must have completed a compliance statement (form EIS1) and submitted this to HMRC. HMRC will then consider the application and, provided the tax officer is happy that all qualifying conditions are satisfied, will authorise the company to issue EIS certificates to each of the investors. HMRC will enclose blank EIS3 certificates to enable this.

Advance assurance

It is possible for the issuing company to request a non-binding statutory ruling, known as advance assurance, from HMRC's Venture Capital Reliefs team before the shares are issued, by providing them with all details pertinent to the potential investment.

HMRC have long felt that this facility was being strained by speculative enquiries (i.e. ones that are unlikely to lead to an actual investment). This might be done in order to test the boundaries of the legislation, so as to develop tax avoidance schemes, for example. Following a consultation in 2017, the following streamlining measures were enacted:

- No opinion will be given if it is apparent that the company is likely to fail to meet the risk-to-capital condition, i.e. there must be a genuine risk of financial loss for the investors (ITA 2007, s. 157A).

- No opinion will be given in relation to speculative enquiries. In practice, this means that the company requesting the opinion will need to demonstrate that it has approached potential investors and must provide the names of all individuals, fund managers or other promoters who are expected to invest.

- If a company is relying on a particular interpretation of the law in order to obtain relief, it will need to provide a full technical analysis demonstrating how the requirements of the law are met. HMRC will not issue an opinion unless it believes that the enquiry is seeking to allay genuine concerns (i.e. not simply testing the boundaries of the rules).

An illustration of how the third point might crop up in practice would be contrasting (a) a company seeking clarification on whether or not a potential investor is connected due to past involvement, with (b) a company sending a number of slightly different scenarios to test the point at which connection is established.

HMRC now only accept advance assurance applications made in a standardised format, which means that the company will need to complete form VCSAA, supply a completed EIS checklist, and explain how the funds will be used to grow and develop its business.

It is possible to do this via email. Full details of the updated requirements and correct correspondence addresses are available online.

Guidance: https://tinyurl.com/yaz4cozd (EIS advance assurance application)

10.2.3   *Termination date*

In practice, the termination date relating to relevant shares is the date when all the relief becomes final – i.e. if all the qualifying conditions have been met throughout the period leading up to this date, there is no longer a risk that this might be withdrawn.

Exactly when the termination date is depends on whether the company was already carrying on the qualifying trade at the time the shares were issued. If it was, the termination date will be the third anniversary of the share issue date. As this is the case with most EIS investments, there is often confusion and an incorrect assumption that the termination date is always three years after the shares were subscribed for. There are instances, however, where this will not be the case.

If the company invested in has not yet commenced the qualifying trade but is preparing to do so, the termination date will be the third anniversary of the date that trade commences. This preparation work can continue for up to two years after the share issue date without jeopardising EIS relief. The termination date can therefore potentially be up to five years after the share issue date.

If an investor makes a disposal of some or all of the shares before the termination date, the income tax relief given will be fully or partially withdrawn, depending on the circumstances. This has a knock-on effect on the availability of the CGT reliefs.

Law: ITA 2007, s. 256

10.3   EIS reinvestment relief

10.3.1   *Overview*

An investor making a qualifying EIS investment is entitled to match the amount invested to any capital gains made within a specified time window (relative to the date of the EIS investment).

Matched gains are then deferred, and do not fall to be charged to CGT until the EIS shares are later disposed of, or until another chargeable event arises. It must be realised that it is the gain itself that is deferred, and not the tax. This is an important distinction because revived gains are charged at the prevailing rate of CGT in the year in which they are revived. Therefore, if the CGT rates increase, more tax may eventually be payable than would have been if the deferral had not been claimed.

Importantly, an investor who does not qualify for EIS income tax relief may still be able to claim CGT deferral relief, as the rules regarding who can claim are less stringent. For example, there is no requirement that the investor must not be connected to the company to claim deferral relief.

Example

Clive worked for Dot Ltd during 2020-21, but left to found a venture capital firm. However, he wishes to make an investment into Dot Ltd in 2021-22, funding this by selling some listed shares from his portfolio and realising £100,000 of gains. Dot Ltd is intending to raise capital via an EIS share issue.

Clive will be precluded from claiming EIS income tax relief as he was connected to the company during Period A. However, he would be able to match the investment to some or all of the £100,000 gains and defer the gain.

At the time of writing there is no restriction on the amount of an individual's gains that can be deferred by qualifying investments, though qualifying investments into a single company are restricted by reference to both an annual and a lifetime limit.

Law: TCGA 1992, Sch. 5B

10.3.2   *Limited window*

If gains are to be matched to an EIS investment, they must arise within a four-year time window, commencing three years before, and ending one year after, the share issue date.

An alternative way of thinking about this is that once the taxpayer realises any capital gains, he has three years to make an EIS investment and defer some or all of them, or he can match them to an EIS investment made within the preceding 12 months.

In some circumstances, HMRC have the power to extend the qualifying time if the EIS investment was not made within three years. Guidance as to when HMRC will do this is given in the *Venture Capital Schemes Manual* at VCM 23030, which states that the time limit will be extended where the claimant can show that he or she:

- had a firm intention to comply with the time limit; but
- was prevented by some fact or circumstance beyond his or her control from complying; and
- acted as soon as he or she reasonably could after ceasing to be so prevented.

It is clear, therefore, that the onus to demonstrate this is on the taxpayer. The guidance also confirms that each case will be considered on its merits.

Law: TCGA 1992, Sch. 5B, para. 1(3)
Guidance: VCM 23030

10.3.3   Gains that can be deferred

Gains that arise from actual disposals of assets can be deferred, as can gains which crystallise because of the disposal of shares – for example, gains deferred under an earlier EIS investment. Certain gains arising on deemed disposals – for example where a revived gain comes back into charge due to the EIS shares ceasing to be eligible shares – can also be deferred.

A gain cannot be deferred using EIS deferral relief if it arises from a disposal of shares in the same company as the one into which the EIS investment is being made.

Law: TCGA 1992, Sch. 5B, para. 1(3)

10.3.4   Who is eligible to claim

Only UK resident individuals, and trustees of a qualifying UK resident settlement, can claim deferral relief. A qualifying settlement is broadly one where all beneficiaries are either individuals or charities.

An individual cannot claim deferral relief if he or she is dual resident and would be treated as resident in another country under the relevant double tax treaty. Additionally, no relief is available if the circumstances are such that if the EIS shares were sold immediately after purchase at a gain, they would not be chargeable to CGT.

There is no restriction on "connected" individuals claiming EIS deferral relief; therefore, existing paid directors and those with a material interest (i.e. more than 30% of the ordinary share capital) are eligible to claim.

There are further conditions, for example that the issuing company must be a "qualifying company". Schedule 5B stipulates that an investment will be a qualifying investment if all of the following conditions are met:

Condition	Notes
Eligible shares are issued to the investor in the permitted reinvestment window, and, if the gain arose after the investment, are still held at the accrual time.	The accrual time is the date on which the gain being deferred arises. Obviously, EIS shares cannot be used to defer a gain if they have already been sold at that point. (If the gain had been realised before the investment then this point will not be relevant.)
The shares are subscribed for wholly in cash.	Bonus shares are excluded from this.
The company is a qualifying company in relation to the shares.	This will be the case if the company meets the requirements set out in ITA 2007, s. 180.
The investment is not made as part of tax avoidance arrangements.	
The annual limit on relevant investments into the company has been observed.	
The company issuing the shares carries on the qualifying activity.	See ITA 2007, s. 183.
The shares are issued to raise money for the purpose of a qualifying business activity, and the money raised is so employed within two years of the issue date.	

Law: TCGA 1992, Sch. 5B, para. 1; ITA 2007, s. 180, 183

10.3.5   Maximum amount to be deferred

There is no current restriction on the amount of an individual's gains that can be deferred by qualifying investments. However, it is important not to overlook the gross assets test and the effect that a particularly large investment in a *single* company, intended to attract deferral relief, might have. This is because the issuing company has to meet the qualifying company status (as set out in the provisions for the income tax relief) if an investment is to be eligible for deferral relief.

Additionally, the maximum amount that can be raised annually by the issuing company (currently £5 million) may need to be considered. Even if the investor is not intending to claim income tax relief (perhaps because he or she is connected to the issuing company), any amount raised through an EIS issue on which deferral relief is to be claimed also counts as a relevant investment for the purposes of the cap. (A compliance certificate has to be obtained from HMRC in order to claim deferral relief, and relevant investments for the purposes of the annual maximum are defined as those for which a compliance certificate has been so obtained.)

The key point is that if the investor is looking to make an investment which would mean the annual maximum relevant investments limit would be breached, he or she would need to invest in more than one qualifying company – possibly through an approved EIS fund. It is important to look at the big picture with every investment.

10.3.6   Mechanics of relief

Deferral relief cannot be claimed before a compliance statement is issued by HMRC. This can mean in practice that the CGT has to be paid and subsequently reclaimed. There is no stipulation as to which gains have to be deferred – i.e. earlier gains do not have to be deferred first – so it is entirely the taxpayer's choice. A relevant entry should be made on the CGT summary pages of the self-assessment tax return showing which gain the taxpayer has chosen to defer.

A gain that would qualify for business asset disposal relief (BADR – see **Chapter 7**) can be deferred via EIS without losing the entitlement. While this is positive, the differential with the top tax rate if the BADR rate were scrapped at some point in the future would need to be considered. This is possibly less likely since the BADR lifetime limit was reduced to just £1 million in 2020, but should always be kept in mind.

The relief simply takes the form of a direct £1 for £1 offset, i.e. £1 of reinvestment defers £1 of gain. Unlike rollover relief there is no restriction to the relief for disposal proceeds *not* reinvested in qualifying shares.

The taxpayer chooses how much of the potential relief to claim. It is therefore possible to claim sufficient relief to leave a gain in charge equivalent to the annual exempt amount, thus ensuring this is not wasted. Available capital losses would need to be factored into this calculation.

A record of which gains have been deferred, and the underlying details, should be kept to enable accurate future calculations.

Law: TCGA 1992, Sch. 5B, para. 2

10.4   EIS reinvestment relief – reviving the gain

10.4.1   Chargeable events

Once a gain is successfully deferred, it is only revived where a chargeable event occurs. The legislation sets out five instances of such a chargeable event:

- The investor disposes of the relevant shares, other than to a spouse or civil partner.
- A spouse or civil partner, having acquired the shares from the investor, disposes of the shares to a third party.
- The investor becomes non-UK resident whilst holding the shares, where the date the non-residency began precedes the termination date of the shares (see below).
- A spouse or civil partner who acquired the shares becomes non-UK resident prior to the termination date (see below).
- The shares cease to be eligible shares, or are treated for the purposes of the deferral relief legislation as so ceasing (see **10.4.2**).

In respect to the third and fourth conditions, as an exception to the general rule, there will not be a chargeable event if the reason for the non-residency is to take up a position of employment or office of which all the duties are performed outside the UK, and if UK residency recommences within three years. This is subject to the further condition that the shares were not sold during the non-resident period.

Additionally, the death of the investor, or of a spouse or civil partner to whom the shares have been transferred, is not treated as a chargeable event. This means that if an investor dies following a successful EIS deferral relief claim, the gain deferred will effectively die with him. This mirrors the position that would arise had the investor died whilst still holding the original asset.

In some instances, for example where the investor makes a part disposal of the shares, it may be necessary to apportion the gain being revived.

Law: TCGA 1992, Sch. 5B, para. 3

10.4.2   Shares ceasing to be eligible

The shares will cease to be eligible in a number of circumstances. Where this occurs, the deferred gain is brought back into charge. A brief summary of these circumstances follows.

Put and call options

If the EIS shares become subject to put or call options in a particular time window, the shares may cease to be eligible. Where such options are granted on or before the share issue date, the shares in question will never be eligible shares.

Where the option date is after the date of the share issue, but before the end of the relevant period, a disposal (and therefore a chargeable event) is treated as taking place on the date of the option grant.

The relevant period referred to is Period A, as defined at **10.2.1** above.

Note that only shares becoming subject to the options cease to be eligible. It follows that only a proportion of the deferred gain is revived in cases where some EIS shares are subject to options and some are not.

Law: TCGA 1992, Sch. 5B, para. 3

Linked loans to the investor

If at any time in the relevant period a "linked loan" is made to the investor (or to any associate of his or hers), the shares will be treated either as not eligible (if the loan was made prior to the share issue date) or as ceasing to be eligible (if afterwards).

Again, the relevant period is Period A. A loan is linked to the investment if it would not have been made, or would have been made on different terms, in the absence of that investment.

Law: TCGA 1992, Sch. 5B, para. 15

Disqualifying arrangements

No deferral relief can be claimed if the shares are issued in consequence or anticipation of, or otherwise in connection with, disqualifying arrangements. See HMRC's guidance at VCM 12100 for details about which arrangements are "disqualifying".

Law: TCGA 1992, Sch. 5B, para. 11A
Guidance: VCM 12100

Pre-arranged exits

Shares will not be treated as eligible if there are arrangements related to their issue that constitute pre-arranged exits. This broadly means that there is some mechanism that reduces the risk to the investor by, for example, guaranteeing re-purchase of the shares at some later date.

Law: TCGA 1992, Sch. 5B, para. 11

Value received by the investor

The deferral period will therefore end if the investor receives value within the "period of restriction". The period of restriction is Period C, which begins one year before the share issue date and ends immediately before the termination date.

Value is received, according to TCGA 1992, Sch. 5B, in the following circumstances:

> "**13(2)** For the purposes of this paragraph an individual receives value from the company if the company–
>
> (a)   repays, redeems or repurchases any of its share capital or securities which belong to the individual or makes any payment to him for giving up his right to any of the company's share capital or any security on its cancellation or extinguishment;
>
> (b)   repays, in pursuance of any arrangements for or in connection with the acquisition of the shares, any debt owed to the individual other than a debt which was incurred by the company–

      (i)   on or after the date of issue of the shares; and

      (ii)   otherwise than in consideration of the extinguishment of a debt incurred before that date;

(c)   makes to the individual any payment for giving up his right to any debt on its extinguishment;

(d)   releases or waives any liability of the individual to the company or discharges, or undertakes to discharge, any liability of his to a third person;

(e)   makes a loan or advance to the individual which has not been repaid in full before the issue of the shares;

(f)   provides a benefit or facility for the individual;

(g)   disposes of an asset to the individual for no consideration or for a consideration which is or the value of which is less than the market value of the asset;

(h)   acquires an asset from the individual for a consideration which is or the value of which is more than the market value of the asset; or

(i)   makes any payment to the individual other than a qualifying payment."

Qualifying payments include reasonable remuneration for services, allowable expenses, payment for goods or assets which do not exceed a market value, or ordinary dividends not exceeding a normal rate of return.

Where the value received is "insignificant", being less than £1,000 or insignificant when considering the overall level of investment, it may be possible to ignore it. Refer to the examples in VCM 23390 for further information.

It is also possible to return the value received to avoid triggering the revival in some circumstances.

Law: TCGA 1992, Sch. 5B, para. 13
Guidance: VCM 23390

Breach of qualifying conditions

A chargeable event occurs if certain conditions relating to the issuing company are breached in Period A, i.e. in the period beginning two years prior to the share issue date and ending immediately before the termination date (see **10.2.3**). The relevant conditions are summarised below:

Event	Date of chargeable event
Company ceases to be a qualifying company.	The date the company ceases to be so qualifying.
Qualifying activity is not carried on by issuing company or qualifying 90% subsidiary.	The date the activity ceased being carried on by the issuing company or qualifying 90% subsidiary.
Money raised was not intended to be used for the purposes of a qualifying business activity.	Shares will be treated as never eligible – deferment will be reversed and cancelled.
Money was intended to be used for the purposes of a qualifying activity, but was not employed before the deadline.	The date the deadline passes, unless the claim was not yet made in which case shares will never be treated as eligible shares.

Law: ITA 2007, Pt. 5, Ch. 3-4

10.4.3   Share identification – mixed holdings

Where there is only a single subscription of shares to which deferral relief applies, it is relatively straightforward to identify the revived gain. For example, if 100,000 shares were issued at £1 each, and were used in full to defer a gain of £100,000, a disposal of all the shares will bring £100,000 of gain back into charge, or a disposal of 30,000 shares will bring in £30,000 of gain, and so on.

In some circumstances, it may transpire that an investor holds a mix of shares in the issuing company acquired on the same day that attracted either income tax relief, CGT deferral relief, both or neither, depending on the particular prevailing conditions at the time the respective share issues took place. If this is the case then the shares disposed of must be carefully identified in accordance with the special identification rules set out in the legislation.

The identification rules are relatively easy to follow, and essentially provide that the shares are not pooled as normal, but are treated as being disposed of on a first-in, first-out basis. In circumstances where shares attracting different relief are acquired on the same day, the rules stipulate that shares to which no relief is attached are treated as being disposed of first, followed by shares only attracting deferral relief, shares only attracting income tax relief, and finally shares attracting both.

Law: TCGA 1992, Sch. 5B, para. 4

10.4.4   Takeovers etc.

When a buying firm purchases all the share capital in a target which has issued shares under EIS there is a disposal, so any deferred gains will be revived. In practice, however, it is often the case that the buying company will issue its own shares in exchange for existing shares in the target company. Whether or not this causes a gain to be revived is complex. HMRC's guidance at VCM 23230 should be referred to.

Law: TCGA 1992, Sch. 5B, para. 8
Guidance: VCM 23230

10.5   EIS exemption on disposal relief

10.5.1   Basic principles

Where the shares issued under EIS are held throughout Period A (see **10.2.1**) before being disposed of, there are provisions in TCGA 1992 to exempt any gain arising from CGT, while allowing any losses (subject to adjustment). Ordinarily, a disposal that would be exempt if it produced a gain cannot be allowable if, in fact, it produces a loss. An example of this would be a disposal of qualifying corporate bonds (QCBs).

Gains will only be exempt if income tax relief has been claimed and not wholly withdrawn. Special consideration needs to be given to circumstances where relief has been withdrawn in part – for example, because of a part disposal before the termination date.

Law: TCGA 1992, s. 150A

10.5.2   Some income tax reduction is crucial

An essential requirement of the CGT exemption is that income tax relief must have been claimed on the relevant shares. It is not sufficient that relief would have been available, there has to be at least some relief claimed by the investor. There has to be some reduction attributable to the EIS investment.

This requirement was examined in *Ames,* where the taxpayer had invested in qualifying shares, but not made any claim to EIS income tax relief because his income did not exceed the personal allowance for the year in question. There was also no scope to carry back the relief. As it

235

transpired, the only way to have done so would have been for him to disclaim part of the personal allowance, and as he had not done this within the prescribed time limits HMRC refused his claim, as they did not feel that he had a reasonable excuse (for the lateness). The First-tier and Upper Tribunals both found that the legislation was unambiguous, and so agreed the principle that there can be no exemption in the absence of some income tax relief. The Upper Tribunal did, however, remit back to HMRC the question regarding the late claim to disclaim the personal allowance, as it felt that HMRC had not followed their own guidance.

A point raised was that it appeared extremely unfair comparing the position of a person with no taxable income making an identical investment to a person with £1 of taxable income. The former would pay full CGT, whereas the second would pay nothing.

Law: TCGA 1992, s. 150A

Case: *Ames v HMRC* [2015] UKFTT 337 (TC)

10.5.3   Disposal relief not restricted

Where income tax has been claimed and has not subsequently been withdrawn at all, a disposal after the end of Period A will be fully exempt in respect of the shares which attracted the EIS income tax relief.

Example

Gemma invests £100,000 in EIS shares on 6 April 2018. The termination date relating to the shares is 6 April 2012. Gemma claims income tax relief and holds the shares for the required period. She sells the shares on 1 December 2021 for £400,000. The gain is exempt from CGT.

If the original investment was greater than the permitted annual limit, the exemption is available on a *pro rata* basis (discussed below).

The disposal on which the exemption is being claimed should be included in the CGT summary pages on the tax return, with the relief then claimed to offset it, and an explanatory note inserted in the white space (i.e. the additional information box on the CGT summary pages).

Law: TCGA 1992, s. 150A

10.5.4   Disposal relief is restricted

In circumstances where income tax was not given in full, for example where the investor exceeded the maximum permitted investment limit or where some shares were made subject to options in Period A, it may be necessary to restrict the disposal exemption.

Example

Joanna invests £1.5 million into A Ltd in 2016. She claims EIS income tax relief on £1 million of the shares. However, the other £500,000 is in excess of the investment limit. Joanna has no scope to make a carry-back claim. Joanna sells the shares for £4.5 million in 2021. Two thirds of the £3 million gain (i.e. £2 million) is exempt, but the remaining third will be chargeable.

Things can be more complicated where there is a combination of excess investment and a clawback of income tax relief. Refer to VCM 20030*ff.* for full commentary.

Law: TCGA 1992, s. 150A(3), 150B
Guidance: VCM 20030*ff.*

10.6   EIS loss relief

10.6.1   Overview

As mentioned previously, in most circumstances where a disposal would be exempt from CGT if it produced a gain, any loss arising on such a disposal would be non-allowable. This is not the case here, as while gains are exempt, losses are still allowable. This works because the legislation specifically disapplies the provision preventing a disposal from being a chargeable event where a loss arises.

In calculating the loss, the allowable costs have to be reduced by the amount of income tax relief given and not subsequently withdrawn.

Example 1

Penelope invests £1 million in shares in an EIS qualifying company, claiming the full £300,000 EIS income tax relief. No relief is withdrawn. The shares eventually become worthless and the company is liquidated. The capital loss of £1 million is reduced by the £300,000 income tax relief given and not withdrawn, meaning the allowable loss is £700,000.

In the event that there is only a part disposal, the reduction is made on a *pro rata* basis.

Example 2

Thomas invests £1 million in shares in an EIS qualifying company, claiming the full £300,000 EIS income tax relief, which is not subsequently withdrawn. He later sells half of the shares for £50,000. The loss of £450,000 is reduced by £150,000 (i.e. half of the income tax relief not withdrawn).

10.6.2   Sideways loss relief

Losses arising on disposals of "qualifying shares" may be offset against general income rather than against other capital gains.

Shares are automatically qualifying shares for these purposes if EIS relief is attributable to them. Because of the wording of the legislation, it would not matter if (following the end of the minimum holding period) the company had ceased to carry on a qualifying trade.

Where losses are to be relieved against general income, they can be relieved against income for the year in which the loss arose, or the preceding year, or both. If a claim is made in a tax year then the maximum possible loss relief must be used, i.e. if sufficient losses are available total income must be reduced to nil, wasting the personal allowance for that year. It is possible to offset both the years' income if the loss exceeds the income for one of the years. The loss, however, may be insufficient to cover in full the income for both years. If a claim is being made to relieve income in both tax years, the taxpayer should specify on his or her return which year is to be offset first.

There is a general restriction on sideways loss relief. This restriction limits the maximum offset of the capital loss against income to the higher of:

- £50,000; or
- 25% of the taxpayer's income.

Losses arising on EIS shares which are to be relieved against income *do not* fall within the provisions of this cap – found in ITA 2007, s. 24A – because restrictions are already imposed upon maximum investment amounts attracting income tax relief. This is confirmed by s. 24A (7). Losses in excess of the general restriction limit can therefore be relieved in full provided that they are shares to which EIS relief is attributable.

Having identified that share loss relief is available due to attributable EIS relief, and that there is income to offset, normal procedures for claiming share loss relief should be followed (found in ITA 2007, s. 133).

If all of the loss cannot be relieved against income in the relevant two years (because there is not enough income to relieve the loss fully), the unused balance can be used against capital gains arising in the same year as the loss, or carried forward to offset future capital gains.

Law: ITA 2007, s. 24A, 131, 133

10.7   Seed enterprise investment scheme

10.7.1   Introduction

There are two CGT reliefs available under SEIS:

- reinvestment relief; and
- disposal relief.

Losses are allowable capital losses, after adjusting for any income tax relief not withdrawn, in the same way as losses on EIS shares.

There is no automatic qualification for share loss relief (see **10.6.2**) as there is for the main EIS. However, a company that meets the qualifying conditions for SEIS is highly likely to meet the general requirements for share loss relief in any case.

10.7.2   Reinvestment relief

Instead of simply postponing payment of the tax on a gain matched to a qualifying investment, reinvestment relief exempts part of the otherwise chargeable gain where the proceeds are reinvested in qualifying shares. Provided the shares qualify for SEIS relief, and are held until the end of Period A, that part of the gain is never subject to CGT.

The relief works by reducing the amount of the gain matched with a qualifying SEIS share investment by the relevant percentage, which is 50%. The remaining 50% of the gain remains chargeable; there is no scope under SEIS to defer this remainder. However, in practice an investment under SEIS takes place alongside an investment under EIS, and so the remainder can be deferred using the EIS deferral provisions in these circumstances.

The amount of gains that can be matched using a qualifying investment is subject to an annual cap of £100,000.

Reinvestment window

The gain to be matched must arise in the same tax year as the qualifying investment is made, or treated as being made. If the SEIS investment is subject to a carry-back claim, the amount of shares subject to the claim are treated as being made in the tax year prior to the investment, and so only gains arising in that tax year can be matched to that proportion of the investment.

Mechanics

The relief works by reducing eligible gains by up to 50% of the amount of the qualifying investment in the SEIS company; however this is restricted and cannot exceed:

- the amount of SEIS expenditure specified in the claim;
- the amount of SEIS expenditure that is unused; or
- the part of the gain that is unmatched.

The effect of this is that no more than 50% of a gain can be offset by SEIS reinvestment relief, even if 50% of the qualifying SEIS investment is more than that amount. For example, where the SEIS investment is £100,000 but the gain to be matched is £70,000, the reinvestment relief is restricted to exempt £35,000, not £50,000.

As with the EIS scheme the claim can be restricted so as to use the annual exempt amount for the year.

Restrictions

It may be necessary to restrict the relief in some circumstances, for example where income tax relief is not obtained on the full amount of the SEIS investment, or where there is some clawback of income tax relief.

Law: TCGA 1992, Sch. 5BB
Guidance: VCM 45040*ff.*

10.7.3   Withdrawal of relief

If SEIS income tax relief is withdrawn or reduced, there will be a corresponding withdrawal or reduction of reinvestment relief. If income tax relief is only partly reduced, reinvestment relief is reduced in the same proportion using the following formula:

Reduction in reinvestment relief

$$= \text{original reinvestment relief} \times \frac{R1 - R2}{R1}$$

where:

> **R1** = the SEIS income tax relief prior to applying the reduction; and

> **R2** = SEIS income tax relief following the reduction.

Law: TCGA 1992, Sch. 5BB, para. 5
Guidance: VCM 45090

10.7.4   Disposal relief

The requirements for the SEIS shares to be exempt from CGT on disposal are the same as for EIS shares, namely that some income tax relief must be attributable to them and the termination date must have passed (see **10.5**).

Where income tax was given and not withdrawn or reduced, the shares will be exempt in full. However, where relief has been partly withdrawn there will need to be an apportionment of the gain.

Law: TCGA 1992, s. 150F
Guidance: VCM 40030*ff.*

10.8   Social investment tax relief

10.8.1   CGT reliefs

An investment into a qualifying social enterprise may attract both income tax and CGT reliefs. A qualifying social enterprise must be one or more of the following throughout the minimum holding period of the investment:

- a community interest company;
- a community benefit society, with an "asset lock" (a restriction on transferring assets); or
- a charity (either a trust or a company).

Note that a social enterprise cannot be a member of a partnership during the applicable period.

The CGT reliefs are:

- reinvestment relief; and
- disposal relief.

The SITR provisions are heavily based on the EIS legislation, and in many places are worded almost identically, for example with the provisions for restricting relief on excess investments. However, there are some differences to be aware of.

One key difference is that a qualifying investment may take the form of a loan instead of a share subscription. The disposal relief only applies to capital gains, so a gain made on a share investment would qualify. However, any income profits on a loan do not qualify, for example interest or premium paid.

Again, there is no specific provision for losses to be offset against general income, so shares would need to meet the general criteria (see **10.6.2**). A loss arising following a loan will never qualify for sideways loss relief.

10.8.2   SITR reinvestment relief

Reinvestment relief operates under the same mechanism as under EIS, namely that a qualifying investment may be matched to gains made in the four-year time window, commencing three years before and ending one year after the share issue date. The gain is then deferred until the investment is disposed of, or relief is withdrawn.

A key difference between SITR and EIS reinvestment relief is that, under SITR, the shares must have been eligible for income tax relief in the hands of the investor (even if it was not claimed). This means that connected persons cannot claim reinvestment relief under SITR. It also means that the investor is restricted to £1 million of deferrals in any one tax year because investments in excess of this would not qualify for income tax relief.

Law: TCGA 1992, Sch. 8B

10.8.3   Specific conditions

As well as being eligible for income tax relief, five further conditions must be met. These are referred to as conditions A to E in the legislation.

Condition A is that the gain the investor is looking to defer is one which accrues on:

- the disposal of an asset;
- a qualifying business disposal; or
- a chargeable event related to SITR investments (i.e. a revived gain).

Condition B is that that gain accrues between 6 April 2014 and 5 April 2021 (the cut-off for this period may be extended in a later Finance Bill).

Condition C is that the investor is resident in the UK at the time when the gain to be deferred accrues, and when the social holding is acquired.

Condition D is that the social holding is acquired by the investor on the investor's own behalf.

Condition E is that the social holding is acquired within the time period beginning 12 months before the gain accrual time, and ending three years afterwards.

10.8.4   Reviving a gain

The deferred gain will be revived in any of the following circumstances:

- The investor disposes of the assets otherwise than to a spouse or civil partner.
- A spouse or civil partner who has received the assets on a no gain/no loss basis disposes of the assets.
- The asset is cancelled, extinguished, redeemed, or repaid.
- Any of the ongoing conditions that must be met in respect of the investor being a qualifying investor, or the social enterprise being a qualifying social enterprise, ceases to be met.

Law: TCGA 1992, Sch. 8B, para. 5

10.9   Venture capital trusts

10.9.1   Overview

A VCT is designed to be less risky than EIS investments, as the investor's money is spread across several companies. VCTs are required to use investments raised to fund smaller unquoted companies, and are heavily restricted in terms of what they can invest into; however, VCTs are permitted to invest a proportion of their funds in publicly listed companies.

As such, the tax reliefs on offer are considerably less generous than for EIS investments. There is no longer a mechanism to defer gains using a VCT investment (this ceased in 2004).

In fact, from a CGT perspective the only relief is the disposal exemption. Losses are not allowable losses, and so cannot be offset against income or gains.

A VCT has approved status from HMRC, and so there should be no uncertainty as to whether an investment will qualify if the investor is eligible.

10.9.2   Disposal relief – conditions

The conditions which must be met are that the company in which the shares were held:

- was a VCT at the time the shares were acquired; and
- was a VCT at the time the shares were disposed of,

and that the disposal was a "qualifying disposal".

A disposal is a qualifying disposal if:

- it is made by a person who is at least 18 years old;
- it is made in respect of shares that were not acquired in excess of the permitted annual maximum; and
- the individual acquired the shares for *bona fide* commercial reasons, and not as part of a scheme in which one of the main intentions was the avoidance of tax.

Shares do not have to have been subscribed for in order to qualify for the CGT exemption, so shares acquired second-hand from another person can qualify subject to the permitted annual maximum condition.

It may be the case that, upon a disposal, some of the shares are eligible and some are not. In this case, the investor must follow the two sets of share identification rules specified in s. 151A(4), (5) and s. 151B.

If the VCT loses its approval from HMRC, the right to claim any disposal relief will be lost on any subsequent disposals. Additionally, if the approval was only provisional, any prior disposals will become taxable as the VCT is treated as never being approved.

Law: TCGA 1992, s. 151A(1), (2), (4), (5), 151B

11. Replacement of business assets (rollover relief)

11.1 Introduction

Replacement of business assets relief, also known as rollover relief, is a CGT relief that allows a trader (or other qualifying activity – see **11.2.2**) to defer the capital gain that arises on the disposal of a business asset.

For relief to be available, there must be a disposal of a qualifying asset (see **11.3**) that is used in the trader's business, and an acquisition of a new qualifying asset within the relevant time-frame (see **11.3.2**). That new asset should also be acquired for use in the trade.

The way rollover relief is given depends on whether the new asset is a depreciating asset or a non-depreciating asset.

In the case of a non-depreciating asset, relief is effectively given by reducing the base cost of the new asset by the amount of deferred gain (see **11.5**). Where a depreciating asset is acquired, the gain arising on sale of the old asset is effectively held over until a taxing point occurs (see **11.7**).

11.2 Who can claim

11.2.1 General rules

Rollover relief is available to a "person carrying on a trade".

There are two key words here: "person" and "trade".

Person

The term "person" casts a wide net, and includes individual sole traders, companies and partnerships, including LLPs (see **11.9**).

Companies are, generally, beyond the scope of this book.

Rollover relief can also be available where an individual disposes of and acquires qualifying assets to be used in a trade carried on by his or her personal company (see **11.11**).

Trade

The term "trade" takes the same meaning as for income tax purposes, meaning that it also includes activities such as farming and furnished holiday letting businesses (see **11.10**).

Law: TCGA 1992, s. 152(1)

11.2.2   Extension of availability

Section 158 extends the availability of rollover relief, allowing it to apply to other activities, including (among others):

- the discharge of the functions of a public authority;
- the occupation of woodlands where the woodlands are managed by the occupier on a commercial basis and with a view to the realisation of profits;
- a profession, vocation, office or employment (see Statement of Practice 5/86 for employees and office-holders); and
- the activities of a body of persons whose activities are carried on otherwise than for profit and are wholly or mainly directed to the protection or promotion of the interests of its members in the carrying on of their trade or profession as are so directed.

Law: TCGA 1992, s. 158
Guidance: SP 5/86

11.2.3   More than one trade

Where a person, either successively or at the same time, carries on two or more trades, then for the purposes of rollover relief they are treated as a single trade.

HMRC confirm in SP 8/81 that if a trader ceases to carry on the trade and commences carrying on another trade, HMRC will regard the trades as having been carried on successively within the meaning of s. 152(8), provided that the interval between cessation and commencement does not exceed three years. Note that this does not override the requirement in s. 152(3) for the acquisition to take place within the usual time limits (see **11.3.2**).

Law: TCGA 1992, s. 152(3), (8)
Guidance: SP 8/81

11.3   Qualifying assets

11.3.1   Types of qualifying asset

For rollover relief to be available, both the old asset disposed of, and the new asset acquired, should be qualifying assets.

Note that an asset is also qualifying if it is an interest in an asset.

A range of different assets may qualify for rollover relief. The full list is outlined in s. 155, but it includes:

- any building or part of a building and any permanent or semi-permanent structure in the nature of a building, occupied (as well as used) only for the purposes of the trade (see **11.3.5**);
- any land occupied (as well as used) only for the purposes of the trade (see **11.3.5**);
- fixed plant or machinery that does not form part of a building or of a permanent or semi-permanent structure in the nature of a building (see **11.3.7**);
- ships, aircraft and hovercraft;
- satellites, space stations, and spacecraft;
- goodwill;
- milk and potato quotas;
- ewe and suckler cow premium quotas;
- fish quota;
- payment entitlements under the farming single payment scheme;
- payment entitlements under the farming basic payment scheme;
- rights of a member of a Lloyd's syndicate; and
- Lloyd's members' agent pooling arrangements.

In the legislation, the above assets are broken down into different "classes". However, this has no practical implication for current rollover relief claims.

Law: TCGA 1992, s. 155

11.3.2   Time limits

Under s. 152(3), rollover relief is available if the acquisition of the new asset takes place, or an unconditional contract for the acquisition is entered into, between:

- the 12 months prior to the disposal of the old asset; and
- three years after the disposal of the old asset.

This, in practice, provides a four-year window during which time the acquisition of a qualifying business asset is eligible for rollover relief.

Example 1

A building used exclusively in Josephine's trade is sold in December 2021 for £250,000, realising a gain on disposal of £100,000.

A new building used exclusively in Josephine's trade is purchased in June 2022 for £300,000. Full rollover relief is available if Josephine wishes to make a claim.

Example 2

In June 2021, Miss Bows purchases a new building to be used exclusively in her trade for £600,000.

A few months later, in January 2022, Miss Bows sells a different building that she had used exclusively in her trade for £550,000, realising a gain on disposal of £300,000.

Full rollover relief is available on the gain arising from the disposal of the building in January 2022, if Miss Bows wishes to make a claim.

HMRC may allow an extension of the above time limits.

Section 152(4) goes on to state that where an unconditional contract for the acquisition exists, a rollover relief claim may be given on a provisional basis without waiting to ascertain whether the new assets, or the interest in the new assets, is acquired in pursuance of the contract.

Once details are known, all necessary adjustments are then made by making or amending assessments or by repayment or discharge of tax without regard to the usual time limits.

Law: TCGA 1992, s. 152(3), 152(4)
Guidance: CG 60300

11.3.3   Trading condition

Rollover relief will not normally be available unless the new asset was acquired for the purpose of being used in the trade and is immediately so used following purchase. In other words, an asset that is purchased with the intention of being used, but is not actually used in the trade after purchase, is not usually a qualifying asset.

Similarly, the old asset disposed of must have been used in the trade to be qualifying. For partial rollover relief claims, see **11.6**.

Law: TCGA 1992, s. 152(1)
Guidance: CG 60270

11.3.4   Purpose of acquisition

Rollover relief is not available where the new asset was acquired, whether wholly or partly, for the purpose of realising a gain from the disposal of the new asset.

Law: TCGA 1992, s. 152(5), 155
Guidance: CG 60270

11.3.5   Land and buildings

Buildings and land are separate assets for rollover relief purposes, meaning that separate rollover relief claims may be made in respect of each. In such cases, this may mean apportioning proceeds/costs as required.

Additionally, land and buildings are qualifying assets provided they are both occupied and used only for trade purposes. Whether these two tests are met is a question of fact.

However, land/buildings are not qualifying assets for rollover relief purposes where the trade is one of:

- dealing in or developing land; or
- providing services for the occupier of land in which the person carrying on the trade has an estate or interest.

The exception to this is where the trade is one of dealing in or developing land, but a profit arising on the sale of any land does not form part of the trading profits. In such cases, rollover relief may still be available on the land.

Let properties

As there are two tests for land and/or buildings to meet when considering whether they are qualifying assets for rollover relief purposes (i.e. the occupation and trade use tests, discussed above) certain types of activities, namely the letting of property, run into particular difficulty when considering eligibility for relief.

This issue is considered in detail at CG 60281:

> "Where land and buildings are let by the owner upon terms which give the tenant the right to occupy to the exclusion of all others, they are not normally qualifying assets of the owner for the purposes of the owner's trade."

Exceptions to this rule are:

- land and buildings let to a partnership by an acting partner;
- land and buildings let to an individual's family or personal company (see **11.11**);
- lessors of tied premises;
- lessors of furnished premises and caravan sites where the owner provides services in circumstances which amount to trading by the owner; and
- commercial letting of furnished holiday accommodation.

Where premises are let in circumstances such that the owner remains the legal occupier of the land or buildings, a claim to relief is not prevented solely because there is also occupation by others. Examples of such lettings are:

- a hotel or guest house (except any part not used exclusively for trade purposes);
- licensed premises owned and managed by a brewer; and
- a house let to an employee who is required to occupy those premises (and no other) for the proper or better performance of the duties of the employment.

Law: TCGA 1992, s. 156
Guidance: CG 60280, 60281

11.3.6   Improvements

There is a specific extra-statutory concession (ESC D22) which provides that, where a trader uses the proceeds from the disposal of an old asset on capital expenditure to enhance the value of other assets the trader owns, said capital expenditure may be considered a "new asset" and so is eligible for rollover relief.

This is provided that:

- the other assets on which the capital expenditure is incurred are used only for the purposes of the trade; or
- on completion of the work on which the expenditure was incurred, the assets are immediately taken into use and used only for the purposes of the trade.

Guidance: ESC D22

11.3.7   Fixed plant or machinery

Under s. 155, a qualifying asset for rollover relief purposes includes "fixed plant or machinery which does not form part of a building or of a permanent or semi-permanent structure in the nature of a building".

"Fixed plant or machinery" in this instance takes its ordinary meaning.

HMRC guidance at CG 60282 states that the word "fixed" is a description of the physical state of the asset in the use to which it is put.

The guidance also outlines four basic tests to determine whether an item is fixed plant and machinery, noting that the answer is determined by fact and degree:

- The first test is whether, in the context of the particular trade, the object is plant or machinery as opposed to, for example, trading stock, or part of a building.
- The second test is whether the trader intends to hold the object in a particular location indefinitely for use in the trade he or she carries on. For example, if the trade is to hire out the object for use by another, it is unlikely that the lessor intends it to be fixed in the function which it performs in the lessor's trade. This is so even though it may be fixed in its use in the lessee's trade.
- The third test is whether the location of the object in a particular site is essential to its function in the trade. For example, it will not normally matter precisely where in an office a desk or bookcase is located. If, however, the items are on display in an historic house and are intended to show how a particular historic figure lived and worked, the precise location of the

object could be important if it is intended to be historically accurate.

- The final test is to consider the nature of the object to determine what means of permanent fixing is available, or necessary, without rendering the object part of the land or buildings and without damaging or destroying the object.

Mobile or fixed?

Mobile plant and machinery is, as perhaps the name suggests, not considered to be fixed plant and machinery within the meaning of s. 155.

For example, a car that is actively used in a trade would not be treated as fixed plant or machinery. Other items that would not be treated as fixed plant or machinery include shop fixtures and fittings (e.g. shelves and counters) and moveable partitions.

There are some exceptions – such as washing machines and dryers in a launderette – that are treated as fixed (although they are, strictly speaking, moveable).

Guidance: CG 60282

11.3.8 Depreciating assets

It is also important to identify whether an asset is a depreciating asset. This is because the way rollover relief is applied differs if the asset being acquired (the new asset) is a depreciating asset.

A depreciating asset is one that is either a "wasting asset" within the definition of s. 44 or it is an asset with a maximum life of 60 years (i.e. it will become a wasting asset within ten years).

For further discussion on depreciating assets, see **11.7**.

11.3.9 Extra-statutory concession D25

ESC D25 specifies that where a trader uses the proceeds from the disposal of an old asset to acquire a further interest in another asset that is already in use in the trade, the further interest is treated as a new asset that is taken into use in the trade for rollover relief purposes.

Guidance: ESC D25

11.4   Consideration

11.4.1   Allocation of consideration

One of the requirements of rollover relief is that the proceeds from the sale of the old asset must be used (i.e. reinvested) in acquiring the new asset. See **11.6.2** for how rollover relief applies where proceeds are not fully reinvested.

This potentially gives rise to a practical issue: does the claimant need to keep evidence of such reinvestment? If so, how can this be achieved in practice?

CG 60270 confirms that:

> "Except where extension of the time limit in Section 152 (3) is requested, it is not necessary to establish a link between the disposal proceeds and their application. To do so would deny relief in almost every case because:
>
> - where acquisition precedes disposal, it would never be possible to show that the consideration for disposal of the old assets was applied in acquiring the new assets; and
>
> - in almost every other case, the consideration for disposal of the old assets will be applied, initially, to some other purpose such as the acquisition of a debt upon lodgement of the funds into a bank account."

As a result, provided the acquisition of the new asset is made within the time limit (see **11.3.2**) there is a default presumption that the consideration on disposal of the old asset was wholly reinvested in the acquisition of the new asset. The exception to this is where there are proceeds not reinvested (see **11.6.2**).

In addition, it does not matter if the old asset was financed by way of a loan, nor does it matter if the new asset is acquired through loan finance or similar.

Example

In September 2021, Natalie sells fixed plant and machinery that has been used in her trade for £50,000 and realises a gain on disposal of £30,000.

That same month, Natalie purchases a freehold building for use in her trade for £300,000, and partly funds the purchase by way of a loan for £250,000.

The fact that the new asset is part funded by way of loan is not taken into consideration when determining Natalie's entitlement to rollover relief. Full rollover relief will still be available.

The base cost of the freehold building, following a rollover relief claim, is £270,000 (£300,000 – £30,000).

Guidance: CG 60270

11.4.2   Priority of provisions

Section 152(10) confirms that any provisions within TCGA 1992 that fix the amount of the consideration deemed to be given for the acquisition or disposal of assets shall be applied before the rollover relief provisions are applied.

An example of where an amount of consideration would be "fixed" is where there is a transaction between connected persons within s. 18 (in such cases, the market value is typically used).

Law: TCGA 1992, s. 152(10)

11.4.3   Deemed acquisitions/disposals

Rollover relief may also be available where a qualifying asset is deemed to be disposed of, or deemed to be acquired (provided the other conditions for rollover relief are also met).

Guidance: CG 60270

11.4.4   Multiple assets

It is possible that a person can purchase and/or dispose of multiple assets that qualify for rollover relief.

In such cases, it falls to the trader's own discretion as to how (or if) rollover relief is allocated.

Example

A trader disposes of a qualifying asset in October 2021 for £75,000 which originally cost £25,000, meaning a gain on disposal of £50,000.

Subsequently, the trader purchases two new qualifying assets; one is freehold land and the other a depreciating asset. The assets cost £495,000 and £80,000 respectively.

The trader can choose whether to roll over the gain of £50,000 against the cost of the land, meaning a revised base cost of £445,000, or to claim rollover relief in respect of the depreciating asset. If the latter option is chosen, this would mean that the base cost of the depreciating asset remains £80,000 and the gain of £50,000 is held over until a crystallisation event occurs (see **11.7.2**).

The trader may well prefer in the above example to roll the gain over against the base cost of the land, as rollover relief into a non-depreciating asset does not carry specific crystallisation events and the deferred gain only comes into charge if the replacement asset is sold.

There may also be instances where it makes more sense for rollover relief *not* to be claimed. For example, if there are allowable capital losses to use, or the gain on disposal of the original asset falls within an individual trader's annual exempt amount.

Guidance: CG 60294

11.5   Computation of relief

Where the conditions for rollover relief are met, the general effect of the relief is to defer the capital gain arising on the disposal of the old business asset.

Putting aside consideration of depreciating assets (see **11.7**), rollover relief is broadly given by rolling the gain arising on the disposal of the old asset into the base cost of the new asset (i.e. by deducting the gain from the base cost).

This, in turn, increases the amount of capital gain that will ultimately arise when the new asset is disposed of, by an amount equal to the capital gain arising on disposal of the original asset.

Example 1

Barry sells a building used exclusively in his trade in December 2021 for £200,000 and makes a capital gain on disposal of £100,000.

He subsequently purchases another building from a third party (Collin) for exclusive use in the trade for £500,000 in February 2022. The whole of Barry's proceeds on sale are reinvested in the purchase of the new building.

Barry claims rollover relief, meaning that the base cost of the new building is reduced by £100,000.

	£
New building purchase price	500,000
Less: rollover relief	(100,000)
Revised base cost	400,000

When the new building is ultimately sold, the capital gain on sale will be £100,000 higher than it otherwise would have been, representing the capital gain arising on the original building's sale.

The rollover relief provisions only apply to the person claiming relief – similar adjustments to base cost etc. are not made in the hands of the person who is on the other end of the transaction.

Example 1 (cont.)

As seen above, the base cost of Barry's new building is £400,000 following a claim for rollover relief.

However, the person who disposed of the new building (Collin) would still record sales proceeds of £500,000 – Barry's claim to rollover relief has no bearing on how Collin should calculate his capital gain on disposal.

The above is a very high-level example of how the relief operates.

The exact way that rollover relief is given is outlined in s. 152, which states that a claim for relief has the following effects:

- The consideration for the disposal of, or of the interest in, the old asset is deemed to be an amount that would secure a no gain/no loss on disposal (in other words, proceeds equal allowable costs).

- The consideration for the acquisition of, or of the interest in, the new asset is reduced by the same amount as that by which the consideration for the disposal of the old asset is reduced.

Example 2

In January 2015, Mary purchases a freehold building for £200,000, which is to be used exclusively in her trade. In January 2022, Mary sells the building for £350,000, resulting in a gain of £150,000.

In June 2022, Mary purchases a new freehold building for £400,000, for use in her trade.

If Mary claims rollover relief, it is calculated as follows:

	£
Consideration	350,000
Less adjustment for rollover relief	(150,000)
Revised consideration	200,000
Less base cost	(200,000)
Chargeable gain	Nil

Base cost of purchase of new freehold building in June 2022

	£
Cost	400,000
Less: rollover relief	(150,000)
Revised base cost	250,000

For ease of understanding, for the remainder of this chapter any reference to a gain being rolled into the base cost of a new asset also assumes that the adjustment has been made regarding the consideration for the asset disposed of, as per the above example.

Where a depreciating asset is acquired, relief is given in a different way (see **11.7**).

Law: TCGA 1992, s. 152(1)
Guidance: CG 60290

11.6   Restriction of rollover relief

11.6.1   Introduction

Notwithstanding the additional occupation test applies to land and buildings (see **11.3.5**), full rollover relief is only available where:

- the qualifying asset sold, and the asset acquired, are solely used for the purposes of the person's trade; and
- the proceeds of sale arising on disposal of the original asset are fully reinvested in the acquisition of the new asset.

Where one (or both) of the above conditions are not met, the amount of rollover relief available is restricted.

11.6.2   Partial reinvestment

Sometimes, when a trader sells the old business asset, the proceeds are higher than the cost of the new business asset.

Full rollover relief is therefore not available. Instead, s. 153 allows for partial rollover relief, provided that the amount of proceeds retained is less than the gain that the person wishes to roll over.

The amount of proceeds that have been reinvested in the purchase of the new qualifying asset is the amount eligible for relief.

The remainder of the gain will be immediately chargeable to tax.

Example 1 – proceeds partially reinvested

On 30 September 2021, Tara disposes of a business asset used in her trade for £350,000, realising a chargeable gain on sale of £200,000.

In April 2022, she purchases a new business asset for £225,000. This means she has retained sales proceeds of £125,000 (£350,000 – £225,000) following the sale of the original business asset in September 2021.

The amount of gain that can be rolled over is restricted to £75,000 (being the gain on sale of the original asset of £200,000, less the sales proceeds not reinvested of £125,000). The remaining £125,000 of gain in September 2021 is chargeable to CGT in the tax year in which the original disposal took place (i.e. 2021-22).

The base cost of the new business asset, after taking rollover relief into account, is as follows:

	£
Cost	225,000
Less: rollover relief	(75,000)
Revised base cost	150,000

Example 2 – proceeds retained exceed gain

In January 2022, Julie sells a business asset for £150,000, and realises a gain on disposal of £50,000.

In February 2022, she purchases a new business asset, but at a much lower price of £75,000. As Julie has retained proceeds of £75,000 (£150,000 – £75,000) following the sale of the old business asset, rollover relief will not be available, as this amount exceeds the chargeable gain arising on disposal of the original business asset of £50,000.

This means that the gain of £50,000 cannot be deferred (i.e. it is immediately chargeable in the tax year of disposal). Similarly, the base cost of the new business asset will remain unchanged at £75,000.

Again, these provisions only apply to the person claiming rollover relief – no adjustments are made from the perspective of the other party to the transaction (see **11.5**).

Practical tip

One quick way to see whether rollover relief may be available where proceeds have been only partially reinvested is to identify how much of the proceeds on sale of the original asset have been retained (i.e. not reinvested in the purchase of the new asset):

- If the amount of proceeds retained is higher than the gain arising on the disposal of the original asset, no rollover relief is available.
- If the amount of proceeds retained is lower than the gain arising on the disposal of the original asset, partial rollover relief should be available.

Law: TCGA 1992, s. 153
Guidance: CG 60291

11.6.3   Partial trade use

Where the old and/or new asset is not solely used in the trade, partial rollover relief may be available. There are two main provisions here:

- buildings (s. 152(6)); and
- part trade use over time (s. 152(7)).

Section 152(6) states that:

> "If, over the period of ownership or any substantial part of the period of ownership, part of a building or structure is, and part is not, used for the purposes of a trade, this section shall apply as if the part so used, with any land occupied for purposes ancillary to the occupation and use of that part of the building or structure, were a separate asset, and subject to any necessary

apportionments of consideration for an acquisition or disposal of, or of an interest in, the building or structure and other land."

Section 152(7) goes on to state that:

"If the old assets were not used for the purposes of the trade throughout the period of ownership this section shall apply as if a part of the asset representing its use for the purposes of the trade having regard to the time and extent to which it was, and was not, used for those purposes, were a separate asset which had been wholly used for the purposes of the trade, and this subsection shall apply in relation to that part subject to any necessary apportionment of consideration for an acquisition or disposal of, or of the interest in, the asset."

Where rollover relief concerns a building, it is therefore possible for the relief to be restricted where:

- only part of the building is used for the trade; and/or
- the building was used in the trade, but only for certain times during the period of ownership.

In the case of other assets, partial rollover relief is available where the asset was only used in the trade at certain times during the period of ownership (i.e. there is not a concept of a "part" of an asset if that asset is not a building – at all relevant times it is either qualifying or not qualifying).

Note that the period of ownership of an asset for rollover relief purposes is considered to be the period of beneficial ownership and possession – see CG 60292.

Example 1 – partial business use of building

Cindy purchases a building to use in her trade for £200,000 in March 2015. She uses the building 75% of the time for her trade and uses it 25% privately.

In March 2022, Cindy sells the building for £500,000, resulting in a gain of £300,000.

In December 2023, Cindy purchases a new building for £500,000 and uses the building 90% of the time in her trade.

To calculate the rollover relief available, two separate calculations are required.

Step 1 – identify the capital gain arising on disposal of the original asset

The capital gain arising on the disposal of the original building should be apportioned according to business and non-business use; effectively the building is treated as being two separate assets, one asset qualifying for rollover relief, the other not.

Gain on disposal – business portion

	£
Proceeds on sale (£500,000 x 75%)	375,000
Less: base cost (£200,000 x 75%)	(150,000)
Capital gain	225,000

Gain on disposal – private portion

	£
Proceeds on sale (£500,000 x 25%)	125,000
Less: base cost (£200,000 x 25%)	(50,000)
Capital gain	75,000

The private portion of the gain (the £75,000) will be chargeable to CGT. No rollover relief is available, as this portion of the gain does not qualify.

To determine how much of the business portion of the gain of £225,000 is eligible for rollover relief, we proceed to step 2.

Step 2 – identify the proceeds reinvested

The new building was purchased for £500,000, with 90% business use and 10% private use. The cost of the new building should also be split into two separate parts – a qualifying business part, and a non-qualifying non-business part.

In this case, the cost of the business part is £450,000 (90% x £500,000) while the cost of the non-business part is £50,000 (10% x £500,000).

Once we have identified the cost of the business portion of the building, we can determine whether proceeds have been fully reinvested.

In this case, the proceeds on sale of the business part of the old building were £375,000, and the cost of the business part of the new building is £450,000. The proceeds on sale have, therefore, been fully reinvested, and full rollover relief (on the business part of the building) is available.

Following a claim to rollover relief, the base cost of the new building is reduced as follows:

Base cost

	Business use	Private use	Total
	£	£	£
Purchase price (£500,000 x 90%/10%)	450,000	50,000	500,000
Less: rollover relief	(225,000)	n/a	(225,000)
Revised base cost	225,000	50,000	275,000

Example 2 – partial relief by time

Sally purchases some fixed plant on 1 June 2010 for £50,000. She sells it on 31 May 2021 for £150,000, leaving an initial gain of £100,000.

During her ownership, Sally used the fixed plant exclusively in her trade between 1 June 2010 and 31 May 2018, exclusively for private purposes between 1 June 2018 and 31 May 2020, and then exclusively in her trade again between 1 June 2020 and 31 May 2021.

In December 2021, Sally buys qualifying freehold land for £140,000, used 100% for business purposes.

Step 1 – identify the capital gain arising on disposal of the original asset

The capital gain arising on the disposal of the original fixed plant should be apportioned based on when it was used for trading and private purposes.

Sally used the fixed plant exclusively in her trade between 1 June 2010 and 31 May 2018, and between 1 June 2020 and 31 May 2021 – nine years in total. Sally used the asset exclusively for private purposes between 1 June 2018 and 31 May 2020 – two years in total. A just and reasonable apportionment would therefore be 9/11th for business use, and 2/11th for non-business use.

Gain on disposal – business portion

	£
Proceeds on sale (£150,000 x 9/11)	122,727
Less: base cost (£50,000 x 9/11)	(40,909)
Capital gain	81,818

Gain on disposal – private portion

	£
Proceeds on sale (£150,000 x 2/11)	27,273
Less: base cost (£50,000 x 2/11)	(£9,091)
Capital gain	18,182

The private portion of the gain (£18,182) will be immediately chargeable to CGT. No rollover relief is available as this portion of the gain does not qualify.

To determine how much of the business portion of the gain of £81,818 is eligible for rollover relief, we proceed to step 2.

Step 2 – identify the proceeds reinvested

The new land was purchased for £140,000 and is exclusively occupied and used in the trade.

The proceeds on sale of the business part of the fixed plant were £122,727, and the cost of the land is £140,000. The proceeds on sale of have therefore been fully reinvested, and full rollover relief (on the business part of the gain arising on disposal of the fixed plant) is available.

Following a claim to rollover relief, the base cost of the land is reduced as follows:

	£
Purchase price	£140,000
Less: rollover relief	(£81,818)
Revised base cost	£58,182

It is also quite possible for an asset (if it is a building) to have been partly used in the trade throughout its ownership, and to have been used at set times in the trade during ownership (in other words, both examples 1 and 2 above apply).

In such cases, the same approach as in the examples above would be taken – i.e. identify:

- the business part of the building that has been disposed of (taking into account both the time the asset has been used in the business, and the percentage of business use during ownership);
- how much of the proceeds on sale of the business part of the original building have been reinvested in the purchase of the business portion of the new asset; and
- how much rollover relief to apply to the business portion of the new qualifying asset.

Any apportionments should be made on a just and reasonable basis.

Law: TCGA 1992, s. 152(6), (7)
Guidance: CG 60292

11.7   Depreciating assets

11.7.1   Definitions and examples

For the purposes of rollover relief, a depreciating asset is one that is either:

- a wasting asset within the definition of s. 44; or
- an asset with a maximum life of 60 years (i.e. assets that will become wasting assets within ten years).

Common examples of depreciating assets are fixed plant and machinery, as well as leases of 60 years or less.

However, where land and buildings are concerned, there are a couple of points to consider.

Although, for rollover relief purposes, land and buildings are separate assets (see **11.3.5**), when identifying whether an asset is a depreciating asset, the life expectancy of both a building and land is determined by the length of tenure of the land on which the building stands. CG 60285 gives the example of a building that is constructed on leasehold land with a term remaining of less than 60 years; this is a depreciating asset.

Freehold land is not considered a depreciating asset. However, a building on freehold land can be considered as such if its expected life is 60 years or less (e.g. as a result of planning permissions/other legal obligations).

Where fixed plant and machinery is part of the fabric of a building (e.g. a lift), then it is considered to be part of the building rather than a separate asset. In such cases, fixed plant and machinery may not be considered a depreciating asset (see **11.3.7**).

Law: TCGA 1992, s. 154, 155
Guidance: CG 60285

11.7.2   Application of rollover relief

Where a person purchases a depreciating asset, rollover relief is not given in the same way as outlined in **11.5**.

Rather than effectively deducting the amount of gain on the sale of the old asset from the base cost of the new asset, the gain arising on disposal of the old asset is held over (or "frozen"), and the base cost of the new depreciating asset is not adjusted.

The held-over gain then becomes assessable at the earliest of the following three events:

- the new asset is sold;
- the new asset ceases to be used in the trade (however, where cessation of use arises due to the death of the claimant, this is not an occasion of charge); and
- ten years after the new asset was acquired.

In practice, this means that the latest the gain may be held over is ten years after its purchase (unless the gain is "parked" – see **11.7.3**).

Example

Sean sells a building used exclusively in his trade in October 2021. Proceeds on sale are £300,000, with a gain on disposal of £100,000.

Sean purchases a depreciating asset for use in his trade for £250,000 in January 2021.

If Sean claims rollover relief, the computation of the relief is as follows:

Step 1 – Identify if any proceeds have not been reinvested

In this example, £50,000 of proceeds are not reinvested in the purchase of the depreciating asset. This £50,000 will be immediately chargeable to CGT in 2021-22.

Step 2 – Identify the rolled-over gain

The amount of gain eligible for rollover relief is £50,000 (being the gain on disposal of the original asset of £100,000 less the £50,000 of proceeds not reinvested).

Step 3 – Calculate the base cost of the new depreciating asset

The cost of the depreciating asset is £250,000. As the new asset is a depreciating asset, the base cost is not adjusted.

Instead, the £50,000 of rollover relief is effectively set aside and frozen. The base cost of the depreciating asset remains £250,000.

The held-over gain of £50,000 will crystallise at the earliest of when:

- the depreciating asset is sold;

- the depreciating asset ceases to be used in the trade; and

- January 2031, being ten years after the depreciating asset was acquired.

Sean subsequently sells the depreciating asset in January 2025 for £400,000.

A gain on sale of £150,000 would arise (being £400,000 less £250,000).

The sale of the depreciating asset also crystallises the gain of £50,000 that was held over on the sale of the building in October 2021.

This leads to total chargeable gains of £200,000 in 2024-25.

It is worth repeating that this difference in rollover relief treatment for depreciating assets only applies where a depreciating asset is *acquired*. It does not apply where a depreciating asset is sold and a non-depreciating asset is acquired; in such cases, rollover relief would be calculated as discussed at **11.5**.

11.7.3   *Parking*

There is a further nuance to rollover relief for depreciating assets that can provide an effective planning tool.

Take the following situation:

- an old qualifying business asset (Asset 1) is sold;
- a new qualifying depreciating asset (Asset 2) is acquired and the gain on sale of Asset 1 is held over; and
- a further non-depreciating asset (Asset 3) is acquired before the held-over gain crystallises.

In such a case, it is possible for the gain that was initially held over on disposal of Asset 1 to be rolled over into the base cost of Asset 3. This is commonly referred to as "parking" as, in essence, the gain arising from the sale of Asset 1 is "parked" with Asset 2 until the non-depreciating asset (Asset 3) is purchased. This can extend the amount of time by which a gain can be deferred.

Note that the other conditions to qualify for relief remain unchanged, as do the usual time limits to make a claim (see **11.3** and **11.8**).

Once a claim is made to roll over the gain from Asset 1 into the base cost of Asset 3, the initial rollover relief claim made in respect of Asset 2 is effectively treated as withdrawn.

Example 1 – adapted from CG 60285

In March 2017 Emma buys a freehold shop for £150,000 which she uses and occupies exclusively for trade purposes until March 2022, when it is sold for £298,000. The chargeable gain on the disposal is £148,000.

Also in March 2022, Emma acquires a 50-year lease of a larger shop at a cost of £320,000. She moves the trade to the new premises and claims rollover relief. In March 2024, Emma assigns the lease for £350,000.

The sale of the first shop should be dealt with as if the disposal consideration were reduced by £148,000 to £150,000. Because the new asset is a depreciating asset, the gain of £148,000 is held over.

On assignment of the lease, the chargeable gain on the second shop is computed in the normal way. In addition, the held-over gain of £148,000 is assessed as accruing at the date of the assignment.

However, if in February 2024 Emma buys the freehold of a third shop for £340,000 and makes a claim, the cost of that shop should be reduced by

£148,000 to £192,000 and the held-over gain will not become chargeable in 2023-24.

Partial reinvestment

If the reinvestment in Asset 2 is insufficient (see **11.6.2**) then part of the original gain will be immediately charged to tax and only the balance will be parked. The parked element can then be rolled over on a subsequent investment in Asset 3, but the amount initially charged will remain chargeable (subject, of course, to any other reinvestment being made within the appropriate time limits based on the original disposal of Asset 1).

Example 2 – adapted from CG 60285

In March 2022 Dan sells a freehold shop for £200,000, realising a gain of £60,000. In 2024 he acquires an item of fixed machinery for £180,000 and claims relief. The held-over gain is £40,000, being the balance of the gain (£60,000 – £20,000) after accounting for the proceeds that have not been re-invested (£200,000 – £180,000). The chargeable gain in 2021-22 is therefore £20,000.

In February 2026, while the machinery is still being used in the trade, he acquires a further freehold shop for £260,000 and makes a claim to apply s. 154(4). The gain that can be rolled over is limited to £40,000. The cost of the new freehold shop is reduced to £220,000 and the chargeable gain in 2021-22 is not affected.

Where full rollover relief has been given (i.e. there has been full reinvestment of proceeds from the sale of Asset 1 in the acquisition of Asset 2) consideration must still be given as to how much of the gain held over in Asset 2 can be set against the cost of Asset 3 (i.e. the new non-depreciating asset).

For example, if there has been a partial reinvestment of proceeds from the disposal of Asset 1 compared to the cost of Asset 3, the held-over gain is split into two separate parts – one part deducted from the base cost of the new non-depreciating asset, and the other part remaining held over until one of the three crystallisation events occurs.

Example 3

In March 2022, Maddie sells a qualifying freehold shop for £200,000 and realises a gain on disposal of £150,000.

At the same time, Maddie acquires a qualifying depreciating asset for £250,000. As proceeds have been fully reinvested, the gain on disposal of the freehold shop of £150,000 is held over until a crystallisation event occurs.

In March 2024, Maddie disposes of the depreciating asset for £300,000. This is a crystallisation event.

Just before selling the depreciating asset, Maddie acquires a new qualifying freehold shop for £180,000. If Maddie claims to roll over the gain from Asset 1 to Asset 3 (following the practice of "parking") £20,000 of the held-over gain would be chargeable in 2023-24, being the amount of proceeds not reinvested between Asset 1 (£200,000) and Asset 3 (£180,000).

The cost of the new freehold shop can therefore be reduced by £130,000 (being the gain on sale of Asset 1 of £150,000 less £20,000).

Law: TCGA 1992, s. 154
Guidance: CG 60285

11.8   Making a rollover relief claim

11.8.1   Introduction

A claim for rollover relief may be made as part of, or outside of, a tax return. However, HMRC do state that, wherever possible, the claim should be attached to the tax return to which it relates (or an amendment to that return).

Guidance: CG 60310

11.8.2   Claiming in a tax return

Persons who complete an income tax self-assessment return can complete form HS290 and attach it to the CGT summary pages.

When completing the CGT summary pages of the return, code ROR should be entered in box 8 and/or box 20 to indicate that a claim for rollover relief is being made. This is unless more than one code applies, in which case code MUL should be used (see HMRC's capital gains summary notes and form HS290 for further information). See **11.8.5** for provisional rollover relief claims.

Where multiple claims are being made, multiple copies of the form may be used.

Note that form HS290 is optional; it is possible to make a claim in any form, providing it is in writing and identifies the following:

- the claimant;
- the claimant's unique taxpayer reference (UTR) number;
- the asset(s) disposed of;
- the date of disposal of each asset(s);
- the consideration received for the disposal of the asset(s);
- the asset(s) that have been acquired;
- the dates of acquisition of the asset(s), or the dates on which unconditional contracts for the acquisition of the asset(s) were entered into;
- the consideration given for the asset(s); and
- the amount of consideration received for the disposal of each specified asset(s) that has been reinvested in the acquisition of the replacement asset(s).

Guidance: CG 60310; Form HS290; Form HS290 guidance; HMRC CGT summary notes

11.8.3   *Claiming outside a tax return*

It is possible for a rollover relief claim to be made outside of a tax return.

The claim should be signed by the claimant and sent to the capital gains general enquiries postal address (Capital Gains Tax Queries, HMRC, BX9 1AS, UK).

11.8.4   *Time limits for claims*

Broadly, the time limit is four years from the end of the tax year to which the claim relates.

However, it is possible for the old and new asset to be sold/acquired in different tax years.

As a result, "tax year" should be taken to be the later of when the old asset is sold or the new one is acquired.

Example

Camilla makes a disposal during 2021-22 and made a qualifying purchase during 2020-21. The time limit to make a rollover relief claim is 5 April 2026.

11.8.5   Provisional claims

Section 153A allows a provisional rollover relief claim to be made where a trader has disposed of an old asset and intends to use whole or part of the consideration to reinvest in the purchase of a new qualifying asset (see **11.3.1**) within the qualifying timeframe (see **11.3.2**).

The provisional claim should be made in the tax return for the chargeable period in which the disposal of the old asset takes place.

The taxpayer can also choose to make a provisional rollover relief claim using form HS290. The relevant code within box 8 and/or box 20 of the capital gains summary pages is PRO, or MUL where more than one code applies (see HMRC CGT summary notes for further information).

Alternatively, a claim can be made in writing specifying:

- the claimant;
- the claimant's UTR number;
- the asset(s) disposed of;
- the date of disposal of the asset(s);
- the consideration received for the disposal of the asset(s); and
- the amount of the consideration received for the disposal of each of the specified assets that is to be reinvested in the new asset(s).

As noted above, where a provisional claim is made, it must be attached to the tax return for the year in which the old asset was sold. The tax return should also be completed as though an actual acquisition of the new asset had occurred and an actual rollover relief claim made for the amount specified (in other words, full or partial rollover relief is calculated, depending on factors such as whether proceeds are to be fully reinvested – see **11.6.2**).

Law: TCGA 1992, s. 153A
Guidance: CG 60310

Effect of a provisional claim

Where a provisional claim has effect, no tax is payable by the claimant in respect of the disposal of the old asset (unless rollover relief is only partially available).

A provisional claim will cease to have effect when any of the following occur (the earliest taking priority):

- an actual claim to rollover relief is made under s. 152 or 153;
- the claimant notifies HMRC of a change of intention and that he or she will no longer reinvest (i.e. the provisional claim is withdrawn); and
- the "relevant day", which is three years from the 31 January following the tax year in which the disposal of the old asset takes place.

Where a provisional rollover relief claim is withdrawn, or the provisional claim lapses by reference to the relevant day, the claimant will have to pay the amount of tax that had been deferred, along with interest calculated from the date on which the tax was originally due to be paid, to the date on which it is actually paid.

Example 1 – provisional claim for full relief

Joe sells a qualifying asset in July 2021 for £75,000, realising a gain on disposal of £50,000.

He makes a provisional claim for rollover relief under s. 153A. As part of the provisional claim, he confirms he intends to reinvest the full amount of the disposal proceeds when purchasing the new asset.

The gain of £50,000, which would otherwise be chargeable to tax, is deferred.

Example 2 – provisional claim for partial relief

Penny sells an old qualifying asset for £30,000 on 15 May 2021 and makes a gain of £25,000. Penny makes a provisional claim for rollover relief under s. 153A.

As part of the provisional claim, Penny confirms that she only intends to reinvest £20,000 in acquiring new qualifying assets.

Tax on £15,000 of the gain (being £25,000 – (£30,000 – £20,000)) can be deferred.

As £10,000 of the disposal proceeds are not being reinvested, £10,000 of the gain is chargeable to tax in 2021-22.

Example 3 – provisional claim withdrawn

Billy sells an old qualifying asset in June 2021 for £30,000 and realises a gain on disposal of £10,000.

A provisional claim for rollover relief is made under s. 153A. As part of the provisional claim, Billy confirms that he intends to reinvest the full amount of the disposal proceeds when purchasing the new asset.

Despite intending to buy a new qualifying asset, Billy realises during the 2023-24 tax year that he does not, in fact, need to purchase the replacement asset. Billy notifies HMRC that he is withdrawing his provisional rollover relief claim.

The original gain of £10,000 that was deferred becomes payable, with interest accruing from 31 January 2023 (when payment should have originally been made) until Billy pays the tax owing.

11.9   Partnerships

11.9.1   *Nature of a partnership*

Subject to very limited exceptions, a partnership (whether a general, limited, or limited liability partnership (LLP)) is considered transparent for income tax and CGT purposes.

In other words, it is necessary to "look through" the partnership, and the partnership's underlying partners/members are subject to tax on their allocation of the partnership's income and gains (for further information on partnership taxation, see **Chapter 17**).

11.9.2   *Calculating relief*

The above transparency principle means that a partnership cannot ordinarily make a claim for rollover relief on its own behalf. Instead, a rollover relief claim may be made by a partner in that partnership, in relation to that partner's interest in the old and new assets respectively. Note that the old/new assets that form the rollover relief claim may be used for trade purposes either by the partner personally, or in partnership.

When calculating the amount of rollover relief a partner is eligible for, it is necessary to determine how much consideration on disposal of the old asset, and how much of base cost of the new asset, is attributable to each partner.

Example

A and B are in partnership and have for many years split profits and gains equally.

A and B acquired a building for use in their trade in April 2005, purchasing it for £200,000 (divided equally).

In August 2021, the building is sold for £300,000.

In July 2021, a new building is purchased for use in the partnership trade for £380,000, with A taking an interest of 80% in the new building and B a 20% interest.

The calculation of the amount of rollover relief available to each partner should be broken down into the following steps.

Step 1 – Calculate the gain arising to each partner on disposal of the building in August 2021

Ratio: 50/50	A £	B £
Proceeds on sale (£300,000 x 50%)	150,000	150,000
Less: base cost (£200,000 x 50%)	(100,000)	100,000)
Gain on sale	50,000	50,000

Step 2 – Calculate the cost of the new asset for each partner

Ratio: 80/20	A £	B £
Purchase price (£380,000 x 80%/20%)	304,000	76,000

Step 3 – Calculate the amount of rollover relief due

First, it is necessary to determine whether the proceeds on sale of the old building have been fully reinvested into the purchase of the new building.

For A – proceeds on sale were £150,000 and the cost of the new building was £304,000. Proceeds have been fully reinvested, and full rollover relief is available.

This means that A's gain of £50,000 can be rolled into the base cost of the new asset, leaving A with an adjusted base cost of £254,000 (£304,000 – £50,000) for the new building.

For B – proceeds on sale were £150,000 and the cost of the new building was £76,000. Proceeds have not been fully reinvested, as £74,000 has not been reinvested. In this instance, no rollover relief will be available for B, as the proceeds not reinvested are higher than the original gain of £50,000. This means that, for B, the gain of £50,000 will be immediately chargeable to CGT (see the example in **11.6.2** for further explanation of this point).

Guidance: CG 62093

11.9.3   Statement of practice D11

It is also worth noting the short SP D11, which states that, provided the other conditions for rollover relief are satisfied, relief is available to the owner of assets that are let to a trading or professional partnership of which the individual partner is a member, and that are used for the purposes of the partnership trade or profession.

This means rollover relief remains available even in cases where the partnership pays rent to a partner to use an asset in the partnership trade.

Law: TCGA 1992, s. 59, 59A
Guidance: SP D11; CG 60286

11.9.4   Limited liability partnerships

As mentioned in **11.9.1**, an LLP is also typically considered to be transparent for income tax and CGT purposes. This means that, when determining the amount of rollover relief available to a member of an LLP, the same process should be followed as outlined in **11.9.2**.

However, there are specific circumstances which, when met, cause an LLP to become opaque (i.e. transparencyfalls away and the LLP is taxed as a body corporate) – see **Chapter 17**.

When it comes to rollover relief, s. 156A outlines that, where an LLP ceases to trade and, immediately before the cessation, a member of the LLP holds any deferred gains by virtue of a rollover relief claim, that member shall be treated as if a chargeable gain equal to the amount of deferred gain accrued to the member immediately before the cessation (i.e. immediately before the LLP's transparent tax status ceases to apply).

This charging provision applies regardless of whether the rollover relief claim was made under s. 152 or 153, or the gain was held over on acquisition of a depreciating asset under s. 154.

Law: TCGA 1992, s. 156A

11.10 Furnished holiday lettings

11.10.1   General rules

Rollover relief is available to persons who carry on a trade, with "trade" given the same meaning as for income tax purposes.

This means that activities that are considered trades, such as the commercial letting of furnished holiday lettings (FHL), are also eligible for rollover relief.

One of the quirks of the legislation is that all FHLs situated in the UK are treated as a single UK FHL trade, while all FHLs situated within the EEA (which does not include the UK) are treated as a single EEA FHL business. Usually, the two trades must be kept separate (e.g. no losses on a UK FHL business may be used against profits of an EEA FHL business).

However, s. 152(8) provides that, where a person, either successively or at the same time, carries on two or more trades, for rollover relief purposes the trades are considered a single trade. For example, this means that a gain arising on disposal of a UK FHL can actually be rolled over against the purchase of a new EEA FHL (or *vice versa*) provided the conditions within s. 152(8) are met.

For further information, see *Furnished Holiday Lettings: A Tax Guide* from Claritax Books.

Law: TCGA 1992, s. 152(8)

11.10.2   Private residence relief

The other point to bear in mind with rollover relief and FHLs is instances where:

- a gain has been rolled over under s. 152 or 153 TCGA against the base cost of FHL accommodation; and
- that accommodation is subsequently sold and the gain is eligible for PRR under s. 222 TCGA (see **Chapter 9**).

On the disposal of that accommodation, the amount of PRR available under s. 223 is restricted to the part of the chargeable gain that exceeds the amount of the gain rolled over. An example is provided by HMRC at CG 60287.

Law: TCGA 1992, s. 222, 223, 241(6), 241A(8)
Guidance: CG 60287

11.11 Personal companies

Where an individual disposes of an old qualifying asset and acquires a new qualifying asset, and the trade in question is carried on by that individual's personal company at the time both of disposal and acquisition, rollover relief is still available.

The definition of personal company here is a company where the individual can exercise at least 5% of the voting rights in a personal capacity.

Where s. 152(8) is being relied upon for relief (i.e. two or more trades treated as a single trade) the trades need to be carried on by the same personal company in order to access rollover relief.

Law: TCGA 1992, s. 152(8), 157
Guidance: CG 60260

11.12 Non-residents

Non-residents are eligible for rollover relief in specific circumstances. For example, rollover relief can be available where a non-resident person disposes of assets that are chargeable assets at the time of disposal, provided the new assets are also chargeable assets immediately after they are acquired.

An asset is a chargeable asset where it would be chargeable to CGT under s. 1A(3).

Rollover relief may be available where a person first disposes of the old asset when non-resident, but is resident in the UK when subsequently acquiring the new asset. There are exceptions to this, namely where, immediately after the new assets are acquired:

- the person is a dual resident; and
- the new assets are prescribed assets (i.e. by virtue of a double taxation agreement, the individual is not liable to tax on gains arising on disposal of the asset in the UK).

There is a separate legislative provision in s. 159A regarding the availability of rollover relief where there is a disposal of interests in UK land by non-residents.

Broadly, rollover relief is available where the old asset disposed of is an interest in UK land (under s. 1C) and it is a chargeable asset (as above), and the new asset acquired is also an interest in UK land.

Law: TCGA 1992, s. 159, 159A
Guidance: CG 60260

12. Holdover relief

12.1 Introduction

Ordinarily, where an asset is gifted outright (i.e. for no consideration) or where an asset is sold at less than market value, the provisions within TCGA 1992, s. 17 apply, such that the donor is considered to have disposed of the asset at market value.

There are exceptions to this, such as a gift made to a spouse or civil partner – see **3.2.6** for further information.

This means that situations can arise where, in the absence of any reliefs, a donor ends up with a capital gain when, in reality, little or no consideration has been given for the asset.

Relief is available in such situations in two ways, under:

- s. 165 – relief for gifts of business assets; and
- s. 260 – gifts on which inheritance tax (IHT) is chargeable.

These two reliefs are commonly referred to as "holdover" or "gift" relief. For the purposes of this chapter, we refer to the relief as "holdover relief".

Strictly, a gift of an asset means that the asset has been given to the donee for no consideration. However, holdover relief can also apply in instances where below market consideration is paid by the donee to the donor (see **12.6.2**). In this chapter, any reference to a "gift" includes an asset gifted outright or an asset where the consideration received is less than market value.

Both s. 165 and s. 260 operate broadly in the same manner, by rolling the gain that would have arisen on the donor against the base cost of the asset in the donee's hands (i.e. deducting the gain from the base cost – see **12.5**).

It is important to note from the outset that relief under s. 260 takes precedence over relief under s. 165.

Holdover relief can assist numerous taxpayers and businesses. For example, s. 165 can provide effective relief where parents are considering passing on business assets such as shares to their children. It may also be attractive as an alternative to incorporation relief (see **Chapter 13**) in some instances.

As the mechanism of relief under s. 165 and s. 260 operates in broadly the same manner, this chapter primarily focuses on holdover relief as it operates under s. 165, in sections **12.2** to **12.12**. Consideration is given to the mechanics of relief under s. 260 at **12.13**.

Law: TCGA 1992, s. 17, 165, 260
Guidance: CG 66450

12.2   The donor

There are two parties to a holdover relief claim: the donor and the donee (referred to in the legislation as transferor and transferee respectively).

The legislation states that a donor should be an individual or the trustee of a settlement. While companies cannot be donors, they can be donees (see **12.3**).

Although the operation of holdover relief is broadly the same whether the donor is an individual or trustee, any differences are highlighted in the relevant sections of this chapter.

There is no requirement that a donor must be UK tax resident. However, a non-UK resident donor may only claim holdover relief on disposals of certain assets. This is discussed in greater detail at **12.9**.

Law: TCGA 1992, s. 165(1); Sch. 7, para. 2
Guidance: CG 66882

12.3   The donee

12.3.1   Introduction

While there are restrictions on who may be a donor, the types of entities that may receive a gifted asset as donee and access holdover relief are broader.

12.3.2   Individuals

Generally, an individual donee should be UK tax resident. There are exceptions (see **12.9**).

12.3.3   Trustees

A trustee donee should again generally be UK tax resident. There are exceptions (see **12.9**).

There are other instances where a trustee donee is unable to access holdover relief (see **12.10**).

12.3.4   Partnerships and limited liability partnerships

Due to the transparency principle of most partnerships (see **Chapter 17**), where a partnership (including an LLP) is the donee and receives a gifted asset, the transaction is treated as if there were a series of individual gifts to each partner/member of the partnership, based on each partner's interest in the partnership.

See **12.6.7** for the holdover implications where an LLP becomes opaque for tax purposes.

12.3.5   Companies

As with other donees, generally a company donee should be UK tax resident to qualify for holdover relief under s. 165. There are similar exceptions for companies as for individuals and trustees (see **12.9.2**).

Another instance where a company cannot access holdover relief as donee is where there is a gift of shares or securities (see **12.6.8**).

Companies are also restricted when it comes to holdover relief under s. 260 (see **12.13.3**).

Law: TCGA 1992, s. 166, 167, 167A
Guidance: CG 66883

12.4   Qualifying assets

12.4.1   Introduction

Holdover relief is available on the disposal of:

- assets used in a trade, profession or vocation (see **12.4.2**);
- shares or securities of a trading company (see **12.4.3**);
- settled property (see **12.4.4**); and
- agricultural property (see **12.4.5**).

12.4.2   Assets used in a trade, profession or vocation

Section 165(2) specifies that for an asset (or an interest in an asset) to qualify for holdover relief, the asset must be used in the trade, profession or vocation of:

- the donor;
- the donor's personal company (see below); or
- a member of a trading group of which the holding company is the donor's personal company (these terms are defined below).

Law: TCGA 1992, s. 165(2)

Trade, profession or vocation

The concept of trade, profession or vocation has the same meaning as for income tax purposes – see *Income Tax* 2021-22, from Claritax Books.

There is also specific allowance for the occupation of woodlands to be included as a trade for holdover relief purposes under s. 165, where the woodlands are managed by the occupier on a commercial basis and with a view to the realisation of profits.

In this chapter these are all hereafter collectively referred to as a "trade".

Law: TCGA 1992, s. 165(8), (9)

Personal company

For holdover relief purposes, "personal company", in relation to an individual, means a company where the individual can exercise at least 5% of the voting rights.

Law: TCGA 1992, s. 165(8)(a)

Trading group

A "trading group" is a group of companies:

- one or more of whose members carry on trading activities; and
- the activities of whose members, taken together, do not include, to a substantial extent, activities other than trading activities.

Law: TCGA 1992, s. 165(8), 165A

Holding company

A "holding company" is a company that has one or more 51% subsidiaries.

Law: TCGA 1992, s. 165(8), 165A

12.4.3   Shares and securities

Holdover relief is also available where the asset gifted is shares or securities of a trading company (see below), or the holding company of a trading group (see **12.4.2**) provided:

- the shares or securities are not listed on a recognised stock exchange; or
- the trading company or holding company is the donor's personal company (see **12.4.2**).

Law: TCGA 1992, s. 165(2)

Trading company

A "trading company" is a company that carries on trading activities, and whose activities do not include, to a substantial extent, activities other than trading activities.

Law: TCGA 1992, s. 165(8), 165A

12.4.4   Settled property

Assets gifted by the trustees of a settlement can qualify for holdover relief where:

- the asset, or interest in the asset, is used for the purposes of a trade, profession or vocation (see **12.4.2**) carried on by:
  - o the trustees making the disposal; or
  - o a beneficiary who had an interest in possession in the settled property immediately before the disposal; or
- the asset is shares or securities of a trading company (see **12.4.3**), or the holding company of a trading group (see **12.4.2**), where:
  - o the shares or securities are not listed on a recognised stock exchange; or
  - o not less than 25% of the voting rights exercisable by shareholders of the company in general meeting are exercisable by the trustees at the time of the disposal.

Law: TCGA 1992, Sch. 7, para. 2
Guidance: CG 66884

12.4.5   *Agricultural property*

Where there is a gift of an asset (including an interest in an asset) that is agricultural property within the meaning of IHTA 1984, Pt. 5, Ch. 2, the disposal can still qualify for holdover relief under TCGA 1992, s. 165 even if the agricultural property is not used for the purposes of a trade.

Section 165(1) applies in relation to the disposal if:

- a reduction in respect of the asset is made under IHTA 1984, Pt. 5, Ch. 2 in relation to a chargeable transfer taking place on the occasion of the disposal;

- a reduction would have been so made if the gift had been a chargeable transfer; or

- a reduction would be so made but for the restrictions imposed by IHTA 1984, s. 124A (transfers within seven years before death of transferor).

While the above concerns the ability to claim holdover relief under s. 165, it should be remembered that s. 260 (see **12.13**), where available, takes priority.

Law: TCGA 1992, Sch. 7, para. 1, 3

12.5   Computation of relief

Under s. 165(4), where a claim for holdover relief is made in respect of a qualifying disposal, two adjustments are made:

- The amount of any chargeable gain which would accrue to the donor on the disposal is reduced by an amount equal to the held-over gain.

- The amount of the consideration for which the donee would be regarded as having acquired the asset is reduced by an amount equal to the held-over gain.

In practice, there are instances where the amount of relief might be restricted (see **12.6**).

The following example shows how holdover relief operates at its most fundamental level.

Example

In February 2022, Julie gifts a building used in her trade to her daughter Michelle for no consideration.

The market value of the building at the time of the gift is £500,000. Julie originally purchased the asset for £200,000.

If no claim for holdover relief were made, Julie would be subject to a capital gain on disposal of £300,000.

If both Julie and Michelle make a claim for holdover relief, then Julie's gain of £300,000 is reduced by £300,000, so that no gain arises to her.

In turn, Michelle is deemed to have acquired the building for a base cost of £200,000 (being £500,000 less £300,000). This will result in a higher capital gain for Michelle when the building is ultimately sold.

Law: TCGA 1992, s. 165(4)

12.6   Restrictions on relief

12.6.1   Introduction

In some situations, the amount of holdover relief may be restricted. This section considers the following scenarios:

- sale at undervalue (see **12.6.2**);
- non-trade use of assets (see **12.6.3**);
- non-trade use of buildings (see **12.6.4**);
- shares and securities (see **12.6.5**);
- use of asset at point of gift (see **12.6.6**);
- limited liability partnerships (see **12.6.7**); and
- other restrictions (see **12.6.8**).

12.6.2   Sale at undervalue

A donee may pay some consideration for the asset they receive. Where that consideration is less than the market value of the asset, a sale at undervalue has occurred.

Under s. 165(7), where there is actual consideration (less than market value at disposal) and that consideration exceeds the donor's allowable costs under s. 38, there is a restriction on the amount of gain that may be held over.

The restriction is equal to the amount of consideration exceeding the donor's allowable costs.

The amount of gain that is not held over is immediately charged to CGT.

Example

In January 2022, Carol sells a building to Oscar, which Carol has used exclusively in her trade. Carol originally acquired the building for £175,000.

Oscar pays Carol £200,000 for the building. At the date of the sale, the building is worth £300,000.

Step 1 – identify the capital gain arising on the disposal

The capital gain that would arise to Carol, in the absence of any claims for relief, would be £125,000, being the market value of the building of £300,000, less the building's cost of £175,000.

Step 2 – identify any excess proceeds

Carol received £200,000 for the building and has allowable costs of £175,000. This means she has excess proceeds of £25,000.

Step 3 – restrict the holdover relief

The amount of gain that may be held over is therefore restricted by £25,000 to £100,000.

Step 4 – calculate the gain arising

The gain arising to Carol, following a holdover relief claim, would be:

	£
Market value	300,000
Less cost	(175,000)
Gain	125,000
Less holdover relief s. 165	(100,000)
Gain chargeable	25,000

Step 5 – Calculate the base cost of the asset

The base cost of the building in Oscar's hands would, following a holdover relief claim, be:

	£
Market value	300,000
Less holdover relief s. 165	(100,000)
Base cost	200,000

Note that s. 165(7) only operates to restrict holdover relief where the consideration given exceeds the donor's allowable costs under s. 38.

Practically speaking, this means that if the consideration given is less than the donor's allowable costs, full holdover relief should be available, provided all other relevant conditions are met.

Example (continued)

Returning to the above example, let us say that Oscar instead gave Carol £150,000 as consideration.

As £150,000 is less than Carol's allowable costs under s. 38 (i.e. the £175,000 base cost) **Steps 2** and **3** are not relevant and there is no restriction on the amount of holdover relief available.

Following a holdover relief claim, Carol's position would be:

	£
Market value	300,000
Less cost	(175,000)
Gain	125,000
Less holdover relief s. 165	(125,000)
Gain chargeable	Nil

The base cost of the building in Oscar's hands would, following a holdover relief claim, be:

	£
Market value	300,000
Less holdover relief s. 165	(125,000)
Base cost	175,000

Trustees

Where the donor is a body of trustees, the above restriction under s. 165(7) does not apply where a disposal is deemed to arise on:

- a beneficiary becoming absolutely entitled to settled property under s. 71; or
- on the termination of a life interest on the death of the entitled person under s. 72.

Law: TCGA 1992, s. 71, 72, 165(7), and Sch. 7, para. 2(3)
Guidance: CG 66882

12.6.3   Non-trade use of assets

Where the asset gifted was used for the purposes of a trade (see **12.4.2**) relief under s. 165 is restricted if the asset has not been used in the donor's trade throughout the donor's period of ownership.

The amount of held-over gain in such cases is reduced by multiplying the gain by the fraction:

$$\frac{A}{B}$$

where:

- **A** = the number of days in the period of ownership during which the asset was used in the trade; and
- **B** = the total number of days in the whole period of ownership.

Example

Harry purchased an asset on 1 November 2010 for £30,000.

Harry's use of the asset was as follows:

- between November 2010 and October 2015, the asset was used in his trade;
- between November 2015 and October 2020, the asset was used for non-trade purposes; and
- since November 2020, the asset has been used in his trade.

On 1 November 2021, Harry gifts the asset to Sofia. The market value of the asset at that time is £100,000.

In the absence of any reliefs, the gain arising to Harry would be £70,000 (£100,000 – £30,000).

Where holdover relief is claimed under s. 165, the amount of relief available to Harry would be restricted by the formula A/B, i.e. by 2,191/4,018 days. This means the amount of holdover relief available is £38,171.

Following a holdover relief claim, Harry's position would be as follows:

	£
Market value	100,000
Less cost	(30,000)
Gain	70,000
Less holdover relief s. 165	(38,171)
Gain chargeable	31,829

Sofia's position, following a holdover relief claim, would be:

	£
Market value	100,000
Less holdover relief s. 165	(38,171)
Base cost	61,829

Exceptions

This restriction does not apply where:

- the gift is a chargeable transfer for IHT purposes and a reduction is made in respect of agricultural property under IHTA 1984, Pt. 5, Ch. 2;
- if the gift were a chargeable transfer, a reduction would have been so made; or
- a reduction would have been so made but for the restrictions imposed by IHTA 1984, s. 124A (transfers within seven years before death of transferor).

Law: TCGA 1992, Sch. 7, para. 5
Guidance: CG 66886

12.6.4   Non-trade use of buildings

Where the asset being disposed of is a building or structure, and only part of the building/structure was used in the donor's trade over the period of ownership, a just and reasonable apportionment, based on the fraction of trade use, is used to restrict the amount of gain eligible for holdover relief.

Example

Steve acquires a building in March 2018 for £125,000. Throughout his period of ownership, part of the building (60%) was used for trade purposes and the other 40% was used for non-trade purposes.

In April 2021, Steve gifts the building to his daughter Mia. At that time, the market value of the asset is £300,000, meaning a gain of £175,000.

If holdover relief is claimed, the amount of gain held over would be restricted, as only 60% of the gain is eligible.

Following a holdover relief claim, Steve's position would be:

	£
Market value	300,000
Less cost	(125,000)
Gain	175,000
Less holdover relief s. 165 (£175,000 x 60%)	(105,000)
Gain chargeable	70,000

Following a holdover relief claim, Mia's position would be:

	£
Market value	300,000
Less holdover relief s. 165	(105,000)
Base cost	195,000

The exceptions discussed at **12.6.3** also apply.

Law: TCGA 1992, s. 17, 38, 165(7), (8); Sch. 7, para. 6
Guidance: CG 66886

12.6.5   *Shares and securities*

Where shares are gifted, the company may hold assets that are not business assets.

If this is the case, and either:

- at any time within 12 months before the disposal, not less than 25% of the voting rights exercisable by shareholders of the company in general meeting are exercisable by the donor (where the trustees of a settlement are the donor); or
- the donor is an individual and, at any time within that period, the company is his or her personal company (see **12.4.2**),

the amount of the held-over gain is reduced by multiplying it by the fraction:

$$\frac{A}{B}$$

where:

- **A** = the market value on the date of the disposal of the chargeable business assets of the company; and
- **B** = the market value on that date of all the chargeable assets of the company.

Business asset

An asset (including an interest in an asset) is a business asset in relation to a company or a group (see *Holding company* below) if it is used for the purposes of a trade (see **12.4.2**) carried on by the company or by a member of the group.

Examples of assets that would not be used in a company's business are shares that are purchased for the purposes of yielding investment income, or an investment property.

Chargeable asset

An asset is a chargeable asset in relation to a company or a group at any time if, on a disposal at that time, a gain accruing to the company/member of the group would be a chargeable gain.

Examples of assets that a company may hold that are not chargeable include those that fall under the chattels rules, cash, or cars (see **Appendix 2**).

Example

Janine gifts shares in her personal company, Starlight Limited, to Michael. Janine acquired her shares for £1,000 and gifted them to Michael at a time when they were worth £115,000.

At the time of disposal, Starlight Limited's balance sheet was as follows:

- cash – £10,000;

- shares held for investment purposes – £5,000; and

- business premises – £100,000.

Cash is not a chargeable asset, and so is not considered further.

The shares are held for investment purposes, and so are not business assets.

The business premises are used in the company's trade and are therefore a business asset.

The amount of holdover relief available to Janine and Michael, in the absence of any restriction, would be £114,000 (£115,000 – £1,000).

Once the restriction is applied (by using the A/B formula above) the held-over gain becomes £108,571, being £114,000 multiplied by A/B, which is the business assets of £100,000 divided by the company's chargeable assets of £105,000 (£100,000 + £5,000).

Following a holdover relief claim, Janine's chargeable gain would be £5,429 (£114,000 – £108,571).

Holding company

Where the shares gifted are shares in the holding company of a trading group (see **12.4.2**), the restriction is calculated based on the chargeable assets and chargeable business assets of the whole group.

However, any ordinary share capital held by one group member in another group member does not count as a chargeable asset.

In addition, where the whole of the ordinary share capital of a 51% subsidiary of the holding company is not owned directly or indirectly by that company, the value of the chargeable assets of the subsidiary is reduced by multiplying it by the fraction:

$$\frac{A}{B}$$

where:

- **A** = the amount of the ordinary share capital of the subsidiary owned directly or indirectly by the holding company; and
- **B** = the whole of that share capital.

Law: TCGA 1992, Sch. 7, para. 7
Guidance: CG 66886

12.6.6   Use of asset at point of gift

While it is possible for an asset to be partly eligible for holdover relief under s. 165 where there has been an element of non-trade use (see **12.6.3** and **12.6.4**) relief is only available in instances where the qualifying asset is, at the point of the gift, being used in the trade.

Where an asset is not being used in the trade at all when it is gifted, holdover relief under s. 165 is not available.

It is worth underlining a distinction between relief under s. 165 and s. 260 at this stage, in that relief under s. 260 is not restricted to business assets – see **12.13**.

12.6.7   Limited liability partnerships

An LLP ceases to be considered transparent on the earlier of:

- the appointment of a liquidator; or
- the making of a winding-up order by the court.

If at this point a member of the LLP holds an asset (or an interest in an asset) that has been subject to a holdover claim (under either s. 165 or s. 260) then the gain held over is deemed to accrue to that member immediately before the LLP's transparent status ceases.

Law: TCGA 1992, s. 59A, 169A

12.6.8   Other restrictions

There are other specific circumstances in which holdover relief under s. 165 is denied. These include where:

- there is a disposal of shares or securities, and the donee is a company;
- there is a disposal of qualifying corporate bonds and a gain is deemed to accrue by virtue of s. 116(10)(b) (reorganisations, conversions and reconstructions, see **5.3.6**); and

- section 260(3) applies in relation to the disposal (or would apply if a claim for relief were made under that section). See **12.13** for more information.

Law: TCGA 1992, s. 165(3)

12.7   Claims

A claim for holdover relief must be made by both the donor and donee.

The exception to this is where the trustees of a settlement are the donee. In such cases, the claim should be made by just the donor.

Where a gift is made to a partnership or LLP, and the partnership is considered transparent for CGT purposes (this is likely to be the majority of partnerships/LLPs – see **Chapter 17**) a claim should be made by each of the partners who receive a share of the asset.

Irrespective of whether the claimants need to complete an income tax self-assessment return, the actual claim for holdover relief is made via form HS295 (relief for gifts and similar transactions). If the claimant does file self-assessment returns, the form can be included as an attachment to the relevant return.

HMRC have confirmed that, because of Covid-19 restrictions, at the time of writing the claim form can be completed using digital signatures, as opposed to physical signatures.

Claims for holdover relief must be made within four years from the end of the tax year in which the gift occurred.

Example

Martin gifts Danielle a business asset during the 2021-22 tax year and would like to claim holdover relief.

Both Martin and Danielle should make a claim for holdover relief under s. 165 by 5 April 2026.

Law: TMA 1970, s. 43
Guidance: CG 66889; https://tinyurl.com/xf9f43ah (digital signatures)

12.8   Valuations

Given that holdover relief, by its nature, involves a gift of an asset (or a disposal that is not at arm's length), it is necessary to determine the market value of the asset at the date of disposal to compute the amount of gain that can be held over.

HMRC's Statement of Practice (SP) 8/1992 confirms that, in many cases, the market value at disposal does not need to be agreed with HMRC provided that certain conditions are met, including that:

- a joint application is made by the donor and donee;
- details concerning the asset and its history (or alternatively a calculation incorporating informally estimated valuations if necessary) is provided; and
- a statement is given that both parties have satisfied themselves that the value of the asset at the date of transfer was in excess of the allowable expenditure to that date.

However, the SP does highlight that there are instances where a valuation may be required – namely where a holdover relief claim is restricted where there has been part business use or where shares are gifted in a company that has non-business assets (see **12.6.3** to **12.6.6**).

If a valuation is required, taxpayers will no doubt wish to obtain professional valuations. HMRC will normally involve the Valuation Office Agency (for gifted land in the UK) or the Shares and Assets Valuation (for unquoted shares and securities, other intangible assets – e.g. trademarks or goodwill – foreign shares, foreign residential property, bloodstock, chattels, boats, and aircrafts).

Guidance: SP 8/92; CG 66890

12.9   Residency

12.9.1   Individuals

There is no restriction on the residence status of an individual donor for holdover relief to apply (i.e. both UK residents and non-UK residents disposing of qualifying assets can make gifts of assets that are eligible for holdover relief).

However, holdover relief is – with exceptions – not available where the donee is not resident in the UK.

This exclusion from holdover relief also applies where the donee is an individual and, although they are resident in the UK, they:

- are regarded for the purposes of any double taxation relief arrangements as resident in a territory outside the UK; and
- by virtue of the arrangements, would not be liable in the UK to tax on a gain arising on a disposal of the asset occurring immediately after its acquisition.

The exception to this is where the asset gifted is a direct or indirect interest in UK land. In such cases, the donee may be non-UK resident (see **12.9.3**).

Law: TCGA 1992, s. 166

12.9.2   *Foreign-controlled companies*

A company, as established at **12.2**, is not eligible to be a donor for holdover relief purposes.

Although a company can be a donee for holdover relief purposes under s. 165 (see **12.13.3** for its application to relief under s. 260), holdover relief is denied where the donee:

- is a company controlled by a person who (or by persons each of whom) is not resident in the UK; and
- that person(s) is, or is connected with, the person making the disposal (under the connected persons rules in s. 286).

(FA 2021 introduced a small amendment ("is, or is connected" replacing the former "is connected") to clarify when holdover relief will be denied in these situations. This amendment has effect for disposals on or after 6 April 2021.)

A person who (either alone or with others) controls a company by virtue of holding assets relating to that, or any other, company and who is resident in the UK, is still regarded as not resident in the UK if:

- they are regarded for the purposes of any double taxation relief arrangements as resident in a territory outside the UK; and
- by virtue of the arrangements, they would not be liable in the UK to tax on a gain arising on a disposal of the assets.

Note that FA 2021 introduced a small amendment to the legislation to clarify when holdover relief will be denied in these situations.

Law: TCGA 1992, s. 167; FA 2021, s. 41
Guidance: CG 66883

12.9.3   *Gifts of direct or indirect interests in UK land*

Since April 2015, there has been a gradual movement to bring non-UK residents into the charge to UK tax in respect of disposals of direct or indirect interests in UK land.

Because of this, the remit of holdover relief has been expanded to bring gifts of such land into scope where gifts are made to/by non-UK residents. This means that, in such instances, the donor and donee can be non-residents, going against the general principles outlined in **12.3**.

The types of assets that are in scope for holdover relief (under both s. 165 and s. 260) include:

- gifts of a direct or indirect interest in UK land by a non-UK resident to a UK resident donee, where that disposal, save for any holdover relief claim, would be chargeable as an interest in UK land under s. 1A(3)(b) (see **Chapter 18**);
- gifts of assets that derive at least 75% of their value from UK land, which are made by a non-UK resident to a UK resident donee, where the non-resident donor has a substantial indirect interest in that land and would otherwise be chargeable under s. 1A(3)(c) (see **Chapter 18**); and
- gifts of a direct or indirect interest in UK land to a non-resident donee (irrespective of the residence status of the donor).

Law: TCGA 1992, s. 1A(3), 165(7A)(7D), 167A, 260(6ZA)-(6D), 261ZA
Guidance: CG 66884, 73922, 73930

12.9.4   *Emigration of donee*

There are also implications on the availability of holdover relief where a donee, who receives a gifted asset while UK resident, ceases to be UK resident within six years of the gift. See **12.11.2** for more information.

12.10 Trusts

12.10.1   *Gifts to settlor-interested settlements*

Holdover relief (whether under s. 165 or s. 260) is not available where there is a gift to the trustees of a settlor-interested settlement.

A settlement is settlor-interested if:

- the settlor (see **12.10.2**) or certain other related parties benefit in any way, these parties being the settlor's:
  - spouse;
  - civil partner;
  - minor child; or
  - minor step-child;

- there are arrangements under which a settlor may acquire an interest (see **12.10.3**); or

- in computing the gain on the gift in the absence of holdover relief, a deduction in the acquisition cost would be required in relation to a previous holdover relief claim by another individual; and immediately after the gift:

  o that individual has an interest in the settlement; or

  o an arrangement subsists that such an interest may or will be acquired by them.

There are exceptions, for example a settlement is not considered settlor-interested if the settlement is, or could be, a heritage maintenance fund within the meaning of ITA 2007, s. 508.

A similar exception is available if the terms of the settlement apply the property and income for the benefit of a disabled person. To qualify here, if one or more settlors is an interested settlor then each of these must be a disabled beneficiary immediately following the gift.

There are also instances where holdover relief may be clawed back if a settlement becomes settlor-interested. See **12.11.3** for further information.

Law: TCGA 1992, s. 169B, 169D
Guidance: CG 66883

12.10.2   Definition of settlor

The definition of a settlor for holdover relief purposes is very broad and is given in s. 169E.

A person is a settlor in relation to a settlement if:

- he or she is an individual; and

- the settled property consists of, or includes, property originating from that person (i.e. property provided by that settlor directly or indirectly for the purposes of the settlement, and property that wholly or partly represents that property or any part of it).

Property which a settlor has provided directly or indirectly is taken to include references to property which has been provided directly or indirectly by another person in pursuance of reciprocal arrangements with that settlor, but does not include references to property which that settlor has provided directly or indirectly in pursuance of reciprocal arrangements with another person.

12.10.3   Definition of interest in a settlement

An individual is considered to have an interest in a settlement if any of the following applies:

- any property which is or may at any time be part of the settlement, is, will, or may become payable to or applicable for the benefit of the individual or their spouse/civil partner;

- the individual or his or her spouse or civil partner enjoys a benefit deriving directly or indirectly from any property comprised in the settlement; or

- any property that is (or may at any time be) comprised in the settlement, is, will, or may become payable to (or applicable for the benefit of) the individual's dependent child, or the dependent child enjoys a benefit deriving directly or indirectly from any property comprised in the settlement.

"Any property" includes reference to any "derived property", which means:

- income from that property;
- property that directly or indirectly represents:
  - o   proceeds of that property; or
  - o   proceeds of income from that property; or
- income from property which is derived property by virtue of the above.

References to a spouse/civil partner do not include a spouse/civil partner from whom the individual is separated by way of court order, under a separation agreement, or in circumstances where the separation is likely to be permanent. Any widow or widower or surviving civil partner of the individual is similarly excluded.

Exceptions

Relief is still available, however, in the following circumstances:

- a term of a settlement relates to dependent children of an individual, at any time at which the individual has no dependent child;

- an amount becomes payable in the case of a marriage settlement or civil partnership settlement due to the death of both parties to the marriage or civil partnership and of all or any of the children of the family of the parties to the marriage or civil partnership; or
- an amount becomes payable to an individual following the death of their child where the child had become beneficially entitled to the property at an age not exceeding 25.

Law: TCGA 1992, s. 169B, 169E, 169F

12.11 Clawbacks

12.11.1 Introduction

There are two main instances in which holdover relief may be clawed back:

- the emigration of the donee from the UK (see **12.11.2**); and
- a settlement becomes settlor-interested (see **12.11.3**).

Each of these situations is considered in further detail below.

12.11.2 Emigration of donee

Where holdover relief is given (either under s. 165 or s. 260) in respect of a gift to an individual and:

- the donee is resident in the UK at the time of the gift; and
- while still holding the asset the donee ceases to be UK resident within the six years following the end of the year of assessment in which the relevant disposal was made,

the held-over gain becomes chargeable under s. 168, with the gain deemed to arise to the *donee* immediately before the cessation of their UK residency.

Example 1

In July 2021, Rupert gifts a business asset to Sarah, which is worth £50,000 at the time of the gift. Rupert has a capital gain of £15,000 following the gift, and a holdover relief claim is made by Rupert and Sarah to defer the gain.

Sarah is resident in the UK at the time of the gift. However, a few years later, in November 2023, she moves to France on a permanent basis.

As this is still within six years after the end of the tax year in which the gift was made (2021-22), the deferred gain of £15,000 becomes chargeable on Sarah as donee in the year she emigrates from the UK (2023-24).

Where the donee has already disposed of part of the asset (and that represents a proportion of the gain held over) only the remainder of the held-over gain becomes chargeable.

A transfer of the asset from the donee to their spouse or civil partner does not count as a disposal for this purpose (the transfer being at no gain/no loss under s. 58). However, any subsequent disposal of the asset by the recipient spouse/civil partner is treated as though a disposal had been made by the original donee.

Note that, if the donee becomes chargeable to CGT on the disposal of the gifted asset *after* a gain has been deemed to accrue under s. 168 then no reduction in the donee's acquisition cost needs to be made in respect of the held-over gain in the resulting computation.

Law: TCGA 1992, s. 168

Exceptions

There are exceptions to the clawback provision if:

- the asset is an interest in UK land (see below); or
- the reason the donee ceases to be UK resident is that they have an employment or office, all the duties of which are performed outside the UK, and they become UK resident again within three years and they have not disposed of the asset in that time.

Law: TCGA 1992, s. 168(5)

Interests in UK land

If the gift in question is an interest in UK land (within the meaning of TCGA 1992, s. 1C – see **Chapter 18**), and the donee emigrates from the UK and triggers the clawback provisions (see above), the donee may elect to delay the charge arising under s. 168 (i.e. the held-over gain does not become chargeable at the time they cease to be UK resident).

Instead, the whole or a corresponding part of the held-over gain is treated as accruing on a subsequent disposal by the donee of the whole (or part) of the interest in UK land.

This gain is in addition to any gain or loss that actually accrues on the subsequent disposal. Note the held-over gain is now effectively "frozen" and is no longer rolled over against the base cost; the base cost of the asset is now the unadjusted market value at the date of the gift.

Law: TCGA 1992, s. 168A

Recouping the tax

Where the conditions of s. 168 are met, the held-over gain becomes chargeable on the donee at the time immediately before they cease to be UK resident.

If the donee does not pay the tax due within 12 months beginning with the date the tax becomes payable, the donor can be assessed and charged (in the name of the donee) to all, or any part, of that tax.

However, HMRC can only make an assessment on the donor within the six years following the end of the tax year in which the gift was made.

In addition, if the donor pays the tax assessed on behalf of the donee, the donor is entitled to recover a corresponding sum from the donee.

Example 2

Continuing Example 1 above, Sarah, who emigrated to France within six years of receiving a gifted business asset, became assessable on the held-over gain of £15,000 in 2023-24 (the tax year she emigrated).

CGT on the gain should have been paid by 31 January 2025. However, Sarah decides that she does not wish to settle her UK tax liabilities.

If Sarah does not pay by 31 January 2026, HMRC can assess Rupert (the donor) to tax on Sarah's behalf.

Should Rupert pay the CGT due, he is entitled to recover the amount he paid from Sarah.

Law: TCGA 1992, s. 168(7)-(9)
Guidance: CG 66888

12.11.3   Settlement becomes settlor-interested

Section 169C operates to claw back/deny holdover relief where:

- a gift which qualified for holdover relief (whether under s. 165 or s. 260) is made by a donor to the trustees of a settlement; and

- that settlement becomes settlor-interested (by satisfying any of the three conditions outlined in **12.10.1**) within the "clawback period", i.e. the period starting after the relevant disposal is made and ending six years after the end of the tax year in which that disposal was made.

When these conditions are met, a chargeable gain equal to the amount that was originally held over is deemed to accrue to the donor. If the donor fails to pay the tax due within 12 months of it becoming due and payable, HMRC can assess the donee to recover the tax (see **12.12.5**).

Any subsequent chargeable gains/allowable losses of the trustees of the settlement, or any person whose title to any property derives directly or indirectly from them, are determined on the assumption that neither s. 165(4)(b) nor s. 260(3)(b) ever applied to that disposal, i.e. the base cost will not be reduced by the gain originally deferred.

The definitions of "settlor" and "interest in a settlement" are the same as at **12.10.2** and **12.10.3**.

Claim for holdover relief not already been made

As might be expected, should any of the conditions be satisfied for a settlement to become settlor-interested between the time at which the gift is made and the making of a holdover relief claim, then no such claim (whether under s. 165 or s. 260) will be allowed.

Exceptions

The above clawback provisions do not apply if the donor is an individual who dies before the settlement becomes settlor-interested.

Law: TCGA 1992, s. 169C
Guidance: CG 66888

12.12 Payment

12.12.1 General rules

Where full holdover relief is available, no CGT charge arises on the gift of the qualifying asset. Instead, the gain is effectively deferred until the gift is subsequently disposed of by the donee.

However, there are instances when CGT will still be due following a gift. This might be where:

- a gift does not qualify for holdover relief;
- holdover relief is only partially available; or
- holdover relief has been clawed back.

Where any CGT does become chargeable immediately following an asset being gifted (or arises following a clawback provision – see **12.11**), the tax is payable by reference to the usual payment deadline for the person concerned (see **Chapter 2**).

Example

In May 2021, Deepti disposes of a business asset to Michael, and a gain arises on disposal of £60,000. Full holdover relief is not available, as Deepti receives some consideration (below market value) for the asset from Michael (see **12.6.2**).

As a result, the amount of holdover relief that she can claim is restricted to £45,000, leaving a gain immediately chargeable of £15,000.

The £15,000 gain will be chargeable on Deepti in the 2021-22 tax year. The deadline to pay the CGT is 31 January 2023.

However, there are instances when a person can settle their CGT in instalments, as outlined below.

12.12.2   *Consideration payable by instalments*

Gifts typically do not involve consideration. See, however, **2.4.4** for further information if relevant.

Law: TCGA 1992, s. 280
Guidance: CG 14910

12.12.3   *Tax paid by instalments over ten years*

Where the whole or part of an asset is disposed of by way of a gift, it may be possible for a person to elect to pay the CGT arising on the gift in ten equal yearly instalments. This also applies if there is a deemed disposal under s. 71(1) (person becoming absolutely entitled to settled property) or s. 72(1) (termination of life interest on death of person entitled).

For instalments to be available:

- holdover relief could not have been fully available on the gift; or
- relief was clawed back where a settlement became settlor-interested (see **12.11.3**).

This instalment option is also available in instances where no holdover relief was available (e.g. where a gift was not a qualifying asset within the remit of s. 165 or s. 260).

To be eligible for instalment payments the gift should be:

- land, or an estate or interest in land;
- a controlling holding of shares or securities of a company; or
- a holding of shares or securities of a company that is not listed on a recognised stock exchange.

To pay in instalments, the taxpayer must make the election in writing to HMRC at any time prior to the deadline for the payment of tax.

Once a valid election has been made, the first instalment falls due on the day on which the tax would normally be payable. Note that interest is still applied, with the interest on the unpaid portion of the tax added to each instalment.

Tax becoming immediately payable

Where tax is being paid in instalments, any tax remaining (including interest) becomes due and payable immediately if:

- the disposal was by way of gift to a person connected with the donor or was deemed to be made under s. 71(1) or 72(1); and
- the assets are disposed of for valuable consideration under a subsequent disposal (whether or not the subsequent disposal is made by the person who acquired them under the first disposal).

In the case of tax relating to the clawback of relief where a settlement becomes settlor-interested (**12.11.3**), the tax remaining (including interest) becomes due and payable immediately where any part of the assets transferred in the original gift is subsequently disposed of for valuable consideration by the trustees to whom the relevant disposal was made, or by some other person.

Law: TCGA 1992, s. 281
Guidance: CG 66452

12.12.4   Clawbacks

There are clawback provisions should a donee become non-UK resident within six years (see **12.11.2**).

If a trust is not settlor-interested at the time holdover relief was given, but subsequently becomes settlor-interested within six tax years following the tax year in which the gift was made, there can be a clawback of holdover relief (see **12.11.3**).

12.12.5   Recovery of tax from donee

If a chargeable gain accrues to any person on the gift of an asset (i.e. any transaction otherwise than by way of a bargain made at arm's length), and the CGT due is not paid by the person assessable (i.e. the donor) within 12 months of the tax becoming payable, it is possible for HMRC to assess the donee to CGT instead (in the name of the donor).

To do this, HMRC must make an assessment not later than two years from the date when the tax became payable by the donor. The amount assessed is capped at the lower of the amount of the gain accruing on the gift or the amount that brings into charge the tax unpaid.

If the donee pays the CGT on behalf of the donor, then the CGT assessment of the donor is correspondingly reduced. Section 282 also includes a provision that entitles the donee to recover that sum from the donor.

The above provisions also apply where a chargeable gain arises under the clawback provisions within s. 169C (settlement becomes settlor-interested – see **12.11.3**). In such instances, where the donor fails to pay the CGT due, HMRC may instead assess the trustees to whom the relevant disposal was made.

Example – adapted from CG 66451

In 2021-22, Douglas gives a property to Amber. Both are higher rate taxpayers. The chargeable gain arising to Douglas as a result of the gift is £48,000. Douglas has gains on disposals of other assets which amount to £15,300 and allowable losses of £3,000. The net gains are chargeable at 28%.

Douglas filed his return which included CGT as follows:

	£
Net chargeable gains	60,300
Less annual exempt amount	(12,300)
Chargeable	48,000
Tax due: (£48,000 x 28%)	13,440

Douglas fails to pay any of the tax. In December 2024, an assessment is made on Amber to recover the tax on the gift.

That assessment should be made for 2024-25 (see *Hamar*) and cannot exceed the lesser of:

- the amount of the gain arising on the gift (£48,000); and

- the amount which brings into charge the tax unpaid (also £48,000, as Douglas and Amber have the same marginal rate for residential property 28%).

The *Hamar* decision referred to above (and in the original HMRC example) was a successful taxpayer appeal concerning the year for which an assessment was correctly made.

Law: TCGA 1992, s. 282
Case: *Hamar v HMRC* [2011] UKFTT 687 (TC)
Guidance: CG 66451

12.12.6 Deductions for inheritance tax paid

The nature of holdover relief means that certain gifts that qualify for relief may also be subject to an IHT charge, for example as a result of a chargeable lifetime transfer.

In such cases, when computing the chargeable gain accruing to the donee when he or she ultimately disposes of the gifted asset, a deduction is allowable for the IHT paid on the gift, although the deduction cannot create a loss.

Law: TCGA 1992, s. 165(10), (11)
Guidance: CG 66887

12.13 Holdover relief under s. 260

12.13.1 Introduction

Holdover relief under s. 260 is available in a similar fashion to that given on gifts of business assets under s. 165.

Section 260 relief is available where gifts are made on which IHT is chargeable.

Where relief under s. 260 is available, it takes priority, meaning that relief under s. 165 is not available.

The mechanics of holdover relief under s. 260 operate in broadly the same fashion as that under s. 165 (i.e. the gain that would have arisen to the donor on the gift is deducted from the donee's acquisition cost, which is the market value of the asset at the date of the gift).

However, there are some differences between the operation of holdover relief under s. 260 and under s. 165.

The most significant difference is that there is no requirement under s. 260 that the asset should be a business asset for relief to be available. Under s. 165, the gift must be of a business asset.

Further differences between these two reliefs, and a summary of how the s. 260 relief operates, are discussed in brief detail below.

See also *Inheritance Tax: Lifetime Transfers and the Death Estate*, from Claritax Books.

12.13.2 Qualifying disposals

Relief is available under s. 260 where a donor makes a disposal otherwise than under a bargain at arm's length (i.e. a gift) to an individual or the trustees of a settlement, and the disposal is a chargeable transfer within the meaning of the IHTA 1984, even in instances where no IHT is due by virtue of the annual exemption or a nil-rate band.

Other gifts can also qualify for relief, such as exempt transfers to political parties, exempt transfers to maintenance funds for historic buildings, or exempt transfers of designated property.

A full list is provided in s. 260(2). Note that if only part of the gift is a qualifying disposal, then holdover relief is only available in respect of that part.

Relief is also available on the direct or indirect disposal of UK land – see **12.9.3**.

However, relief under s. 260 is expressly not available where the gift is a potentially exempt transfer for IHT purposes.

It is also not available where there is a disposal of assets under s. 115(1) (qualifying corporate bonds) on which a gain is deemed to accrue by virtue of s. 116(10)(b) (reorganisations, conversions and reconstructions) (see **5.3.6**).

Law: TCGA 1992, s. 260
Guidance: CG 67033

12.13.3   Donor and donee

As with s. 165 (see **12.2**) the donor should either be an individual or the trustees of a settlement. There are no requirements as to the residency of the donor (see **12.2** and **12.9**).

Unlike s. 165, relief is only available where the donee is an individual or the trustees of a settlement (i.e. companies, for the purposes of s. 260, cannot be donees).

The same residency requirements apply for donees as under s. 165, in that they must usually be UK resident. See **12.9** for further discussion.

Law: TCGA 1992, s. 260(1)
Guidance: CG 67031, 67032

12.13.4   Computation and restrictions

Holdover relief under s. 260 operates in much the same way as under s. 165 (see **12.5**).

Example 1

Manish gifts outright a qualifying asset to the trustees of a discretionary settlement in June 2021. Manish originally acquired the asset for £50,000, and it is worth £200,000 at the time of the gift. Manish therefore has a capital gain of £150,000 on disposal.

As the gift is to a discretionary settlement, it is considered a chargeable transfer for IHT purposes, meaning that holdover relief under s. 260 is available.

Where holdover relief is claimed, the gain arising to Manish would be:

	£
Market value	200,000
Less cost	(50,000)
Gain	150,000
Less holdover relief s. 260	(150,000)
Gain chargeable	Nil

The base cost of the asset in the trustees' hands would be:

	£
Market value	200,000
Less holdover relief s. 260	(150,000)
Base cost	50,000

The above is a simple example – no consideration was paid by the donee to the donor, and there were no other circumstances to restrict relief.

However, there are instances when relief under s. 260 may be restricted. They are considered in further detail below.

Consideration

As is the case with relief under s. 165 (see **12.6.2**), where the donee pays the donor consideration, and that consideration exceeds the donor's allowable costs under s. 38, relief under s. 260 is restricted.

Example 2

Eva purchased a qualifying asset that she later sold to a discretionary trust. At the time of the disposal, the asset was worth £30,000. However, Eva agreed to sell the asset for £15,000, less than market value. Eva paid £10,000 to acquire the asset.

As the asset has not been given as an outright gift, we need to determine the amount of excess proceeds received by Eva. In this case, Eva received £15,000 for the asset, but has allowable costs of £10,000. This means she has excess proceeds of £5,000.

The amount of gain that may be held over is therefore restricted by £5,000.

Following a holdover relief claim, the gain arising to Eva would be:

	£
Market value	30,000
Less cost	(10,000)
Gain	20,000
Less holdover relief s. 260 (£20,000 – £5,000)	(15,000)
Gain chargeable	5,000

The base cost of the asset in the trustees' hands, following a holdover relief claim, would be:

	£
Market value	30,000
Less holdover relief s. 260	(15,000)
Base cost	15,000

The above restriction does not apply where the disposal is deemed to occur on a person becoming absolutely entitled to settled property under s. 71 or the termination of a life interest on the death of the entitled person under s. 72.

Apportionment of gain

The advantage of holdover relief under s. 260 is that relief is not confined to business assets. Provided the disposal is a qualifying one (see **12.13.2**) holdover relief is available. This means that the restrictions on relief considered in **12.6.3** to **12.6.6** under s. 165 are not in point where relief under s. 260 is in scope.

However, where the gifted asset only partly qualifies for relief, or an exemption operates to provide a reduced charge, then holdover relief is only available in respect of that qualifying part.

Law: TCGA 1992, s. 260(3)-(5), (9)-(10)
Guidance: CG 67034

12.13.5 Credit for inheritance tax

Where the disposal is a chargeable transfer and IHT is payable as a result, the gain accruing to the donee on a subsequent disposal of the asset is reduced by this amount. This reduction cannot create a loss.

Law: TCGA 1992, s. 260(7)
Guidance: CG 67034

12.13.6 Claims

As with a claim under s. 165, for relief under s. 260 to apply, it must be claimed jointly by the donor and donee. Where the trustees of a settlement are the donee, the donor may make the claim alone.

The time limit to make a claim is four years from the end of the tax year in which the gift occurred.

Claims should be submitted using form HS295. See **12.7** for further information.

Law: TCGA 1992, s. 260(1)(c)

13. Incorporation of a business

13.1 Introduction

Many businesses start as a sole trader or partnership rather than as a company.

This is for a variety of reasons, including simplicity and minimal administration, and the fact that relief for trading losses – often incurred in early years – is more favourable for unincorporated businesses.

At some point in their journey, however, many businesses find that the next logical step is to undertake an incorporation.

It is possible to incorporate into a limited liability partnership (LLP) or a company.

The tax implications of trading through a LLP are broadly the same as those of a traditional partnership. Specifically:

- ITTOIA 2005, s. 863(1) provides that for income tax purposes the activities of the LLP are treated as being conducted in partnership by its members.
- TCGA 1992, s. 59A provides that for CGT purposes assets owned by the LLP are treated as held by the members as partners.

Incorporation into an LLP therefore has little effect for tax purposes.

The focus on this chapter will therefore be on incorporation into a company.

13.2 Key definitions and concepts

13.2.1 Incorporation

Incorporation is the process by which a sole trader or partnership transfers the business to a company.

A company is a legal entity with a separate identity from its directors and shareholders. Most companies are limited liability companies where the liability of the members is limited by shares or guarantee.

Once a business is carried on through a corporate wrapper, the directors will have an annual obligation to file statutory accounts and a confirmation statement and to prepare and submit a corporation tax return.

13.2.2   Types of company

Private company limited by shares

Most limited companies are private companies limited by shares. These companies have a share capital, and the liability of each member is limited to the amount, if any, unpaid on their shares. Shares cannot be offered to the general public.

This is by far the most popular type of company. There are, however, also other types of company.

Private company limited by guarantee

This is a more unusual type of company where there is no share capital. Instead, its members are guarantors rather than shareholders. The members' liability is limited to the amount they agree to contribute to the company's assets if it is wound up.

Private unlimited company

An unlimited company may or may not have a share capital but there is no limit to the members' liability.

Public limited company

A public company has a share capital and limits the liability of each member to the amount unpaid on their shares. It may offer its shares to the general public and may be listed or unlisted.

13.3   Reasons to incorporate

Many reasons for incorporation have their basis in commerciality rather than tax. Some of the reasons are:

- limited liability minimises the risk of running the business, as shareholders and directors cannot normally be sued for the actions of the company;
- companies tend to pay lower rates of tax than individuals;
- directors can set their own levels of dividends and salary, which allows flexibility as to when they take income;
- it can be easier to raise finance; and

- it may be perceived that there is a certain level of prestige from running a company.

13.4   Income tax implications

Although beyond the scope of this chapter and book, transferring a business from a sole trade or partnership to a company will also have income tax implications, including:

- cessation of the existing business will require application of the closing year rules, including claiming relief for any brought-forward overlap profits;
- transfer of capital items may require valuations and will result in balancing adjustments for capital allowances purposes, unless the transferor chooses to elect to transfer at tax written-down value (CAA 2001, s. 266);
- transfer of stock is deemed to be at market value, triggering taxable trading profits, but the transferor can elect to transfer it at the higher of cost or price paid (ITTOIA 2005, s. 177-178); and
- assets transferred (e.g. cars) may give rise to a benefit on the directors going forward.

13.5   SDLT implications

The company will be a party connected with the transferor, so if land or property is transferred there will be a deemed market value disposal for stamp duty land tax (SDLT) purposes, regardless of the sale value.

The SDLT consequences of any incorporation should therefore be considered before undertaking any transfers.

For more detail see *Stamp Duty Land Tax* from Claritax Books.

13.6   CGT implications – overview

On incorporation of a business into a company in which the transferor owns the shares, the connected party rules apply and it is a deemed market value transfer for CGT purposes (see **3.2.2**).

Chargeable assets owned by the business, including property and goodwill, will be taxed as if sold at market value when they are transferred, regardless of the value agreed between the company and the individual.

This could be costly in terms of the CGT that becomes payable, with no cash proceeds to pay the tax. For this reason, there are various reliefs available that allow the CGT to be deferred. These are considered below:

- relief for gifts of business assets under TCGA 1992, s. 165 (see **13.7**);
- incorporation relief under s. 162 (see **13.8**); and
- business asset disposal relief (BADR) (see **13.9**).

If relief is not available, any CGT liability must be included on the self-assessment tax return for the tax year in question on the CGT pages. Where the transfer includes a residential property, this would fall under the 30-day reporting rules.

13.7 Relief for gifts of business assets

13.7.1 Introduction

The first of the reliefs available to a sole trader or partnership wishing to incorporate is commonly referred to as "holdover" or "gift" relief. This book uses the term "holdover". The relief is covered more fully in **Chapter 12**.

This relief is available for business assets that are "gifted" to a company i.e. given away for no proceeds or transferred at below market value. It is mainly used where a sole trader or partnership has a valuable asset such as a factory or a shop standing at a large gain.

A gift is a disposal for CGT purposes whether the parties are connected or not. When a gift is made the transferor is taxed on a gain calculated using proceeds equivalent to the market value of the asset. The transferee receives the asset with market value as base cost.

Relief is available to defer this tax liability. If claimed, some or all of the gain is deducted from the base cost of the asset. The gain is, in effect, passed to the recipient rather than being paid by the transferor (see **12.5**).

The implications of a loss on transfer are discussed at **13.7.7**.

Law: TCGA 1992, s. 17, 165

13.7.2 Qualifying assets

Section 165 allows the transferor to claim holdover relief when gifting certain shares in trading companies and other specified assets – see **12.4**.

However, when the transferee is a company, a transfer of shares and securities is precluded from receiving relief.

Example

Roger owns a shop which is used in his sole trader business. He has invested his profits in shares in an unconnected company, which have grown significantly in value in recent years.

He decides to incorporate the business and gift the property into the company. He would like to gift the shares to the company too, so that he has all his assets in one structure.

He would be able to claim holdover relief on the transfer of the property into the company. The company would inherit his base cost. However, any gain on the shares would become taxable.

There may be other, more tax-efficient, ways of transferring his shares into the company, such as a share-for-share exchange.

Law: TCGA 1992, s. 165, 165A

13.7.3   Restrictions

There are some important restrictions to claiming holdover relief (e.g. where consideration is received or where there is non-business use of assets). These are covered at **12.6**.

Law: TCGA 1992, s. 165 and Sch. 7

13.7.4   Claiming holdover relief

Joint election

A holdover relief claim under s. 165 requires a joint election between the parties. The donor cannot make an election without the written consent of the recipient. See **12.7**.

HMRC's *Helpsheet HS295* includes a form to assist taxpayers.

Time limits

The time limit for claiming holdover relief is four years from the end of the tax year of disposal. Therefore, for a gift in the 2021-22 tax year, a holdover relief claim is only valid if it is made on or before 5 April 2026.

13.7.5   Residence issues

Claiming relief

The rules preclude anyone who is within the charge to UK CGT from transferring assets to a party outside the scope of UK CGT and claiming relief, as the deferred gain would then ultimately escape the charge to tax.

Traditionally, holdover relief could therefore only be claimed if the transferee was resident in the UK.

As all UK property (i.e. land and buildings) is now subject to UK CGT, the rules have been modified in recent years to enable holdover relief to apply also on UK property gifted to non-resident transferees. From 6 April 2019 the transfer must be made to a resident in the UK or to a non-resident who is subject to UK CGT under the non-resident CGT 2019 rules. See **12.9.3** for further details.

In the context of incorporation, the transferee will be a company. Note that in certain circumstances relief will be denied where the company is controlled by non-residents. For the detailed rules see **12.9.2**.

Clawback

The s. 168 clawback provisions for an emigrating transferee discussed at **12.11.2** do not apply where the transferee is a company.

On migration, companies must make arrangements to pay corporation tax and this liability could be affected by previous holdover claims. The detail of this is beyond the scope of this book.

13.7.6   Instalments

Where a transferor gifts a non-business asset and holdover relief cannot be claimed, it is possible to apply to pay the tax over ten years in ten equal instalments. See **12.12.3**.

Only certain assets qualify for the instalment option, such as land and buildings or unquoted shares. Instalments can be claimed on quoted shares but only where the transferor controls the company (i.e. has more than 50% of the voting rights).

Law: TCGA 1992, s. 280, 281

13.7.7   Losses

Losses arising from disposals to connected persons are only available to offset gains arising in relation to disposals to the same person. Therefore, if a loss arises on a gift of an asset to a company, the loss can only be used against gains on subsequent transfers to that company.

13.8   Incorporation relief

13.8.1   Introduction

While holdover relief (see **13.7**) is concerned with the transfer of individual business assets, incorporation relief (s. 162) is concerned with the transfer of a business in its entirety.

The relief applies when the business is exchanged for shares or a combination of shares and cash (the cash could be left in the company in the form of a loan – see **13.9.2**).

Where the conditions are met, incorporation relief is automatic, so does not have to be claimed.

As such, there is no opportunity for a taxpayer to restrict incorporation relief where share consideration is received. However, it is possible to receive a combination of shares and cash to restrict how much incorporation relief applies (see **13.8.2**).

If there are any gains left in charge after incorporation relief then it may be possible to claim BADR on these (see **13.8.3, 13.9**).

13.8.2   Conditions

Three conditions must be satisfied:

- The business being transferred must be a going concern.
- All assets of the business (except cash) must be transferred to the company. This is in practice a very important condition. If the sole trader wishes to retain any assets outside the company, such as land and buildings, incorporation relief will not be available.
- The consideration paid to the individual by the company must be wholly or partly in shares.

The relief is calculated by working out the total gains arising on the transfer and then apportioning these gains using a fraction that compares the value of the share consideration to the value of the total consideration. If the full consideration is given entirely in shares, the fraction is one and therefore the whole gain can be deferred.

The gain is then deferred by deducting it from the base cost of the shares.

Example 1

Bobby has a business that he feels would be better run as a company. He trades from a freehold property that he owns. This is now worth £250,000 and he originally paid £150,000 for it. After consulting with his accountant, they agree that, based on the trading position, the business has £50,000 in goodwill. The cash in the bank is £25,000.

Bobby is transferring the whole business, except the cash, to the company as a transfer of going concern. In return he will receive shares in the business.

The total gains arising on the transfer are £150,000 (£100,000 on the property and £50,000 on the goodwill). The shares issued to Bobby as consideration in his new company will be worth £300,000 (i.e. the sum of the market value of the assets the company now owns, being the property and the goodwill).

In this instance, Bobby can apply incorporation relief to the total gains and there will be no CGT to pay.

The company buys the assets from Bobby at market value in exchange for shares, so the shares were acquired at a cost of £300,000. The gains of £150,000 are deducted from this meaning that, for tax purposes, they will effectively inherit Bobby's base cost of £150,000.

The additional £150,000 gain will be taxed when these shares are sold or otherwise disposed of.

So, if Bobby were to sell his shares five years later for £500,000, the total gain at that point would be £500,000 less £150,000 which equates to £350,000, i.e. the increase in value of the shares of £200,000 plus the £150,000 gain deferred.

Example 2

Bobby (from **Example 1**) decides instead to sell his business to a company owned by his friend and receives £100,000 in share capital and £200,000 in cash on sale. There will be a restriction on the amount of incorporation relief available.

The amount of gain that could be deferred would be:

$$£150,000 \text{ (gains)} \times \frac{£100,000 \text{ (shares issued)}}{£300,000 \text{ (total consideration)}}$$

This gives a deferral of £50,000. The additional £100,000 of gains would become chargeable.

The base cost of the shares in this instance would be £50,000 (£100,000 – £50,000), so if Bobby sells the shares for £175,000 in five years' time, he would pay tax on a gain of £125,000.

It is possible to structure the consideration so that a gain is left in charge sufficient to use the annual exempt amount for the year. This would be beneficial if it would otherwise be wasted. As current year capital losses are used before the annual exempt amount, these should be factored into the calculation.

13.8.3   Disapplying the relief

Although incorporation relief is given automatically where the conditions are met, there may be situations where the taxpayer does not want the relief to apply. This may be achieved by electing to disapply it.

For example, a taxpayer qualifying for BADR (see **Chapter 7**) may want to exploit the 10% CGT rate on the way in to the company and pay tax now at this low rate to avoid the risk of a higher rate on a later disposal. This may be because of potential rule changes over time, or because there is a risk that the taxpayer may not meet the conditions for BADR on a future disposal.

To obtain BADR on a subsequent disposal of shares, the taxpayer would have to meet the "personal company" rules described at **7.3.2**. Broadly, this requires a 5% holding in the company for a two-year period during which time the shareholder is an officer or employee of the company. So if there are any doubts as to whether these conditions will be met at the time of the future disposal, the taxpayer should consider disapplying incorporation relief in order to obtain BADR at the point of incorporation.

Note, however, that where there has been an incorporation that qualifies for incorporation relief, and a subsequent disposal, the two-year test for ownership and involvement in the business may instead be applied to the unincorporated business at the point of incorporation, so if the business would have qualified for BADR at that point it will also qualify when the shares are sold. The issue here, therefore, is whether the taxpayer would pass the 5% test at the point of disposal.

Disapplying the relief would also allow the taxpayer to use capital losses and the annual exempt amount.

The time limit for making the election to disapply incorporation relief is normally the second anniversary of 31 January following the tax year of incorporation (e.g. 31 January 2025 for an incorporation in 2021-22).

There is a separate rule if the taxpayer disposes of all of the shares by the end of the tax year following that in which the incorporation takes place. In this case the deadline is brought forward one year (so to 31 January 2024 for an incorporation in 2021-22).

Law: TCGA 1992, s. 169I(7ZA-7ZB)

13.8.4   *Meaning of business*

Section 162 refers to the transfer of a "business". This is different from the concept of trading that is used in many other areas of the legislation, such as for BADR.

Many activities are clearly within this definition. However, the position is sometimes less clear cut. For example, renting can cause uncertainties.

The concept of "business" is not defined in tax legislation, so it is necessary to give the word its normal meaning. The *Oxford English Dictionary* (OED) defines a business as being:

- "a person's regular occupation, profession or trade"; or
- "a commercial activity".

In contrast to a business, the OED defines an "investment" as being:

> "the action or process of putting money into financial schemes, shares, property or a commercial venture with the expectation of achieving a profit".

However, these definitions do not necessarily help to distinguish a business from mere investment activities.

HMRC have therefore issued guidance in this area to assist their staff when considering claims for relief under s. 162. The guidance acknowledges that there is no definition of a business and that it is therefore a question of fact as to whether a particular activity being undertaken should be treated as a business. HMRC have to consider how the activities are run on a day-to-day basis before being able to reach a decision.

Case law in this area suggests that there needs to be more than merely a modest amount of "activity". For example, where a considerable amount of time is devoted to managing, maintaining and planning, this is more likely to be a business activity than the position of a person who is merely in receipt of a passive income.

Property portfolio

A person with a residential property portfolio, for example, may or may not be actively involved in running the portfolio as a business at a strategic level. Undertaking most or all of the following duties would help to demonstrate that the activities amount to a business:

- being regularly briefed by the property managing agent (if there is one);
- assisting with the sourcing of new properties for the portfolio;
- vetting new tenants;
- overseeing the accountancy side;
- ensuring that the property managing agent follows up new opportunities and resolves disputes in a timely manner; and
- taking ultimate responsibility for making decisions regarding the portfolio (other than the day-to-day decisions that are necessarily delegated to the managing agent).

Ramsay v HMRC

This lack of any definition resulted in an FTT case, *Ramsay*. The taxpayer was the landlord of a property which had been converted into ten flats, of which five flats were occupied by tenants.

The taxpayer and her husband transferred this property to a company in exchange for shares and claimed incorporation relief. Following an enquiry, HMRC issued a closure notice on the basis that the relief did not apply, following which Mrs Ramsay appealed to the tribunal.

The FTT had to decide whether the taxpayer's activities in connection with the letting and administration of the property created a passive income (i.e. an investment activity), or whether those activities were sufficient to constitute a business, thereby qualifying for s. 162 relief. The FTT found against the taxpayer, but her appeal to the Upper Tribunal (UT) was successful.

The FTT had held that the activities undertaken by the taxpayer were normal and incidental to the owning of an investment property, particularly when the property consisted of flats. In addition, Mrs Ramsay had declared the property income under what was then Schedule A, rather than as trading/business income.

However, the UT decided that property letting can be a business for the purposes of incorporation relief and that whether it is run as a business is a question of fact. It is a business if the letting activity has the characteristics of a business, specifically if it:

- is a "serious undertaking earnestly pursued" or a "serious occupation" which is pursued with regularity;
- produces a material turnover;
- is conducted in a regular manner;
- is carried out on sound and recognised business principles; and
- is pursued with a view to making a profit.

The tribunal stated that all activities should be considered to assess the general degree of activity carried out, rather than individual activities in isolation. It ruled that "in the context of property investment and letting, the same activities are equally capable of describing a passive investment and a property investment or rental business". The main differentiator as to whether the activities constitute a business is "the degree of activity undertaken".

Case: *Ramsay v HMRC* [2013] UKUT 226 (TCC)

HMRC guidance

Since this case HMRC have paid particular attention to the actual time spent working in the business when determining whether the business qualifies for s. 162 relief.

HMRC consistently argue that lettings do not constitute a business and that carrying out additional services and work is commensurate with a larger portfolio of properties rather than being indicative of a running a business.

Although the tribunal did not include any specific threshold of days or hours worked, HMRC's interpretation of the judgment (at CG 65715) does impose a minimum threshold of 20 hours per week, as per the particulars of the *Ramsay* case:

> "You should accept that incorporation relief will be available where an individual spends 20 hours or more a week personally undertaking the sort of activities that are indicative of a business. Other cases should be considered carefully."

It used to be possible to apply to HMRC for a non-statutory clearance on business status for s. 162 purposes. However, this is no longer possible, so it is important that the taxpayer is sure about transferring a business before relying upon s. 162.

13.8.5   Transfer of going concern

To qualify for incorporation relief, the business must be transferred as a going concern.

A transfer of a going concern (TOGC) is a phrase commonly used in connection with VAT and there is significant guidance as to what it actually is. Although the following analysis is based on VAT guidance, it is difficult to imagine a circumstance in which HMRC could refuse to apply the same definition of TOGC, and indeed business, for CGT purposes. In particular, the VAT guidance considers in detail the circumstances in which the transfer of a property rental business will qualify as a TOGC.

The main conditions to qualify as a TOGC for VAT purposes are:

- The assets must be sold as part of TOGC.
- The assets must be used by the purchaser with the intention of carrying out the same kind of business as the seller.
- There must not be a significant break in the normal trading pattern of the business before or immediately after the transfer.
- There must not be a series of immediately consecutive transfers of the business.

The VAT guidance also lists out specific scenarios in which property rental activities are transferred where HMRC will accept that it is a TOGC for VAT purposes, and also specific scenarios that they consider would not qualify as a TOGC.

In relation specifically to incorporation relief, HMRC make reference to an Australian case, with the concept of having the doors "open for business". And HMRC make the point that the transferor must not take steps "to prevent the transferee company from carrying on the business without interruption as it wishes" after the transfer.

Law: TCGA 1992, s. 162, 162A

Guidance: CG 65710; https://tinyurl.com/w85tp47f *(VAT Notice 700/9)*

13.9   Business asset disposal relief

13.9.1   Availability and operation

BADR is discussed at length in **Chapter 7**. Broadly, it will be available on incorporation provided the business has been owned and run for two years. This is subject to the lifetime cap on the amount of BADR available to an individual (currently £1 million, for disposals on or after 11 March 2020).

It will be applicable if:

- incorporation relief is not available (as the business is transferred for cash or some assets are retained);
- incorporation relief is only partially available (as the business is transferred for a combination of shares and cash); or
- holdover claims are not possible, or have not been made, or there are still gains in charge following any claims made.

On incorporation the taxpayer may receive cash or choose to lend it back to the company, leaving it on loan account. Tax would be chargeable in both circumstances and BADR would be available. This is discussed at **13.9.2**.

The sale of properties will attract BADR providing they meet the conditions and are used in the business. The main assets that will attract CGT are goodwill and properties.

However, goodwill may not attract BADR if the disposal is to a close company – see **7.8.2** for a full discussion.

Following incorporation, BADR might be available on a subsequent disposal of the shares, provided the conditions are met. This is discussed at **13.8.3**.

Law: TCGA 1992, s. 169LA

13.9.2   Sale and loan account

When planning incorporation, most taxpayers will consider the option of leaving cash proceeds in the company in the form of a loan from the owner to the business.

The owner will then draw down from the loan account over a number of years until it is exhausted.

When undertaking this route gains will occur on the transfer to the company so there will be an element of CGT payable (at 10% if the conditions for BADR are met).

Even though there may be tax to pay on chargeable assets such as property or goodwill on incorporation, creating a loan account can still be beneficial as future profits can be extracted from the company without any further tax liability.

It can also be useful if:

- the vendor wants to receive some proceeds in the form of cash at incorporation to trigger capital gains, for example to exploit an annual exempt amount (see **13.8.2**); but
- the company has no actual cash to pay at the point of incorporation.

14. Other reliefs

14.1 Introduction

Previous chapters have covered the best known CGT reliefs. This chapter considers other reliefs that may apply:

- chattels – see **14.2**;
- trading losses – see **14.3**;
- share loss relief – see **14.4**;
- irrecoverable loans to traders – see **14.5**;
- cultural gifts – see **14.6**;
- employee shareholders – see **14.7**; and
- employee-ownership trusts – see **14.8**.

14.2 Chattels – exemption, loss restriction and marginal relief

A chattel is an asset that is both tangible and moveable. "Tangible" simply means that the asset is physical and can be touched, e.g. a war medal, in contrast to intangible assets such as shares or goodwill.

In some cases, an asset may consist of a combination of tangible and intangible assets. A personalised car number plate is tangible, but most of the value is represented by the intangible right to use the particular combination of characters. In such cases, a just and reasonable apportionment of disposal value must be made.

"Moveable" follows the general law meaning. An asset will be moveable if it can be moved easily without damaging its surroundings. Complications may arise where an asset has been attached to a building or structure. If the asset is attached in such a way that it becomes part of the building, then it is likely that it will lose its status as a chattel.

As discussed at **6.2**, a disposal of a chattel that is a wasting asset will not realise a chargeable gain for CGT purposes. Similarly, any loss arising will not be allowable.

There is no wholesale exemption for chattels that are not wasting assets, but reliefs are available in the following circumstances (using gross proceeds before incidental disposal costs):

- asset bought and sold for £6,000 or less (exempt disposal);
- asset sold at a loss, with proceeds less than £6,000 (restricted loss); and
- asset sold at a gain, with proceeds greater than £6,000 (marginal relief available).

Exempt disposal

If the disposal proceeds in respect of a non-wasting chattel do not exceed £6,000, any gain arising will be exempt from CGT.

Example 1

Wendy purchases a painting for £1,000. Some years later, she sells the painting for £5,000. The gain is exempt.

Restricted loss

If the above exemption does not apply, and the disposal is made at a loss, then the loss will be allowable. However, this loss must be restricted if the consideration is less than £6,000.

The loss is restricted by substituting £6,000 for the actual consideration in the CGT computation.

Example 2

Hannah was the original owner of the painting in Example 1 above. Hannah bought the painting at auction for £8,000, and so realised a loss of £7,000 on the disposal to Wendy. However, the loss must be restricted by substituting £6,000 for the actual £1,000 disposal proceeds, i.e. Hannah's allowable loss will be £2,000.

Where the disposal consideration is £6,000 or more, any loss is calculated in the normal way with no restriction.

If the allowable expenditure and disposal consideration are both £6,000 or less, any loss will not be allowable for CGT purposes.

Marginal relief

If the gain is not exempt, a form of marginal relief is available where the consideration exceeds £6,000 but does not exceed £15,000.

The relief works by restricting the chargeable gain to 5/3 of the excess of the consideration above £6,000 (using gross proceeds). This is the maximum chargeable gain. This is then compared to the actual gain and the lower figure is the chargeable gain for CGT purposes.

Where the disposal consideration exceeds £15,000, the maximum chargeable gain will always exceed the actual chargeable gain so no marginal relief will be available.

Example 3

Bert and Tom both purchase chattels for £1,000. Bert sells his for £12,000 a few years later. Tom holds onto his for several more years and eventually sells it for £16,000.

The actual gains are £11,000 for Bert and £15,000 for Tom.

Bert can take advantage of marginal relief which will restrict his gain to 5/3 x (£12,000 – £6,000) = £10,000.

However, using the marginal relief calculation Tom's maximum chargeable gain is 5/3 x (£16,000 – £6,000) = £16,667 so no marginal relief is available, and he will simply be taxed on the £15,000 actual gain.

Sets of assets

In the absence of specific rules, it would be possible to split assets that comprise a set or collection into individual disposals to ensure each of them qualifies for the full exemption, or marginal relief.

For example, an antique table with four chairs is worth £20,000 as a set. However, the owner could collude with a buyer to make five separate purchases of the individual items for £4,000 each. Overall, the total consideration is the same but because the consideration for each individual item does not exceed £6,000, the aim is to secure the chattels exemption on the entire set.

Unsurprisingly, there are anti-avoidance rules preventing this. Where the rules apply, the individual transactions are treated as a single transaction, and the availability of the exemption or marginal relief is measured by reference to the total consideration. So, the seller of the table and chairs would be treated as having made a single transaction with total consideration of £20,000, so neither the exemption nor marginal relief would be available.

These anti-avoidance rules apply where:

- a taxpayer has made disposals of two or more assets;
- the assets form part of a set of articles;

- they have all been owned at one time by that taxpayer; and
- the disposals are made to the same person or to persons who:
  - are acting in concert; or
  - are connected persons.

HMRC guidance indicates that to be regarded as a set of articles for these purposes, the individual assets must not only be essentially similar and complementary, but the value when taken together must also be greater than the total value of the individual items.

See **3.2.5** for further commentary and an example.

Law: TCGA 1992, s. 262
Guidance: CG 76632

14.3   Trading losses

Where a taxpayer suffers a trading loss for income tax purposes, this will generally be offset against other income, or future profits from the same trade, in accordance with one of the available options under ITA 2007.

If the loss qualifies for relief under ITA 2007, s. 64 (sideways loss relief) then relief is also available against net capital gains where either:

- the taxpayer makes a claim under that section, but there is some excess loss that cannot be offset; or
- the loss would be eligible, but there is no income available to offset.

In these circumstances it is possible to make a claim under TCGA 1992, s. 261B to offset the otherwise unrelievable amount against net capital gains for the tax year after accounting for brought-forward and in-year losses, but before deduction of the annual exempt amount.

It is usually preferable to use losses against income rather than gains because income tax rates are higher so the savings would be greater. However, using the loss against gains may be an attractive option if carrying the trading loss forward is likely to lead to it being wasted, e.g. if future trading profits are likely to be largely covered by the personal allowance.

It may also be desirable if it is unlikely that the trade will be sufficiently profitable to use the losses efficiently within a reasonable length of time, i.e. the taxpayer may prefer to accept a lower amount of effective relief now rather than waiting several years.

Note that this availability of offsetting unused income losses against capital gains also applies to losses that are employment losses under ITA 2007, s. 128, to unused relief for post-cessation trade under s. 96, and to property relief under s. 125.

Any losses relieved under TCGA 1992, s. 261B-261E obviously cannot be used subsequently to reduce taxable income, i.e. the loss may only be used once.

Law: TCGA 1992, 261B-261E; ITA 2007, s. 64, 96, 125, 128

14.4 Share loss relief

14.4.1 Overview and general conditions

Complementary to the CGT relief for trading (and certain other income) losses (see **14.3**), capital losses realised on certain shares made by individuals (but not trustees) can be offset against general income by virtue of ITA 2007, s. 131. The shares must be those of an unquoted trading company.

Shares that have been issued under either the EIS or the seed EIS (SEIS) (see **Chapter 10**) automatically qualify under s. 131.

Relief is also available on a deemed loss on shares arising from a negligible value claim (see **3.5.5**).

These reliefs reduce the cash risk of an investment into such companies, as the effective rate of relief can be higher under income tax (where the maximum rate is 45%) compared with the CGT rate applicable to shares (20%).

This is an income tax rather than a CGT relief, but is included here for completeness as the relief derives from an underlying capital loss.

To qualify, the shares must be:

- ordinary shares; and
- subscribed for, i.e. issued directly to the taxpayer by the company, and not acquired second-hand from a third party.

However, if the shares are transferred from a spouse or civil partner who originally subscribed for them, the recipient will be treated as having made the subscription directly and relief will be available.

HMRC may request evidence that the shares were actually subscribed for and subsequently issued, e.g. by checking the annual return and register of members.

In *Alberg*, the company had received £250,000 from one of its subscriber shareholders, which he believed was in exchange for further shares. The company later went into liquidation, whereupon the shareholder made a claim under s. 131 for share loss relief.

HMRC requested evidence that the shares had been issued and, despite some board minutes and the draft shareholders' agreement appearing to demonstrate that the shares were to be issued, certificates were never actually produced, and the register of members was never written up. The tribunal agreed with HMRC that, unfortunately for the shareholder, the £250,000 investment that he had genuinely lost could be nothing other than a loan to the company.

A further requirement is that the disposal giving rise to the loss must be either:

- a disposal for full consideration made on arm's length terms;
- made in connection with a dissolution or winding up of the company; or
- a deemed disposal due to a successful negligible value claim (see **3.5.5**).

The disposal should not be part of a scheme of exchange or arrangements with a motive of tax avoidance.

Law: ITA 2007, s. 131, 134-143
Case: *Alberg v HMRC* [2016] UKFTT 621

14.4.2   *Company requirements*

The company must also meet three conditions (conditions A, B and C in the legislation) to be a *qualifying* company. Much of the content is similar to parts of the EIS legislation.

Condition A

To satisfy this condition, at the date of disposal the company must meet the following four requirements, discussed in detail below:

- trading;
- control and independence;
- qualifying subsidiaries; and
- property management subsidiaries.

Alternatively, the company will satisfy condition A if it has *previously* met the above four requirements, has ceased to do so in the three-year period ending with the disposal, and since that date has not been:

- an excluded company (one dealing in shares, land, etc.);
- an investment company (other than a holding company of a trading group); or
- a trading company.

The trading requirement

The trading requirement is that the company's business is the carrying on of one or more qualifying trades, with no non-qualifying activities permitted, other than to an insignificant degree.

This requirement can also be met if the company is the parent company of a trading group that, as a whole, has insubstantial non-qualifying activities.

Most trades are qualifying trades, but ITA 2007, s. 192 lists those that are specifically excluded, being the same as those that are excluded for EIS purposes.

The company must still be trading at the share disposal date. However, provided that it has been done for genuine commercial reasons and not for tax avoidance purposes, a company (or any subsidiaries) will not be regarded as ceasing to meet the trading company condition if:

- it is in administration or receivership; or
- a resolution has been passed, or an order made, for the winding-up of the company, or it is otherwise dissolved provided that during the winding-up process it continues to be a trading company.

The control and independence requirement

The control and independence requirement will be met if the issuing company is not a 51% subsidiary of another company (or otherwise under the control of another company) and does not control any another company other than a qualifying subsidiary (see below).

The qualifying subsidiary requirement

The company must have no subsidiaries other than qualifying ones. A subsidiary will be qualifying if it is a 51% subsidiary and no person but the issuing company or another of its subsidiaries has control of it.

The property management subsidiaries requirement

The company must have no property management subsidiaries other than qualifying 90% subsidiaries. A property management subsidiary is one whose business consists wholly or mainly in the holding or managing of land or any property deriving its value from land.

Condition B

Condition B is that the company has either:

- met all the requirements of condition A for a continuous period of six years ending with:
  - the date of disposal ("that date"); or
  - the time it ceased to meet the requirements if within three years before the disposal date ("that time"); or
- met each of those requirements for a shorter continuous period ending on that date or at that time and has not before the beginning of that period been an excluded company, an investment company or a trading company.

Condition C

Condition C will be satisfied if, at the date of issue, the shares meet:

- the gross assets requirement; and
- the unquoted status requirement.

The gross assets requirement

The gross assets requirement is that the company's gross assets (or the aggregate gross assets of a trading group) must not exceed £7 million immediately before the share issue or £8 million immediately afterwards.

The unquoted status requirement

The unquoted status requirement is that the company must not be listed on a recognised or designated stock exchange at the time of the share issue, and there must be no arrangements in place for the company to become so listed.

Law: ITA 2007, s. 131, 134-143

14.4.3   Operation of relief

Where relief is available under ITA 2007, s. 131, it may be claimed in:

- the tax year in which the loss is incurred;
- the preceding year; or
- both.

Where a claim is made for both years, the first year the relief is given must use the loss as far as possible before the excess is deducted from income in the other year. The taxpayer should therefore specify which year is to apply first. A claim must be made by the first anniversary of 31 January following the end of the tax year in which the loss arises.

As the relief is an income tax relief, it is subject to the general restriction to the higher of £50,000 and 25% of adjusted total income in each tax year by virtue of ITA 2007, s. 24A.

Law: ITA 2007, s. 24A, 132, 133

14.5   Relief on irrecoverable loans to traders

In general, simple debts are not chargeable assets for CGT purposes, so losses are not allowable losses. However, there is an exception on certain loans made to traders.

Loss relief may be claimed to the extent that a qualifying loan made to a trader becomes irrecoverable other than by reason of:

- the terms of the loan; or
- any act or omission by the lender.

For example, if the terms of the loan included a clause that the loan would be forgiven if the trader did not become profitable within a set time limit then no relief would be available if these terms were met.

The operation of relief is broadly similar to the negligible value provisions in respect of shares, so the loss is treated as accruing when it is claimed, or at an earlier specified time.

The lender and borrower must not be spouses or civil partners.

A loan is a qualifying loan if the money is used for the purpose of a borrower's trade, profession or vocation that is not a debt on a security (see **6.6.2**). The commercial letting of furnished holiday accommodation is treated as a qualifying trade for these purposes.

Example

Ernie loans £15,000 to Ellie who is trying to start a florist business. Initially the business is successful and Ellie pays Ernie back £3,000 over the first three years of trade. However, due to the coronavirus pandemic, Ellie is forced to close her business in 2021. Ernie can claim a loss of £12,000.

Where the loan is subject to a guarantee, the guarantor may also claim relief for any payment made to the lender under the guarantee. The original loan can be a debt on a security.

If relief is claimed, but subsequently some or all of the amount is recovered, an equivalent chargeable gain is deemed to accrue at the time of recovery.

Law: TCGA 1992, s. 253

14.6   Cultural gifts

Under the Cultural Gifts Scheme, an individual can claim a deduction from hir or her income tax or CGT liability (or a mixture of both) if the individual makes a gift of a "pre-eminent" property to the nation. The deduction is 30% of the agreed value of the qualifying gift as set out in the agreed terms.

To be a qualifying gift, it must be made in the following circumstances:

- the person offers to give pre-eminent property to be held for the benefit of the public or the nation;
- the person is legally and beneficially entitled to the property and the property is not owned jointly (or in common) with others;
- the offer is made in accordance with a scheme set up by the Secretary of State for the purposes of Sch. 14;
- the offer is registered in accordance with the scheme;
- the offer, or a part of the offer, is accepted in accordance with the scheme; and
- the gift is made pursuant to the offer, or the part of the offer that was accepted.

Pre-eminent property means:

- any picture, print, book, manuscript, work of art, scientific object or other thing that the relevant minister is satisfied is pre-eminent for its national, scientific, historic or artistic interest;

- any collection or group of pictures, prints, books, manuscripts, works of art, scientific objects or other things if the relevant minister is satisfied that the collection or group, taken as a whole, is pre-eminent for its national, scientific, historic or artistic interest; or

- any object that is or has been kept in a significant building if it appears to the relevant minister desirable for the object to remain associated with the building.

The taxpayer can opt to offset the deduction against income tax in priority to CGT (or vice versa). If no instruction is received, income tax will automatically be relieved first. The taxpayer can also elect to spread the relief over up to five years, as long as each one is either the tax year the offer registration date falls into, or one of the four subsequent years.

Law: FA 2012, Sch. 14

14.7 Employee shareholders

The short-lived Employee Shareholder Status scheme was withdrawn from 1 December 2016. However, shares held under agreements that employees signed prior to this date continue to benefit from the limited CGT exemption arising on any gain on a disposal.

If the relevant share agreement was signed before 17 March 2016, CGT is restricted to shares that were valued (using the unrestricted market value) at more than £50,000 at the date of acquisition.

Where this limit is exceeded, the first £50,000 worth of shares are exempt.

The qualifying shares may have been acquired in tranches, and so the cumulative acquisition values must be examined to see if the limit was breached for a particular tranche. If so, the acquisition must be apportioned so that an appropriate proportion will be treated as being acquired separately and before the others using the formula:

$$\frac{£50,000 - B}{T}$$

where:

- **B** is the initial value of the qualifying shares held before the acquisition day of the relevant tranche; and
- **T** is the total value of qualifying shares acquired on the day.

HMRC's guidance at CG 56725 contains a useful example, adapted below.

Example

Bernadette enters into an employee shareholder agreement with her employer, D Ltd. This is her only employee shareholder agreement. Neither B nor anyone connected with her has, or has had, a material interest in D Ltd.

In consideration of the agreement, she acquires over a period of time three successive tranches of shares in D Ltd. Each tranche comprises 10,000 ordinary £1 shares in D Ltd. Tranche 1 has a value of £15,000; tranche 2 £20,000 and tranche 3 £25,000.

All the shares in tranches 1 and 2 are exempt employee shareholder shares. Of the shares in tranche 3 a proportion: (50,000 – 35,000)/25,000 are treated as acquired before the others. Thus 6,000 shares of tranche 3 (having a value of £15,000) are exempt employee shareholder shares. The remaining 4,000 are not exempt.

If the relevant share agreement was signed on or after 17 March 2016 things are far less complicated. Each individual has a lifetime limit of £100,000 that can be used to exempt the relevant gains.

Law: TCGA 1992, s. 236B
Guidance: CG 56725

14.8   Employee-ownership trusts

An employee-ownership trust (EOT) is a special trust used to facilitate a business that is wholly or mainly owned by its employees. It is relatively new, having been introduced in 2014. Perhaps the best known example is John Lewis and Partners.

The EOT is intended to encourage shareholders to consider employee ownership via indirect holding. The tax reliefs are only available to shareholders, though of course an unincorporated business such as a partnership could take advantage by incorporating and then establishing the EOT.

Once established, the existing shareholders must sell a majority controlling interest to the trustees at their agreed market value. A qualifying transfer will be treated as being made for consideration that means neither a gain nor a loss arises, i.e. the transferor can claim a form of rollover relief.

Certain requirements must be met:

- The company must be a trading company, or the parent company of a trading group.
- The trustees must use the settled property for the benefit of all eligible employees on the same terms – though the trustees may distinguish between employees on the basis of remuneration, length of service and hours worked.
- The EOT must hold more than 50% of the ordinary share capital, and have majority voting rights.
- The number of continuing shareholders (and any other 5% participators) who are directors or employees (and any persons connected with such employees or directors) must not exceed 40% of the total number of employees of the company or group.

In addition to the CGT relief, there are also income tax and IHT benefits to using an EOT. See *Employee-Ownership Trusts*, due to be published by Claritax Books in early 2022.

Law: TCGA 1992, s. 236H-236U

PARTICULAR TAXPAYERS

15. Trusts and settlements

15.1 Introduction

Trust law has its roots far back in history; its origins can be traced to the Magna Carta in 1215.

The concept of a trust often causes confusion, but while trust taxation can be a complex area the basis of trusts is simple. A trust is a mechanism to protect assets while maintaining an element of control. The vehicle of a trust was used to protect assets long before there were any taxation benefits.

By establishing a trust, an individual is making a transfer of assets which binds the trustees to control and administer the trust property for the benefit of the beneficiaries. The trustees have a fiduciary duty to hold the trust property on behalf of the beneficiaries as governed by the terms of the trust deed.

For many years, trusts were an effective tax planning (some would say, tax avoidance) vehicle. As such, they acquired a bad reputation with HMRC. However, over the years, the rules have evolved (resulting in much of the complexity that exists) to level the playing field between individual and trust ownership of assets.

Trusts remain an effective way to pass current value and future capital growth outside the estate of an individual, but many of their additional tax benefits have been eroded over the years.

For further information see *Financial Planning with Trusts* from Claritax Books.

15.2 Key definitions and concepts

15.2.1 Trust, settlor, beneficiary and trustee

Trust

A trust is a vehicle used to manage assets (cash, investments, property) on behalf of other people (beneficiaries).

Settled property is defined in TCGA 1992, s. 68 as any property held within a trust, except that to which the bare trust rules apply.

Beneficiary

The beneficiaries of a trust are the ultimate beneficial owners of the trust assets.

Some beneficiaries only have an interest in the income of the trust (life tenant – see **15.2.5**) but other beneficiaries may have a potential interest in both income and capital.

Settlor

The settlor is the individual (or sometimes company) that establishes the trust.

In the case of an individual, this may be during lifetime (lifetime trust) or on death (will trust).

The settlor can also be a trustee of the trust. Very often the settlor and his or her spouse will become trustees of the trust to retain control over the assets.

The settlor can also be a beneficiary (see **15.2.8**).

Trustee

The trustees are the legal owners of the trust property, but they are not the beneficial owners. They are responsible for ensuring that the assets are protected for the beneficiaries and have fiduciary duties to the trust.

Trustees are normally individuals, but they can be corporate trustees.

15.2.2 Types of trust

There are many different types of trust in existence, such as:

- bare trusts (see **15.2.3**);
- discretionary trusts (including accumulation and maintenance trusts – see **15.2.4**);
- interest-in-possession trusts (also known as life interest trusts – see **15.2.5**);
- vulnerable beneficiary trusts (see **15.2.6**);
- employee trusts (see **15.2.7**);
- settlor-interested trusts (see **15.2.8**); and
- non-resident trusts (see **15.2.9**).

15.2.3   Bare trust

A bare trust is effectively a nominee arrangement. The individual has beneficial ownership of the asset but it is owned legally in another person's name.

The property may remain in a trust structure but the beneficiary is absolutely entitled to the assets as against the trustees.

Guidance: CG 34300

15.2.4   Discretionary trust

Where assets are held in a discretionary trust the income and capital of the trust is paid out to the beneficiaries at the discretion of the trustees.

No individual beneficiary is entitled to income or capital from the trust. It is completely at the discretion of the trustees to decide when and if beneficiaries receive anything from the trust.

A discretionary trust will normally have a wide class of beneficiaries, such as children and grandchildren, and can include unborn children.

An accumulation and maintenance trust is a type of discretionary trust that used to receive favourable IHT treatment. It is now taxed like all other discretionary trusts.

Very often, the settlor of a discretionary trust will provide a letter of wishes to the trustees, setting out why the settlor chose to set up the trust. Although not legally binding, it can be used by the trustees when exercising their discretion for distributing income and capital to beneficiaries.

15.2.5   Interest-in-possession trust

This type of trust is also known as a life interest or fixed interest trust.

Under this type of trust arrangement, one or more beneficiaries has a right to the income of the trust for life, or for a fixed period of time.

This type of trust might be used where the settlor wants to give an individual the right to income from assets in a trust but wants the capital to pass to someone else.

Example

Mrs S has married for a second time and has prepared a will leaving her property portfolio to her husband via a life interest trust on her death, giving him an entitlement to income during life (the life tenant) but

345

leaving the capital to the children of her first marriage (the remaindermen) on the death of her second husband.

15.2.6   Vulnerable beneficiary trust

A trust qualifies under these rules if it is for the benefit of :

- someone aged under 18 whose parent has died;
- a disabled person who is eligible for disability living allowance, attendance allowance, personal independence payment, disablement pension, constant attendance allowance or armed forces independence payment; or
- someone who is unable to manage his or her own affairs due to a mental health condition covered by the *Mental Health Act* 1983.

Law: FA 2005, s. 23, 38, 39

15.2.7   Employee trust

The concept of "trusts for benefit of employees" – generally referred to as employee trusts – is an IHT term.

Very often an employee trust is a discretionary trust set up to acquire and hold shares in a company on behalf of employees. The settlor will be the company setting up the trust and the beneficiaries will be the employees. The trustees will be appointed to look after the interests of the employees.

Law: IHTA 1984, s. 86

15.2.8   Settlor-interested trust

A settlor-interested trust is broadly one in which the settlor or the settlor's spouse or civil partner can benefit. See **15.4.4** for a fuller definition.

Law: ITTOIA 2005, s. 625

15.2.9   Non-resident trust

A non-resident trust is a trust that is controlled by individuals, or a trust corporation, resident outside the UK.

If all the trustees are UK resident, the trust is UK resident. Conversely, if all the trustees are non-UK resident, the trust is non-UK resident.

If there is a mixture of resident and non-resident trustees, the status of the settlor of the trust must be considered. If the settlor was UK resident or domiciled at the time the trust was set up, the trust will be UK resident.

Residence is determined by reference to the statutory residence test.

Law: TCGA 1992, s. 69; FA 2013, Sch. 45

15.3   Trust gains – basic calculation

15.3.1   Introduction

The trustees will have to calculate the net chargeable gains, after exemptions and reliefs.

They will then calculate tax due in accordance with the rules that apply to the particular type of trust (see **15.9**).

15.3.2   Chargeable disposals

UK trustees are taxable on worldwide capital gains and are taxed as a single entity.

They are taxed on a chargeable disposal, which occurs when they:

- sell assets from the trust; or
- distribute assets out to beneficiaries.

There are also special rules in relation to certain deemed disposals, which are discussed at **15.8**.

Any gain is calculated on the same principles as for an individual (see **Chapter 3**), i.e. the trustees can deduct allowable costs from the proceeds (or deemed market value).

Law: TCGA 1992, s. 1A(1), 18, 62

15.3.3   Allowable cost

If the trustees acquire the asset at arm's length this forms the base cost for CGT purposes.

Assets transferred into trust by settlors as a gift will be deemed to be made at market value. Where the gift is made subject to a holdover election (see **Chapter 12**), the base cost will effectively be the base cost of the settlor.

If the settlor claimed holdover relief but the transfer was also later subject to IHT, the IHT payable is available as a deduction against the capital gain on a later disposal of the asset.

If the trust is created on death, the trustees will be deemed to acquire the assets at their market value on the date of death.

Law: TCGA 1992, s. 38, 165(10), 260(7)

15.4   Reliefs

15.4.1   Introduction

Various tax reliefs are available to trustees in the same way as to individuals:

- private residence relief (PRR) (see **15.4.2**);
- business asset disposal relief (BADR) (see **15.4.3**); and
- holdover relief (see **15.4.4**).

15.4.2   Private residence relief

This relief is covered in detail in **Chapter 9**.

A claim for PRR can be made by the trustees when they sell a property that the trust owns. To qualify it must be:

- the main residence;
- for a beneficiary;
- who is entitled to live in the property under the terms of the trust.

It is not available where the settlor held over a gain on the way into the settlement (see **15.4.4**).

The relief is calculated in the same way as for individuals.

A claim must be made for the relief. This is a very important difference from the relief as it applies to individuals, which is automatic and does not have to be claimed.

Where the trustees are already within self-assessment, it is simple to make the claim by including it on the tax return and claiming the relief. However, many life interest trusts are not in the self-assessment system as there is no income arising in the trust. In this case, it is necessary to write to HMRC to make the claim in the first instance and, if required, HMRC will request a tax return from the trustees. Under TMA 1970,

Sch. 1, a signed written claim should be sufficient where a tax return has not been issued.

Example

Mr Jones dies on 31 March 2012 and leaves a life interest trust for his son. The main asset in the trust is a property that the son is entitled to live in for the remainder of his life. On the son's death, the property is to be divided between Mr Jones's two grandchildren.

On 30 June 2020, Mr Jones's son decides the property is too large for him, and he asks the trustees to sell it and purchase a smaller one. They duly do so and crystallise a gain of £30,000 due to an increase in the property's value since Mr Jones's death.

As the son has lived in the property since his father's death and the property is held by a trust in which he has a life interest, PRR will apply. However, it is necessary for the trustees to make a claim to HMRC, which they will make via a separate election or in the tax return for the relevant year.

Law: TMA 1970, Sch. 1; TCGA 1992, s. 225(1)
Guidance: CG 65400

15.4.3   *Business asset disposal relief*

This relief is covered in detail in **Chapter 7**.

Trustees pay a 10% CGT rate on qualifying gains if they sell:

- assets used in a beneficiary's business, which has ceased (see below); or
- shares or securities in a company that is the personal company of a beneficiary (see below).

This is subject to the lifetime limit, which has altered over the years. From 11 March 2020 it is £1 million.

The relief is only available if the beneficiary has a life interest in the trust, which must include the assets that are sold. No relief is therefore available to discretionary trusts.

BADR must be claimed jointly by the trustees and the qualifying beneficiary. Effectively the beneficiary is giving up his or her entitlement to the relief.

Example 1

Miss S has a life interest in a trust which owns 80% of the shares in her trading company. She owns the remaining 20% and has done since the company was incorporated ten years ago.

The company is sold realising a gain of £1 million. Miss S jointly elects with the trustees that they can use part of her lifetime allowance to cover their 80% shareholding. This means that she receives relief on her 20% and the trustees apply the 10% rate on their 80%. However, Miss S has now used her £1 million lifetime allowance and any future gains she makes personally can no longer benefit from the 10% rate.

Assets used in beneficiary's business

For the trustees to claim relief for assets used in a qualifying beneficiary's business, the following conditions must be satisfied:

- the asset must have been used for the qualifying beneficiary's business for at least two years ending within the three years up to the date of the trustees' disposal;
- the qualifying beneficiary must have ceased to carry on that business on the date of disposal or within the three years before the date of disposal; and
- the qualifying beneficiary must have had the interest in possession for the relevant two-year period.

Shares in a personal company

For the trustees to claim relief on the sale of shares or securities the following conditions must be satisfied:

- the company must be the personal company of the beneficiary (see **12.4.2**), and a trading company, for at least two years ending on the date of the trustees' disposal of the shares, or no earlier than three years before the date of the disposal;
- throughout the same two-year period, the beneficiary must have been an officer or employee of the company; and
- the qualifying beneficiary must have had the interest in possession for the relevant two-year period.

More than one beneficiary

If there is more than one beneficiary with a life interest in the settlement, then only a part of the gain will be covered by the relief.

Example 2

Miss A has a life interest in a farming business that is owned by a family trust. She is entitled to 50% of the income from the farm.

She has farmed the land for 15 years and ceased to farm it on 2 June 2021, when the trustees sold it to a local farmer realising a gain of £500,000.

It is possible for Miss A and the trustees to make a joint election for the trustees to claim BADR. However, the claim will be restricted to £250,000 (50% x £500,000).

This means Miss A has a lifetime limit of £750,000 to carry forward against future disposals.

Beneficiary and trustee – priority of disposals

For the purposes of allocating the relief between the beneficiary and the trustees, any disposals by the beneficiary are deemed to take place in priority to those of the trustees. So, if the beneficiary and trustees make disposals on the same day, the relief is first allocated to the beneficiary.

Example 3

Mr C has a life interest in a trust which owns 60% of his trading company shares. The company is sold realising a gain of £3 million.

The shares are all disposed of on the same day.

Although Mr C is a qualifying beneficiary in relation to the trust, his personal gain is £1.2 million. Therefore, he will use all of his BADR and there is nothing to "give" to the trustees, who will pay the full 20% CGT charge.

Beneficiary and trustee – ownership of assets

To obtain relief the beneficiary must personally own sufficient shares. Trustees can often be caught by these rules.

Many years ago it was common for the owners of trading companies to sell their entire shareholding to a trust to obtain the benefits of the then current retirement relief. Some older trusts and companies may now find there is an issue with the tax position when the shareholders sell their shares, or the company undertakes a purchase of its own shares.

There have been instances in practice where the individuals considered they "owned" the shares, but the legal reality was that there was a trust in existence which actually owned them. This can be problematic if discovered close to or after the disposal date, as the two-year ownership period will not be met. However, if the issue is discovered early enough, it is possible to put planning in place to prevent this from occurring.

Example 4

The Inchling trust owns all the shares in the Inchling Trading Company Ltd. Although the trust legally owns the shares, the family members consider that they are each entitled to 25% of the company.

One of the family members is retiring and the rest of the family suggests that the company buys his shares back as a means of exiting the business.

If the individual had owned the shares directly, he would have met the tests for capital treatment and the company would have qualified for BADR so he would pay 10% on the gain. However, as the accountants prepare the paperwork, they realise the shares are not held by the individual but through a trust.

As none of the individuals are qualifying beneficiaries, the trust cannot claim BADR and the share buy-back is no longer an effective method.

Deadline for claims

BADR must be claimed in writing by the first anniversary of the 31 January following the end of the tax year in which the disposal takes place. For example, if the disposal takes place during the 2021-22 tax year then a claim must be made by 31 January 2024.

The claim may be amended or revoked during this period.

Law: TCGA 1992, s. 169H
Guidance: CG 63950

15.4.4 Holdover relief

This relief is covered in detail in **Chapter 12**.

In certain circumstances, trustees may hold over a gain when they transfer assets to beneficiaries.

This means that there will be no tax payable by the trustees on the transfer; instead the beneficiary will pay tax when he or she sells the asset.

Such holdover claims can apply to deemed disposals as well as actual disposals.

Claim under s. 260

Holdover relief can apply to business assets under TCGA 1992, s. 165. However, the relief that is more often claimed by trustees is under s. 260. This is the relief that applies when a transfer is subject to both the CGT and IHT regimes.

An IHT charge will usually arise when assets are transferred out of, or into, a "relevant property" trust. Most trusts will be caught here, the major exception being interest-in-possession trusts where the life interest arises from the deceased's will and commences immediately on death. This is known as an "immediate post-death interest" (IPDI). Another exception would be a transitional serial interest (TSI) trust.

Transfer out of trust

A transfer out of a relevant property trust will be both a disposal for CGT purposes and an exit from the trust under the IHT rules. Without the holdover provisions, the trustees might suffer both tax charges.

A claim under s. 260 will allow the trustees to hold over any CGT that might otherwise become due. Such a claim is available to the trustees regardless of whether they actually pay any IHT. The only condition is that IHT *could* arise on the transfer. So, if there is no exit charge under the IHT provisions, this does not preclude a claim under s. 260 from being made.

Example 1

The trustees of Mrs Morris Family Trust, which is a relevant property trust set up in 2016, decide to transfer a property from the trust to one of the beneficiaries, Janice.

At the point of transfer this crystallises a gain of £50,000 which is inherent in the property.

As the trust is a relevant property trust, there is also a potential exit charge when the property leaves the trust. For this reason, the trustees may claim holdover relief under s. 260 to prevent any tax becoming payable.

When Janice sells the asset, her base cost will be that of the trustees and therefore Janice will pay CGT on both her own gain (since the date of transfer) and the gain that had already arisen when the asset was transferred.

Unless an asset qualifies as a business asset, there is no holdover relief available when assets are transferred from a trust that is not within the relevant property regime, such as an IPDI or a TSI.

Example 2

Mrs Jones died and left a rental property to her son in her will through a trust in which he had a life interest. This therefore created an IPDI which means that the property would be in the estate of the son for IHT purposes.

The trustees later decide to distribute the property to the son in his own name. As the trust is an IPDI and not within the relevant property regime, the gain cannot be held over and the trustees will have to pay any CGT due on the transfer.

Transfer into trust

Holdover relief can also be claimed by a settlor when transferring assets into a trust (see **15.15**). Again, the most usual provision under which holdover relief is claimed is s. 260. This is because there is potentially a charge to IHT on the way into the settlement, although, in reality, most lifetime trusts are set up within the IHT nil rate band and so no tax charge arises.

Clearly, if the trust is established on death, there will be no CGT charge on its creation.

Restrictions

There are restrictions on when holdover relief can be claimed by trustees.

Settlor-interested trusts

It is not possible for holdover relief to be claimed when an individual transfers assets into a settlor-interested settlement.

A trust is settlor-interested if the settlor, the settlor's spouse or civil partner or minor child/stepchild can benefit from the trust. A trust will also be settlor-interested if there are any arrangements in place that enable the settlor to benefit from the trust in the future.

There is a clawback of the relief if the trust becomes settlor-interested within six years after the end of the tax year in which the transfer is made.

Non-resident trusts

If the trust becomes non-resident within six tax years after the end of the tax year in which the transfer was made, any holdover relief will be withdrawn.

There is no requirement for the transferor to be resident. It would therefore be possible for a non-resident transferor to claim holdover relief into a UK resident trust (assuming it meets the qualifying conditions).

Private residence relief

Where a settlor claims holdover relief on a property that is settled into trust, the trustees are precluded from claiming any PRR (see **15.4.2**) on a subsequent sale of that property.

It is therefore important to establish the intentions of the trustees when considering whether a holdover relief claim should be submitted on setting up the trust.

If the intention is for a beneficiary to live in the property going forward, then it may be better for the settlor to pay the tax on the way into the trust and the trustees to claim relief on the sale of the property in the future.

Example 3

Mr Jones is considering settling a property that he owns into trust for his two adult children. The property cost him £150,000 and is now worth £170,000. His advisers have told him that he can hold over the gain into the trust and pay no tax now.

However, the intention is for Mr Jones's eldest daughter to live in the property as a beneficiary. She is likely to be living in the property for most of her life.

In this instance, it is very important to consider whether the tax arising now should be paid, to enable the trustees to make a claim for PRR in the future.

Claims for relief

The claim for holdover relief is made on Form HS295 and is signed by both transferor and transferee (apart from transfers into a settlement, when only the transferee has to sign).

The time limit to make a claim is four years from the end of the tax year in which the gift occurred.

Law: TCGA 1992, s. 165, 169B, 260
Guidance: CG 66880

15.5 Annual exempt amount

Trusts have an annual exempt amount (AEA) in the same way as individuals. This is often referred to as the annual exemption.

The AEA for a trust is half of that of an individual (so currently £6,150 for tax year 2021-22).

The AEA is likely to be reduced if the settlor has set up more than one trust since 6 June 1978. The AEA is divided by the number of all settlements made by the settlor since 6 June 1978 in existence during the relevant tax year. For this purpose, non-resident trusts, charitable trusts and pension funds are not counted as additional trusts.

The reduced AEA will never fall below 10% of that available to an individual. Where there is more than one settlor, the AEA is determined by reference to the settlor who has the greatest number of settlements in existence for that tax year.

Where there is a vulnerable beneficiary, the AEA is that of an individual. However, if the same settlor has set up more than one trust for vulnerable beneficiaries, the AEA is reduced by dividing by the number of such settlements subject to the overall 10% minimum described above.

Law: TCGA 1992, Sch. 1C, para. 5, 6

15.6 Losses

Losses are calculated for trustees in the same way as for individuals.

Losses are covered in detail at **3.5**.

15.6.1 Current-year losses

Losses that arise during a tax year are first deducted from total chargeable gains for that year.

To the extent that the losses are greater than the gains, the excess is carried forward to later years. There is no time limit within which these losses have to be used.

There is no ability to carry losses back to earlier years.

Law: TCGA 1992, s. 1(3), 16

15.6.2   Brought-forward losses

Brought-forward losses are set against subsequent years' gains in such a way as to preserve the AEA for the year.

Law: TCGA 1992, s. 1K(4)

15.6.3   Claiming capital losses

As with individuals, capital losses have to be claimed to be carried forward. This is normally done on the Trust and Estate Tax Return. The normal time limit of four years from the end of the year of assessment to which they relate applies.

15.6.4   Restrictions

Loss on distribution of assets

A distribution of assets to a beneficiary is a deemed disposal for CGT purposes. The consideration is at deemed market value as it is a connected party transaction and no consideration changes hands.

To the extent a loss arises on a distribution to a connected party, this loss is "clogged" (ring-fenced) and can only be set against gains with the same connected party.

Loss when a beneficiary becomes absolutely entitled to trust assets

When a beneficiary becomes absolutely entitled to trust assets and a loss arises, it can be deducted against gains in that year on:

- other trust assets distributed; or
- other gains within the trust.

If the loss cannot be used in this way, it can be transferred to the beneficiary to use against any future gain on disposal of that particular asset. The loss cannot be used against any other asset.

Loss on assets transferred between settlements

When assets are transferred between settlements, the losses are treated in the same way as a loss arising when a beneficiary becomes absolutely entitled, above.

Purchased losses

There are anti-avoidance rules which prevent trusts from purchasing losses.

Interaction with holdover relief

Losses may not be set against gains where:

- the gain has been calculated after deduction of holdover relief;
- the transferor who claimed holdover relief has an interest in the settlement (or could have such an interest in the future); and
- any person has received consideration in relation to the acquisition of an interest in that settlement.

This is to prevent a person purchasing an interest in a trust that has made capital losses, transferring assets standing at a gain into the trust and claiming holdover relief. The loss restriction then applies when the held-over gain is crystallised on a subsequent disposal by the trust.

Law: TCGA 1992, s. 18, 79A

15.7 Exempt assets

Trustees do not pay CGT on the usual exempt assets. See **Appendix 2**.

15.8 Deemed disposals

15.8.1 Introduction

There are occasions when trustees are deemed to dispose of assets for CGT purposes.

The main two situations to which this applies are when:

- a beneficiary becomes absolutely entitled to an asset, either under the terms of the trust deed or when the assets are appointed to him or her; and
- certain qualifying interest-in-possession trusts come to an end.

Where these rules apply, the trustees are deemed to have disposed of the asset for market value and reacquired it at market value as bare trustees.

Law: TCGA 1992, s. 71(1)

15.8.2   Holdover relief

Any gain arising on a deemed disposal is taxable unless the trustees are able to hold over the gain:

- under s. 165 (gift of business assets);
- under s. 260 (where an IHT event also arises);
- where the trust is for a bereaved minor; or
- where it is an 18-25 trust.

See **15.4.4**.

15.8.3   Death of beneficiary

There is no taxable gain where a beneficiary of a qualifying interest-in-possession trust dies and, as a result, the settlement comes to an end. This is because there is a tax-free uplift on death.

If the settlor has become absolutely entitled to the assets on death, the trustees are deemed to make a no gain/no loss transfer and the settlor is deemed to have reacquired the trust property with a market value equal to that at the time the trustees acquired it.

If anyone other than the settlor is entitled to the assets, then the trustees are deemed to have made an exempt disposal of the assets and the beneficiary is treated as having acquired the asset at the market value at that date.

Law: TCGA 1992, s. 73(1)

15.8.4   Not all beneficiaries become entitled

A special rule applies when a beneficiary becomes absolutely entitled to undivided shares of land while the remaining beneficiaries are not entitled. At this point there is no disposal. The disposal will occur when all the beneficiaries become absolutely entitled to the land.

Case: *Crowe v Appleby* (1974) 51 TC 457

15.8.5   Interest in possession comes to an end but settlement continues

Where a qualifying interest in possession comes to an end and the settlement continues, there will be a deemed disposal for CGT purposes.

Where this has happened on the death of a beneficiary, the gain is exempt from taxation. The trustees will have an uplifted base cost in those assets going forward.

Where a qualifying interest in possession comes to an end on an occasion other than the death of a beneficiary, and the trust property remains settled, there is no deemed disposal by the trustees.

Law: TCGA 1992, s. 62

15.9 Taxing trust gains

15.9.1 Overview

Different types of trusts will be taxed using different rules and different rates:

- trusts in general (see **15.9.2**):
- bare trusts (see **15.9.3**)
- vulnerable beneficiary trusts (see **15.9.4**);
- employee trusts (see **15.9.5**); and
- non-resident trusts (see **15.9.6**).

15.9.2 Taxing gains generally

Most trusts are taxed at 28% on residential property and carried interest (i.e. the share of profits arising from participation in an investment vehicle) and at 20% on everything else (e.g. commercial property or shares).

This treatment would apply to:

- discretionary trusts (including accumulation and maintenance trusts);
- interest-in-possession trusts; and
- settlor-interested trusts.

15.9.3 Taxing gains in a bare trust

A bare trust is effectively a nominee arrangement. The individual has beneficial ownership of the asset but it is owned legally in another person's name.

This type of arrangement is often seen for minor children and grandchildren, for example where a parent or grandparent buys shares for a child. The child has beneficial ownership of the shares and will have absolute entitlement at age 18.

Any gains arising will be taxed on the child, who will have a full AEA (£12,300 for 2021-22) to set against the gain. The child will then be taxed on any gain based on the type of asset and on his or her marginal income tax position. So a child with no income will be taxed on the first £37,700 of gains at 10% (or 18% if it is residential property).

This can be very tax-efficient. However, it should be remembered that the asset belongs to the child, who therefore has a legal entitlement to it from age 18 and who may then choose to sell it. This is an important consideration from an asset protection point of view.

Law: TCGA 1992, s. 60

15.9.4   *Taxing gains in a vulnerable beneficiary trust*

If a trust is set up for the benefit of a disabled beneficiary, or an orphaned child who meets the criteria of a vulnerable beneficiary (see **15.2.6**), the beneficiary and the trustees can jointly sign a vulnerable beneficiary election.

This election means that the trustees pay the same amount of CGT on the trust gains as the beneficiary would if the gains were made in a personal capacity.

Where the beneficiary is a non-taxpayer or basic rate taxpayer this can be tax advantageous.

From a practical point of view, when the trustees make a vulnerable beneficiary election, the trustees are then entitled to a CGT deduction. This is calculated by working out how much tax would be due based on the trust rules relevant to that trust. The trustees then work out what the vulnerable beneficiary would have paid in tax if the gains had been received directly. The trustees can claim the difference between these two amounts as a deduction from their own liability.

This special treatment is not available in the tax year in which the beneficiary dies.

To claim the special treatment, the trustees must complete form VPE1 and have it signed by the vulnerable person or their attorney. A separate VPE1 must be signed for each vulnerable beneficiary.

The special tax treatment takes effect from the date elected for on the form. The election must be made no later than 12 months after 31 January following the tax year in which it is to start.

Any gains arising prior to the elected date will be taxed normally.

Depending upon the trust's circumstances the trustees can then choose each tax year whether to make a claim or not.

The time limit for making the claim is the first anniversary of 31 January following the end of the tax year in question.

Where there is a vulnerable beneficiary election in place, it is necessary to tick the relevant box on the Trust and Estate Tax Return, SA900.

This treatment is no longer available to the trustees after the death of the beneficiary or the date he or she ceases to be vulnerable.

The trustees have 90 days to inform HMRC that the election has ceased, otherwise a penalty might be payable.

Law: FA 2005, s. 30-32, 37

15.9.5   Taxing gains in an employee trust

On basic principles, employee trusts are subject to the same rules as other trusts (see **15.9.2**).

For the purposes of ascertaining the level of AEA available it is necessary to establish how many trusts the employer has set up and therefore it will be necessary to consider all group companies.

However, where an employee receives an asset from the trust by way of remuneration, there is potentially a CGT charge in the trust and an employment income charge on the individual receiving the asset.

Section 239ZA prevents a charge to both income tax and CGT by providing that the disposal by the trustees is not a chargeable gain in their hands.

15.9.6   Taxing gains in a non-resident trust

If trustees are treated as non-resident (see **15.2.9**) for UK tax purposes, the trust is chargeable on assets which are situated in the UK and used in the trust's UK branch or agency for the purposes of a trade, profession or vocation in the UK.

They are also chargeable on sales of UK land (see **4.3.9**) and assets (such as shares) which derive at least 75% of their value from UK land and the trust has a substantial interest in the asset, i.e. ownership of 25% or more.

Furthermore, beneficiaries of offshore trusts may be taxed on gains attributed to them.

For more detail see **Chapter 18**.

15.10 CGT on terminating a trust

The trustees pay the tax liability when assets are distributed or sold from the trust, see **15.8**.

15.11 CGT on changes under the terms of a trust deed – interest-in-possession trusts

Where a beneficiary becomes absolutely entitled to trust property, the CGT on the trustees will be based on the market value of the assets at the date the beneficiary becomes entitled to them.

On transfer of assets to a beneficiary when he or she becomes absolutely entitled, it is likely that there will be costs incurred by the trustees. The beneficiary may bear the costs of the transfer. He or she can either deduct the costs of the transfer on a later sale of the asset, or can allow the trustees to deduct these costs on calculation of the disposal. However, only one method is allowed.

Law: TCGA 1992, s. 52(1)

15.12 CGT position on death of a beneficiary – interest-in-possession trusts

Where the trust is an interest-in-possession trust that was set up before 2006 or an IPDI or TSI for IHT purposes (see **15.4.4**), there will be a CGT uplift when the beneficiary dies as the assets of the trust are within the beneficiary's estate for IHT purposes.

As there is an uplift to market value, there will be no CGT when the asset is distributed to the remainderman under the terms of the trust.

If the trust becomes discretionary, the assets will be carried forward at the market value at the date of death.

Law: TCGA 1992, s. 72
Guidance: CG 36542

15.13 Sub-funds

15.13.1 Introduction

It is common for trustees to decide to earmark specific assets for certain beneficiaries. This can be referred to as either a sub-fund or a sub-trust.

15.13.2 Usual treatment – no CGT disposal

Providing that the assets remain within one legal entity, the sub-funds are all pooled and continue to be treated as remaining within one trust for CGT purposes.

The trustees have to exercise their power of appointment into the sub-fund so it is important that the trust deed allows them to do this.

However, to prevent a CGT charge arising when the sub-funding takes place, it is important that this appointment does not give the trustees the authority to remove the assets from the original settlement. The assets must remain within the same settlement for CGT purposes.

To ensure that the trustees have not inadvertently created separate settlements, it is best practice to make the appointment of the sub-fund as a revocable appointment (this means that the trustees have power to revoke the sub-fund at a future date if they have reason to). There should be nothing in the appointment documentation which suggests there is no possibility that the funds will ever be held in the main fund again.

Furthermore, it is important that the documentation used to appoint assets onto the sub-funds ensures that the duties with regards to the appointed assets (the new sub-funds) still fall to the trustees of the original settlement in their capacity as trustees of that settlement.

15.13.3 Alternative treatment – election for CGT disposal

It is possible to make an irrevocable sub-fund election in relation to the sub-funds. In simple terms, this means that they would be treated for tax purposes as separate trusts going forward.

By making this election, the trust makes deemed disposals at market value of the capital assets within the sub-fund, therefore any inherent capital gains in those assets are realised.

It is only possible to defer the capital gain under s. 260 if there is a charge to IHT when the sub-fund is created. For example, a transfer from an IPDI trust (which is in the life tenant's estate) to a sub-fund which is held on discretionary powers for the life tenant's children. This would be a chargeable lifetime transfer and, as such, any gain arising could be held over under s. 260.

Similarly, holdover relief can be claimed if the trust assets qualify under s. 165.

Once the election is made, the sub-fund becomes known as the sub-fund settlement and the original trust is known as the principal settlement.

The trustees of the sub-fund settlement are deemed to have reacquired the assets at market value at the date of the election, unless holdover relief is claimed.

Allowable losses on sub-funding assets are dealt with under s. 71(1) which allows losses to be used against gains arising on those same assets. Otherwise, they are not allowable.

Law: TCGA 1992, s. 71(1), (2)
Guidance: CG 37200; TSEM 3510

15.14 Reporting trust gains to HMRC

15.14.1 Self-assessment

Trustees report gains to HMRC on the Trust and Estate Tax Return, known as SA900.

The SA900 CGT pages have to be completed if any of the following apply:

- the trust disposes of chargeable assets in the year worth more than £49,200 (in 2020-21);
- the trustees were required to file non-resident CGT returns in the year;
- the total chargeable gains before the deduction of losses is more than the annual exempt amount for the trust; or
- the trustees have to make a claim for losses or any other kind of CGT claim or election.

All gains should be included (apart from exempt assets).

If the gain has already been reported under the 30-day reporting, the trustees must tick the relevant box on the tax return and claim credit for the tax already paid.

15.14.2   30-day reporting for UK residential property

From 6 April 2020, UK resident taxpayers within the scope of CGT, i.e. individuals, personal representatives, trustees and partnerships, have to report the disposal of UK residential land and property and pay any CGT due within 30 days of the date the transaction is completed.

These rules are covered at **2.3.3**, **2.4.3**, and **4.3.2**

15.14.3   Penalties

Self-assessment penalties for late reporting and late payments are discussed at **2.6**.

15.14.4   Trust registration

A UK trust must register with HMRC when a capital gain arises. It must also register if there is income tax, IHT, SDLT or SDRT. Furthermore, it must register if the trustees wish to claim a tax relief.

For a non-resident trust, the trustees must register it if it becomes liable for tax on UK income or UK assets.

The deadline for an unregistered trust liable for CGT for the first time is 5 October following the tax year the gain arises in.

For example, if the trust first becomes liable for CGT during the 2021-22 tax year, it must register by 5 October 2022.

If the trust has been liable for income tax or CGT before then, the deadline is 31 January in the tax year following the year in which the gain arises.

For example, if the trust is liable for CGT during 2021-22 and it has been liable for tax before, it must register by 31 January 2023.

15.15 CGT on transferring assets into a trust

15.15.1   Effect on settlor

Tax on transferring assets into a trust is paid by the person or persons making the transfer (the settlor).

Under basic principles any transaction is deemed to be made at market value as the settlor is connected to the trust for tax purposes. The individual will be taxed at their marginal rate (either 18% for residential property or 10% on other assets where the settlor is within his or her basic rate band or 28%/20% where they are higher/additional rate taxpayers).

If the transfer into the trust creates a loss, the loss is described as "clogged" (ring-fenced). This means that it can only be used against gains made between the same parties and cannot be used as a general loss against other gains.

15.15.2   Holdover relief

Most lifetime trusts created since 2006 and discretionary trusts prior to this date are within the relevant property regime. This means that a transfer into a discretionary trust is a chargeable lifetime transfer for IHT purposes.

As the transfer into trust is also within the IHT regime, holdover relief can be claimed under s. 260 (as otherwise there would be a double charge to tax under both IHT and CGT on the same transfer for the same person).

Holdover relief is covered in detail in **Chapter 12**.

A claim can be made to hold over under s. 260 even if there is no IHT payable. All that is required is that there has to be a *charge* to IHT, not a liability.

There are exceptions to claiming holdover relief. The settlor cannot claim holdover relief if the trust is settlor-interested. "Settlor" here includes:

- the settlor;
- the settlor's spouse; and
- minor unmarried child, including step-children.

To claim holdover relief, the transferee generally has to be UK resident, unless the asset gifted is a direct or indirect interest in UK land.

Holdover effectively defers the tax on the gains until the recipient (the trustees) sell the assets so preventing a "dry" tax charge (which is a tax charge that arises without receiving any sales proceeds).

Example

Mr Wolverine decides to transfer his share portfolio into a trust for the benefit of his grandchildren. There is a gain of £100,000 inherent in the portfolio.

Without claiming holdover relief, this gain would become chargeable and taxed on him even though he receives no money for the transfer.

However, he can claim holdover relief as the trust is not settlor-interested, and the tax will be deferred until the trustees sell the shares in the future.

A claim has to be made for holdover relief, see **12.7** and **12.13.6**.

It is important that the settlor is aware that if a gain on residential property is held over on the way into the trust, the trustees cannot claim PRR going forward if a beneficiary lives in the property (see **15.4.2**).

15.16 Disposal of trust interest

An interest in a settlement is a form of property in the hands of the beneficiary.

A disposal of a trust interest is generally exempt from CGT. This is to prevent a double charge to taxation when a beneficiary becomes absolutely entitled to trust property,

However, there are certain exceptions to this rule:

- where the beneficiary acquired the trust interest by way of payment (or derives the interest from someone who paid for it);
- where the interest is a non-resident settlement; or
- where the settlement in which the interest is held has been non-resident previously.

Guidance: CG 38000

15.17 Employee-ownership trusts

There is a relief from CGT on disposals of shares in a trading company or the holding company of a trading group where they are sold to an employee-ownership trust (EOT).

To obtain CGT benefits it is it is necessary to meet certain conditions:

- The company has to be a trading company or the holding company of a trading group.
- All employees should be able to benefit from the EOT, though there can be a qualifying employment period of up to one year.
- Any benefits must be provided on the same terms to all beneficiaries.

Certain types of beneficiaries are excluded from benefiting such as those who have held (within the last ten years), now hold, or are able to hold, 5% or more of the share capital (any class of shares) and are also entitled to 5% or more of assets on a winding up. Any person connected with them is included for the purposes of meeting the 5% test.

The EOT must not hold a controlling interest in the company before the tax year in which the acquisition is made. When the sale takes place the EOT must acquire a controlling interest and it must continue to own this interest throughout the remainder of the tax year of acquisition.

Continuing shareholders (and any other 5% participators who are directors, employees or persons connected with them) must not exceed 40% of the total number of employees of the company or group.

Connection is determined in the usual way by s. 286. However, the definition is extended to include uncles, aunts, nephews, and nieces.

Law: TCGA 1992, s. 263I-236M, 236U(3)

16. Deceased estates

16.1 Introduction

There is no CGT on death. Instead, the deceased's assets form his or her estate and will be subject to IHT.

However, once those assets have passed to the personal representatives (PRs), they are subject to a different set of rules that are summarised in this chapter.

For further details see *Personal Representatives – A Guide for Tax Practitioners* from Claritax Books.

Law: TCGA 1992, s. 62(1)

16.2 Key definitions and concepts

16.2.1 Estate

The estate represents the possessions of the deceased that are administered by the PRs. These will be the money and other assets that belonged to the deceased. The estate may also include gifts with reservation of benefit and potentially exempt transfers that were made in the seven years before death.

16.2.2 Personal representatives

The PRs are responsible for dealing with the affairs of a deceased person. PRs may be either executors (if there is a valid will) or administrators (if not).

16.2.3 Administration period

The administration period is the time when the PRs are dealing with the finances of the estate. It starts on the date of death and usually ends for tax purposes when the residue has been determined.

If there are disputes about the will, the administration period will not be concluded until they are resolved.

16.2.4 Residue

The residue of the estate is the remaining funds after all the assets have been identified and all the liabilities paid.

16.2.5   Legatee

A legatee is defined for CGT purposes as including any person benefiting from a testamentary disposition (normally a will), or on an intestacy or a partial intestacy.

For this purpose, legatees include trustees of a settlement arising under the terms of the will or intestacy.

Law: TCGA 1992, s. 64(2)-(3)

16.3   CGT position of PRs

The PRs take over the deceased's assets at market value at the date of death (probate value).

With regards to CGT they must account for and settle any liabilities of:

- the deceased on disposals before death; and
- the estate on disposals during the administration period.

16.4   CGT liabilities of the deceased

16.4.1   Overview

The PRs are responsible for ensuring that any disposals that arose during the tax year up to the date of death are declared to HMRC and any relevant CGT paid.

This is normally done by way of self-assessment, if the deceased was within the self-assessment regime.

If the individual is not registered for self-assessment, then the PRs may calculate the tax due and settle with HMRC informally (subject to the rules for registering complex estates, see **16.6.5**).

The PRs will also take on responsibility for any tax returns that are outstanding. They will need to settle any outstanding CGT liabilities from earlier years and any enquiries that were not concluded by the deceased's death.

16.4.2   Held-over gains

Any gains held over by the deceased, for example under TCGA 1992, s. 165 or 260 (see **Chapter 12**) or deferred using EIS (see **Chapter 10**), will be extinguished on death.

The PRs receive such assets at their market value and no adjustment is made for any previous gains deferred or held over.

16.4.3   Annual exempt amount

The deceased will have a full annual exempt amount (AEA) in the year of death regardless of when they die.

16.4.4   Losses in the year of death

If the deceased sold or otherwise disposed of assets in the tax year of death, then losses may have arisen on these disposals.

The normal rules apply here (see **3.5.1**) in that such losses should be set against any chargeable gains in the same year, even if this reduces the net chargeable gains to below the AEA.

If the PRs have allowable losses for the deceased remaining after offsetting against any gains, then those excess losses may be carried back and offset against gains arising in the three tax years prior to the year of death. This is on a last-in, first-out basis, so the losses must be set against gains made in later years rather than earlier.

Losses carried back under these provisions are used to reduce net chargeable gains to an amount equivalent to the AEA for that tax year, which is then applied, thus preserving its benefit.

Any losses not set against gains of the part of the tax year before death and the three previous tax years will be lost.

See **3.5.2** for a numerical example.

It is not possible to transfer any capital losses to the PRs or the legatees in this situation.

Law: TCGA 1992, s. 62

16.5   CGT in administration period

16.5.1   Overview

During the period of administration, the PRs will be liable to CGT if they sell or otherwise dispose of any of the assets in the estate.

This only applies to assets that are held within the estate, so does not apply to assets that are to be passed to legatees under the terms of the will. Any such assets are held absolutely for the beneficiaries, and the

PRs will simply be acting here as trustees of a bare trust (see **15.2.3** and **15.9.3**).

Otherwise, during the period of administration, the PRs have absolute control over the assets which are not left directly to legatees. As they are not holding these assets on behalf of the legatees the PRs are chargeable on any gains arising until the estate assets are formally transferred to legatees.

Where an estate intends to sell an asset at a gain, it is often worth the PRs considering whether they should appropriate it to one or more of the legatees prior to sale. If the legatee makes the disposal that would trigger the gain in his or her computation and would allow the legatee to offset his or her AEA, preserving the PR's AEA (see **16.5.2**). If the asset is to be sold for the benefit of a number of beneficiaries, appropriating it to them before the sale would enable more than one AEA to be used.

16.5.2   Annual exempt amount

The PRs of an estate have an AEA equal to that of an individual for the tax year in which the individual dies, and for the following two tax years.

Law: TCGA 1992, s. 1K(7)

16.5.3   Residence issues

Other than in relation to UK property, individuals who are treated for tax purposes as non-resident in the UK are not liable to CGT.

The PRs of a deceased individual are treated as a single and continuing body of persons having the same residence and domicile status as the deceased.

For this reason, if the deceased was not resident in the UK before death, then the PRs will not be liable on disposals, even if they are themselves resident in the UK.

Where, despite being not resident, the deceased would still have been liable to CGT on the disposal of certain assets (for example, where the assets had been used in a trade carried on in the UK through a permanent establishment or on the sale of UK property), then the PRs will also be liable on disposal of those assets.

Law: TCGA 1992, s. 62(3)

16.5.4   Calculating the gains

For the purposes of calculating gains and losses, most of the normal CGT rules apply to PRs in the same way as they do to individuals.

However, any assets that were owned by the deceased at the date of death are treated as though they had passed to the PRs at the date of death at their market value at that date.

This value forms the base cost of the asset for any subsequent sale.

Where the PRs acquire assets during the administration of the estate, the actual cost or value of those assets is used in calculating gains or losses on their disposal.

Law: TCGA 1992, s. 62(1)

16.5.5   Rate of CGT

The rate of CGT that applies to PRs is the same as applies to trustees. Any residential property gain is taxed at 28%, other gains are taxed at 20%.

16.5.6   Expenses incurred by PRs

PRs often incur legal and other expenses in the administration of the estate, for example in obtaining a grant of probate.

If the PRs then sell or dispose of some of the assets of the estate, they may wish to deduct some of that expenditure for the purposes of calculating the gains or losses (in addition to usual deductions).

However, given the way that professionals charge for their services, it may not be possible to ascertain the allowable expenditure.

For this reason, HMRC will allow calculations which include deductions for costs of establishing title that are based on an agreed scale.

However, PRs can claim the actual expenditure where this is known.

Guidance: *Statement of Practice* SP 02/04

16.6   Reporting gains to HMRC

16.6.1   Self-assessment

Disposals by the deceased

PRs report any gains up to the date of death to HMRC on the Individual Tax Return (SA100).

Disposals by the PRs

If the PRs have to register the estate as a complex estate on the trust register, they will need to complete Form SA900, Trust and Estates Tax Return, and report any gains made during the period of administration. Otherwise, they will use the SA100.

PRs will need to complete the CGT pages on either SA100 or SA900 if any of the conditions listed at **15.14.1** apply.

All gains should be included, apart from exempt assets.

If the gain has already been reported under the 30-day reporting (below), the PRs must tick the relevant box on the tax return and claim credit for the tax already paid.

16.6.2   *30-day reporting for UK residential property*

From 6 April 2020, UK resident taxpayers within the scope of CGT, i.e. individuals, PRs, trustees and partnerships, have to report the disposal of UK residential land and property and pay any CGT due within 30 days of the date the transaction is completed.

There are different requirements for non-UK residents.

These rules are covered at **2.3.3**, **2.4.3** and **4.3.2**

16.6.3   *Penalties*

Self-assessment penalties for late reporting and late payment are discussed at **2.6**.

16.6.4   *Trust register*

PRs must register a complex estate (see **16.6.5**) with HMRC when a capital gain arises. They must also register it if there is income tax, IHT, SDLT or SDRT. Furthermore, they must register the trust with HMRC if the trustees wish to claim a tax relief.

For a non-resident trust, the trustees must register it if it becomes liable for tax on UK income or tax on UK assets.

16.6.5   When to register

An estate is complex, and the PRs will need to register it, if:

- the value of the estate exceeds £2.5 million;
- the value of assets sold by the PRs in any one tax year exceeds £500,000; or
- total tax due exceeds £10,000.

The registration deadline for a trust liable to tax for the first time is 5 October following the tax year the tax arises in.

For example, if the estate first becomes liable for CGT during the 2021-22 tax year, it must register by 5 October 2022.

If the estate has been liable for tax before, the deadline is 31 January in the tax year following the year in which the gain arises.

For example, if the estate is liable for CGT during 2021-22 and it has been liable for tax before, it must register by 31 January 2023.

16.7   Transfer to legatees

16.7.1   Base cost for legatees

Asset belonged to deceased

When PRs complete the administration of the estate, they will pass the assets to the legatees in accordance with the wishes of the deceased in the will, or under rules of intestacy where there is no will in place.

There is no CGT payable at the point the PRs pass the estate assets to the legatees. They are treated as though they were owned by the legatee at the date of death at their market value.

Law: TCGA 1992, s. 62(1), (4)

Asset acquired by PRs

If the PRs acquire assets during the administration period, and these are passed to legatees under the terms of the will, they are treated as though they were acquired by the legatees themselves on the date the PRs acquired them, at the PRs' cost.

Law: TCGA 1992, s. 62(4)

Subsequent disposal

If the legatee sells or otherwise disposes of those assets, the normal rules of CGT will apply.

16.7.2   Valuations

The PRs will need to value the assets held by the estate to calculate IHT on death. This same valuation will become the base cost for CGT purposes for the legatees receiving the assets.

There will be times when HMRC do not need to consider the valuation for IHT purposes, such as where all the assets pass to the spouse or there is a relief such as business property relief available.

In these circumstances HMRC reserve the right to consider the valuation of the asset at death on a subsequent disposal of the asset.

16.7.3   Losses

The legatee is not able to use unused losses of the deceased or of the PRs, or any of the expenses incurred by the PRs. However, the legatees may be able to offset expenditure incurred by them or by the PRs relating to the actual transfer of the asset to the legatee.

16.7.4   Partial transfers

There may be times when only part of an asset is transferred to a legatee, such as a property being split between several beneficiaries. Here, the acquisition cost of each legatee's share is an appropriate fraction of the market value of the holding or asset acquired by the PRs.

16.8   Variation of terms of will or intestacy

The beneficiaries of the deceased may decide to alter the terms of the will or (if no will is left) of the intestacy. This is normally for IHT purposes, for example to prevent older family members who are likely to be subject to IHT from having more assets pushed into their estate, or to distribute assets in a fairer way.

Where the document is legally valid and certain conditions are met:

- the variation will be treated for CGT purposes as not being a disposal; and
- the rules in this chapter will apply as they would if the variation had in fact been the original terms of the will.

All of the following conditions must be satisfied:

- The variation must be effected by an instrument in writing made within two years of the deceased's death.
- The persons who wish to give up all or part of their entitlement under the will or intestacy provisions must be parties to the instrument.
- There must be no consideration in money or money's worth for the variation other than consideration in the form of a disclaimer or variation of other dispositions of the same estate.
- The instrument must contain a statement that the parties intend s. 62(6) to apply.

Where these conditions are not met, the terms of the deed of variation will result in disposals by some of the parties, which may have CGT consequences.

In some instances, a trust is created as part of the deed of variation. If this trust replaces an absolute gift of assets under the will then the person who gave up their entitlement under the will is the settlor of that trust for CGT purposes.

Law: TCGA 1992, s. 62(6)-(9)

17. Partnerships

17.1 Introduction

17.1.1 What is a partnership?

A partnership is defined in the *Partnership Act* 1890 as "the relation which subsists between persons carrying on a business in common with a view of profit."

For there to be a partnership, there must be at least two people party to the business arrangement These may be individuals, companies or even certain types of other partnership. The arrangement must be one that does not amount to an employment or joint venture and that is more than mere joint ownership.

Example

Aria and Meredith jointly own a flat in Weymouth. This is let on a long-term basis to a tenant. It is unlikely that this would be considered to be a partnership arrangement. However, if the flat was a furnished holiday let, it might be possible to structure the business as a formal partnership.

A partnership cannot be a limited company – although the relatively new concept of limited liability partnerships (LLPs) can offer similar protection to the members.

HMRC consider relationships that do not amount to one of partnership in their *Partnership Manual*:

> "Not all associations between persons for business purposes constitute partnerships. An arrangement which falls short of a partnership is often called a joint venture. Business associates may claim that their relationship is only a joint venture and not a partnership. It is most likely that you have a joint venture and not a partnership in cases:
>
> - where two or more persons, already carrying on a business of their own, co-operate in some way on a single project but
> - do not calculate and share the net profits or losses resulting from this.

> The letting of jointly owned property does not normally constitute a partnership. Most cases will fall short of the degree of business organisation needed to constitute a business. The provision of significant additional services in return for payment may be an indicator of such business organisation."

Broadly, if there is an arrangement between two or more persons to carry on a business with a clear profit motive, a partnership is likely to exist. In recent years, the profit motive has been examined in relation to a number of tax avoidance schemes.

A partnership (other than an LLP) does not need a formal written agreement to exist; its existence is instead a question of fact. However, it is usual for there to be a written partnership agreement setting out how profits are to be shared and other terms.

An LLP *must* be incorporated by registration at Companies House, together with a statement of compliance confirming that two or more persons (the designated members) have subscribed to an incorporation document with a view to carrying on a lawful business with a view to profit (*Limited Liability Partnership Act* 2000, s. 2).

For the purposes of this chapter, we will assume that the partnerships discussed are established, and their existence is not in question. In-depth commentary about the status of partnerships, including relevant case law, is included in *Taxation of Partnerships*, from Claritax Books.

Law: PA 1890; LLPA 2000, s. 2
Guidance: PM 131800

17.1.2   Types of partnership

There are a number of recognised partnership types, some of which have slightly different applicable rules. A brief description of the most common types is given below.

General partnerships

A general partnership is one whose partners are all general partners, i.e. all the partners are jointly liable for all debts and obligations of the partnership.

Husband and wife partnerships

It is common for spouses, and more recently civil partners, to divide income-producing assets between them to maximise tax efficiency, e.g.

to use two income tax basic rate bands as far as possible. Traders may seek to do this by incorporating their business and bringing in the spouse or civil partner as a director shareholder. This increases the options for profit extraction. However, there are many reasons why a company may not be a desirable option, and an alternative could be to form a partnership instead.

HMRC consider that the settlements legislation can apply to husband and wife partnerships, such that the profits transferred to one partner continue to be assessed on the other. This will depend on the partnership terms and the contribution of the incoming partner.

In particular, the settlements legislation may apply where there is an arrangement under which the property received by one spouse or civil partner is wholly or mainly a right to income.

HMRC provide an example in the *Trusts, Settlements and Estates Manual* at TSEM 4215.

HMRC example

Mr Y, an architect, commences business as a sole trader. The business is successful and a few years later annual profits are in the region of £80,000. The business is transferred to a new partnership of Mr and Mrs Y. A deed is executed under which income profits are to be shared equally but the rights to share in capital profits belong solely to Mr Y.

Mrs Y subscribes no new capital and carries out no work whatsoever for the partnership, that is to say she is a sleeping partner. Profits for the year are £80,000 and £40,000 belongs to Mrs Y. This is a bounteous arrangement transferring income from one spouse to another. The settlements legislation will apply, and Mrs Y's share of the profits will continue to be assessed on Mr Y.

Limited partnerships

A limited partnership (LP) is one in which – for at least one partner – a limit is placed on that partner's liability for the debts and obligations of the partnership. There must also be one "general" partner, with unlimited liability, who is essentially the "manager" of the business.

LPs must be registered at Companies House, and are subject to the *Limited Partnerships Act* 1907 (LPA 1907) in addition to the *Partnership Act* 1890 (PA 1890).

Limited liability partnerships

LLPs are relatively new, and are subject to LLPA 2000. The liability of a member of an LLP for partnership debts and obligations is limited to that member's capital contribution, in much the same way that a company shareholder has limited liability.

Unlike LPs, LLPs are considered to be distinct and separate from the individual members. Generally, and despite this separate legal entity, the tax consequences for LLPs are the same as for other types of partnership (i.e. they are fiscally transparent). However, there are some important exceptions, discussed later in this chapter.

A key difference from LPs is that a member of an LLP can take part in the management of the business, even though that member's liability is limited.

Mixed partnerships

A mixed partnership is any partnership, including an LLP, that has both real and legal persons (e.g. individuals and companies) as partners. Mixed partnerships are subject to anti-avoidance rules to prevent profits and losses being diverted between corporate and non-corporate members to secure tax advantages.

Scottish partnerships

A Scottish partnership is considered a legal person (PA 1890, s. 4(2)). This stands in contrast to English, Welsh or Northern Irish general or limited partnerships.

In practice, this has very few tax consequences. For income tax purposes, ITTOIA 2005, s. 848 directs that, unless otherwise indicated, a partnership is not regarded as an entity separate and distinct from the partners

Law: PA 1890; LPA 1907; LLPA 2000; ITTOIA 2005, s. 848
Guidance: BIM 82065; TSEM 4215

17.1.3   Types of partner

There are a number of different categories of partner. As discussed above, a general partner is one who is jointly (and severally in Scotland) liable for all debts and obligations of the partnership incurred while a partner.

An indirect partner is a member of a partnership that has a separate legal identity, e.g. an LLP, that is itself a partner in another partnership. A person can also be an indirect partner in a partnership if the person is a partner in:

- a partnership that is a partner in the underlying partnership; or
- any partnership that is an indirect partner in the underlying partnership.

Example

Partnership A allocates profits to partnership B, and partnership B then allocates profits to Person C.

Partnership B is a partner in partnership A. Person C is a partner in partnership B. Person C is therefore also an indirect partner in partnership A.

The liability of a limited partner in a limited partnership, for partnership debts and obligations, is restricted, typically to the level of that partner's capital contribution. A limited partner must not take part in the management of the partnership's business; nor may the limited partner bind the partnership, i.e. by entering into contracts on its behalf.

A general partner in a limited partnership is a partner with no restriction on liability.

A nominated partner is the partner responsible for managing the partnership's tax return, i.e. submitting the return to HMRC and dealing with matters that may arise from HMRC enquiries into the return. The nominated partner is also responsible for the partnership's record keeping.

The term "salaried partner" can refer either to a genuine partner, who has entitlement to the first share of partnership profits, or (depending on the facts) to an employee to whom the title of partner is conferred for prestige and in name only.

There are specific anti-avoidance provisions for LLPs to determine whether a member of an LLP is a genuine partner or a partner in name only.

17.1.4   *How a partnership is taxed*

The parties to the arrangement are referred to as "partners", though the term "member" is often used – particularly with LLPs.

There are several types of partnership in the UK, for example ordinary, LP, LLP, etc., as discussed in **17.1.2**. However, for tax purposes the treatment of all of them is virtually identical: they are "fiscally transparent" in that they are not taxed on their income and gains directly. Instead, the partners are treated as receiving a share in the profits, losses and gains and are taxed individually, reporting the results on their self-assessment returns. There are particular rules with CGT for LLPs in cases of liquidation or court-ordered winding up (see **17.3**).

Despite this fiscal transparency, partnerships must complete a partnership tax return each year, including a split of the results allocated to each partner.

For CGT purposes, the legislation is largely silent on how gains are to be taxed, so most of the detail (of how normal tax principles are applied to partnerships) is contained in Statement of Practice D12 (SP D12). This was first published in 1975, but various supplementary statements have been issued subsequently.

The concept of fiscal transparency in respect of gains is, however, put on a statutory footing in TCGA 1992, s. 59:

"(1)   Where two or more persons carry on a trade or business in partnership–

(a)   tax in respect of chargeable gains accruing to them on the disposal of any partnership assets shall, in Scotland as well as elsewhere in the United Kingdom, be assessed and charged on them separately, and

(b)   any partnership dealings shall be treated as dealings by the partners and not by the firm as such."

Section 59A deals with LLPs and is almost identical, save for some minor exceptions.

The sharing ratio for profits may be the same as the capital-sharing ratio, though this is not a requirement, and it is common for more junior partners to be entitled to share in the profits without having an entitlement to a capital interest.

As the charge to CGT is levied on the individual partners rather than the partnership, the residence and domicile status of the partners may need to be considered (see **Chapter 18**).

Law: TCGA 1992, s. 59, 59A
Guidance: SP D12

17.2 CGT for partnerships in detail

17.2.1 The legal basis of SP D12

Statement of Practice D12 does not have any statutory basis, but it has, over the last 40 years, become accepted practice in relation to partnership capital gains. It is, essentially, a non-statutory extension to s. 59 and s. 59A(1).

The Office of Tax Simplification carried out a review of the taxation of partnerships (*Review of partnerships: final report*, January 2015), and concluded that SP D12 provided a reasonable result in most circumstances, but that parts of it should be rewritten to replace out-of-date language and obsolete content. The current version of SP D12 (updated in September 2015) has taken into account those recommendations.

Guidance: SP D12

17.2.2 Valuing partnership assets

Each partner in a partnership is treated as owning a fraction of partnership assets, usually stipulated by the partnership agreement. However, unlike holdings of share capital, there is no concept of discounting for a minority interest; instead, each partner's interest is valued at that partner's fractional interest in the total value.

HMRC's manual advises at CG 27220 that a partner's fractional interest in a partnership asset should be determined by reference to:

- any specific agreement that sets out how capital assets are to be allocated; or (if there is no such agreement)
- any agreement or other evidence that sets out how capital profits are to be shared; or (if there is no such agreement or evidence)
- any agreement or other evidence that sets out how income profits are to be shared; or (if there is no such agreement or evidence)

- *Partnership Act* 1890, s. 24(1), which provides that assets should be treated as held by the partners in equal proportions.

It is common for the capital-sharing ratio to be set out in writing. For example, if partnership ABC owns a building worth £500,000, and partner A's partnership share according to the partnership agreement is 15%, A's financial share of the asset is 15% of £500,000 = £75,000.

Law: PA 1890, s. 24(1)
Guidance: SP D12; CG 27220, 27250

17.2.3   Allocating the base cost

Establishing the base cost of a partnership asset needs to be approached with care, as not only do the basic statutory provisions have to be considered, but the allocation of base cost between the partners can also be complex.

The basic statutory position is that the base cost of an asset comprises the original cost of acquiring the asset, plus any expenditure incurred wholly and exclusively for the purpose of enhancing the value of the asset. Any enhancement expenditure must be reflected in the state or nature of the asset at the time of disposal.

When an asset is acquired by the partnership, its base cost is allocated to the partners in accordance with the agreed capital-sharing ratio or otherwise in accordance with the rules in **17.2.2**.

However, there will likely be changes to the sharing ratios throughout the life of the partnership – either through partners joining or leaving, or via agreed changes to the ratios. Such changes represent disposals and acquisitions of fractional interests and, in the absence of SP D12, would mean capital gains and losses were frequently being made.

17.2.4   Disposals and distributions of partnership assets – sales to third parties

Where assets are disposed of by the partnership to an outside party, each partner will be treated as disposing of his or her fractional share in the asset.

The disposal proceeds will be allocated according to how they are dealt with by the partnership, which will usually be in accordance with an agreed capital-sharing ratio, or in accordance with the normal profit-sharing ratio. However, if there is no formal agreement on how profits are to be shared, the default position under PA 1890 is to share profits equally. If there is an agreement outside the accounts as to how the proceeds on a disposal are to be shared, that will be used as a basis for computing the gain for each partner.

Example – sale of property

Jack and Jill are business partners who have operated a flour mill for many years. The mill cost them £80,000 and they are now selling it for £400,000. Jill contributed most of the original capital and is entitled to 65% of capital assets. The computation is as follows:

	Jack	Jill
	£	£
Sale proceeds (35%/65%)	140,000	260,000
Base cost	28,000	52,000
Gains	112,000	208,000

The partners each pay tax on the respective gains, subject to such reliefs as may be available.

The position is more complex if there has been a change in profit-sharing ratios, for example when a partner joins or leaves the partnership. See **17.2.4**.

17.2.5   Distribution of assets to the partners

Where assets are distributed to the partners in kind, often on dissolution of the partnership:

- Partners who do not receive a share of the asset on distribution will be treated as making a disposal for CGT purposes. The asset is treated as being sold at market value.

- Partners who receive a share of the asset on distribution will have a gain, but this is deferred. They will be treated as having acquired the asset with a base cost that is made up of their own share of the original base cost, plus the aggregate market value taken into account in computing gains for the partners giving up a share of that asset.

When the partners who received a share in the asset on distribution dispose of the asset, their share of the gain that was deferred will fall into charge, together with any further gain in respect of their share in that asset. This means that over the entire period of ownership of the asset by partners of the partnership, the whole gain will have been charged, albeit at different times.

HMRC example (CG 27400)

A and B carry on a business in partnership and hold equal interests in partnership assets.

The partnership owns a freehold property which cost £400,000.

On the dissolution of the partnership the property was distributed to Partner B.

The market value of the property at the time of the distribution was £640,000.

The chargeable gain arising on the disposal by A of his fractional interest in the asset at the time of the distribution and the notional gain arising on B's fractional interest in the asset are computed as follows:

	Partner A £	Partner B £
Disposal proceeds based on market value		
£640,000 x 50%	320,000	320,000
Less acquisition cost	200,000	200,000
Chargeable gain	120,000	
Notional gain		120,000

Partner A

The gain accruing to Partner A, £120,000, will be chargeable at the time of the distribution.

Partner B

The notional gain accruing to Partner B is not chargeable as the effect of the distribution is that his interest in the asset has increased. His CG base cost on a future disposal of the property will be the market value of the asset at the time of the distribution reduced by the notional gain:

	£
Market value of asset	640,000
Notional gain on distribution	120,000
CG base cost	520,000

Note that Partner B acquired a 50% interest in the asset for £200,000 on its acquisition by the partnership. At the time of the distribution he acquired a further 50% interest for an amount equal to the disposal consideration taken into account for Partner A, ie £320,000. His total acquisition cost is therefore £520,000.

Guidance: SP D12, para. 3; CG 27400

17.2.6   Changes in sharing ratios

Change in sharing ratio with no revaluation

Where the chargeable assets are not revalued on a change in sharing ratio, and no consideration is paid for the change, no chargeable gains or losses will arise. Each partner's base cost is simply reallocated in accordance with the new ratio.

Example 1

There are three equal partners in the Trading Partnership, A, B and C. The partnership acquired its premises, paying £300,000. The base cost for each of the partners is £100,000.

The partners agree to change the profit-sharing and capital-sharing ratios, so that A will take 45%, B 40%, and C 15%. The property is now worth £480,000. When the change in the capital-sharing ratios takes effect, C will make a disposal of part of his interest in the property. However, because the partnership has not revalued the asset, which is shown in the accounts at the original cost of £300,000, the gain is not charged.

Instead, the base cost of the asset is reallocated between the partners so that the revised share of base cost is: A £135,000, B £120,000, C £45,000. The partnership must keep a note of these base costs, as it will be required when there is a chargeable disposal of the property.

In these circumstances, a CGT charge will only arise if the transaction is deemed to take place at market value, for example if it is made between connected persons or otherwise than by way of a bargain on arm's length terms.

It should be noted that while partners in a partnership are generally connected with one another, this connection is ignored for transfers between partners as long as they are undertaken for genuine commercial reasons – unless the partners are otherwise connected, e.g. family members.

Change in sharing ratio with revaluation

If a capital-sharing ratio changes following a revaluation of the underlying asset on the balance sheet, a capital gain will arise for the partner(s) whose interest is reduced.

Example 2

The Trading Partnership instead decides (i.e. in a different approach from Example 1) to revalue the property before changing the capital-sharing ratio between the partners.

On revaluation, the property will be shown as a fixed asset in the balance sheet with a value of £480,000. The revaluation will be credited to each of the partners' capital accounts in the partnership in proportion to their current capital-sharing ratios. Each capital account will therefore increase by £60,000.

This upward revaluation will not be the occasion of charge. However, when the partners change the capital-sharing ratio, C gives up part of his interest in the property, and as there has been a revaluation, this change will be the occasion of charge.

C's gain will be computed as follows, reflecting the reduction from a one third interest (say 33.34% for the example) to a 15% interest, so a disposal of 18.34% of the total:

	£
Proceeds, based on balance sheet value of the property 480,000 x (33.34% – 15%)	88,032
Base cost 100,000 x 18.34/33.34	55,009
Net gain 88,032 – 55,009	33,023

A's base cost of the property will be £156,016:

(88,032 x 11.67/18.34 = 56,016) + 100,000

B's base cost of the property will be £132,016:

(88,032 x 6.67/18.34 = 32,016) + 100,000

C's base cost of the property will be £44,991 (100,000 − 55,009).

Change in sharing ratio with consideration

Where a payment is made outside the accounts, for example one partner pays another to acquire a greater fractional share of the asset, a gain will accrue to the partner receiving the payment, and the partner making the payment will take the payment into account in establishing his or her base cost for the asset acquired.

Example 3

A few years later, the property owned by the Trading Partnership has increased in value to £600,000. A has agreed to acquire part of B's interest in the partnership, so that the capital will be shared in the proportions: A 70%, B 15%, C 15%.

A has agreed to pay B £24,000 for the 25% interest in the partnership that she is acquiring. There will be no further revaluation in the accounts to reflect the increase in value in the property. The gain accruing to B will be computed as follows:

	£
Proceeds, based on the balance sheet value plus the consideration received from A (480,000 x 25% = 120,000) + 24,000	144,000
Base cost 132,016 x 25/40	82,510
Net gain 144,000 − 82,510	61,490

B's remaining base cost will be £49,506 (132,016 x 15/40).

A's base cost will be £300,016 (156,016 + 120,000 + 24,000).

C's base cost will remain at £44,991.

Once the base cost at the date of disposal is correctly identified, it is deducted from the fractional share of disposal proceeds (or market value as appropriate) to calculate the gain.

Law: TCGA 1992, s. 17, 18, 59, 59A

Guidance: SP D12; CG 27500*ff.*

17.2.7   Contributions of assets

An individual partner may make an asset, e.g. a commercial building, available for use by the partnership. Where this is done by a transfer of the asset, the individual will have made a part disposal equal to the fractional share acquired by the other partners. Unless the market value rule applies, the consideration will be the amount paid by the partnership in exchange for the part disposal.

The computation is similar to the computation on a change in profit-sharing ratios, although because the asset does not have a balance sheet value the approach is usually to apportion the allowable costs on a fractional basis, rather than using the statutory A/A + B formula that would usually apply on a part disposal.

Example

Joanne owns a workshop that she would like to contribute to a partnership in which she has a 75% interest. The remaining 25% in the partnership is held by Catherine. The workshop is currently worth £200,000 and cost £160,000.

Joanne is disposing of a 25% interest in the property when she contributes it to the partnership. Her disposal consideration is, therefore, £50,000.

Her base cost is £40,000 (160,000 x 50,000/(50,000 + 150,000)).

Joanne's remaining base cost for the workshop is £120,000 (160,000 – 40,000).

Catherine's base cost for her share of the workshop is £50,000.

Law: TCGA 1992, s. 42

Guidance: SP D12; CG 27900

17.3   Special rules for LLPs

LLPs that carry on a commercial trade or business are treated as fiscally transparent like other partnerships, even though they are a distinct and separate legal entity from their members. Upon a cessation of trade, the fiscal transparency continues if:

- the cessation is temporary; or
- an informal winding-up process is started following a permanent cessation, provided the winding-up is not connected with the avoidance of tax, and the period of winding up is not unreasonably prolonged. This would apply, for example, where the members decide to cease trade and sell the assets of the LLP in an orderly way.

However, an LLP will cease to be fiscally transparent, instead being treated as a corporate entity, if a liquidator is appointed or a winding-up order is issued by a court. Any gains arising following the relevant date will be calculated as if the LLP had never been fiscally transparent. Each member will be treated as making a disposal of a capital interest in the LLP (i.e. not the underlying asset), the allowable cost being the capital contributions made by each of the members as if the LLP had never been treated as transparent.

Law: TCGA 1992, s. 59A
Guidance: CG 27050

17.4   Reliefs available for partnership gains

17.4.1   Overview

A number of reliefs may be available on disposals of partnership interests or assets, including in particular:

- business asset disposal relief (see **17.4.2**);
- rollover relief (see **17.4.3**); and
- gift holdover relief (see **17.4.4**).

17.4.2   Business asset disposal relief

BADR (covered in depth in **Chapter 7**) is an important relief for partnerships and partners.

Key principles that apply include the following:

- An individual who disposes of (or of interests in) assets used for the purposes of a business carried on by the individual on entering into a partnership which is to carry on the business is to be treated as disposing of a part of the business.

- The disposal by an individual of the whole or part of the individual's interest in the assets of a partnership is to be treated as a disposal by the individual of the whole or part of the business carried on by the partnership.

- At any time when a business is carried on by a partnership, the business is to be treated as owned by each individual who is at that time a member of the partnership.

In accordance with normal BADR principles, the relief is available on the disposal of an interest in a partnership (a material disposal) but not on a disposal of partnership assets by the partnership.

BADR is also available on a disposal of assets held by the partner but used for the trade of the partnership, so long as that disposal is associated with a relevant material disposal.

Where an individual owns shares in a corporate partner in a trading partnership, it is possible to claim BADR on a disposal of shares in that company, so long as the company can be treated as a trading company taking into account:

- the activity of the partnership (in respect of which there is a look through); and

- any activity carried on by the company itself.

Law: TCGA 1992, s. 169I-169V
Guidance: CG 64020, 63950P

17.4.3   Rollover relief

Rollover relief (covered in depth in **Chapter 11**) is another important relief for business partners.

Where a partnership disposes of a qualifying asset, for example land and buildings, goodwill, various quotas and single-payment entitlements, and uses the whole of the proceeds to acquire new qualifying assets that are brought into use for the purposes of its trade, the gain on the disposal of the old asset can be rolled into the acquisition of the new asset. As a result, the base cost of the new asset is reduced by the rolled-over gain.

The amount of the gain that can be rolled over is reduced where only part of the proceeds from the old asset are reinvested and/or if the old asset has not been used for the purposes of the trade throughout the period of ownership.

Assets owned personally

Where a partner owns an asset personally, but the asset is used for the purposes of the partnership's trade, it is possible to claim rollover relief. However, where the asset is jointly owned with individuals who are not partners in the partnership, relief can be claimed only on the part owned by the partner in the partnership.

Law: TCGA 1992, s. 152-160
Guidance: CG 60250C

17.4.4   Gift relief

Holdover relief, also referred to as gift relief, is covered in depth in **Chapter 12**.

A gift is not an arm's length bargain, so market value is used to compute the gain, whether or not the parties are connected for CGT purposes. However, a claim for relief can be made for gifts of business assets, as a result of which the asset is treated as being transferred at a price that gives rise to neither a gain nor a loss on the disposal. In most cases, this means that the transferor's base cost transfers to the transferee.

The transferor and the transferee must make a joint claim to relief, unless the transferees are trustees, in which case the claim is made by the transferor alone.

Where the partnership is carrying on a trade, and the CGT transaction involves an asset used for the purposes of the trade, gift relief usually takes care of any difference between the market value of the asset and any consideration received. However, it is important to ensure that the full measure of any consideration received is taken into account, as consideration in non-cash form can be overlooked. If an asset is transferred in exchange for something else, or there are reciprocal transactions, the transfer of the asset is not by way of gift, so relief for gift of business assets may not be available.

Partnership assets may also include assets that are not used for the purposes of the partnership's trade. The partnership could, for example, hold rental property or land that is simply not used for the purposes of the trade. Gift relief would not be available on a disposal at undervalue of those assets.

Law: TCGA 1992, s. 165, 166, 168
Guidance: CG 66880P

18. Non-resident capital gains tax

18.1 Introduction

Historically, non-UK resident individuals were generally not subject to CGT on the disposal of assets, wherever the assets were situated in the world. Only those who were temporarily non-resident (see **18.8**) or operating in the UK via a permanent establishment, branch, or agency were subject to UK CGT.

This meant that once a person had left the UK and successfully established non-UK residence, they would not pay tax on gains realised on any UK assets, including property, that they owned.

Since 2013, UK tax residency has been determined by the statutory residence test (SRT). Provided an individual was non-resident under the terms of the SRT, they were outside the scope of UK CGT.

While this is still the case for many assets such as shares or investments, from 6 April 2015 the UK CGT regime was extended so that non-UK residents became subject to CGT on the disposal of UK residential property. This was called the non-resident CGT regime (NRCGT).

The NRCGT regime in its original form was focused solely on residential property. However, further amendments were introduced in 2019 to widen its scope to cover all UK land and property. Broadly, this requires a relevant disposal to be reported to HMRC within 30 days of completion.

This chapter will consider the current, i.e. the NRCGT 2019, regime in the first instance, with references to the NRCGT 2015 rules as appropriate.

A non-resident taxpayer who is taxed under the NRCGT rules will be taxed based upon the taxpayer's legal status. This means that the relevant annual exemption will be available to individuals, PRs and trustees.

18.2 Key definitions and concepts

18.2.1 Persons within the scope of NRCGT 2019

All non-resident taxpayers are within the NRCGT 2019 regime. For these purposes, this includes individuals, personal representatives, trustees, partnerships, companies and collective investment vehicles.

Law: TCGA 1992, s. 1A(3), 1C-1D, 2B(4)-(6)

18.2.2   Disposals within the scope of NRCGT 2019

To come within the scope of NRCGT 2019, the disposal must take place in a tax year in which the person is non-resident or, where there is a split tax year, it must be in the part that relates to the overseas residence.

Example

Roger leaves the UK on 31 July 2021. He claims split-year treatment for the 2021-22 tax year. He sells his house on 20 February 2022. This is during the part of the tax year that he is non-resident and therefore the sale will fall within the NRCGT rules.

Partnerships are taxed based on the underlying member entity, i.e. either an individual or a company (as relevant) based on the structure of the partnership.

From 2019, a disposal of an interest in UK land can either take the form of a direct disposal, i.e. one where the taxpayer owns the interest outright, or an indirect disposal.

Where an option is granted that binds the owner to sell an interest in the land, the rules treat this as a disposal of that interest. The date of the grant is the date that triggers the 30-day reporting window (see **18.6.1**).

This is different from the basic principles of CGT. See **6.5** for a discussion of the CGT treatment of options.

Law: TCGA 1992, s. 1A(3)-(5), 1G, 2B(4)-(6)

18.2.3   Indirect disposal

An indirect disposal is one where the taxpayer does not own the relevant asset directly.

75% test

An indirect disposal of an asset (such as shares) for the purposes of NRCGT is one that derives at least 75% of its value from UK land where the taxpayer has a substantial indirect interest in that land. Such a disposal includes a straightforward sale of an asset, but can also include a gift, a transfer or an exchange of the asset. Therefore, the definition is wide for these purposes.

The typical scenario is where a taxpayer owns shares in a company and the company owns the UK property, and it is the shares that are disposed of. In this situation, if the company derives 75% or more of its value from

UK land, the taxpayer is deemed to have disposed of their interest in the land.

Example

Pierre, who is non-UK resident for tax purposes, owns 100% of the share capital in a Jersey resident company which in turn owns properties in the UK and in France. The UK property makes up 85% of the value of the company. When he sells the shares in the company, he is deemed to have disposed of the underlying UK properties.

Before these rules came into force in 2019, the CGT regime related to the annual tax on enveloped dwellings (ATED) operated to tax the sale of UK residential property. These rules were abolished when the NRGCT 2019 regime came into effect.

25% test (substantial indirect interest)

In addition to meeting the 75% test, it is necessary for the taxpayer to have an effective investment of 25% or more in the entity that owns the land. This is known as a "substantial indirect interest". This has to be held for the two-year period before the date of disposal.

When deciding whether a non-resident has an effective 25% investment in the entity that owns the land, the investment directly held by the non-resident and any investments held by anyone connected with the non-resident must be included in the calculation. The definition of "connected persons" for this purpose is given in CG 73936 (the definition at s. 286 being modified for these purposes by Sch. 1A, para. 10).

To establish whether there is a substantial indirect interest, it is necessary to consider:

- voting power;
- entitlement to company assets on disposal;
- entitlement to income distribution; and
- the right to assets in the event of a winding-up.

The condition is met when a non-resident is entitled to at least 25% of any of these.

Restricted preference shares and normal commercial loans made by the non-resident or a connected person to the company are ignored.

The substantial indirect interest condition is measured over the two years prior to the date of disposal. This condition is met if the non-resident's effective investment is at least 25% at any point in this period.

25% test – insignificant proportion exclusion

However, there is a concept of "insignificant proportion" in the rules. This is an exclusion if the non-resident holds a substantial indirect interest for only an insignificant proportion of that two-year period (or of the entire period of ownership, if this is less than two years).

Where this rule applies, the holding is ignored, and the condition is treated as not being met.

There is no definition of "insignificant proportion" in the legislation. However, for most purposes HMRC consider a holding to be insignificant where the proportion held is 10% or less.

Law: TCGA 1992, s. 1A, 1D, 286; Sch. 1A, para. 3-10
Guidance: CG 73936, 73938

18.2.4   Interest in land

An interest in UK land includes an estate, interest, right or power over land in the UK. It will also include the benefit of an obligation, restriction or condition that affects the value of an estate, interest, right or power over land. This is a wide definition that includes both freehold and leasehold interests.

The rules include all buildings and structures and any land under the sea or otherwise covered by water.

There are limited exemptions to the definition of interest in land as follows:

- security interests (i.e. a mortgage);
- licences to occupy;
- tenancies at will;
- advowsons;
- franchises granted by the Crown; and
- manors.

Law: TCGA 1992, s. 1C(2), (3), (6)
Guidance: CG 73922

18.2.5   UK residential property interest

It is still necessary to consider the NRCGT 2015 rules for disposals after 5 April 2019 which were wholly or partially chargeable before this date (see **18.3**).

When NRCGT 2015 was introduced, the rules applied only to disposals of UK "residential property interests". This meant that only UK dwellings (subject to some exceptions listed below) were within the scope of the regime.

The definition of residential property for the purposes of NRCGT is similar to that for stamp duty land tax and ATED but there are some differences. A UK residential property interest is an interest in UK land which has either:

- consisted of, or included, a dwelling at any time in the relevant ownership period, which is the period from the date of acquisition (or 6 April 2015 if later) to the date of disposal;
- consisted of a right which exists, at any time in the relevant ownership period, for the benefit of the land (such as an easement or planning permission); or
- been acquired off-plan (in which case, it is treated as being a dwelling throughout its period of ownership, even though the land may have been purchased prior to construction of the dwelling itself or before an existing building had been adapted for use as a dwelling).

Due to the widely drawn definition, it is possible for the NRCGT 2015 rules to apply to a disposal which is not actually residential property at the time it is disposed of.

Where a property has been converted into a different use, say commercial use, but had previously been a dwelling (after 6 April 2015), any gain would be apportioned between the different uses, to ensure that only the part of the gain attributable to the period during which the dwelling existed would be charged to CGT.

Where a person has different interests in the same land (e.g. leasehold and freehold) which were acquired at different times, then the "relevant ownership period" begins on the date the first interest was acquired.

Law: TCGA 1992, Sch. B1, para. 1(5)

18.2.6   Dwelling

The definition of "dwelling" for the NRCGT 2015 rules has similar elements to other areas of the legislation but also has very specific exclusions.

A dwelling is:

- a building, or part of a building, which is used as, or is suitable for use as, a dwelling;
- a building, or part of a building, which is in the process of being constructed or adapted for use as a dwelling; or
- land that is, or is intended to be, occupied or enjoyed as garden or grounds of a dwelling at any time during the ownership period.

Any period where the residence is temporarily unfit for use as a dwelling is normally ignored when calculating the NRCGT 2015 gain.

The main exceptions to this are where:

- the building is not available for use due to accidental damage, or to other damage beyond the owner's control, and the damage means that the building cannot be used for at least 90 consecutive days; or
- the building is in the process of being demolished or converted to non-residential use and the demolition/conversion is in accordance with any required planning permission or consent.

Where one of these exceptions applies, the unavailable period is taken into account when calculating the gain or loss on disposal chargeable under the NRCGT 2015 rules.

Although there are similarities, the dwellings excluded from the NRCGT 2015 rules are different from the ATED exclusions. An example is properties rented to third parties, which are excluded from a charge to ATED but are within the NRCGT 2015 rules.

The following buildings are not treated as being used as a dwelling:

- residential accommodation used by school pupils or members of the armed forces;
- homes or institutions providing residential accommodation to children, old age pensioners, disabled people, people with mental illness, or those dependent on alcohol or drugs;
- a hospital, hospice or prison;

- a hotel or inn;
- residential accommodation with at least 15 bedrooms which is purpose-built or converted for occupation by students and is occupied by them for at least 165 days in the tax year; and
- residential accommodation used as an institution that is the main residence of its residents (and not covered by one of the exclusions listed above). This may include dwellings such as monasteries and other communal accommodation.

Law: TCGA 1992, Sch. B1, para. 4, 6, 8

18.3   Calculating NRCGT 2019 gains and losses

18.3.1   *Overview*

Under the NRCGT 2019 rules, the gain or loss on a disposal is calculated with reference to the category into which it falls. These categories are:

- direct disposals of pre-6 April 2015 UK land which is *fully* chargeable before 6 April 2019. This is residential land or property held from 6 April 2015 (or date of acquisition if later) to 5 April 2019 and is taxable under the NRCGT 2015 rules (see **18.3.2**);
- direct disposals of pre-6 April 2015 UK land which was *partly* chargeable before 6 April 2019. This is land or property that was partly residentially held from 6 April 2015 and is taxed under the NRCGT 2015 rules (see **18.3.3**);
- disposal of an asset that was not chargeable before 6 April 2019 (i.e. indirect disposals of residential and disposals of non-residential property) (see **18.3.4**); and
- disposal of an asset purchased on or after 6 April 2019 (see **18.3.5**).

Law: TCGA 1992, Sch. 4AA, para. 1
Guidance: CG 73960

18.3.2   *Disposals of pre-6 April 2015 UK land fully chargeable before 6 April 2019*

Where the interest in UK residential land is held directly by the non-resident and the land was wholly residential in nature in the period between 6 April 2015 (or the date of acquisition, if later) and 5 April 2019, the gain is calculated using the NRCGT 2015 rules.

Although the normal CGT rules apply for the purposes of calculating the gain or loss, only the gain arising after 5 April 2015 is chargeable. This means there is an effective uplift to 5 April 2015.

Under these provisions, there is no uplift to April 2019.

If wholly residential land is sold, the taxpayer can choose any of the following possible methods of calculation to work out the gain or loss:

- default method (rebasing to 5 April 2015);
- election for straight-line time apportionment; or
- election for retrospective basis of computation.

Default method (rebasing to 5 April 2015)

This is the default position and the calculation which must be used if no election is made for one of the other bases.

Under this option, only the increase in value from the rebased date (if any) is taxable. This is a straightforward calculation, but requires a valuation to determine the value at 5 April 2015.

It is advisable to obtain a professional valuation at this date to substantiate the uplift. For the purposes of this calculation, it is possible to deduct any professional valuation costs.

However, it is not possible to deduct the cost of valuation fees if one of the other two methods is chosen following a valuation, as it is not required for the purposes of carrying out those calculations.

Election for straight-line time apportionment

Under this method, the chargeable proportion of the gain is calculated on a time-apportioned basis, with only the post-5 April 2015 proportion being within the scope of the NRCGT 2019 charge. No valuation is needed under this method. As a basic example, if the taxpayer purchased the property on 6 April 2005, and sells it on 5 April 2022 this basis would exclude 10/17ths of any gain from charge. However, any loss would be similarly restricted.

Election for retrospective basis of computation

This method brings into charge the entire gain, not just the post-5 April 2015 element. This election is most likely to be useful where the disposal results in a loss as, under this method, the entire loss is allowable.

For a worked example, see CG 73962.

It will be necessary to produce calculations of the gain or loss under all three methods to decide which provides the most beneficial outcome for the taxpayer.

Law: TCGA 1992, Sch. 4AA, para. 6-10
Guidance: CG 73962

18.3.3   *Direct disposal of UK land partially chargeable before 6 April 2019*

Where the interest in UK land is held directly by the non-resident and the land was partly residential in the period between 6 April 2015 (or the date of acquisition, if later) and 5 April 2019, the NRCGT 2015 rules will apply to *part* of the gain.

For example, this would apply to flats above a shop. The flats would be taxable under the NRCGT 2015 regime, but the shop would not.

The value of the property in this example would need to be split between the residential element and the non-residential element. It is suggested that a professional valuation is undertaken to establish the respective valuations of the different parts of the building.

The gain will be calculated in the normal way, but only the part of the gain arising since 6 April 2015 for the residential element and 6 April 2019 for the commercial element would be chargeable.

In this situation, the following two alternative methods of calculation can be used to determine the gain or loss:

- default method (rebasing to 5 April 2015 and 5 April 2019); or
- election for retrospective basis of computation.

Default method (rebasing to 5 April 2015 and 5 April 2019)

This is the calculation which must be used if no election is made. The asset must be valued as at 5 April 2015 (if acquired before that date) and as at 5 April 2019.

In relation to the gain or loss arising between 6 April 2015 (or date of acquisition, if later) and 5 April 2019, only the proportion during which the land was a dwelling is chargeable.

The post-5 April 2019 gain or loss is fully chargeable or allowable.

Election for retrospective basis of computation

Under this method, the entire gain is chargeable, not just the post-5 April 2015 proportion. Therefore, this election is most likely to be useful where the disposal results in a loss as, under this method, the entire loss is allowable.

For a worked example, see CG 73974.

It will be necessary to produce calculations of the gain or loss under both methods to decide which is the most beneficial for the taxpayer.

Law: TCGA 1992, Sch. 4AA, para. 12-15
Guidance: CG 73974

18.3.4   Disposal of an asset not chargeable before 6 April 2019

Although the normal rules apply for the purposes of calculating the gain or loss arising, only the gain arising after 5 April 2019 is chargeable under the NRCGT 2019 rules. There are two methods of calculation to choose between:

- default method (rebasing to 5 April 2019); or
- election for retrospective basis of computation.

Default method (rebasing to 5 April 2019)

This is the default option and is used if no election is made.

Under this option, the asset must be valued at 5 April 2019 and this becomes the base cost figure in the capital gains calculation. This means that only the increase or decrease in value from 5 April 2019 is within the scope of the NRCGT 2019 regime.

Election for retrospective basis of computation

Under this method, the entire gain is chargeable, not just the post-5 April 2019 proportion. Therefore, this election is most likely to be useful where the original cost exceeds the 5 April 2019 market value as it would reduce a gain or increase a loss.

Note, though, that if this is an indirect disposal, any loss arising under this method is not allowable.

It will be necessary to calculate the gain or loss under both methods to decide which is the most beneficial to the taxpayer.

Law: TCGA 1992, Sch. 4AA, Pt. 2
Guidance: CG 73980

18.3.5   Disposal of an asset acquired on or after 6 April 2019

Where the asset being disposed of has been acquired on or after 6 April 2019, the whole gain falls within the NRCGT 2019 regime. This means that the gain or loss is calculated under normal CGT principles and there is no need for any rebasing.

Law: TCGA 1992, Sch. 4AA, para. 2-5
Guidance: CG 73960

18.4   Private residence relief

18.4.1   Introduction

One of the most valuable CGT reliefs available to any taxpayer, whether UK resident or otherwise, is PRR (see **Chapter 9**).

To protect the Treasury from potential abuse, various changes were made to the PRR rules to ensure a fair interaction with NRCGT 2015. The one most often seen in practice is the concept of "non-qualifying tax years", which affects UK resident taxpayers as well as non-residents.

18.4.2   Non-qualifying tax years

These rules effectively introduced a day count condition where the property is situated in a country where the individual is non-resident. The same rules apply whether it is a property owned in the UK by a non-resident or a property outside the UK that a UK resident is claiming to be their main residence.

For the day count condition to be met, the individual must spend at least 90 days in the house in question during the tax year. If this is the case the whole of the tax year will qualify for relief.

A day is counted for these purposes if the individual is present in the house at midnight or has spent some time in the house that day and the next day and has stayed overnight in the house (i.e. he or she was not actually present in the house at midnight but has stayed overnight).

If a spouse or civil partner occupies the house separately, these days can be counted. However, if they occupy together, then the days are only counted once so there is no duplication.

It is also possible to count days spent in other properties owned in the same country. So, if an individual had two UK properties and spent 15 days in one and 85 days in the other, this would constitute 90 days in total and therefore would meet the test.

18.4.3   Main residence nomination

For the purposes of NRCGT, the usual two-year deadline for making a main residence nomination does not apply.

In this instance, the non-resident individual may make an irrevocable main residence notification on the NRCGT return. This nomination can apply retrospectively to any period of ownership of the UK residential property, and it will supersede any previous elections made with HMRC. Where spouses or civil partners live together, they are only entitled to one main residence and therefore it is important to note that the election will affect both parties.

If spouses or civil partners are both within the NRCGT regime, they must both file a NRCGT return in respect of the same property containing the same nomination for it to be valid.

Where the spouse or civil partner does not need to file a return, then the individual must attach a written notification from the spouse to their NRCGT return confirming their agreement to the terms of the nomination.

If this is not followed, then the nomination will not be valid and the calculation of the NRCGT 2019 gain will be incorrect.

18.4.4   Relevant periods

Where NRCGT is calculated using the default method, PRR is only given based on the facts since 5 April 2015. Where NRCGT is calculated using the total ownership period, then PRR is given based on this whole period.

It may still be possible to qualify for relief for deemed periods of occupation based on the usual PRR rules.

Law: TCGA 1992, s. 222A(7)

18.5 Allowable losses arising under the NRCGT regime

To the extent that losses arising within the NRCGT regime are allowable, the normal CGT loss rules discussed at **3.5** apply.

For a loss to be allowable and available to a non-resident, it must have arisen on the disposal of an asset that would have been taxable on the non-resident.

Losses arising under NRCGT relating to disposals on or after 6 April 2019 can be used against any chargeable gains arising to non-residents.

Unused losses that arose under the NRCGT 2015 regime can be carried forward and set against any chargeable gains arising to non-residents.

It is possible that the taxpayer might have losses available from disposals made prior to becoming non-UK resident. These losses are "clogged" (ring-fenced) meaning they cannot be used against NRCGT gains that arise during the period of non-residence.

These losses brought forward from a period of residency are carried forward until the taxpayer becomes UK resident again, when they can then be used in the normal way.

If the taxpayer becomes UK resident again then any brought-forward NRCGT losses arising in the period of non-residence can be used in the same way as any other brought-forward allowable losses and set-off in the most tax efficient way.

18.6 Compliance

18.6.1 30-day reporting requirement

Non-resident taxpayers within the scope of CGT, i.e. individuals, personal representatives, trustees and partnerships, have to report the disposal of UK land and property and pay any CGT due within 30 days of the date the transaction is completed.

These rules are covered at **2.3.3** (reporting property and land disposals) and **4.3.2** (residential property).

For UK residents, the 30-day reporting requirement only applies to residential property, whereas non-resident taxpayers have to report all UK property disposals in this manner.

Furthermore, non-resident individuals need to report the transaction whether there is a gain, a loss, or break even. UK residents only report the transaction if there is tax due.

Under the provisions of the SRT, it can in practice be difficult to establish whether individuals are UK resident during the tax year in question, as the SRT provisions are factual and retrospective. A number of the SRT tests will require the taxpayer to look back over the tax year while the 90-day test requires consideration of the previous two years.

For this reason, it may not be possible to determine with certainty whether an individual will be non-resident in the tax year at the point when the NRCGT return would be due. In such a case, the individual must complete the paperwork to the best of his or her knowledge at that time.

If it becomes apparent later in the tax year that the residency position of the individual was incorrect, the 30-day report should be amended as soon as practical.

18.6.2   Penalties

Penalties for late reporting and late payments are discussed at **2.6**.

18.6.3   Self-assessment tax return

If the taxpayer is required to file a self-assessment tax return for the tax year, any NRCGT disposals made in the year must also be reported on that return. They will also need to report any CGT already paid so that it is not double counted.

18.7   Taxation of the gain in the country of residence

If the taxpayer is resident in another country, then the sale of the UK property might also be taxable in the other jurisdiction under its rules.

The taxpayer will need to take local tax advice.

Under the terms of most tax treaties, the UK will have taxing rights over UK *situs* assets. However, to avoid double taxation, the other jurisdiction will need to give credit to the taxpayer for any tax paid in the UK on the asset.

The taxpayer will effectively pay the higher of the tax charges in the two jurisdictions.

Example

Miss S lives and is resident in Spain. She sells her property in the UK and pays tax of £5,000 under the NRCGT rules. This is an effective rate of 28%. The rate of tax charged on the property in Spain is 35%. She will therefore receive a credit for the 28% tax paid in the UK and will need to pay the additional 7% to the Spanish authorities.

The UK and Spanish computations may result in a different gain, because of differences in the calculation rules.

18.8   Temporary non-residence rules

18.8.1   *Introduction*

Without rules to prevent it, it would be possible for a taxpayer to secure tax advantages by leaving the UK on a short-term basis and disposing of assets once non-resident.

Some assets, such as shares, would then be outside the tax net completely. UK land and property would be taxable under the NRCGT regime but could potentially benefit from a base cost uplift to either 2015 or 2019 value, depending upon the type of asset.

There are therefore specific rules in place for temporary non-residents.

18.8.2   *Conditions for temporary non-residence*

The rules apply if the individual leaving the UK:

- had sole residence in the UK for either the whole or a part of at least four out of the last seven years prior to the year of departure;
- becomes non-resident; and
- has a period of non-residence not exceeding five years.

Non-residency is determined using the SRT.

18.8.3   *Effect of the rules*

If a taxpayer is caught by the rules then any gains or losses realised during the period of absence that were not subject to UK tax become chargeable or allowable in the tax year of return.

Under basic principles, any foreign tax suffered on the sale of an asset can be relieved when the gain becomes chargeable in the UK. So, if an asset is sold while the taxpayer is resident in another jurisdiction and the gain is taxed in that country, then relief is given by way of tax credit for the tax already paid when the gain is subsequently charged to UK tax on the return of the taxpayer.

Example

Mariam was formerly UK resident. While living in Portugal, she sells her UK share portfolio, realising a gain of £50,000. This gain is taxed in Portugal at 15%. For personal reasons, Mariam returns to the UK and becomes tax resident again after three years away.

The gain will become taxable in the UK on her return under the temporary non-residence rules. Her tax liability is 20% but she is given credit for the 15% already paid to the Portuguese authorities.

18.8.4 Excluded gains and losses

Gains and losses on assets acquired after leaving the UK are normally excluded from the scope of the temporary residence rules, i.e. disposals of such assets during the period of absence would not be brought into charge on a subsequent return to the UK.

An exception to this is where the assets acquired after the period of non-residence begins are connected to an earlier period of UK residence. The exceptions broadly cover three categories:

- assets acquired under no gain/no loss rules, for example an asset transferred to the taxpayer from a spouse or civil partner;
- assets that have had their acquisition cost reduced by rollover relief where the gain deferred arose on the disposal of an asset acquired before the date of departure; and
- assets into which a gain has been deferred where the original gain arose on an asset acquired before the date of departure, e.g. a QCB following a share reorganisation.

Law: TCGA 1992, s. 10A-10AA
Guidance: CG 26610, 26630

18.8.5 Non-resident companies and settlements

The gains and losses of non-resident companies and settlements can also be chargeable on a return to the UK under the temporary non-residence rules, specifically:

- gains accruing to a closely controlled non-resident company, attributed to the participators (s. 13 attributed gains – see **18.11**);

- gains accruing to settlor-interested non-resident settlements that are attributed to a UK resident and domiciled settlor (s. 86 attributed gains); and

- gains attributed under the matching rules in relation to capital payments from offshore trustees (s. 87 attributed gains).

If any of the above gains or losses arose in the period of temporary non-residence and would have been chargeable or allowable on the individual if they had retained UK residence, they will be treated as accruing to the individual in the year of return.

Law: TCGA 1992, s. 13, 86, 87
Guidance: CG 38570C, 38430P, 57200P

Example

Mr Song is the settlor of a non-resident settlement, and he is attributed income and gains on an arising basis. He leaves the UK to become non-UK resident and remains outside the UK for three tax years. Due to personal circumstances, he returns to the UK during the fourth tax year.

During the three years that he was non-resident, he will not have been taxed on the attributed gains from the trust. However, when he once again becomes resident in the UK (within the five year period) he is taxable on all of the gains arising during that period under the temporary non-residence rules.

18.8.6   Remittance basis

The remittance basis may apply where relevant if the individual is non domiciled and the asset sold during their absence is non-UK *situs*.

Law: TCGA 1992, s. 10A
Guidance: CG 26650

18.8.7   Interaction with NRCGT

The NRCGT 2015 rules (see **18.2** and **18.3**) take priority over the temporary non-residence rules. This means that where an individual who is temporarily non-resident holds residential UK property, the temporary non-residence rules only apply to gains arising on that property to the extent that they relate to the period before 6 April 2015.

18.9 Section 86 CGT settlor charge on non-resident settlement

18.9.1 Introduction

To prevent taxpayers settling assets into offshore trusts and obtaining a tax advantage, there are various anti-avoidance provisions that are designed to ensure that the relevant amount of taxation is suffered in the UK.

Section 86 contains the settlor provisions that tax capital gains arising in an offshore trust directly on the settlor.

For these provisions to apply the settlor must be UK domiciled and resident in the year that the assets are settled into the trust. The SRT determines residency for these purposes.

Section 86 does not apply in the tax year in which the settlor dies. Instead, s. 87 (see below) will apply.

For s. 86 to apply the trust must be non-resident, which requires the trustees to be non-resident for a whole tax year. If the trustees are UK resident for as little as one day in a tax year these rules will not apply. Establishing the trust's residency is therefore important to determine whether these rules apply.

Trust residency is discussed at **15.2.9**.

Law: TCGA 1992, s. 86
Guidance: CG 38445

18.9.2 Qualifying settlement

Since 6 April 1999 all offshore settlements are qualifying settlements unless they are protected settlements.

Law: TCGA 1992, s. 86(1)(a)
Guidance: CG 38520

18.9.3 Protected settlement

A protected settlement is a settlement that was created before 19 March 1991 in which the beneficiaries are:

- children of the settlor or of his or her spouse/civil partner who are under 18 at the beginning of the tax year;

- unborn children of the settlor or of his or her spouse/civil partner or of his or her future spouse/civil partner and any future spouse/civil partners of those children;
- a future spouse/civil partner of the settlor; or
- persons who are not defined persons in relation to the settlor (see **18.9.4**).

The definition above does not include the settlor's grandchildren, so any trust that can benefit grandchildren is not a protected settlement. However, HMRC do not generally consider grandchildren as causing the protected settlement status to fail.

A protected settlement loses its protection and comes within the scope of s. 86 if it tainted following the 1991 and 1999 changes.

A protected settlement is tainted if a defined person is added as a beneficiary (or receives a benefit from the settlement), a child attains age 18 without being excluded as a beneficiary, new property is added to the settlement, or the trustees become non-resident.

Law: TCGA 1992, Sch. 5
Guidance: CG 38430P, 38520

18.9.4   Defined person

Defined persons for the purposes of s. 86 are:

- the settlor;
- the settlor's spouse or civil partner;
- any child of the settlor or of the settlor's spouse or civil partner;
- the spouse or civil partner of such a child;
- any grandchild of the settlor or the settlor's spouse or civil partner;
- the spouse or civil partner of any such grandchild;
- a company controlled by a person or persons listed above; and
- a company associated with such a company.

Child includes step-child for these purposes.

It is possible for the settlor to be excluded but to have an interest in the settlement under s. 86 by virtue of a defined person benefiting from the settlement.

Law: TCGA 1992, Sch. 5, para. 2(3)

18.9.5   Settlor-interested trust

For s. 86 to apply the settlor must have an interest in a settlement during the tax year.

A settlor has an interest if, at any time during the tax year, settlement property or income may become payable to, or applied on behalf of, a defined person, or a defined person enjoys a direct or indirect benefit from the settlement.

This is a wide definition of settlor-interested.

Any settlement created before 17 March 1998 will be a qualifying settlement if a defined beneficiary can continue to benefit from it on or after 17 March 1998.

To prevent a charge arising under s. 86, it is necessary for all defined beneficiaries to be excluded in the year before any gains accrue under s. 86.

Law: TCGA 1992, s. 86(1)(d) and Sch. 5, para. 2A(1)-(2)

18.9.6   Attribution of the charge under s. 86

Gains are attributed to the settlor in the year in which they accrue to the trustees.

If a loss is incurred, it is not attributed to the settlor but instead is carried forward against the trustees' gains of the following tax year.

The attributed gains are treated as the settlor's top slice of gains. Therefore, if the settlor pays tax at 20% or 28% on the attributed gains, then this is the amount that he or she can recover from the trustees (see **18.9.8**).

The settlor's annual exempt amount and any personal capital losses are set against their other gains first.

Where a settlor is resident for part of the tax year under split-year treatment, the s. 86 gains are deemed to have accrued in the part of the year that the individual was tax resident.

If the settlor is charged under the temporary non-residence rules (see **18.8**) then they will be chargeable on any s. 86 gains that accrued during the period of non-residence.

Relief will be given for any gains that may have been taxed under s. 87 during the same period.

Guidance: RDRM 12000; CG 38535

18.9.7   *Calculation of the charge under s. 86*

The gains are calculated as if the trustees were UK resident for the tax year in question.

The trustees are not entitled to claim the annual exemption. Losses may be set against gains and carried forward providing the settlement remains with the s. 86 regime.

Losses that arose prior to 19 March 1991 are not available to carry forward.

Where the trustees are participators in a non-resident company that would be caught by the s. 3 (formerly "s. 13") rule (see **18.11**), it will be included in the gains attributed to the settlor providing that the property in which the gain arises originates from the settlor.

Property is treated as originating from the settlor if the settlor has settled shares in the company or funds that have been used to purchase those shares.

Law: TCGA 1992, s. 86(1)(e)

18.9.8   *Settlor's right of recovery*

Settlors have a statutory right of recovery of the tax paid under s. 86.

The fact that the settlor receives reimbursement from the trustees will not create taxable income or capital payments for the purposes of other tax provisions.

18.10 Section 87 CGT beneficiary charge on non-resident settlement

18.10.1   *Introduction*

These rules impose a charge on beneficiaries of a trust where the settlor is not taxable under s. 86.

Gains accruing to non-UK resident trustees are deemed to accrue to the beneficiaries when they receive capital payments from the trust.

Section 87 applies to any non-resident settlement regardless of when it was set up, but it does not apply to capital payments received before 10 March 1981.

Section 87 applies to any year in which the trustees are non-resident for the whole tax year. If the trustees are resident in the UK for at least one day s. 87 will not apply, and the trustees will be taxed on any gains accruing during the tax year.

Trust residency is discussed at **15.2.9**.

18.10.2   Calculation of the charge under s. 87

The trustees' gains for the year are called their s. 2(2) amount. This is defined in s. 87(4) as:

- the amount on which the trustees would be chargeable to tax under s. 2(2) if they were UK resident; less
- any amount of those gains taxed on the settlor under s. 86.

The trustees do not have an annual exempt amount to deduct in calculating the s. 2(2) amount.

Trustees' losses can be set against gains and, if unused, can be carried forward and set against gains in later years.

Losses are not attributed to beneficiaries.

Losses are restricted in certain circumstances, such as where the gains accrue on the disposal of assets that were transferred into the trust under a holdover relief claim, the transferor acquired an interest in the trust and the transferor gave consideration for that acquisition.

Any foreign tax paid by the trustees is deducible in calculating the trustees' s. 2(2) amount.

Reliefs apply in the normal way, such as private residence relief, where applicable.

Where s. 3 (see **18.11**) attributes gains to a non-resident trust, these gains form part of the trustees' s. 2(2) charge.

18.10.3   Beneficiaries under s. 87

A beneficiary for these purposes includes anyone named in the trust deed, either by name or class, as well as anyone who receives a capital payment from the trust. This applies even if the payment is a breach of the trust deed.

Where a beneficiary dies having received unmatched capital payments, those payments cannot be matched against trustees' gains for the tax years after the year of death. They may, though, be matched against trustees' gains in the tax year of death, even if they arose after the actual date of death.

18.10.4   Capital payment

A capital payment for the purposes of s. 87 is very wide. It is defined as any payment other than a payment that would be chargeable to income tax if received by a UK resident or treated as income if received by a non-resident, or a distribution where the recipient does not pay market value (i.e. a transaction not made at arm's length).

18.10.5   Unused capital payments

If, once all of the capital gains in the settlement have been attributed to beneficiaries, there are excess capital payments, the excess is carried forward and matched in future years.

18.10.6   Beneficiary's tax position

The matched payment is added to the beneficiary's other gains for the tax year in question and will be taxed according to their marginal rates of tax at either 10% or 20%. Since the introduction of NRCGT (see **18.2** and **18.3**), it is unlikely they will be taxed on residential and commercial property gains.

The beneficiary cannot offset personal losses against the gains.

18.10.7   Payment to non-UK residents

Prior to the changes enacted in FA 2018, it was possible to "wash out" gains by making distributions to non-UK residents. This is no longer possible as, since 2018, capital payments to non-UK resident beneficiaries are disregarded when calculating the gains to be matched

18.10.8   Onward gifts

FA 2018 also introduced new anti-avoidance rules to prevent a non-resident or non-domiciled individual receiving a capital payment and then making a subsequent gift to a UK resident.

The rules create a charge on the recipient of the distribution where a capital payment is made to a person who is non-resident, or non-domiciled in the UK, and there is an arrangement or intention to pass the original payment to another person who will be UK resident when they receive the payment. This gift has to be made within three years.

These rules are very widely drawn and cover most types of payment.

Law: TCGA 1992, s. 87J-87LL

18.10.9   *Capital payments made to close family of the settlor*

FA 2018 also introduced further anti-avoidance rules to prevent payments being made to close family members of a UK resident, living settlor.

In this case, the liability to tax moves to the settlor, not the beneficiary.

A close family member of the settlor includes spouse, civil partner and minor children. It also includes couples living together as spouses.

If s. 86 already applies, then these provisions are not relevant.

Law: TCGA 1992, s. 87I-87M

18.10.10 *Supplementary charge*

As well as paying CGT in the UK, the beneficiary may suffer a supplementary charge if the capital payments are matched to gains that are more than two years old.

These are known as "stockpiled" gains.

The supplementary charge is calculated as a percentage of the CGT due for the tax year.

The percentage is 10% for each tax year that the gains are stockpiled in the trust up to a maximum charge of 60%, illustrated as follows:

Tax year of gains	Increase in CGT rate
2020-21	0%
2019-20	0%
2018-19	20%
2017-18	30%
2016-17	40%
2015-16	50%
2014-15	60%

18.11 Section 3 – attribution of gains of non-resident companies

18.11.1 Introduction

Under s. 3 (formerly s. 13), gains are attributed to members of non-resident companies.

For these rules to apply, the company would have to be a close company if resident in the UK.

A close company is defined at CTA 2010, s. 439. It is generally a UK company controlled by five or fewer participators (and their associates) or controlled by any number of participators (and their associates) who are directors.

These rules prevent taxpayers from setting up non-resident companies and realising gains that are not subject to CGT or corporation tax. This is achieved by attributing the gains realised by such non-resident companies to the UK resident participators.

To the extent that the profit is covered by the NRCGT rules (see **18.2** and **18.3**), they are not also chargeable under s. 3. Therefore, for example, if a UK residential property was owned by a non-resident company prior to the NRCGT 2015 rules applying, the earlier portion of the gain would be taxed under these provisions and the later portion (post 2015) would be taxable under the NRCGT rules.

18.11.2 Participator

A participator in the company must be resident in the UK during the tax year in which the gain was realised for these rules to apply.

Participator has the meaning attributed in CTA 2010, s. 454.

Section 13 can apply to individuals who are resident in the UK, companies resident in the UK, trustees are resident in the UK, and trustees who are not resident in the UK but are taxable under s. 86 or s. 87).

If a gain is attributed under s. 3 to an individual who is a participator in a company, and the individual is non-domiciled in UK during that year, he or she can elect for the remittance basis to apply to the gain if the asset on which the gain arose is situated outside the UK.

18.11.3   Section 3 amount

The amount attributable to UK participators is calculated as follows:

- calculate the chargeable gain that would have accrued to the company if it had been resident in the UK;
- establish which participators are within the charge to UK tax;
- calculate the gain due to each of the participators; and
- ensure this is a just and reasonable allocation of the gain.

The amount attributed to the UK resident taxpayer should be reported in the UK in the appropriate way.

Law: TCGA 1992, s. 3
Guidance: CG 57275

APPENDICES

Appendix 1 – tax rates

The rates here are for 2021-22. Details of rates for all years are at: https://www.gov.uk/guidance/capital-gains-tax-rates-and-allowances.

Rates of CGT – individuals

The UK has a number of applicable rates of CGT. The main rates are as follows:

	Residential property or carried interest gains	All other types of asset
Lower rate	18%	10%
Higher rate	28%	20%

The higher rates apply if the individual has income in excess of the basic rate band (£37,700 for 2021-22). If the individual's income does not exceed the basic rate band, the lower rates apply to the difference. For example, if the taxable income is £27,700, the first £10,000 of any gains after deducting the annual exempt amount in the tax year will be charged at the lower rates, with any excess charged at the higher rates.

The main UK basic rate band applies for this purpose, even if the individual is a Scottish or Welsh taxpayer.

Special rates

Gains qualifying for business asset disposal relief are charged at 10%, subject to a lifetime limit of £1 million.

Gains qualifying for investors' relief are charged at 10%, subject to a lifetime limit of £10 million.

Trustees and personal representatives

The higher rates of 28% and 20% (as appropriate) apply to gains realised by trustees of settlements and personal representatives of a deceased person's estate.

Appendix 2 – exempt assets and gains

This table details the main types of asset or gain that enjoy a statutory exemption from a charge to CGT under TCGA 1992, in the order they appear in the Act. See **1.3.4**.

TCGA 1992 section	Description	Notes
21	Sterling	Exchanging sterling into and from other currency may, however, give rise to a foreign exchange gain.
45	Chattels that are wasting assets	A wasting asset is one with an expected useful life not exceeding 50 years. Plant and machinery is always treated as a wasting asset, irrespective of the actual expected useful life. For plant, there is an additional requirement that the asset has been used in a trade carried on by the owner.
51	Gambling winnings and compensation	Amounts won from betting (including pool betting), lotteries and games with prizes are not chargeable gains. Compensation to rectify a wrong or injury, suffered by an individual in person or in his or her profession or vocation, such as damages awarded to a plaintiff or claimant, is not a chargeable gain. However, compensation paid for damage, destruction or loss of an asset may realise a capital gain. See **6.4.2**.
72	Termination of a life interest upon death	Where a person entitled to an interest in possession (i.e. a life tenant) dies, the trustees are treated as disposing of and immediately reacquiring the asset at its market value (or part thereof, as appropriate). No chargeable gain arises – even if the asset is transferred to a beneficiary. However, if a person becomes absolutely entitled to the settled property otherwise than upon the death of the life tenant the deemed disposal may realise a chargeable gain accruing to the trustees.

TCGA 1992 section	Description	Notes
72 (cont.)	Termination of a life interest upon death (cont.)	This mirrors the position for non-settled property, i.e. where a lifetime transfer may be a chargeable event but death is not, by virtue of s. 62. For further information on the CGT position of trusts, see **Chapter 15**.
76	Disposal of a beneficial interest in settled property	Where a beneficiary disposes of an interest in a settlement, including an annuity or life interest (or the reversion to either of these), no chargeable gain arises unless the beneficiary acquired it for money or money's worth, or derives the title from someone who acquired the interest in this way. There are exceptions in the case of non-resident settlements.
115	Gilts and qualifying corporate bonds	Gilts are securities issued by the government, and are essentially a form of interest-bearing loan stock, issued only by the government's Debt Management Office instead of the board of a corporate body. Any gain realised on the disposal of gilts is not chargeable. A corporate bond is the private sector equivalent and will generally pay a higher interest rate (reflecting the greater risk of a company going bankrupt compared to the UK government).
		Qualifying corporate bonds (QCBs) are corporate bonds that meet the criteria in s. 117, one of which is that they must be expressed in sterling. Gains on the disposal of a QCB are not chargeable gains. It is possible for loan notes to be structured as QCBs (though there are advantages and disadvantages of doing so), which can be important in corporate takeovers.
		The exemption under s. 115 extends to a disposal of options over gilts or QCBs.

TCGA 1992 section	Description	Notes
121	Government non-marketable securities	Disposals of savings certificates and non-marketable securities issued by the state-owned National Savings and Investments are exempt from CGT. This covers children's bonus bonds, premium bonds, etc.
150	Shares issued under EIS, SEIS or the business expansion scheme (BES)	Subject to the relevant conditions being met – generally that income tax relief has been given and not withdrawn – any gain made on shares issued under the enterprise investment scheme (EIS), or its predecessor, the business expansion scheme, or the seed enterprise investment scheme (SEIS) are exempt from CGT. See **Chapter 10**. Additionally, the SEIS permits otherwise non-exempt gains to be matched to qualifying investments in the same year the investment is made (or treated as made) and to be partly exempted from CGT.
151	ISAs, etc.	Certain investments into UK savings accounts offer tax benefits, subject to annual investment limits. Personal equity plans (PEPs) were replaced in 1999 by individual savings accounts (ISAs), and pre-existing PEP accounts automatically became stocks and shares ISAs from 6 April 2008. Junior ISAs were introduced in November 2011 and offer the same benefits – albeit with a lower investment limit. Gains made on investments within the ISA wrapper are exempt from CGT, as long as the investment limits have been observed.
151A	Shares in venture capital trusts	If an investment is made into shares in a qualifying venture capital trust, any gain on the shares will be exempt if the conditions for the disposal relief are met. See **10.9**.

TCGA 1992 section	Description	Notes
222	Main or only residence	If a dwelling has been the individual's only or main residence throughout the period of ownership, relief is available to exempt the gain in full. Partial relief is also available where it was the only or main residence for only part of the ownership period. See **Chapter 9**.
236B*ff.*	Shares acquired under an employee shareholder scheme before 1 December 2016	This short-lived scheme came to an end in 2016, but any qualifying shares acquired before that date are exempt from CGT. See **14.7**.
237, 271	Pensions, etc.	Where investments are held by a registered pension scheme (or certain similar schemes), any gains realised within the wrapper are exempt from CGT.
250	Qualifying woodland	Any proceeds on woodland are split into the consideration for the land itself, and the consideration for the trees and underwood. Only the consideration for the land is taken into account when calculating the taxable gain. If the woodland is occupied commercially, there are further tax breaks (see **4.3.8**).
251	Debts other than securities	If a debt (or an interest in a debt) is sold or assigned, no gain or loss will accrue to the original debt holder, unless the debt is a security.

TCGA 1992 section	Description	Notes
252	Foreign currency accounts	Withdrawing money from a bank account denominated in a currency other than sterling will not lead to a gain or loss for CGT purposes. However, buying and selling investments listed in a foreign currency, e.g. shares listed on an overseas stock exchange, can lead to foreign exchange gains (or losses).
255B	Social investment tax relief (SITR) investments	Qualifying investments into a social enterprise will not incur CGT if sold at a gain, as long as income tax relief was given (and not withdrawn). See **10.8**.
258	Art works and similar assets	If the conditional exemption for heritage property for IHT purposes is potentially available, no CGT will apply on a disposal. This will cover situations such as when a valuable art collection is given to a museum, if the museum is a recognised body.
262	Moveable tangible property	Chattels enjoy an exemption from CGT if the proceeds paid, or deemed to be paid, do not exceed £6,000. If the proceeds exceed this, partial relief is potentially available (see **Chapters 6** and **14**).
263	Cars	If a vehicle is of a kind commonly used as a private vehicle, it is not a chargeable asset for CGT. So, the sale of a collection of motor cars would be exempt, but the sale of a vintage military tank would not be.
263AZA	Renewable energy generation	
268	Decorations for valour etc.	A gain realised on the disposal of war medals or other decorations for conduct, etc., will not be a chargeable gain, unless the seller acquired it for money or money's worth.

TCGA 1992 section	Description	Notes
269	Foreign currency for personal expenditure	A gain realised on a disposal of currency acquired for personal usage, e.g. at a foreign exchange bureau for a holiday, is not a chargeable gain.

Appendix 3 – reliefs and exemptions

Exempt assets are listed at **Appendix 2**. The following list shows other key CGT reliefs and exemptions.

TCGA 1992 (starting section)	Description	Notes	Coverage in this book
s. 1K	Annual exempt amount	£12,300 for 2020-21 and all years to 2025-26	1.3.1
s. 1K, Sch. 1C	AEA for trustees	Trustees' AEA is in most cases half that of an individual	15.5
s. 58	Transfers between spouses and civil partners	Deemed to take place for consideration that gives rise to no gain/no loss	1.3.1 3.2.6
	Enterprise investment scheme:		Chapter 10
s. 150C, Sch. 5B	• EIS reinvestment relief		10.3
s. 150A	• EIS exemption on disposal		10.5
ITA 2007, s. 24A	• EIS loss relief		10.6
s. 150F, Sch. 5BB	Seed enterprise investment scheme: • SEIS reinvestment relief • SEIS disposal relief		10.7
s. 151A	VCT disposal relief		10.9

TCGA 1992 (starting section)	Description	Notes	Coverage in this book
s. 152	Rollover relief (replacement of business assets)	A trader can defer all or part of the capital gain on disposal of a business asset when a new qualifying asset is acquired	Chapter 11
s. 162	Incorporation relief	Applies when a business is transferred to a company in exchange for shares or shares and cash	13.8
s. 165	Holdover relief for gifts of business assets	The donor's gain is relieved by holding it over against the base cost of the asset in the donee's hands. Relief under s. 260 takes precedence if both are available	Chapter 12
s. 169H	Business asset disposal relief	BADR replaced entrepreneurs' relief from April 2020. The relief applies a flat tax rate of 10% on eligible gains up to a maximum lifetime limit (currently £1 million)	Chapter 7

TCGA 1992 (starting section)	Description	Notes	Coverage in this book
s. 169VA	Investors' relief	The relief gives investors in unlisted trading companies a tax rate of 10% on relevant gains up to a lifetime limit (currently £10 million)	Chapter 8
s. 222	Private residence relief PRR lettings relief	The relief provides full or partial exemption for the gain on a dwelling-house that has been occupied as the taxpayer's only or main residence. If there are two or more properties, the taxpayer can elect which is the main residence	Chapter 9
s. 236A	Employee shareholders	The Employee Shareholder Status scheme has been withdrawn but relief still applies to shares held under agreements signed before 17 March 2016	14.7
s. 236H	Employee-ownership trusts	Transfers to trustees of an EOT are treated as being made for consideration that gives rise to no gain/no loss	14.8

TCGA 1992 (starting section)	Description	Notes	Coverage in this book
s. 248A	Exchanges of joint interests in land	This provides a form of rollover relief when landowners rearrange their holdings	Chapter 4
s. 253	Irrecoverable loans to traders	A capital loss can be claimed to the extent that a qualifying loan made to a trader becomes irrecoverable	14.5
s. 255A, Sch. 8B	Social enterprise investments: • SITR reinvestment relief • SITR disposal relief		10.8
s. 257	Gifts to charities	Gifts to charities (and other eligible bodies) are treated as made for consideration that gives rise to no gain/no loss	3.2.6
s. 258, FA 2012, Sch. 14	Gifts to the nation	Under the Cultural Gifts Scheme, an individual can claim a tax deduction for the gift of a pre-eminent property to the nation	14.6

TCGA 1992 (starting section)	Description	Notes	Coverage in this book
s. 260	Holdover relief for gifts on which IHT is chargeable	Takes precedence over relief under s. 165 where both are available	12.13
s. 261B, ITA 2007, s. 64	Relief for trading losses	Allows a trading loss for income tax purposes to be set against capital gains	14.3
s. 262	Chattel exemption	Disposal of a non-wasting chattel is exempt if proceeds do not exceed £6,000. Marginal relief applies if proceeds do not exceed £15,000	14.2
ITA 2007, s. 131	Share loss relief	Capital losses on shares in an unquoted trading company can be offset against general income	14.4
Statement of practice D12	Partnerships	SP D12 sets out some points of practice for CGT and partnerships. These include non-statutory deferral relief where some partnership events, such as changes in sharing ratios, would otherwise give rise to frequent capital gains and losses.	Chapter 17

Appendix 4 – leases – wasting assets

A lease with a duration of 50 years or less is treated as a wasting asset. Expenditure is assumed to be written off at a rate fixed in accordance with the table below, which is reproduced from TCGA 1992, Sch. 8.

Years	Percentages	Years	Percentages
50 (or more)	100	24	79.622
49	99.657	23	78.055
48	99.289	22	76.399
47	98.902	21	74.635
46	98.490	20	72.770
45	98.059	19	70.791
44	97.595	18	68.697
43	97.107	17	66.470
42	96.593	16	64.116
41	96.041	15	61.617
40	95.457	14	58.971
39	94.842	13	56.167
38	94.189	12	53.191
37	93.497	11	50.038
36	92.761	10	46.695
35	91.981	9	43.154
34	91.156	8	39.399
33	90.280	7	35.414
32	89.354	6	31.195
31	88.371	5	26.722
30	87.330	4	21.983
29	86.226	3	16.959
28	85.053	2	11.629
27	83.816	1	5.983
26	82.496	0	0
25	81.100		

If the duration of the lease is not an exact number of years the percentage to be derived from the Table above shall be the percentage for the whole number of years plus one-twelfth of the difference between that and the percentage for the next higher number of years for each odd month counting an odd 14 days or more as one month.

Appendix 5 – compliance deadlines and penalties

Deadlines

Task	Deadline	Law
Filing of return and estimated payment of CGT following disposal of UK residential property where relevant via UK Property Reporting Service	30 days following completion of conveyance	FA 2019, Sch. 2
Filing of online self-assessment tax return	31 January following end of relevant tax year	TMA 1970, s. 8, 12AA
Filing of paper self-assessment tax return	31 October following end of relevant tax year	TMA 1970, s. 8, 12AA
Filing of online self-assessment tax return when notice to file is issued after 31 October following relevant tax year	Three months from issue date of notice to file	TMA 1970, s. 8, 12AA
Filing of paper self-assessment tax return when notice to file is issued after 31 July following relevant tax year	Three months from issue date of notice to file	TMA 1970, s. 8, 12AA
Filing of electronic return where taxpayer wishes any eligible underpayment of tax to be collected via his or her PAYE tax code	31 December following relevant tax year	SI 2003/2682, reg. 186
Filing of paper return where taxpayer wishes any eligible underpayment of tax to be collected via his or her PAYE tax code	31 October following relevant tax year	SI 2003/2682, reg. 186
Notify HMRC of chargeability to tax if no notice to file a tax return is issued	5 October following relevant tax year	TMA 1970, s. 7

Task	Deadline	Law
Payment of tax due for a tax year (balancing payment)	31 January following end of relevant tax year	TMA 1970, s. 59B
First payment on account for a tax year (payments on account do not take account of CGT part of tax liability)	31 January in the tax year concerned	TMA 1970, s. 59A
Second payment on account for a tax year (payments on account do not take account of CGT part of tax liability)	31 July following the end of the relevant tax year	

Penalties

Task	Penalty	Law

Filing of online self-assessment tax return	a. initial late filing penalty of £100;
	b. continued failure to file for more than three months, £10 per day penalty up to a maximum of 90 days, i.e. £900;
	c. failure to file within six months, tax-geared penalty of higher of:
	    • £300; and
	    • 5% of the tax due (see **2.1.7**);
	d. failure to file within 12 months, same penalty as above unless there has been deliberate withholding of the tax return, in which case the following applies:
	    • deliberate withholding – 70% of the tax due;
	    • deliberate and concealed withholding – 100% of the tax due.
		FA 2009, s. 106, Sch. 55

Filing of paper self-assessment tax return		
Filing of online self-assessment tax return when notice to file issued after 31 October following relevant tax year		
Filing of paper self-assessment tax return when notice to file is issued after 31 July following relevant tax year	There is a minimum in both cases of £300. Reductions are available for unprompted disclosure resulting in the minimum penalty being between 20% and 30%, and between 35% and 50% where there has been prompted disclosure. See HMRC compliance check factsheet CC/FS18a.	

Task	Penalty	Law
Notify HMRC of chargeability to tax if no notice to file a tax return is issued	Based on potential lost revenue, so if tax due is not paid by the due date of 31 January the following applies: • failure to notify – 30%; • deliberate but not concealed – 70%; • deliberate and concealed (i.e. makes arrangements to conceal the situation) – 100%. Reductions in the above penalties are available as follows: _see table below_ See HMRC compliance check factsheet CC/FS11	FA 2008, s. 123, Sch. 41
Payment of tax due for a tax year (balancing payment)	• 31 days late – 5% (3 March unless a leap year when 2 March); • six months late – an additional 5%; • 12 months late – a further additional 5%.	FA 2009, Sch. 56

	Standard %	Min. % if unprompted disclosure	Min. % if prompted disclosure
Any other case	30%	Nil if disclosure within 12 months, otherwise 10%	15%
Deliberate but not concealed	70%	20%	35%
Deliberate and concealed	100%	30%	50%

Task	Penalty	Law
First payment on account for a tax year (payments on account do not take account of CGT part of tax liability)	No penalties for late payment, but interest charged on a daily basis.	
Second payment on account for a tax year (payments on account do not take account of CGT part of tax liability)		

Task	Penalty	Law
Inaccuracy in return	Based on potential lost revenue with a reduction to standard % for the quality of disclosure on the following basis: |	Standard %	Min. % if unprompted disclosure	Min. % for prompted disclosure
---	---	---	---
Careless inaccuracy	30%	Nil	15%
Deliberate but not concealed	70%	20%	35%
Deliberate and concealed	100%	30%	50% | "Careless" means a failure to take reasonable care. The above penalties apply for each inaccuracy in the return if more than one inaccuracy. The minimum penalties for deliberate behaviour are increased by 10% if it has taken the taxpayer a "significant" time (three years or more) to correct/disclose. See HMRC compliance check factsheet CC/FS7a.	FA 2007, s. 97, Sch. 24, Pt. 1, 2
Failure to notify HMRC of an error in an assessment within 30 days of the date of the assessment	30% of potential lost revenue with reductions to a minimum of nil if unprompted disclosure or 15% if prompted.	FA 2007, Sch. 24, para. 2, 4C
Failure to keep adequate records	Up to £3,000	TMA 1970, s. 12B (5)

Task	Penalty	Law
Offences involving an offshore matter	Potentially up to 200% of tax due in the UK, depending on country ("territory") involved. See HMRC compliance checks factsheet CC/FS17 and CH 100000	SI 2011/976; SI 2013/1618

Table of primary legislation

Taxes Management Act 1970

Index of cases

General index